An Emerging Intellectual Property Paradigm

QUEEN MARY STUDIES IN INTELLECTUAL PROPERTY

The Centre for Commercial Law Studies at Queen Mary, University of London, has teamed up with international social science publisher, Edward Elgar Publishing Ltd, to re-launch its prestigious book series, Queen Mary Studies in Intellectual Property. Already established as an important forum for acute and relevant debate in the field of intellectual property, the series aims to build further upon its success, publishing books by renowned guest editors who will commission original and often provocative work by both leading scholars and specialist practitioners on key subjects and issues in IP. Combining volumes that are theoretical in their analysis with others that seek to explore the issues from a more practical perspective, all will be rigorous, as well as international in origin, outlook and appeal. The scope of the series will be wide-ranging and its approach will be to synthesize insights from a range of disciplinary backgrounds. The books in this series will not only provide unique sources of reference for researchers and students in IP, but will offer a level of insight to lawyers, policymakers and legislators that is consistent with the reputation of the Centre.

Titles in the series include:

US Intellectual Property Law and Policy
Edited by Hugh Hansen

Emerging Issues in Intellectual Property
Trade, Technology and Market Freedom: Essays in Honour of Herchel Smith
Edited by Guido Westkamp

An Emerging Intellectual Property Paradigm
Perspectives from Canada
Edited by Ysolde Gendreau

An Emerging Intellectual Property Paradigm

Perspectives from Canada

Edited by

Ysolde Gendreau

Professor of Law, Université de Montréal, Canada

QUEEN MARY STUDIES IN INTELLECTUAL PROPERTY

Edward Elgar
Cheltenham, UK • Northampton, MA, USA

Published by
Edward Elgar Publishing Limited
The Lypiatts
15 Lansdown Road
Cheltenham
Glos GL50 2JA
UK

Edward Elgar Publishing, Inc.
William Pratt House
9 Dewey Court
Northampton
Massachusetts 01060
USA

A catalogue record for this book
is available from the British Library

Library of Congress Control Number: 2008935947

PEFC
PEFC/16-33-111
CATG-PEFC-052
www.pefc.org

ISBN 978 1 84720 597 1

Typeset by Cambrian Typesetters, Camberley, Surrey
Printed and bound in Great Britain by MPG Books Ltd, Bodmin, Cornwall

Contents

PART 3 OVERLAPPING ISSUES

Biographical notes

Elizabeth Adeney is a Senior Lecturer in the School of Law at Deakin University, Melbourne, Australia. She holds the degrees of Doctor of Philosophy from the University of Melbourne (Arts) and from Monash University (Law) and is admitted to practise in the Supreme Court of Victoria. She has published widely on moral rights – in Australia, Germany, the UK and Canada – and is the author of a treatise on the subject: *The Moral Rights of Authors and Performers: an international and comparative analysis*, published by Oxford University Press.

Mélanie Bourassa Forcier is a doctoral candidate and a researcher with the CIPP at the Faculty of Law, McGill University. Mélanie's research focuses on patents and access to health care services. She worked in the field of intellectual property law and policy, holding the positions of In-House Legal Counsel, policy analyst within the Patent Policy Division of Industry Canada and Health Policy Analyst for the OECD. Mélanie holds a MSc in International Health Policy from the London School of Economics, a LLM in Biotechnology Law from the University of Montreal and a LLL (Summa Cum Laude) from the University of Ottawa.

Dianne Daley, LLB (Hons.), LLM (McGill) is an Attorney-at-Law and a founding partner of the Law Firm of Foga Daley & Co. based in Jamaica. Admitted to the Jamaican Bar in 1990 Dianne has a Master of Laws Degree in Comparative Law from McGill University with International Copyright as an area of specialization. She lectures Intellectual Property Law in the Master of Laws Programme at the Faculty of Law, University of the West Indies and is a member of ATRIP and INTA. Dianne was a founding member of the Jamaica Intellectual Property Office Advisory Board and its acting chairman from January 2006 to September 2007. She has been the Honorary Secretary of the Jamaican Copyright Licensing Agency for several years. Dianne has been published in *Copyright World*, *Intellectual Asset Management*, *IP Value: Building and Enforcing Intellectual Property Value*, the International Law Office and *Managing Intellectual Property*.

Abraham Drassinower, PhD, LLB is Associate Professor at the University of Toronto Faculty of Law; Chair in the Legal, Ethical and Cultural Implications of Technological Innovation; and Director of the Centre for Innovation Law and Policy. He joined the Faculty of Law in 1999, held a Postdoctoral Fellowship in the Department of Political Science at the University of Toronto (1993–1995) and lectured principally on political philosophy at York University (1993–1995) and at the University of Toronto (1995–1998). He served as a Law Clerk to Mr Justice John C. Major of the Supreme Court of Canada (1998–1999). Professor Drassinower's interests include property, intellectual property, copyright, legal and political philosophy, critical theory, and psychoanalysis. He has published and spoken widely and internationally in the areas of charitable trusts, unjust enrichment, intellectual property, copyright, and psychoanalysis and political theory. He is currently working on a book on the public domain in copyright law.

Ysolde Gendreau, BCL, LLB, LLM (McGill University); docteur en droit (Université de Paris II) is professor at the Faculty of Law and researcher at the Centre de recherche en droit public of the Université de Montréal where she teaches intellectual property law and competition law. She has also been guest professor at several universities. Her publications mainly focus on copyright and include *The Retransmission Right: Copyright and the Rediffusion of Works by Cable* (Oxford, ESC Publishing Ltd, 1990), *La protection des photographies en droit d'auteur français, américain, britannique, et canadien* (Paris, L.G.D.J., 1994), *Copyright Administrative Institutions* (Montreal, Yvon Blais, 2002). Her articles appear in Canadian and foreign journals and she is the Canadian contributor to Paul Geller's *International Copyright Law and Practice*.

She was President of the *Association for the Advancement of Teaching and Research in Intellectual Property* (ATRIP) in 2003–2005 and is currently the President of the Canadian group of the Association littéraire et artistique internationale (ALAI). She is also an associate member of the International Academy of Comparative Law.

Daniel J. Gervais, LLB, LLM, DIUHÉI, Doctorate (Nantes), is the Acting Dean, Osler Professor and University Research Chair in Intellectual Property at the Faculty of Law of the University of Ottawa (Common Law Section). Prior to his teaching career, Prof. Gervais was successively Legal Officer at the GATT (now WTO); Head of Section at the World Intellectual Property Organization (WIPO); Deputy Secretary General of the International Confederation of Societies of Authors and Composers (CISAC); and Vice-President, International of Massachusetts-based Copyright Clearance Center, Inc. (CCC). He also served as consultant to the Organisation for Economic Co-operation and Development (OECD) in Paris. He is Editor in Chief of the *Journal of World Intellectual Property*.

Robert G. Howell has been with the Faculty of Law at the University of Victoria since 1980. He specializes in Intellectual Property Law and Policy, Managing Intellectual Property Law, Telecommunications Law and related areas. He has published nationally and internationally in these areas and has organized and participated in national and international conferences in his areas of specialization. In 1999 and 2002 he completed Reports on Databases and Canadian laws for Canadian Federal Ministries. From 2002 to 2007 he has Co-Directed the International Intellectual Property Summer Studies Program, a joint venture of the University of Victoria Faculty of Law, St Peter's College University of Oxford, and the University of Illinois College of Law, USA.

Jean-Frédéric Morin is professor at Université Libre de Bruxelles (ULB) where he holds a chair in international relations. He has an interdisciplinary background, including a dual Ph.D. in political science and law. Prior to joining ULB in 2008, he was researcher at the Centre for Intellectual Property Policy (CIPP) of McGill University, where he taught international intellectual property law and led a research project on access to medicines. Professor Morin has published several peer-reviewed articles on various issues, including patent lawmaking, biodiversity governance, social movements, and international investment law.

Pierre-Emmanuel Moyse joined the McGill Faculty of Law in 2006 as a Wainwright Junior Fellow. The same year, he successfully defended his thesis at the University of Montreal entitled 'Le droit de distribution – Analyse historique et comparative en droit d'auteur' (Yvon Blais/Carswell, 2007). He was appointed assistant professor in 2007. Professor Moyse is also a member of McGill's Centre for Intellectual Property Policy, an interdisciplinary research centre focusing on the nexus between intellectual property, creativity, innovation and trade.

Before being appointed assistant professor, Professor Moyse practiced for several years commercial and intellectual property law with the Montreal-based firm Leger Robic Richard. Most recently, he pleaded successfully before the Supreme Court of Canada in the 2007 case *Euro-Excellence v. Kraft Canada*, the first Canadian case where copyright misuse theory has been invoked.

Mark Perry is jointly appointed to the Department of Computer Science and the Faculty of Law at The University of Western Ontario in London, Canada. He is also an Adjunct Professor of Law at QUT in Brisbane.

Professor Perry's research focuses on the nexus of science and law, and on autonomic computing system development. He has most recently published in the areas of digital rights management, copyright reform and software licensing automation. He holds grants from the Natural Science and Engineering Research Council, IBM, and the Social Science and Humanities Research Council.

Professor Perry is a frequent invited speaker at research-intensive colloquia and classes at universities in Australia, India, New Zealand, United Kingdom, United States and Canada. He has been interviewed by the media around the world for his ideas on technology law issues. In addition to serving on the Executive of ACM SiGCAS, he is a Faculty Fellow at IBM's Center for Advanced Studies, a Barrister and Solicitor of the Law Society of Upper Canada, and serves on many review and editorial boards.

More information can be found at http://www.csd.uwo.ca/~markp.

Teresa Scassa holds a Canada Research Chair in Information Law at the University of Ottawa, Faculty of Law. She has undergraduate law degrees in civil and common law from McGill University, as well as a LLM and an SJD from the University of Michigan. She taught at Dalhousie Law School for 15 years before joining the faculty of law at the University of Ottawa as a full professor in July 2007. She has taught a range of subjects including Intellectual Property, Law and Technology, Public Law, Administrative Law, Public Law and Professional Responsibility. She is co-editor of the *Canadian Journal of Law and Technology*, published by CCH Canadian Ltd, and co-author of the recent book *Electronic Commerce and Internet Law in Canada* (CCH Canadian Ltd.). Her research and scholarship is primarily in the areas of intellectual property law, law and technology, and privacy.

Myra J. Tawfik is a Professor of Law at the University of Windsor and a former Associate Dean of the Faculty. She is a graduate of McGill University with degrees in both common law and civil law and the University of London (LLM – Queen Mary College 1989). Appointed to the Faculty of Law in 1991, Professor Tawfik teaches in the area of intellectual property law including copyright law, trademark law, international intellectual property law and the law of confidential information. Her research centres on intellectual property law, primarily, but not exclusively, in the area of copyright and she has published and spoken nationally and internationally on a wide range of intellectual property law issues. She is the director of the Intellectual Property Legal Information Network, a student-run community legal education initiative that has recently received a substantial grant to develop workshops and mentoring programmes to foster entrepreneurship in a knowledge-based economy. Her current research interests lie in the historical dimensions of intellectual property law and she is completing a monograph on the 19th century origins of Canadian copyright law.

Margaret Ann Wilkinson attended law school at The University of Toronto and was called to the Bar of Ontario in 1980. She practiced law in Toronto for a number of years. Her doctoral dissertation on 'The Impact of the Ontario Freedom of Information and Protection of Privacy Act, 1987 upon Affected Organizations', won the 1992 American Society for Information Science Doctoral Dissertation Award. Dr Wilkinson has spoken and published in the areas of intellectual property, information policy, information and media law, management, professionalism and professional ethics.

On faculty at the University of Western Ontario since 1991, Dr Wilkinson held a joint appointment between the Faculty of Law and the Faculty of Information and Media Studies. A full professor in both faculties, Professor Wilkinson was appointed full-time to Law in 2007 and is Director of the Area of Concentration in Intellectual Property, Information and Technology Law. She is also an Adjunct Professor at The Richard Ivey School of Business. She is the current editor of the *Canadian Intellectual Property Review*.

Preface

Whenever one is confronted with a particular intellectual property issue for which one's national law does not appear to offer an immediate answer, a common reflex is often to enquire whether that issue has already given rise to some discussion in the United States or in the European Union. The state of their technological development and the size of their economies make these two jurisdictions natural leaders in the search for solutions with respect to intellectual property matters. This leadership has also manifested itself on an institutional scale: if several European countries were instigators of the founding intellectual property conventions, the *Paris Convention for the Protection of Industrial Property* of 1883 and the *Berne Convention for the Protection of Literary and Artistic Works* of 1886, the driving force behind the *Agreement on Trade-related Aspects of Intellectual Property Rights* of 1994 has been the United States.

Over a century of events separates these two eras in the development of intellectual property law. It is already possible to appreciate that one of the key differences in the political environment of these instruments is the rise of the developing world as an active participant in the quest for a truly international understanding of intellectual property law. The Doha Declaration on the TRIPS Agreement and Public Health is the most conspicuous manifestation of this evolution. At the forefront of the international process, a North–South dialogue is thus engaged between developing countries and the leaders of the industrialised world.

While this dialogue is taking place, another movement is unfolding: other industrialised and industrialising countries are trying to find their own position amid these circumstances. One of these countries is Canada. Neither a superpower nor a developing country, yet a member of the G8, Canada must have intellectual property rules that are in keeping with international developments, but that remain adapted to its own economic and social realities. The texts that have been brought together in this volume are meant to highlight particular approaches to various issues within intellectual property law that have developed in Canada. Some pertain more to legislative solutions, while others stem mostly from judicial reasonings. All of them betray a preoccupation for solutions that suit national needs that need not necessarily coincide perfectly with those of its international allies. Of course, it has not been possible to be exhaustive. Yet, one hopes that this sampling of Canadian intellectual property issues by some of the foremost experts in the field today will give the reader a taste of the originality of this law.

On a more personal note, I should like to express my gratitude to all the contributors to this volume who have so readily accepted to take part in this project. Many thanks also go to François Senécal who coordinated the revision of the texts, to Mohamed Saifeddine Hichri who completed the table of jurisprudence, as well as to Luke Adams and Nep Elverd and all the members of the editorial team at Edward Elgar Publishing for their professionalism in making this book a reality.

Ysolde Gendreau
Montreal, November 2007

Table of jurisprudence

CANADA

AUSTRALIA

FRANCE

GERMANY

UNITED KINGDOM

UNITED STATES OF AMERICA

EUROPEAN UNION

WORLD TRADE ORGANIZATION (WTO)

PART 1

Industrial property

1. The challenge of trademark law in Canada's federal and bijural system

Teresa Scassa

In November of 2005, the Supreme Court of Canada handed down its decision in *Kirkbi AG v. Ritvik Holdings Inc.*[1] The Court's decision has implications for the interrelationship of the civil and common law traditions in dealing with unregistered trademarks in Canada. It also resolves lingering issues of the constitutional authority of the federal government to legislate with respect to trademarks.

Canada's constitution divides jurisdiction over the full range of legislative subject matter between federal and provincial governments. While intellectual property subjects have typically fallen within federal jurisdiction, some aspects of intellectual property protection are provincial in nature. This is particularly the case in the area of trademarks. Further, Canada is a mixed jurisdiction. While the three territories and nine of the ten provinces draw on the common law legal tradition, Quebec's private law is drawn from the French civil law tradition. This federal and bijural nature of Canada's legal system presents challenges for trademark law that cut across a variety of lines. This chapter will explore the issues which arise from the tension between the federal and provincial levels of government and between the co-existing common and civil law traditions, and will consider the impact of the *Kirkbi* decision on these issues.

I FEDERALISM AND THE CONSTITUTIONAL DIVISION OF POWERS

Legislative authority over various subject matters was divided between federal and provincial levels of government at the time of Canadian confederation in 1867. Throughout the course of Canada's constitutional history, trends in the judicial interpretation of these powers have alternately leaned towards strong

1 [2005] 3 S.C.R. 302, 2005 SCC 65 [*Kirkbi*].

regional or provincial powers or a stronger centralist presence.[2] With an increasingly complex economy, and the growth of international and interprovincial trade, the contemporary trend has been towards recognizing broader federal jurisdiction in key areas. Among the basket of powers accorded to the federal government in the *Constitution Act, 1867*,[3] is the specific authority to legislate with respect to copyrights (s. 91(23)) and patents (s. 91(22)). There is no allocation of legislative authority over trademarks.

Notwithstanding the absence of explicit constitutional authority to legislate with respect to trademarks, the federal government already had in place, at the time of confederation, legislation establishing a system of registration of trademarks. This early statute, *An Act to amend the Act respecting Trade Marks and to provide for Registrations of Designs*,[4] was quite different in structure and scope from the current *Trade-marks Act*.[5] Nevertheless, it marked the assertion of central constitutional authority over registered trademarks. This authority has never been seriously challenged (except in relation to its scope), and it is generally assumed that the basis for federal jurisdiction over trademarks is the federal government's power to regulate trade and commerce.[6] Indeed, in an early case involving the constitutionality of legislation to establish a national trademark, the Privy Council noted the existence of more general trademarks legislation in Canada and stated:

> No one has challenged the competence of the Dominion to pass such legislation. If challenged one obvious source of authority would appear to be the class of subjects enumerated in s. 91(2), the Regulation of trade and commerce. . . . There could hardly be a more appropriate form of the exercise of this power than the creation and regulation of a uniform law of trade marks.[7]

Yet in spite of the general consensus around the authority of the federal government to provide for a national scheme of trademarks registration under the trade and commerce power, there have remained areas of jurisdictional uncertainty and conflict. Even prior to the introduction of registration schemes for trademarks, both the common law tradition of English Canada and the civil

[2] Henri Brun & Guy Tremblay, *Droit constitutionnel*, 2nd ed. (Montreal: Yvon Blais, 1990) at 507.

[3] *Constitution Act, 1867* (U.K.), 30 & 31 Vict., c. 3, reprinted in R.S.C. 1985, App. II, No. 5 [*Constitution Act, 1867*].

[4] *An Act to amend the Act respecting Trade Marks and to provide for Registrations of Designs*, S. Prov. C. 1861 (24 Vict.), c. 21.

[5] *Trade-marks Act*, R.S.C. 1985, c. T-13 [*Trade-marks Act*].

[6] *Constitution Act, 1867*, *supra* note 3, s. 91(2).

[7] *Attorney-General for Ontario v. Attorney-General for Canada*, [1937] A.C. 405 (P.C.) at 417 [*Canada Standard Trade Mark*].

law tradition of Quebec recognized, in one form or another, unregistered trademarks. These marks have generally been protected through actions in tort or delict. The protection of these marks is founded on a recognition that a trader could develop a form of property interest in the goodwill or reputation through the use of a distinctive 'mark'.[8] The provincial power over 'property and civil rights in the province',[9] which includes the power over civil causes of action, has also long been held to give provinces authority over torts and delicts generally. This would include commercial torts such as passing off, or the civil law equivalent, the delict of *substitution*. It also gives jurisdiction over property rights. The ambiguous relationship between trademark protection and certain commercial torts has given rise to challenges to the validity of aspects of the *Trade-marks Act*.

The problems of conflict between spheres of legislative competence are most evident in dealing with small to mid-size enterprises which operate exclusively within the boundaries of a single province. These businesses might incorporate and register their business names under the relevant legislation in their province, and might rely upon common (or civil) law protection for any goodwill established in trade names, marks and indicia. Yet this reliance may turn out to be misplaced, as conflicts often arise between local businesses and those with a more national profile.[10] Further, a registered trademark will prevail over an unregistered trademark in most circumstances.[11] The scope and dominance of the federal scheme has been described as 'unfair', and inconsistent with a proper balancing of federal and provincial powers,[12] although this view is not universally shared.

---

[8] *Consumers Distributing Co. v. Seiko Time Canada Ltd.*, [1984] 1 S.C.R. 583 at 598 [*Seiko Time*].

[9] *Constitution Act, 1867*, *supra* note 3, s. 92(13).

[10] For example, it sometimes occurs that a purely local business (A) acquires goodwill and reputation in association with a mark that it has adopted to distinguish its wares or services. The same mark may have been adopted and used, unbeknownst to A, by another trader elsewhere in Canada (B) for similar wares or services. If B adopted and used the mark before A, and if B subsequently registers the mark, B will have the right to use the mark in association with those wares or services throughout Canada, and B's rights as a registered trademark holder will trump A's rights, even if A adopted the mark in good faith, and with no knowledge of B's prior use. This result is somewhat tempered by s. 21(1) of the *Trade-marks Act*, *supra* note 5, which sets out very limited circumstances in which A will be permitted to continue to use his or her mark.

[11] If the mark is registered by the person who first used it, it will prevail over identical unregistered marks, even if it is only used and known in a limited geographical region of the country. Even if it is registered by someone other than the first user of the mark in Canada, it will prevail if the registration was in good faith and is more than five years old. See *Trade-marks Act*, *supra* note 5, ss. 18, 17(2), 19.

[12] Daniel R. Bereskin, 'Federal v. Provincial Trade-Marks and Trade Name Rights: Is the tension at the Breaking Point?' (1989–90) 6 C.I.P.R. 233.

The source of the difficulties is that the federal *Trade-marks Act* does not limit itself to the regulation of *registered* trademarks, but also governs unregistered trademarks. Unregistered trademarks have long been considered to derive from the common (or civil) law, thus falling within the domain of the provinces. The coexistence of the two regimes creates some overt points of conflict. Indeed, one author has noted that ss. 3 to 11 of the *Trade-marks Act*, which govern unregistered trademarks, will apply to marks even if they are used only within a single province, and thus will have a real impact on the adoption and use of unregistered marks at the provincial level.[13]

The tensions between the spheres of federal and provincial competence have often been expressed as challenges to the constitutionality of the *Trade-marks Act*. Some have questioned the jurisdiction of Parliament with respect to official marks,[14] and others have raised broader objections, citing a number of provisions whose constitutionality they question.[15] Bereskin has argued that the scope of the federal government's constitutional authority over trademarks does not extend to overriding those trademark rights which arise at common law.[16] He argues that s. 19 of the Act, which gives the owner of a registered trademark the right to exclusive use of the mark throughout Canada, should not extend to regions of the country where the owner's mark is unknown. In Bereskin's view, the infringement provisions of the *Trade-marks Act* should be applied, on a case-by-case basis, in a manner that is sensitive to the fact that trademark rights may arise by regulation under the federal scheme or by the operation of provincial common law. Courts should not allow the rights under the federal scheme to run roughshod over rights acquired at common law. Although Bereskin is able to cite some cases where courts have balanced the interests of common law rights holders with those of owners of registered trademarks,[17] the dominant trend in the case law has been to give a firm preeminence to registered marks.

The most contentious provision of the *Trade-marks Act* from a constitutional perspective has been s. 7 (formerly s. 11 of the *Unfair Competition Act*[18]). Section 7 applies to unregistered trademarks, and governs conduct

13 Hugues G. Richard, 'Provincial Trade Marks' (1988–89) 5 C.I.P.R. 301 at 306.

14 An issue regarding the constitutionality of s. 9 was raised, and quickly dismissed, in *Canadian Olympic Association v. Konica Canada Inc.* (1991), 39 C.P.R. (3d) 400 (F.C.A.).

15 Richard, *supra* note 13.

16 Bereskin, *supra* note 12 at 238.

17 *Ibid.* at 240–42. It is worth noting that for registrations of trademarks under s. 12(2) and s. 13 of the Act, which depend upon acquired distinctiveness of the mark, the Registrar may restrict the registration of a mark to those geographical areas of Canada in which the mark has acquired distinctiveness.

18 S.C. 1932, c. 38.

very similar to passing off and to 'unfair competition' more generally. It provides:

> 7. No person shall
> (*a*) make a false or misleading statement tending to discredit the business, wares or services of a competitor;
> (*b*) direct public attention to his wares, services or business in such a way as to cause or be likely to cause confusion in Canada, at the time he commenced so to direct attention to them, between his wares, services or business and the wares, services or business of another;
> (*c*) pass off other wares or services as and for those ordered or requested;
> (*d*) make use, in association with wares or services, of any description that is false in a material respect and likely to mislead the public as to
> (i) the character, quality, quantity or composition,
> (ii) the geographical origin, or
> (iii) the mode of the manufacture, production or performance
> of the wares or services; or
> (*e*) do any other act or adopt any other business practice contrary to honest industrial or commercial usage in Canada.

Paragraph 7(*a*) covers territory most closely associated with the common law tort of injurious falsehood. Paragraphs 7(*b*) and (*c*) address what is commonly understood as 'passing off', and paras 7(*d*) and (*e*) are addressed at regulating honesty in commercial practices.

Section 7 applies to a range of commercial conduct in much the same way that the existing civil causes of action would, and this gives rise to constitutional tension. From a constitutional point of view, the issue is whether the federal government has usurped provincial jurisdiction over a series of commercial torts or delicts that properly lie within the provinces' jurisdiction over property and civil rights.

The constitutionality of para. 7(*e*) was directly challenged in *MacDonald et al. v. Vapor Canada Ltd.*[19] The case made its way to the Supreme Court of Canada, which confirmed that the federal power to legislate with respect to trademarks was rooted in the general trade and commerce power under the constitution. However, the Court found that para. 7(*e*) fell outside the legislative scope of this power, as the provision clearly cast its net far beyond conduct linked to actual trademarks, whether registered or unregistered. Chief Justice Laskin ruled that para. 7(*e*) of the *Trade-marks Act* was *ultra vires* Parliament because it lacked the regulatory scheme required for a valid exercise of the general trade and commerce power. He stated:

---

19 [1977] 2 S.C.R. 134 [*Vapor Canada*].

> One looks in vain for any regulatory scheme in s. 7, let alone s. 7(e). Its enforcement is left to the chance of private redress without public monitoring by the continuing oversight of a regulatory agency which would at least lend some colour to the alleged national or Canada-wide sweep of s. 7(e). The provision is not directed to trade but to the ethical conduct of persons engaged in a trade or in business, and, in my view, such a detached provision cannot survive alone unconnected to a general regulatory scheme to govern trading relations going beyond merely local concern.[20]

The majority of the Court did not find that the *Trade-marks Act* as a whole was unconstitutional. Rather, their view was that s. 7(*e*) did not fit within the general (and otherwise legitimate) regulatory scheme in the *Trade-marks Act*. The Chief Justice noted that paragraph 7(*e*) 'has not been brought under a regulatory authority in association with the scheme of public control operating upon trade marks'.[21]

By requiring the provisions of the *Trade-marks Act* to be associated with a 'scheme of public control' or a regulatory regime, the Court cast the constitutionality of the whole of s. 7 into doubt. The Chief Justice observed: 'Neither s. 7 as a whole, nor s. 7(*e*), if either stood alone and in association only with s. 53, would be valid federal legislation in relation to the regulation of trade and commerce or in relation to any other head of federal legislative authority.'[22] Section 7, standing alone, would be a mere duplication of existing commercial torts grounded in provincial authority over property and civil rights. Nevertheless, although the Court found para. 7(*e*) to be invalid, it distinguished this provision from the other paragraphs of s. 7. The rest of s. 7 could be within federal jurisdiction 'in so far as it may be said to round out regulatory schemes prescribed by Parliament in the exercise of its legislative power in relation to patents, copyrights or trade marks and trade names'.[23] Thus, to the extent that paras. 7(*a*) to (*d*) rounded out a general statutory scheme to regulate trademarks and trade names, they had constitutional validity. Paragraph 7(*e*), however, could not be saved. In the view of the Court, it either duplicated the substance of paras. 7(*a*) to 7(*d*) and thus had no independent meaning, or it went beyond the reach of those provisions and thus prohibited 'any other act' or 'any other business practice contrary to honest industrial or commercial usage in Canada'. Such a general prohibition was simply too broad to be a sustainable exercise of federal jurisdiction.

Following *Vapor Canada*, the accepted view was that the *Trade-marks Act*, to the extent that it provided a comprehensive regulatory scheme for registered and unregistered trademarks, was constitutionally supported by the general

---

20 *Ibid.* at 167.
21 *Ibid.*
22 *Ibid.* at 172.
23 *Ibid.*

trade and commerce power of the federal government.[24] Paragraph 7(*e*), because it went beyond any scheme to regulate trademarks, was *ultra vires* Parliament. Nevertheless, questions remained about the constitutionality of s. 7 generally.[25] This was largely because the remainder of s. 7 appeared to duplicate existing causes of action in tort or delict, and did not provide specific remedies for the infringement of *registered* trademarks.[26] The uncertainty spawned sporadic constitutional challenges.

The constitutionality of s. 7 of the *Trade-marks Act* was most recently, and perhaps most definitively, considered by the Supreme Court of Canada in *Kirkbi AG v. Ritvik Holdings Inc.*[27] The case involved a dispute over whether the appearance of the Lego™ brick constituted an unregistered trademark in the form of a distinguishing guise. The *Kirkbi* Court confirmed the long held view that constitutional authority for the enactment of the *Trade-marks Act* flowed from s. 91(2) of the *Constitution Act, 1867*: the trade and commerce power.[28] The Court also noted that federal power over trade and commerce was limited to international and inter-provincial trade and commerce, or to 'general trade and commerce affecting Canada as a whole'.[29] The Court described these limitations as being necessary to balance 'the otherwise overlapping federal power over trade and commerce (s. 91(2)) and the provincial power over property and civil rights in the province (s. 92(13))'.[30]

The Court situated the *Trade-marks Act* under the general trade and commerce power. It identified five factors required for a valid exercise of that power:

> (i) the impugned legislation must be part of a regulatory scheme; (ii) the scheme must be monitored by the continuing oversight of a regulatory agency; (iii) the

---

24 The view was not, however, unanimous. In *Motel 6, Inc. v. No. 6 Motel Ltd. et al.* (1981), 56 C.P.R. (2d) 44 (F.C.T.D.) [*Motel 6*], Addy J. found s. 7(*b*) of the *Trade-marks Act* to be *ultra vires* the federal government's legislative authority. In *ACA Joe International v. 147255 Canada Inc. et al.* (1986), 10 C.P.R. (3d) 301 (F.C.T.D.), Collier J. followed the decision in *Motel 6*.

25 The constitutionality of s. 7, in whole or in part, was raised in a number of other cases including: *Banquet & Catering Supplies Rental Ltd. v. Bench & Table Rental World Inc.* (1979), 52 C.P.R. (2d) 71 (Que. S.C.), *Seiko Time*, *supra* note 8 and *Les rôtisseries St-Hubert Ltée v. Le Syndicat des Travailleur(euse)s de la rôtisserie St-Hubert de Drummondville (C.S.N.)* (1986), 17 C.P.R. (3d) 461 (Que. S.C.) [*Rôtisseries St-Hubert*].

26 Recourse for the infringement of registered trademarks is provided for in ss. 19, 20 and 22 of the *Trade-marks Act*, *supra* note 5.

27 *Supra* note 1.

28 *Ibid.* at para. 15.

29 *Ibid.*

30 *Ibid.*

> legislation must be concerned with trade as a whole rather than with a particular industry; (iv) the legislation should be of a nature that provinces jointly or severally would be constitutionally incapable of enacting; and (v) the failure to include one or more provinces or localities in a legislative scheme would jeopardize the successful operation of the scheme in other parts of the country.[31]

The Court noted that while the constitutionality of particular provisions of the Act had been challenged in the past, the constitutionality of the Act as a whole had never been conclusively determined. Because of the framework of analysis adopted by the Court in *Kirkbi*, it incorporated into its consideration of the validity of para. 7(*b*) an assessment of the constitutionality of the Act as a whole.

The Court stated that 'if s. 7(*b*) is sufficiently integrated into the scheme of the *Trade-marks Act* as a whole'[32], then it will be constitutionally valid notwithstanding the fact that it encroaches on provincial powers over property and civil rights. Applying the three factors identified in *General Motors of Canada Ltd. v. City National Leasing*,[33] Justice LeBel noted that s. 7(*b*) of the *Trade-marks Act* is remedial and related to the enforcement of substantive provisions of the Act. He noted as well that it protects unregistered trademarks, and in doing so 'merely rounds out an otherwise incomplete trade-mark scheme'.[34] Justice LeBel concluded that 'civil causes of action are *intra vires* Parliament if sufficiently integrated into valid federal legislation'.[35] This conclusion moved him on to the next stage of inquiry: whether the *Trade-marks Act* was valid federal legislation as a whole.

Justice LeBel noted that there was no challenge to the federal government's authority to regulate registered trademarks. What was at issue was whether this scheme could also legitimately address unregistered trademarks. Justice LeBel wrote:

> The protection of unregistered trade-marks is integral to the legitimacy, legal standards and efficacy of registered trade-marks. The *Trade-marks Act* is clearly concerned with trade as a whole, as opposed to within a particular industry. There is no question that trade-marks apply across and between industries in different provinces. Divided provincial and federal jurisdiction could mean that the provincial law could be changed by each provincial legislature. This could result in unregistered trade-marks that were more strongly protected than registered trade-marks, undermining the efficacy and integrity of the federal Parliament's Trade-marks Act. The lack of a civil remedy integrated into the scheme of the Act, applicable to all

31 *Kirkbi*, *supra* note 5 at para. 17.
32 *Ibid*. at para. 23.
33 [1989] 1 S.C.R. 641.
34 *Kirkbi*, *supra* note 5 at para. 26.
35 *Ibid*. at para. 27.

> marks, registered or unregistered, might also lead to duplicative or conflicting and hence inefficient enforcement procedures.[36]

Justice LeBel noted that many provisions of the *Trade-marks Act* addressed unregistered marks. He pointed out that '[t]he primary difference between registered and unregistered trade-marks under the Act is that the rights of a holder of a registered trade-mark are more extensive'.[37] Registration confers additional rights and recourses, yet 'marks remain marks, whether registered or unregistered, because their legal characteristics are the same'.[38]

The Court therefore concluded that a scheme governing both registered and unregistered marks was legitimately within federal jurisdiction over trade and commerce. The final stage in their analysis was to consider the extent to which the impugned provision was integrated into the Act. Justice LeBel found that para. 7(*b*) intruded only minimally into provincial jurisdiction. He stated: 'In its pith and substance, s. 7(*b*) is directly connected to the enforcement of trade-marks and trade-names in Canada: the civil remedy in s. 7(*b*) protects the goodwill associated with trade-marks and is directed to avoiding consumer confusion through use of trade-marks.'[39] He expressed the view that without para. 7(*b*), 'there would be a gap in the legislative protection of trade-marks'.[40] In drawing the conclusion that para. 7(*b*) was sufficiently integrated into the federal scheme, he distinguished it from para. 7(*e*), which was not tied in any way to the existence of a registered or unregistered trademark.

Following *Kirkbi*, it is now clear that the *Trade-marks Act* as a whole is valid federal legislation, and that para. 7(*b*) is also valid to the extent that it rounds out that legislative scheme in relation to trademarks. The Court has accepted that paras. 7(*a*) and (*d*) are also valid, in so far as they relate to patents, trade-marks or copyrights. Although no specific mention is made of para. 7(*c*), it is likely also valid.[41] The invalidity of para. 7(*e*) is confirmed.[42] It would likely be an uphill battle to successfully challenge the constitutionality of other provisions of the *Trade-marks Act*, given the Supreme Court's approach in *Kirkbi*. It is not an objection in and of itself to state that provisions dealing with unregistered marks trench on provincial powers as the Court has clearly accepted that the federal scheme may legitimately address both registered and unregistered marks. The only real issue, on a provision by provision

---

36 *Ibid.* at para. 29.
37 *Ibid.* at para. 30.
38 *Ibid.*
39 *Ibid.* at para. 35.
40 *Ibid.* at para. 36.
41 *Ibid.* at para. 34.
42 *Ibid.* at para. 36.

basis, would be the degree of integration of each provision within the overall regulatory scheme. If paras. 7(*a*) through (*d*) can survive, there is likely not much basis for challenge to other sections of the Act.

It is also clear however that the federal government does not have the competence to regulate 'unfair competition', broadly speaking, and that its authority over other territory normally covered by commercial torts is limited to matters bearing some connection to patents, copyrights or trademarks. For example, para. 7(*a*), which provides that no person shall: 'make a false or misleading statement tending to discredit the business, wares or services of a competitor' could be said to cover much of the same ground as the common law tort of injurious falsehood, although para. 7(*a*) does not appear to require malice, whereas the common law tort does.[43] Nevertheless, the courts have held that para. 7(*a*) depends for its constitutional validity on its rounding out a valid federal scheme. Thus, in one case where allegedly false statements were made with respect to a product for which a patent had not yet been granted Justice Rouleau ruled that para. 7(*a*) could not be said in that case to be rounding out the provisions of the *Patent Act*, as the inventor had yet to acquire any rights under that Act.[44] Where a patent exists, para. 7(*a*) might well play a role in curbing abuses that flowed from patent holders making false claims regarding the scope or extent of their rights.[45] However, where a patent has not yet been granted, any protection of the inventor's invention falls to trade secret protection, 'a matter unquestionably governed by provincial law'.[46] The situation is somewhat different with trademarks, as it has been recognized that the *Trade-marks Act* governs both registered and unregistered marks. Nevertheless, some issues remain unanswered. For example, some have questioned whether this section can legitimately apply where false or misleading statements are made in comparative advertising. Gill & Jolliffe ask whether, in such a context, para. 7(*a*) would apply if the plaintiff's product was referred to by its trademark name, but would cease to apply if the product was merely referenced as 'the leading brand' or in some other oblique manner.[47]

It may also be that in some circumstances, recourse under para. 7(*b*) will not be available. In a case which predates *Kirkbi*, *Dumont Vins & Spiritueux Inc. v. Celliers du Monde Inc.*,[48] the Federal Court of Appeal considered the

---

43 *S & S Industries Inc. v. Rowell* (1966), 56 D.L.R. (2d) 501 (S.C.C.).

44 *Safematic, Inc. v. Sensodec Oy* (1988), 21 C.P.R. (3d) 12 (F.C.T.D.) [*Safematic*].

45 *Riello Canada, Inc. v. Lambert* (1986), 9 C.P.R. (3d) 324 (F.C.T.D.).

46 *Safematic*, *supra* note 44 at 21.

47 Gill & Jolliffe, *Fox on Canadian Law of Trade-marks and Unfair Competition*, 4th ed., looseleaf (Toronto: Thomson Carswell, 2002) at §2.2(b)(ii)(B).

48 [1992] 2 F.C. 634 (F.C.A.), (1992), 42 C.P.R. (3d) 197 [*Dumont #2* cited to F.C.].

extent to which an action brought under para. 7(*b*) is dependent upon the existence of an unregistered trademark. A previous decision of the Quebec Superior Court involving the two parties had found that the distinguishing guise at issue, a bottle, had not acquired distinctiveness, and was thus not an unregistered trademark.[49] The appeal of the Superior Court decision was discontinued. An injunction was later sought from the Federal Court to prevent the marketing of the defendant's product in a somewhat different bottle. The injunction was granted, and the decision was appealed. The Federal Court of Appeal ruled that the decision of the Quebec Superior Court, that the plaintiff's bottle lacked the necessary distinctiveness to be an unregistered trademark, was *res judicata*. Justice Décary then went on to state:

> It seems to me to follow from these reasons that s. 7(*b*) is valid in so far as the passing-off action is connected to a trade mark, registered or not, but that it would not be valid in a case such as the one at bar in which the passing off action, as a result of the fact that the absence of an unregistered trade mark is *res judicata*, is not connected to any trade mark. In my opinion, the same reasoning applies to para. (*c*).[50]

The Court thus denied relief under s. 7 of the *Trade-marks Act* on the basis that it had no jurisdiction.

While s. 7 has been the focus of the majority of constitutional challenges in the trademarks area, it is not the only area where provincial and federal powers converge. The provinces have jurisdiction, as a matter of 'property and civil rights'[51] over the incorporation of businesses. Typically, provinces will regulate the adoption of business names. There is potential for conflict between provincial legislation governing business names and federal trademark legislation, particularly where registered trademarks conflict with business names. In *Reference re Constitution Act, 1867*,[52] the Manitoba Court of Appeal considered, *inter alia*, questions relating to the relationship between the province's *Corporations Act*[53] and *Business Names Registration Act*,[54] and the federal *Trade-marks Act*. Justice Twaddle observed that 'The fact that a word has been registered as a trade mark gives its owner no right to use it

---

49 *Dumont Vins & Spiritueux Inc. v. Celliers du Monde Inc.*, [1990] R.J.Q. 556 (Que. S.C.) [*Dumont* #1].

50 *Dumont* #2, *supra* note 48 at 651.

51 *Constitution Act, 1867*, *supra* note 3, s. 91(13).

52 *Reference re Constitution Act, 1867* (1991), 35 C.P.R. (3d) 289 (Man. C.A.) [*Reference re Constitution Act*].

53 R.S.M. 1987, c. C225.

54 R.S.M. 1987, c. B110.

in his business name. The province may regulate that usage if the business is local in nature.'[55] Nevertheless, he continued:

> . . . the province cannot regulate the use of a trade mark because it has a similarity to an existing business name in the province. So long as the trade mark is used in association with the product or the service which it identifies, the trade mark owner may use it notwithstanding that it may cause confusion between the business of the trade mark owner and that of a local business using a similar name. A dispute over such confusion must be resolved under the federal laws.[56]

Justice Jewers took the matter further. He noted that the *Business Names Registration Act* required a company carrying on business under a trade name other than its business name to register under the Act. The Act also provided that where there is likely to be confusion between a prospective registrant's trade name and another trade name, the registration must be rejected. Justice Jewers noted:

> Under the doctrine of paramountcy, any conflict [between the provincial legislation and the *Trade-marks Act*] must be resolved in favour of the federal legislation. It follows that a corporate body could not be successfully prosecuted for breaches of either s. 191(1) of the *Corporations Act* or s. 2(1) of the *Business Names Registration Act* (and could not be refused registration under the latter) solely because the corporation was exercising its exclusive right to the use throughout Canada of its registered trade mark.[57]

In the opinion of Justice Jewers, the right to exclusive use of a registered trade-mark provided for under s. 19 of the *Trade-marks Act* combined with the presumption of trademark validity, would take precedence over the provisions in the provincial legislation. In consequence, while it remains open to the provinces to regulate the adoption of business names for provincially incorporated businesses, the federal *Trade-marks Act* is paramount over the provincial legislation in areas of conflict. The provincial laws cannot limit the rights of a registered trademark owner to use its trademark, even if the mark is confusing with a provincially registered business name.

II BIJURALISM IN THE CANADIAN CONTEXT: PRINCIPLES OF HARMONIZATION

The coexistence of private law recourses with the federal *Trade-marks Act*

---

55 *Reference Re Constitution Act*, *supra* note 52 at 307.

56 *Ibid.*

57 *Ibid.* at 315.

draws into the picture another particular feature of the Canadian legal system: its bijural nature. A short-lived attempt by the British to substitute English law for the received French law following the conquest of New France in 1763 gave way to the compromise reflected in the *Quebec Act* of 1774.[58] This enactment restored French law in matters relating to property and civil rights, with a few exceptions.[59] Over time, English law came to heavily influence administrative law, civil procedure and the structure of the courts, leaving Quebec with a hybrid or 'mixed' system of laws. The other provinces of Canada received English law, and their private law was the received English common law and equity. In this sense, therefore, the bijural nature of Canada's legal system is predominantly evident in Quebec, where the private law remains based in the civil law tradition, yet is interpreted and applied within a procedural context heavily influenced by the common law.

The pressure to harmonize private law for the greater facilitation of commercial and other relationships among provinces has often had an influence on the development of Quebec's private law. The law of passing off is an example of this. The *Civil Code of Quebec* contains no specific provision outlining a delict of passing off. The core provision governing delictual liability is art. 1457 (formerly art. 1053 of the *Civil Code of Lower Canada*), which reads:

> 1457. Every person has a duty to abide by the rules of conduct which lie upon him, according to the circumstances, usage or law, so as not to cause injury to another.
>
> Where he is endowed with reason and fails in this duty, he is responsible for any injury he causes to another person and is liable to reparation for the injury, whether it be bodily, moral or material in nature.
>
> He is also liable, in certain cases, to reparation for injury caused to another by the act or fault of another person or by the act of things in his custody.

A cause of action equivalent to passing off is considered to fall under this article's broad ambit, but it is only one of a range of recognized recourses for 'concurrence déloyale' or unfair competition that are said to fall within the scope of art. 1457.

Article 1457 has been said to encompass three main categories of actions amounting to unfair competition: acts of confusion, acts of denigration and

---

[58] *Quebec Act, 1774* (U.K.), 14 Geo III, c. 83 reprinted in R.S.C. 1985, App. II, No. 2.

[59] The exceptions included the abolition of the feudal system of land tenure, and the incorporation of the principle of freedom of willing. See John E.C. Brierley & Roderick A. Macdonald, *Quebec Civil Law: An Introduction to Quebec Private Law* (Toronto: Emond Montgomery Publications, 1993) at 16.

acts of disorganization.[60] To give some illustrations by way of comparison with common law actions, passing off would fall within the first general category, actions such as the tort of injurious falsehood or defamation would fall in the second category, and the abuse of confidential information by a former employee would fall within the third. All three of these categories of delictual activity are said to be encompassed by s. 7 of the *Trade-marks Act*.[61]

Passing off is sometimes known by different names in Quebec. In *Demco Manufacturing Inc. c. Foyer d'artisanat Raymond inc.*,[62] the Court of Appeal of Quebec considered an action characterized as a species of unfair competition known interchangeably as '*commercialisation trompeuse*' or the delict of '*substitution*'. Whatever the name of the cause of action, the Court of Appeal stated that it was equivalent to passing off in common law.[63] The Court accepted the elements of the action as being those set out by the Supreme Court of Canada in *Ciba-Geigy*,[64] a case involving the common law tort of passing off. Indeed, in that case the Supreme Court of Canada had stated that: 'The passing-off rules in Quebec are derived largely from the common law.'[65] Although in Quebec the action is brought under art. 1457 of the *Civil Code of Quebec*, in the words of the Court of Appeal: 'rien n'empêche, s'agissant de commercialisation trompeuse, de subsumer sous cette règle générale les éléments mis en lumière par l'énoncé du juge Gonthier [dans l'arrêt *Ciba-Geigy*].'[66] Thus, in Quebec, an action which is the functional equivalent of the common law tort of passing off is available under the *Civil Code of Quebec*.

The similarity between the common law tort of passing off and the civil law recourse for *substitution* or *commercialisation trompeuse* is perhaps even less surprising in light of the presence of paras. 7(*b*) and (*c*) in the *Trade-marks Act*. In spite of the fact that s. 7 has been said to 'codify' the tort of passing off and its civil law equivalent, it has not supplanted those recourses in private law.[67] In common law Canada, an action in passing off may still be brought in a provincial superior court. In Quebec, an action in delict for conduct amount-

---

60 Mistrale Goudreau, 'Concurrence déloyale en droit privé – commentaires d'arrêts' (1984) 15 Rev. Gen. de Droit 133 at 136.

61 *Ibid.* at 138. Note, however, that without s. 7(e), the scope of s. 7 is much less broad.

62 [2006] J.Q. no 222, 2006 QCCA 52 [*Demco*].

63 *Ibid.* at para. 8.

64 *Ibid.* at paras. 9-11.

65 *Ciba-Geigy Canada Ltd. v. Apotex Inc,* [1992] 3 S.C.R. 120 at para. 39, (1992), 44 C.P.R. (3d) 289 (S.C.C.) [*Ciba-Geigy*].

66 *Demco*, *supra* note 62 at para. 12.

67 See, e.g.: *Rôtisseries St-Hubert*, *supra* note 25, where the court, when faced with issues regarding the constitutionality of s. 7 of the *Trade-marks Act* proceeded to deal with the case as one of delict under art. 1053 of the *Civil Code of Lower Canada*.

ing to passing off can also be initiated in a provincial superior court. The basic elements of the tort of passing off are the same whether the action is initiated at common law or under para. 7(*b*) or (*c*). Section 7, which took on its current form with the enactment of the *Trade-marks Act* of 1953,[68] does not merely reflect a codification of the law of passing off as it existed at that time. The courts have consistently applied the same legal tests and precedents to cases whether they are brought under the common law tort or under s. 7(*b*) or (*c*) of the Act. Indeed, in *Kirkbi*, the Supreme Court of Canada said of the common law tort: 'Its principles now inform both statute law and common law.'[69]

The harmonization of the recourse under the statute with the recourse available at common law has had an almost inevitable practical effect of harmonizing as well those principles that will guide the civil recourse under the laws of Quebec. In Quebec, rather than saying that paras. 7(*b*) and (*c*) represent a codification of the common law tort of passing off, the issue has been framed as the civil law recourse being broad enough to encompass the causes of action set out in paras. 7(*b*) and (*c*).[70]

At least one author has criticized an incautious reliance on English common law in informing the law of passing off in Canada. Clearly English common law has been highly influential in shaping the law of passing off in Canada,[71] and being the received law, it is not inappropriate that modern developments be considered. Yet Richard argues that principles of common law from a unitary jurisdiction such as the United Kingdom must be incorporated with caution in a federal state such as Canada, where ten separate provinces have jurisdiction over their private law rules and the federal government has a distinct statutory recourse.[72] Yet this point of view has not carried the day. In *Ciba-Geigy*, the Supreme Court of Canada stated: 'The passing off rules in Quebec are derived largely from the common law',[73] and in *Kirkbi* it stated that para. 7(*b*) of the *Trade-marks Act* amounts to a codification of the law of

68 The predecessor provision, s. 11(b) of the *Unfair Competition Act*, S.C. 1932, c. 38, was, in fact, very similar.

69 *Kirkbi*, *supra* note 1 at para. 63.

70 *Compro Communications Inc. v. Communications Promo-Phone LT Inc.* (1991), 41 C.P.R. (3d) 260 (Que. S.C.).

71 In *Ciba-Geigy*, supra note 65, Justice Gonthier for the unanimous Supreme Court of Canada described the general principle of passing off, and cited in support a line of British cases including: *Perry v. Truefitt* (1842), 6 Beav. 66, 49 E.R. 749; *Singer Manufacturing Co. v. Loog* (1880), 18 Ch.D. 395 (C.A.), aff'd (1882), 8 App. Cas. 15 (H.L.); *Erven Warnink B.V. v. J. Townend & Sons (Hull) Ltd.*, [1979] A.C. 731, [1980] R.P.C. 31 (H.L.) and *Reckitt & Colman Products Ltd. v. Borden Inc.*, [1990] 1 All E.R. 873 (H.L.).

72 Richard, *supra* note 13 at 312.

73 *Ciba-Geigy*, *supra* note 65 at para. 39.

passing off.[74] Such statements imply that there is only one law of passing off for all of Canada, regardless of provincial competencies and even of the distinct private law tradition of Quebec.

In spite of the influences of common law Canada, and the effect of the 'codification' of the tort of passing off in paras. 7(*b*) and (*c*) of the *Trade-marks Act*, there is the potential for distinctive approaches to emerge in the Quebec courts. Civil law methodology is distinct from common law approaches, and the broad statement of principle in art. 1457 of the *Civil Code of Quebec* leaves room for flexibility in application. At the same time, the location of the recourses for unfair competition under the umbrella of art. 1457 poses some challenges in that the general theories of delictual liability require proof of fault on the part of the defendant as well as proof of damage.[75] By contrast, passing off at common law requires neither intent to deceive nor proof of damage.

Goudreau explains these differences in approach to the concept of 'fault'by noting that since competition is inherently socially desirable and therefore not actionable,[76] acts of unfair competition amounting to passing off must be based on fault of some kind. She notes that in the past, this was translated by some courts as a requirement of 'bad faith'.[77] Another line of cases has moved the law away from a requirement of bad faith,[78] focusing instead on the issue of confusion. Writing in 1949, Nadeau rejected a requirement of bad faith, and framed the concept as follows: 'Il suffit qu'il y ait des actes destinés à créer une confusion probable entre des produits similaires, et qu'il en résulte un préjudice chez un concurrent en butte à ces tactiques.'[79] This approach is largely in harmony with contemporary approaches to the tort of passing off. Yet Nadeau's formulation would appear to require actual damage, whereas, at common law, a plaintiff may show either actual damage or a likelihood of damage.[80]

Goudreau is critical of developments in Quebec law that award damages without proof of harm. She argues that proof of harm is a principle of delictual liability in Quebec law. She cites decisions in which Quebec courts have presumed damage once proof of confusion is made.[81] Nevertheless, this

---

74 *Kirkbi*, *supra* note 1 at para. 23.

75 Goudreau, *supra* note 60 at 138.

76 The same point is also made by André Nadeau, *Traité de Droit Civil du Québec*, vol. 8 (Montreal: Wilson & Lafleur, 1949) at 186.

77 Goudreau, *supra* note 60 at 148.

78 *Ibid.* at 150.

79 Nadeau, *supra* note 76 at 187.

80 Note that the requirement for the plaintiff to show harm is emphasized again by Nadeau, *supra* note 76 at 189.

81 Goudreau, *supra* note 60 at 154.

approach is consistent with common law approaches to passing off and, following the Supreme Court of Canada's decisions in *Ciba-Geigy* and most recently *Kirkbi*, it is difficult to maintain that there are significant differences between the two actions.

Notwithstanding these doctrinal controversies, there is also room for the development of distinct approaches that flow from the location of the action within a broader framework for delictual liablility. In *TV Guide Inc./TV Hebdo Inc. v. Publications La Semaine Inc. et al.*,[82] the Quebec Superior Court granted an injunction based on the defendant's counter-claim against the plaintiff due to evidence of a deliberate strategy to 'semer la confusion' or create confusion between the two products. Although the objectionable conduct involved the deceptive use of words which formed part of the claimant's trademark, the court found that the facts fell short of an action in passing off. Nevertheless, the court found that the conduct fell within the language of art. 1053 of the *Civil Code of Lower Canada* (now replaced by art. 1457 of the *Civil Code of Quebec*). The court characterized it as a form of unfair competition.

Canada's mixed system of law supposes to some extent that there is a cross-pollination of principles and ideas between one legal tradition and the other. Yet such cross-fertilization depends to a large extent on the mutual accessibility of legal authorities, be they case law or doctrine, to practitioners in both traditions. In Canada, language plays a role in the interaction between common law and civil law traditions.

With the exception of New Brunswick, which is officially bilingual, Canada's provinces tend to operate for all practical purposes in only one of the two official languages. In the overwhelming number of instances, federally appointed judges of the provincial superior courts in the common law provinces of Canada (again, excepting New Brunswick) deliver their reasons in English, and with very few exceptions, these decisions are not translated into French. In Quebec, judges often issue their reasons in the language in which the litigation was conducted, but in practical terms, this is most often French. Decisions of the Federal Court of Canada and the Supreme Court of Canada are published in both official languages. While there are some francophone or bilingual lawyers outside of Quebec, for the most part, facility in the French language in the English Canadian legal community is relatively limited. The ability to function in both French and English is much higher within the Quebec bar. The result of these dynamics is that while decisions on important issues of law rendered in English in common law Canada may be read by Quebec lawyers and judges, and may influence the development of

---

82 (1984), 9 C.P.R. (3d) 368 (Que. S.C.).

law in that jurisdiction, and while decisions of the federal and supreme courts are equally accessible across the country, decisions emanating from Quebec courts have a relatively low level of penetration into common law Canada. As a consequence, developments in the law of passing off in common law Canada are likely to be more influential than developments in Quebec, notwithstanding the fact that the principles applied may be very similar.

At the same time, the structure of court recourse for trademark infringement allows for a relatively high degree of harmonization between developments in the law across Canada. Actions for the infringement of a registered trademark may be brought in the superior courts of any province where sufficient jurisdictional ties exist. Alternatively, they may be brought in the Federal Court of Canada, which has jurisdiction throughout Canada. A decision rendered by a provincial superior court has precedential value in that province, and has effect within that province. By contrast, a decision of the Federal Court has effect throughout Canada. Actions for the infringement of an unregistered trademark – typically passing off – may be brought under paras. 7(*b*) or (*c*) or at common law in any relevant provincial superior court. However, an action for passing off at common law may not be brought in the federal courts – in the federal court, passing off may only be asserted under paras. 7(*b*) or (*c*). While the Supreme Court of Canada has stated that paras. 7(*b*) and (*c*) are effectively equivalent to the tort of passing off, the separate provincial silos for common law actions in passing off, and for the equivalent Quebec delictual action, do leave some room for distinctive application of the law. It is at the provincial superior court level that language is the greatest factor: as decisions of the federal courts are available in both official languages, these decisions are widely accessible in all jurisdictions. By contrast, decisions of the provincial superior courts will normally be in the dominant language of the relevant province, and decisions from the Quebec Superior Court in particular are likely to be overlooked by courts and lawyers in the other provinces.

Some decisions of Quebec courts do have a broader influence due to the fact that at least one commercial case reporter series, the *Canadian Patent Reporter*, has, from time to time, published translations of what its editors consider to be key intellectual property cases from Quebec. For example, the decision in *Sport Maska Inc. v. Canstar Sports Group Inc.*[83] was considered interesting enough to be translated from French into English and published in the *Canadian Patent Reporter* series.[84] The editorial note attached to the trans-

83 (1994), 57 C.P.R. (3d) 323 (Que. S.C.).

84 It is not uncommon for intellectual property related decisions of the Quebec courts to be published in the Canadian Patent Reporter series. However, they are not always translated, although untranslated decisions are accompanied by short English language head notes.

lation observed that the case was distinctive in that it had attached the words 'contrary to honest industrial or commercial usage' to its passing off analysis. This is present in Nadeau's discussion of the delict of 'concurrence déloyale', where he notes, in general terms, that competition is unfair if it is 'contraire aux "usages honnêtes" de l'industrie ou du commerce'.[85]

CONCLUSION

It is possible to describe the situation in Canadian trademark law as a negotiation of the realities of trademark protection in a bijural and federal state. The result is a set of rules for the protection of registered and unregistered trademarks that has achieved a high level of consistency and harmonization across Canada. This has been facilitated by the policy of bilingual case reporting in the federal court system and at the Supreme Court of Canada.

Yet the situation could also be seen as a one-sided harmonization of private law principles regarding unregistered trademarks and aspects of unfair competition, where the common law has emerged essentially unchanged, and the civil law has become virtually indistinguishable from the common law. Yet the legal principles at issue were very similar at the outset, and there has been relatively little outcry over the loss of distinctive legal doctrines or approaches. What has received more commentary has been the balance struck between registered trademarks and common law marks. Many have seen the dominance of the federal legislative scheme as strongly interfering with the jurisdiction of the provinces over common law trademarks as a matter of property and civil rights in the province. Yet even these concerns have failed to motivate a groundswell of calls for changes to the *Trade-marks Act*. The situation is now largely that described by the Supreme Court of Canada in *Kirkbi*: 'The primary difference between registered and unregistered trade-marks under the Act is that the rights of a holder of a registered trade-mark are more extensive.'[86]

---

[85] Nadeau, *supra* note 76 at 189. Nadeau also states: 'La concurrence cesse d'être licite dès qu'elle comporte la tromperie ou la fraude, dès qu'elle cesse d'être loyale et honnête' (*ibid.* at 186–87).

[86] *Kirkbi*, *supra* note 1 at para. 30.

2. A watershed year for well known or famous marks

Robert G. Howell*

In 2006 concurrent decisions of the Supreme Court of Canada in *Mattel*[1] and *Veuve Clicquot Ponsardin*[2] provided a watershed in the protection of well known or famous marks in Canada even though neither expression 'well known' or 'famous' enjoys any definitional recognition as such in Canadian trademark law. The expressions are used in this chapter simply to identify marks that possess such characteristics. An absence of legal identification has, perhaps, allowed Canadian trademark law to lack overall direction or focus in affording protection.

The focus here is on the two key dimensions that occupied the attention of the Supreme Court in *Mattel* and *Veuve Clicquot Ponsardin*. First, the concept of confusion within s. 6, and second that of depreciation of goodwill within s. 22, *Trade-marks Act*.[3] To begin, however, reference to relevant international obligations should be considered.

INTERNATIONAL OBLIGATIONS

Articles 6 *bis*, *Paris Convention*[4] and 16(2) and (3), *TRIPs Agreement*[5] address

* I thank Ms Lydia Zucconi (University of Victoria, British Columbia, 2007) for her research assistance and Ms Gail Rogers (University of Victoria) for her secretarial assistance.

1 *Mattel, Inc. v. 3894207 Canada Inc.*, [2006] 1 S.C.R. 772 [*Mattel*].

2 *Veuve Clicquot Ponsardin v. Boutiques Cliquot Ltée*, [2006] 1 S.C.R. 824 [*Veuve Clicquot Ponsardin*].

3 *Trade-marks Act*, R.S.C. 1985, c. T-13.

4 *Paris Convention for the Protection of Industrial Property*, 20 March 1883 revised at Brussels, 14 December 1900; Washington, 2 June 1911; The Hague, 6 November 1925; London, 2 June 1934; Lisbon, 31 October 1958; and Stockholm, 14 July 1967, and amended on 2 October 1979. Article 6 *bis* (1) is in the following terms: '(1) The countries of the Union undertake, ex officio if their legislation so permits, or at the request of an interested party, to refuse or to cancel the registration, and to prohibit the use, of a trademark which constitutes a reproduction, an imitation, or a

well known or famous marks. *TRIPs* Article 16(2) extends Article 6 *bis* to services and stipulates a focus on knowledge of the trademark in the relevant sector of the public both within the member country, where it is to be 'obtained as a result of the promotion of the trademark', and extra-territorially. Article 16(3) is the key provision in this context, declaring that Article 6 *bis* is to apply:

> to goods or services which are not similar to those in respect of which a trademark is registered, provided that use of that trademark in relation to those goods or services would indicate a connection between those goods or services and the owner of the registered trademark and provided that the interests of the owner of the registered trademark are likely to be damaged by such use.

Although expressed as *an application* of Article 6 *bis*, Article 16(3) is significantly more. The test of 'confusion' under Article 6 *bis* is replaced by the requirement of simply 'a connection' between a defendant's goods or services and the holder of the registered trademark. It is also inclusive of knowledge of the trademark gained extra-territorially rather than just within the country of registration as provided for in Article 6 *bis*. It is, however, expressly limited in its protection, to registered trademarks.

SECTION 6 *TRADE-MARKS ACT* – 'CONFUSION'

The concept of 'confusion' and the interpretation of s. 6 governing this concept has been the pivotal provision for statutory protection of well known or famous marks. Registration may be refused for a mark confusing with another for which registration is pending (s. 37(1)(c)). In opposition, a mark is not registrable if confusing with a registered mark (ss. 38(2)(b), 12(1)(d) and 14(1)(a)). Invalidity may be found if a mark was not registrable at the date of registration by being confusing with a registered mark (ss. 18(1)(a), 12(1)(b) and 14(1)(a)). Infringement will occur if another person sells, distributes or advertises wares or services in association with a confusing trademark (s. 20). The statutory proceeding in the nature of passing off under s. 7(b), brought

---

translation, liable to create confusion, of a mark considered by the competent authority of the country of registration or use to be well known in that country as being already the mark of a person entitled to the benefits of this Convention and used for identical or similar goods. These provisions shall also apply when the essential part of the mark constitutes a reproduction or any such well-known mark or an imitation liable to create confusion therewith.'

5 *Agreement on Trade-Related Aspects of Intellectual Property Rights*; Annex IC to the *Final Act and Agreement Establishing the World Trade Organization*, 15 December 1993, (1994), 33 ILM 81.

into mainstream trademark practice in 2005 by the Supreme Court in *Kirkbi*,[6] requires a likelihood of confusion in Canada between the respective wares or services of the parties. In all such instances of 'confusion' within the *Trade-marks Act*, s. 6 defines confusion in the manner and circumstances set out in the section and is of mandatory application.[7]

Section 6(2), (3) and (4), to the same effect *mutatis mutandis*, address the combinations of confusion of a trademark with other trademarks and with trade-names. Each of these paragraphs stipulates that a use will be a confusing use:

> if the use of both [trademarks or trademark and tradename] in the same area would be likely to lead to the inference that the wares or services associated with [the mark or name] are manufactured, sold, leased, hired or performed by the same person, whether or not the wares or services are of the same general class.

Three key dimensions are noted. First, the usage of both indicators (mark or name) must be in the same area.[8] This would preclude relief for instances of extra-territorial use with mere reputation without use within Canada. Second, the confusion must concern the actual origin (manufacture, sale, lease, hire or performance) of the wares or services. Expansions of confusion to include confusion of mere association, connection, supervision or quality control measures, or consent to the usage[9] would not, literally, be within s. 6 although such strictness of interpretation is not apparent.[10] Third, confusion as to origin can, however, cross classes of wares or services, providing considerable benefit to holders of famous marks that encompass an association with multiple and diverse products.

---

[6] *Kirkbi AG v. Ritvik Holdings Inc.*, [2005] 3 S.C.R. 302 [*Kirkbi*].

[7] Section 6(1). While s. 7(b) is said to reflect a codification of the tort of passing off, the application of the s. 6 test for confusion as to origin in s. 7(b) presents a narrower focus than that at common law where the test for misrepresentation or confusion is cast in broader terms. See *Positive Attitude Safety System Inc. v. Albian Sands Energy Inc.* (2005), 43 C.P.R. (4th) 418 at paras. 30–32 (F.C.A.).

[8] *Veuve Clicquot Ponsardin*, *supra* note 2 at para. 38. In *Remo Imports Ltd. v. Jaguar Cars Ltd.* (2006), 47 C.P.R. (4th) 1 at para. 310 (F.C.T.D.), Shore, J. interpreted s. 6 as requiring only that the parties be entitled to sell in the same place [rev'd on other grounds, [2008] 2 F.C.R. 132 (F.C.A.)].

[9] These broader descriptions have been used at common law with a consequential broadening of the passing off proceeding. See e.g. *Walt Disney Productions v. Triple Five Corp.* (1994), 53 C.P.R. (3d) 129 (Alta. C.A.). Leave to appeal to SCC denied [1994] S.C.C. *Bulletin of Proceedings*, 1210.

[10] Although source or origin is expressly emphasized by Binnie J. in *Veuve Clicquot Ponsardin*, *supra* note 2 at paras. 19 and 37 there are also broader references in the judgment to 'association' (para. 26), 'affiliation' (para. 36) or third party licensing (para. 36), suggesting some softening of the literal strictness of s. 6(2), (3) and (4) in this respect.

Section 6(5) requires in determining confusion that regard be had 'to all the surrounding circumstances' then stipulates the following non-exhaustive factors to consider:

(a) the inherent distinctiveness of the trade-marks or trade-names and the extent to which they have become known;
(b) the length of time the trade-marks or the trade-names have been in use;
(c) the nature of the wares, services or business;
(d) the nature of the trade; and
(e) the degree of resemblance between the trade-marks or trade-names in appearance or sound or in the ideas suggested by them.

Although 'fame' *per se* is not specifically enumerated, the Supreme Court in *Veuve Clicquot Ponsardin* found it implicit in enumerations (a) (inherent distinctiveness and extent of reputation) and (b) (length of time used) as well as being an important general circumstance.[11] The crux of this test when faced with a well known or famous mark is the balance to be struck between the dissimilarity of products on the one hand and the degree of fame presented by the mark on the other. The inclusion in s. 6(2), (3) and (4) of the extension 'whether or not the wares or services are of the same general class' was found by the Supreme Court in *Mattel* to have enhanced the weighting of fame.[12] Binnie J. (for the court) noted:

> fame *is* capable of carrying the mark across product lines where lesser marks would be circumscribed to their traditional wares and services [emphasis is that of Binnie J.].[13]

Both reputational expansiveness and the commercial reality of product diversification by holders of famous brands are part of the circumstances.[14] Yet, these cannot trump other factors, including the need for some linkage or connection to the wares or services to which the brand name relates.[15] Fame itself is not 'in the ascendant',[16] but neither is the similarity or dissimilarity between the products.[17] Every instance is to be evaluated 'in its full factual context'[18] with the respective weighting of the factors of confusion in s. 6(5) being determined by 'the totality of the circumstances'.[19]

---

11 *Veuve Clicquot Ponsardin*, *supra* note 2 at para. 27.
12 *Mattel*, *supra* note 1 at para. 60.
13 *Ibid.* at para. 63.
14 *Ibid.* at para. 73.
15 *Ibid.* at paras. 64–70.
16 *Ibid.* at para. 72.
17 *Ibid.* at para. 72.
18 *Ibid.* at para. 72.
19 *Ibid.* at para. 63.

The analysis in the companion proceeding *Veuve Clicquot Ponsardin* is to the same effect.[20] A sharper distinction is made between marks that have fame in a very specific product context, from those that transcend product lines.[21] Limited criticism is made of the earlier Federal Court of Appeal decisions in *Pink Panther*[22] and *Lexus*[23] to the effect that these cases had placed too much emphasis on product similarity and dissimilarity.[24] Binnie J. addressed this in greater detail in *Mattel* disapproving of a reference to a finding of confusion to be exceptional in the absence of product connection or similarity[25] as well as the need for 'some resemblance' between the products.[26] However, Binnie J. did ultimately find *Pink Panther* and *Lexus* to have applied the correct overall test and characterized the offending references in those cases as simply *obiter*.[27]

From a factual perspective, *Pink Panther* involved the motion picture series of that name registered in Canada for use with films and sound recordings. An applicant was seeking registration with respect to hair care and beauty supplies. In *Lexus* the dispute involved automobiles and canned foods and fruit juice. Binnie J. agreed that the products in these cases were sufficiently different to constitute the decisive element of the 'surrounding circumstances'.[28] The fame of the marks in both instances was in very specific product contexts. Neither significantly transcended product lines. This was also the position in *Mattel* and *Veuve Clicquot Ponsardin.* The BARBIE mark (*Mattel*) was distinctive or famous only of dolls and doll accessories. This could not be confused with restaurant take-out catering and banquet services.[29] In *Veuve Clicquot Ponsardin* the mark 'Veuve Clicquot' for wine and champagne was alleged to be infringed by the mark 'Cliquot'[30] used for mid-range women's apparel. This significant product difference could not be bridged. There had

---

20 *Veuve Clicquot Ponsardin, supra* note 2 at paras. 21, 27.

21 *Ibid.* at para. 32.

22 *United Artists Corp. v. Pink Panther Beauty Corp.*, [1998] 3 F.C. 534, (1998), 80 C.P.R. (3d) 247 (F.C.A.) [*Pink Panther*].

23 *Toyota Jidosha Kabushiki Kaisha v. Lexus Foods Inc.*, [2001] 2 F.C. 15, (2000), 9 C.P.R. (4th) 297 (F.C.A.) [*Lexus*].

24 *Veuve Clicquot Ponsardin, supra* note 2 at para. 27.

25 *Mattel, supra* note 1 at para. 63.

26 *Ibid.* at paras. 64 and 65 where Binnie J. rejected a need for 'resemblance' when the products 'need not even be of the same *general* class' (emphasis added by Binnie, J.).

27 *Ibid.* at para. 71.

28 *Ibid.* at paras. 64–71.

29 *Ibid.* at paras. 79–85.

30 The difference in spelling – Clicquot and Cliquot – was not significant. *Veuve Clicquot Ponsardin, supra* note 2 at para. 48.

been no expansion of Clicquot to luxury items in general, despite a potential to develop in this direction.[31]

Overall, the Supreme Court in *Mattel* and *Veuve Clicquot Ponsardin* has blunted efforts of holders of famous brands to find 'confusion' from fame, especially when fame is product specific or applied over a narrow range of products. Greater scope exists for brand names used over multi-product lines. Each case is, however, considered in its own factual circumstances.

The nature of the person who is to be confused is 'the somewhat hurried consumer',[32] standing in between the careful and diligent purchaser and the so-called 'moron in a hurry'. The mythical appropriate person is functionally bilingual, English and French, in appropriate markets, and possessed of an average and imperfect memory, and takes ordinary care in observation.[33] Actual confusion need not be established, but its presence or absence is a factor to be weighed.[34] The focus is on the *likelihood* of confusion for which there must be evidence beyond mere speculation.[35]

SECTION 22 *TRADE-MARKS ACT* – DEPRECIATION OR DILUTION

Although *Mattel* and *Veuve Clicquot Ponsardin* have set an appropriate balance between fame and product diversity within an analysis of confusion in s. 6, the requirement of confusion in itself would cause a s. 6 analysis to fall short of compliance with Article 16(3), *TRIPs Agreement* that has dispensed with the test of confusion. As noted earlier, Article 16(3) requires simply a 'connection' between the defendant's goods or services and the owner of the registered trademark with the likelihood of damage.[36] Additionally, if s. 6 is limited to only territorial use of a mark,[37] it would on this ground also fall short of compliance with Article 16.[38] After *Veuve Clicquot Ponsardin*, however, Canada is now substantially in compliance with Article 16 through the recognition by the Supreme Court of a fledgling dilution remedy under s. 22(1), *Trade-marks Act* providing:

---

31 *Ibid.* at para. 23.

32 *Ibid.* at para. 21.

33 *Mattel*, *supra* note 1 at paras. 56–8. The nature and value of the item being purchased is also relevant. In buying ordinary everyday wares a consumer may have more money than time to spend on the purchase (para. 58).

34 *Ibid.* at para. 89.

35 *Veuve Clicquot Ponsardin*, *supra* note 2 at para. 37.

36 See text accompanying note 4.

37 See text accompanying note 8.

38 See text accompanying note 4.

(1) No person shall use a trade-mark registered by another person in a manner that is likely to have the effect of depreciating the value of the goodwill attaching thereto.

Enacted in 1953,[39] this provision was, as Binnie J. noted,[40] intended by law reform sources as an alternative remedy to that of confusion.[41] In this respect, Binnie J., for the Supreme Court, expressly declares s. 22 to be free of any criterion of confusion,[42] and expressed surprise at the minimal level of attention that has been directed to this provision since its enactment. He speculated that:

where there is no confusion claimants may have felt it difficult to establish the likelihood that depreciation of the value of the goodwill would occur.[43]

Surprising? Perhaps. In 1953, the rather succinct and somewhat vague s. 22 would understandably be seen in the nature of an anomaly presenting significant uncertainty as to legislative purpose. A formal 'dilution' remedy was not introduced in the neighbouring United States until 1995 and then was expressed in a far more detailed, focused and comprehensive manner,[44] but still gave rise to uncertainties and narrow interpretation.[45] 1994 saw a similar provision in the United Kingdom.[46] These extra-territorial sources noted by Binnie J.[47] did provide, in 2006, a resource of dilution jurisprudence that the Supreme Court was prepared to adopt in concept and policy within s. 22 in the fortunate circumstance that that section possesses the literal capacity to receive such an incorporation.[48] Yet some earlier fledgling recognition of potential relief in the nature of dilution under s. 22 can be found[49] and this

---

39 Trade Marks Act 1953, S. C. 1952–53, c. 49, s. 22.

40 *Veuve Clicquot Ponsardin, supra* note 2 at paras. 39–40.

41 Christopher Robinson, 'The Canadian Trade Marks Act of 1954 – A Review of Some of Its Features' (1959) 32 C.P.R. 45 at 61, cited in *Veuve Clicquot Ponsardin, ibid.* at para. 39 by Binnie J.

42 *Veuve Clicquot Ponsardin, ibid.* at para. 38.

43 *Ibid.* at para. 46. Earlier, Binnie J. referred to s. 22 as having been treated as 'a poor cousin' (*ibid.* at para. 38).

44 *Federal Trademark Dilution Act of 1995*, 15 U.S.C. § 1125(c).

45 See e.g. *Moseley v. V Secret Catalogue Inc.*, 537 U.S. 418 (2003) [*Victoria's Secret*] and *Restatement (Third) of Unfair Competition* § 25 (1995).

46 *Trade Marks Act 1994* (U.K.), 1994, c. 26, s. 10(3).

47 *Veuve Clicquot Ponsardin, supra* note 2 at paras. 41–45.

48 See David Vaver, *Intellectual Property Law* (Toronto: Irwin Law, 1997) at 216–219 and Robert G. Howell, Linda Vincent & Michael D. Manson, *Intellectual Property Law: Cases and Materials* (Toronto: Emond Montgomery Publications, 1999) at 757, querying whether s. 22 could indeed include dilution.

49 See e.g. *Source Perrier (Sociéte anonyme) v. Fira-Less Marketing Co. Limited*, [1983] 2 F.C. 18, (1983), 70 C.P.R. (2d) 61 (F.C.T.D.) concerning the product

does leave a measure of surprise as to why famous brand holders did not earlier take this opportunity.

A principal context for use of s. 22 was comparative advertising of competing products. The leading interpretation of s. 22 was *Clairol* in the Exchequer Court (now the Federal Court) which interpreted the expression 'use' in s. 22 as being a 'use' as defined in s. 4 to be in association with wares (marked on the wares themselves or on the packaging to give notice of the association of the mark with the wares to the transferee of property or possession at the time of such transfer) or services (displayed in the performance of advertising those services).[50] However, s. 22 was interpreted as not requiring the distinguishing of products, and that confusion is not an element in the interpretation of the provision.[51]

The requirement of interpreting 'use' within s. 4 as determined by *Clairol* is retained by the Supreme Court as the first element to be met in a dilution context.[52] Ordinarily, this would be met in a defendant's merchandising of wares or services in association with another's well known or famous mark. Section 22 refers to use of the actual mark, not a similar or confusing mark. However, in *Veuve Clicquot Ponsardin* the different spelling 'Cliquot' rather than 'Clicquot' meant that the actual mark had not been so used, but the spelling difference was held to be irrelevant given that the actual spelling used could potentially still convey the idea of the brand.[53] This suggests an approach of substantiality as to use of the actual mark. This may be significant with respect to compliance with Article 16(3) *TRIPs Agreement* as that provision extended

---

Perrier water and a political spoof 'Pierre Eh!' with Dube J. finding the spoof 'to dilute the quality of [the plaintiff's] trade marks, to impair its business integrity established over the years, and to cause injury to its goodwill'. See also *Dubiner v. MCA Canada Ltd.* (1976), 30 C.P.R. (2d) 281 (Ont. H.C.) (use of a mark in a title to a television series – no likely depreciation) and *Canadian Council of Blue Cross Plans v. Blue Cross Beauty Products Inc.*, [1971] F.C. 543 (F.C.T.D.) (inference that a non profit organization was now in the 'for profit' business – no depreciation).

50 *Clairol International Corp. v. Thomas Supply & Equipment Co. Ltd.* (1968), 55 C.P.R. 176 at 196, 202 (Ex. Ct.) [*Clairol*] followed in several later cases including *Syntox Inc. v. Apotex Inc.* (1984), 1 C.P.R. (3d) 145 (F.C.A.).

51 *Cie Générales des Établissements Michelin-Michelin & Cie v. CAW-Canada* (1996), 71 C.P.R. (3d) 348 at 363–5 (F.C.T.D.) [*Michelin*]. Teitelbaum J. notes at 363 and 364 that under s. 22 the distinguishing of wares was not required in *Clairol*; at 365 that while the distinguishing of wares or services is needed for s. 20 infringement, it is not for s. 22; and, earlier, at 363–4 that no requirement of confusion exists in s. 22. See also *Tommy Hilfiger Licensing Inc. v. Produits de Qualité I.M.D. Inc.*, [2005] F.C. 10 at para. 126 (F.C.T.D.).

52 *Veuve Clicquot Ponsardin*, *supra* note 2 at paras. 46-48.

53 *Ibid.* at para. 48. However, as a question of fact, it did not in this instance convey any link or connection with the holder of the brand and the s. 22 claim failed accordingly. See text accompanying notes 64–6.

to dissimilar goods and services the provisions of Article 6 *bis*, *Paris Convention* which itself (Article 6 *bis* (1)) refers to a mark 'which constitutes a production, an imitation, or a translation' of the protected mark, as opposed to simply the precise actual mark.

The second element of a s. 22 dilution claim is the establishing of goodwill. The claimant's registered trademark must be 'sufficiently well known to have sufficient goodwill attached to it', even though it need not be well known nor famous.[54] The formulation in *Veuve Clicquot Ponsardin* expressly combines traditional definitions of goodwill, including that of 'reputation and connection' from *Clairol* under s. 22 itself,[55] with the requirements for 'fame' from dilution in the United States – essentially a reputation that transcends the wares and services with which the mark is associated.[56]

This formulation of goodwill for the purposes of dilution under s. 22, is remarkably similar to the distinction drawn earlier by Binnie J. (in the context of confusion under s. 6) between product specific fame and multi-product fame. The product specific fame in both *Mattel* and *Veuve Clicquot Ponsardin* was influential in avoiding confusion.[57] However, in the s. 22 dilution context, Binnie J. found:

> clearly considerable goodwill attaching to the VEUVE CLICQUOT mark that extends beyond wine and champagne

thereby meeting the goodwill criterion under s. 22.[58]

It is suggested that this distinction aptly illustrates the difference between s. 6 confusion and s. 22 depreciation or dilution. No sales or distributions transcended product lines so there was no confusion as to source regarding product. Yet pure *reputation* did exist across multi-product lines. Protection of *reputation simpliciter* as goodwill is consistent with common law developments to redefine goodwill to encompass cross border reputation without any need for a business presence in the local jurisdiction.[59] This is also all that is required for goodwill for the purposes of dilution in this context is relief focused on a loss of source related *reputation*. To this effect in *Veuve Clicquot Ponsardin* Binnie J. expressly noted that s. 22 has no requirement of use of

---

54 *Ibid.* at paras. 46, 54.

55 See *Clairol*, *supra* note 50 at 199 speaking of: 'the whole advantage, whatever that may be, of the reputation and connection, which may have been built up by years of honest work or gained by lavish expenditure of money.'

56 *Veuve Clicquot Ponsardin*, *supra* note 2 at paras. 53 and 54.

57 See text accompanying note 66.

58 *Veuve Clicquot Ponsardin*, *supra* note 2 at para. 55.

59 See *Orkin Exterminating Co. Inc. v. Pestco Co. of Canada Ltd.* (1985), 5 C.P.R. (3d) 433 (Ont. C.A.) and text accompanying note 9.

both marks in the same geographic area. Mere association is enough.[60] This can therefore include extra-territorial reputational spillover to the local jurisdiction.

Binnie J. also noted additional factors to consider in establishing reputational goodwill as: degree of recognition of the mark, sales volume, market penetration, advertising and publicity, geographic reach, inherent or acquired distinctiveness, narrow or multiple channels of trade and identification with quality features.[61] *Clairol* reminds us that the goodwill under s. 22 is that attaching to the particular mark and not the mark holder's business in general.[62] Binnie J. likewise emphasizes the linkage of goodwill with the actual mark.[63]

The third and fourth elements to establish dilution are only subtly distinct. Effectively, factual causation of depreciation of the goodwill must be established. This first requires evidence of the likelihood of a mental association to constitute a link or connection between the holder's mark and the defendant's use.[64] This will not be assumed, nor is any reverse onus to be placed on the defendant user.[65] In *Veuve Clicquot Ponsardin* no such evidence was available.[66] If it had been available, the next stage would have been to determine if such an association would have had the likelihood of depreciating the goodwill attaching to the mark.

Again, it is *Clairol*, involving comparative advertising, where the meaning of depreciate in s. 22 is first defined and this has been consistently followed. Definitional elements include: reducing the advantage of reputation and connection; to take or reduce the custom otherwise expected; to make the mark 'less extensive and less advantageous'; to reduce the esteem of the mark; and to entice away customers[67] or to demonstrate how readily a switch might be made to the defendant's product.[68] A loss of exclusive use by the activities

---

60 *Veuve Clicquot Ponsardin*, *supra* note 2 at para. 38. Contrast the position under s. 6 confusion where a use in the same area is required. See text accompanying note 8.

61 *Ibid.* at para. 54.

62 *Clairol*, *supra* note 50 at 196–7.

63 *Veuve Clicquot Ponsardin*, *supra* note 2 at paras. 50, 69.

64 *Ibid.* at paras. 56–61. See also para. 46 describing this enquiry as to whether the mark was used in a manner to have an effect on the holder's goodwill.

65 *Ibid.* at para. 57.

66 *Ibid.* at para. 61.

67 See e.g. *Michelin*, *supra* note 51 at 371; *Canadian Council of Blue Cross Plans v. Blue Cross Beauty Products Inc.*, *supra* note 49 at para. 39; and *Top Notch Construction Ltd. v. Top Notch Oilfield Services Ltd.* (2001), 13 C.P.R. (4th) 515 at para. 39 (F.C.T.D.).

68 *Interlego AG v. Irwin Toy Ltd.* (1985), 3 C.P.R. (3d) 476 at 487–8 (F.C.T.D.).

of a competitor is excluded,[69] as is a use otherwise than by way of use as a trademark.[70] These interpretations, concerning a reduction of the value attaching to a mark, are consistent with the comparison Binnie J. made with dilution theory in the United States. Described as simply illustrative, the comparison is subject to differing statutory provisions in each jurisdiction and a perceived broader scope in Canada, given that s. 22 is phrased more broadly and still remains to be developed by the courts.[71] The categories of 'tarnishment' and 'blurring' from United States jurisprudence are therefore identified non-exclusively.

Tarnishment is linked with disparagement and a dictionary meaning of depreciate as to 'disparage, belittle, underrate'.[72] It concerns the creating of a 'negative association' with the mark, such as by linkage with illegal or offensive products.[73] Linking a high end market brand with a mid or lower range product could produce a disparagement of this nature. A difference in market level might be helpful to a user in avoiding a claim of confusion[74] but, conversely, may support a claim for dilution.

Blurring concerns the loss of distinctiveness to the holder of a mark by causing a public perception of a connection with other products. Identification with the holder is diminished or lost.[75] Binnie J. does hint at a possible distinction between identifying a holder on the one hand, and loss of goodwill on the other,[76] but continues to accept a loss of distinctiveness as qualifying. This, it is suggested, is appropriate given that s. 22 addresses the goodwill in the mark itself, not the holder's business goodwill.[77] The value or goodwill of a mark can only be the distinctiveness of that mark.

Overall, the Supreme Court, while opening up s. 22 to holders of well known or famous brands, also urged caution in its usage, noting this to be the position in the United States and the European Union, specifically the United

---

69 *Clairol*, *supra* note 50. Presumably this is so because this situation will fall within a regular trademark proceeding under ss. 19 or 20.

70 See *Michelin*, *supra* note 51 at 365–6; and *British Columbia Automobile Assn. v. Office and Professional Employee's International Union* (2001), 10 C.P.R. 423 at para. 167 (B.C.S.C.) concerning use of a mark in a labour relations or employment context rather than on wares or advertised with services in the nature of a trademark.

71 *Veuve Clicquot Ponsardin*, *supra* note 2 at paras. 64–7 where Binnie J. refers to U.S. sources as providing 'useful elucidation of relevant concepts'.

72 *Ibid.* at paras. 63, 66.

73 *Ibid.* at para. 66, noting U.S. authorities concerning linkage of marks with pornographic products or services.

74 This was the position in *Veuve Clicquot Ponsardin*, *ibid.* at para. 37.

75 *Ibid.* at paras. 64–5.

76 *Ibid.* at para. 64.

77 See text accompanying note 62.

Kingdom.[78] Section 22 expressly requires only a *likelihood* of depreciation, a position similarly clarified by legislation in the United States in 2006.[79] This likelihood must, however, be established by evidence. Mere mental association of consumers of the brand mark from a use by another, while necessary to constitute a link or connection,[80] is not sufficient in itself to constitute a likelihood of depreciation.[81]

At this stage there is no guidance in Canada as to what will constitute a likelihood of depreciation. The essence of likelihood is future damage – involving a measure of speculation. It has been a vexed issue in the United States, particularly for blurring that concerns an association that diminishes the distinctiveness of the well known or famous mark. If every usage were found to qualify as depreciation or dilution, then the mark would be seen to possess proprietary protection in gross or in the mark itself and relief would be in the nature of misappropriation *simpliciter*. Although flirted with at common law,[82] there has been no acceptance of this as appropriate trademark theory in Canada. It is indeed, seen as anti-competitive.[83] How, therefore, should the courts proceed once the remedial focus has moved away from the safe harbour of confusion or misrepresentation? How is the mid-way position of depreciation or dilution to be formulated and assessed, while still preserving fair competition? McCarthy describes efforts in the United States to establish factors to be weighed, but acknowledges difficulties, in some instances gravitating back to confusion by weighing the similarity of products, the feature the whole exercise of depreciation or dilution seeks to avoid.[84]

This exercise may be even more problematic in Canada given the absence of even a framework for this purpose in s. 22. However, regard may be had to the 2006 legislative revision in the United States,[85] which does attempt a solution with respect to blurring, the most acute context for formulating a midrange position. Consideration must be given to 'all relevant factors'.

---

78 *Ibid.* at paras. 44–5.

79 See *Trademark Dilution Revision Act of 2006*, Pub. L. No. 109-312, 120 Stat. 1729, s. 2(1) inserting new s. 43(c). See s. 43(c)(2)(B) and 43(c)(5)(A). This changed the 'actual damage' rule that had been stipulated by the United States Supreme Court in *Victoria's Secret*, *supra* note 45. See generally J. Thomas McCarthy, *McCarthy on Trademarks and Unfair Competition*, 4th ed., vol. 4 (St. Paul, MN: West Group, 1996) at s. 24.94.10 (Rel. 40, 12/2006).

80 See text accompanying notes 64–6.

81 *Veuve Clicquot Ponsardin*, *supra* note 2 at para. 43.

82 See the limited theory to this effect as misappropriation of business values – *International News Service v. Associated Press*, 248 U.S. 215 (1918).

83 McCarthy, *supra* note 79 at s. 24:114 (Rel. 40, 12/2006).

84 *Ibid.* at s. 24:94.3 to 24:96 (Rel. 40, 12/2006).

85 *Trademark Dilution Revision Act of 2006*, *supra* note 79.

Enumerated factors are: degree of similarity of the marks; degree of inherent or acquired distinctiveness of the famous brand mark; the extent to which the well known mark is utilized by the holder on an exclusive basis; the degree of recognition of the well known mark; the intention (to associate the marks or not) of the user; and any actual association,[86] no doubt to be established by evidence. These factors do avoid gravitation back to confusion while also denying any recognition of a property in gross in a mark. The factors are focused in a context of injunctive relief. The grant of other remedies depends upon the user having *intended* to cause blurring or tarnishment.[87] No specific factors are given in the Act for dilution by tarnishment.[88]

CONCLUSION

The Supreme Court of Canada has presented holders of well known or famous brand marks with a substantial opportunity through a fledgling interpretation of s. 22 depreciation to provide relief in the nature of dilution formulated with express, though only illustrative, reference to the concepts of blurring and tarnishment in the United States. There is no requirement under s. 22 of a need for the uses of the mark to be in the same area, allowing protection for reputation that has spilled into the jurisdiction from an extra-territorial use. Such relief under s. 22 will likely ensure Canadian trademark law is in compliance with Article 16(2) of the *TRIPs Agreement*, extending Article 6 *bis*, *Paris Convention* to dissimilar goods or services, so long as a test of substantiality is applied in determining whether or not a mark itself is used.

Additionally, the classical focus on s. 6 confusion is still available, though the court has reiterated that 'confusion means confusion' and widely diverging product lines, though only a factor, can dispel the likelihood of confusion despite fame. This is especially likely to be so if the fame is of a single product focus. Section 6 confusion is also limited to the two uses being within the same geographic area. It does, however, encompass use of a similar mark rather than the actual mark itself.

Under ss. 6 and 22 almost every enquiry will depend on thoroughly gathered and effectively presented evidence. Assumptions, implications, and speculations will lead to failure. Facts and evidence are required.

---

86 *Ibid.*, s. 2(1) inserting new s. 43(c). See s. 43(c)(B)

87 *Ibid.*, s. 2(1) – s. 43(c)(5).

88 *Ibid.*, s. 2(1) – s. 43(c)(1)(C) refers just to harming the reputation of the mark.

3. Canada's treatment of geographical indications: compliant or defiant? An international perspective

Dianne Daley

INTRODUCTION

TRIPS: The Trigger for Protection of GIs in the Twenty-first Century

To the connoisseur, the fine distinctions between various wines and spirits are marked by their places of origin. Although such distinctions may elude an ordinary consumer the fact is that names like Champagne,[1] Tequila,[2] Canadian Whisky[3] and Scotch[4] serve to denote a certain quality, characteristic or reputation of each drink that is essentially attributable to its geographical origin. Geographical Indications (GIs),[5] as they have come to be generally described, are names, signs or symbols used on or in association with a product denoting its geographical origin where a special quality, characteristic or reputation of the product is essentially attributable to that origin.[6]

1 The name Champagne is protected in the European Union (EU) as a Protected Designation of Origin (PDO). In France Champagne is protected as a Controlled Appellation of Origin (*Appellation d'Origine Contrôlée*).

2 The name Tequila has been protected as a Geographical Indication since 1977. The liquor derives its name from the town of Tequila located in the state of Jalisco.

3 Canadian Whisky is protected as a Geographical Indication in Canada.

4 The production of Scotch is regulated by the *Scotch Whisky Act 1988* (U.K.), 1988, c. 22.

5 In this work the term 'GIs' is used interchangeably with 'Geographical Indications' where considered appropriate.

6 GIs are classified as a genre of intellectual property rights which have been derived from related concepts such as Indications of Source, Appellations of Origin, Designations of Origin and Trademarks. See Albrecht Conrad, 'The Protection of Geographical Indications in the TRIPS Agreement' (1996) 86 Trademark Rep. 11 at 13, 18. See also Irene Calboli, 'Expanding the Protection of Geographical Indications of Origin under TRIPS: "Old" Debate or "New" Opportunity?' (2006) 10:2 Marquette Intellectual Property Law Review 184.

When the global trade regime and Intellectual Property Rights converged, resulting in the adoption of the World Trade Organization's (WTO) *Agreement on Trade-Related Aspects of Intellectual Property Rights*,[7] a raft of new intellectual property rights obligations, including the obligation to protect GIs from wrongful and misleading uses and unfair competition, was thrust upon many countries.

Canada, a WTO member since 1 January 1995, was among several countries that, prior to the *TRIPS Agreement*, had not accorded any special protection to GIs. Indeed, the concept of a GI was relatively alien or insignificant to Anglo-American countries.[8] The predominant Anglo-American view has been that GIs are a type of trademark and qualify for protection primarily as certification marks or through the tort of passing off under the Common Law.[9]

GIs of European origin have been protected for over a century, through national laws and regulatory regimes in their respective countries of origin. Some European countries such as France, Spain and Switzerland have had special or *sui generis* legislation for GIs while others have granted protection for GIs under unfair competition laws, consumer protection laws and/or laws governing registered and unregistered trademarks and trade names.[10]

It was these European countries that lobbied for protecting this special genre of intellectual property and, in their quest for international protection, were most vociferous in their lobby for its inclusion in the *TRIPS Agreement*.[11] These ardent proponents of GI protection succeeded in obtaining internationally a minimum level of protection for GIs and additional protection for GIs pertaining to wines and spirits. The *TRIPS Agreement*, with its wide geographic membership, globalized the protection of GIs.[12]

---

[7] The *TRIPS Agreement* (1994), Annex 1C of the Marrakesh Agreement establishing the World Trade Organization (WTO), signed in Marrakesh, Morocco on 15 April 1994 (entered into force on 1 January 2005) [*TRIPS* or *TRIPS Agreement*].

[8] See Conrad, *supra* note 6 at 17–21. See also Justin Hughes, 'The Spirited Debate over Geographical Indications' (2006) 58 Hastings Law Journal 299 at 4.

[9] In the United States of America (US) both certification marks and collective marks are available modes of protection of GIs. See Hughes, *supra* note 8 at 308–10. See Conrad, *supra* note 6 at 20–21.

[10] France has protected appellations of origin by way of statute under the Law of 1 August 1905 and indications of source by way of unfair competition law. See Conrad, *supra* note 6 at 15–16. See Hughes, *supra* note 8 at 301, 307–8. Germany initially granted GI protection through unfair competition and also protects GIs as a collective mark. See Conrad, *ibid.* at 19. All members of the EU now implement special regulations to protect GIs (discussed below).

[11] See Conrad, *supra* note 6 at 29–30 noting that it was the European Commission (EC) and Switzerland which pushed for the subject of GIs to be placed on the agenda for the Uruguay Round of negotiations leading to the WTO Agreement.

[12] As at 11 January 2007, 150 countries were WTO members. See Jinghua Zou,

TRIPS requires member states to provide the legal means for interested parties to prevent misleading uses and acts of unfair competition in relation to all geographical indications as defined for the purposes of the Agreement.[13] In relation to GIs for wines and spirits member states are also required to provide the legal means for interested parties to prevent uses of a GI on a wine or a spirit not originating in the place denoted by the GI even where the use is not misleading, the so called 'additional protection' for wines and spirits.[14]

Notwithstanding the overall acceptance of a global regime of GI protection through the *TRIPS Agreement*, conceptual and commercial tensions have emerged in the implementation of obligations by member countries and these have been exacerbated by the Agreement's failure to specify how such protection is to be afforded.[15]

GIs for wines like Champagne and Bordeaux from France, and cheeses like Parmigiano Reggiano and Gorgonzola from Italy, that have enjoyed legal protection and commercial success in their home markets for hundreds of years have long been the object of appropriation or adoption by foreign traders and producers, some of whom, as immigrants from the so called 'old world',[16] carried the processes and formulations of these products with them and crafted their own 'new world'[17] versions while using the same or similar name or derivative, like 'Parmesan cheese' or 'Feta cheese' to market them.[18]

It is therefore not surprising that the protection of GIs in an international context is polarized with mainly European countries being strong proponents of special protection for GIs at the international level and the United States of America (US), Australia, New Zealand and Canada being hesitant to support international treaties which subscribe protection for GIs at a multilateral level.

Increasingly, the lines of demarcation between proponents and opponents of GI protection have become even more vivid as WTO Members debate

---

'Rice and Cheese, Anyone? The fight over *TRIPS* Geographical Indications continues' (2005) 30:3 Brook. J. Int'l L. 1141 at 1152.

[13] *TRIPS*, *supra* note 7, Article 22.

[14] *Ibid.*, Article 23.

[15] The wording of the *TRIPS Agreement* in Articles 22 and 23 allows member countries to choose their own mode of protection. Articles 22(2) and 23(1) commence as follows: ... 'Member[s] shall provide the legal means for interested parties to prevent…' and in relation to protection for wines and spirits gives members the option of enforcement through administrative action.

[16] Europe.

[17] The US, Canada, Australia and Argentina have been collectively described as the new world countries in the context of the debate over GI protection. See Zou, *supra* note 12 at 1143.

[18] See Hughes, *supra* note 8 at 353–4.

whether and how to review the relevant provisions of the *TRIPS Agreement*.[19] The current debates concern the establishment of a multilateral system of notification and registration of GIs for wines and spirits as contemplated by Article 23(4) of the *TRIPS Agreement* and the extension of the additional level of protection accorded to GIs for wines and spirits under Article 23 to all products.[20] It has been observed that such issues divide the WTO Membership 'according to old world/new world lines rather than developed vs. developing countries' and accordingly is not really a development issue.[21]

As a new world developed country Canada's approach to the implementation of its GIs obligations under *TRIPS* is of particular interest when contrasted with the approaches adopted by old world developed countries in the European Union (EU) and the approach of the US and some developing countries.[22] In weighing local industry and foreign trade interests, Canada appears to take contradictory stances by aligning with the EU for reciprocal GI protection on the one hand while staunchly opposing the EU's expanding GI protection agenda on the other hand.

This work looks critically at Canada's implementation of its obligation to provide protection for GIs under the *TRIPS Agreement* and concludes that while Canada is compliant with the commitments under *TRIPS*, its minimalist approach to implementation and overt opposition to the GI extension agenda being propelled by some WTO Members reflect its defiance to the expanding GI protection regime.

I GEOGRAPHICAL INDICATIONS: FROM PARIS TO MARRAKESH

Evolution of Protection

Although the *TRIPS Agreement* represents a modern framework for the protec-

---

19 See WTO, 'TRIPS: Geographical Indications – Background and the current situation', online: <http://www.wto.org/english/tratop_e/trips_e/gi_background_e.htm> and WTO, *Issues Related to the Extension of the Protection of Geographical Indications Provided for in Article 23 of the TRIPS Agreement to Products Other Than Wines and Spirits*, WTO Doc. TN/C/W/25 (18 May 2005), online: <http://docsonline.wto.org> [*Issues Related to the Extension of the Protection of Geographical Indications*].

20 *Ibid.*

21 'TRIPS Council Still Stuck on All Fronts', *Bridges* 9:6–7 (June/July 2005) 13 at 14, online: International Centre for Trade and Sustainable Development <http://www.ictsd.org>.

22 This writer draws some comparisons with the approaches of the US, the EU and Jamaica in assessing Canada's approach.

tion of GIs, the concept is far from modern.[23] It is rooted in the protection of related concepts such as indications of source and appellations of origin which evolved through national decrees and statutes and various agreements dating back to the nineteenth century. Protection for indications of source and appellations of origin was first accorded international recognition in the *Paris Convention for the Protection of Industrial Property* of 1883.[24] Protection for GIs developed along various legal conceptual lines resulting in a cumulative form of protection including the vesting of exclusive rights by statute and rules against unfair competition and passing off.[25] Some countries, for instance Canada, posit that GIs have always been afforded a level of protection under their trademarks system while others, for example France, treat GIs as a separate and distinct legal concept from trademarks.[26]

Indications of source are geographical identifiers denoting the geographical place of origin of a product and are typically included on the label of the product: for example, 'made in Canada'.[27] Appellations of Origin are the actual names of the geographical places of origin of products, but go further than indications of source in that they denote a qualitative link between the product and the place of origin.[28]

Article 10 of the *Paris Convention* provides for the prohibition from, or seizure on, importation of all goods which bear a false indication of the source of the goods or the identity of the producer, manufacturer or merchant.[29] Articles 10 *bis* and 10 *ter* oblige member countries to implement effective protection against unfair competition including the use of an indication in the course of trade which 'is liable to mislead the public as to the nature, the

---

[23] See generally Hughes, *supra* note 8. See also Conrad, *supra* note 6 at 14, 17–20.

[24] The *Paris Convention* was last revised in Stockholm on 14 July 1967 [*Paris Convention*]. The *Paris Convention* has a membership of 171 countries including Canada as at June 2007.

[25] See text accompanying note 10.

[26] See discussion below on Article 22 Protection – Certification Marks.

[27] Article 1(2) of the *Paris Convention* includes 'indications of source' under protected subject matter but does not define the term. Conrad, *supra* note 6 at 13, defines it thus: 'Indication of Source refers to a word, symbol, or device that indicates that a product originates in a specific geographic region.'

[28] Appellations of Origin were later defined in the *Lisbon Agreement for the Protection of Appellations of Origin and Their International Registration*, of 31 October 1958, revised at Stockholm on 14 July 1967 and as at June 2007 [*Lisbon Agreement*]. See Article 2(1) and 2(2).

[29] Article 10 of the *Paris Convention, supra* note 24 applies the provisions on Article 9 thereof pertaining to the seizure on importation of goods which unlawfully bear a mark or trade name to goods bearing false indications as to their source or the identity of the producer.

manufacturing process, the characteristics, the suitability of their purpose, or the quantity, of the goods' and to provide the necessary legal remedies.[30]

Even with its large membership encompassing the so called old world and new world countries, the *Paris Convention* has been considered somewhat inadequate in its protection of these indications. Article 10 *bis* appears to shield only such indications which denote not only the geographical origin but the characteristics of the product in question.[31] In essence, the protection afforded by the *Paris Convention* operates only to prevent the importation of goods which bear a false geographical indication and not necessarily where the use of the indication is merely misleading.

The *Paris Convention* was followed in 1891 by the *Madrid Agreement*[32] which sets out the cases and manner in which seizure may be requested and effected and prohibits use of all indications which deceive the public as to the source of the goods.[33] It also prohibits member countries from treating geographical indications of wines as generic terms.[34] Conceptual differences among the several *Paris Convention* member countries led to an eventually weak accord. The US, Canada and Australia did not sign the *Madrid Agreement* and the majority of its few members hailed from countries in Europe and South America where GI protection was an important economic issue.[35]

The *Lisbon Agreement*[36] which followed in 1958 was an attempt at augmenting the slim protection afforded to indications under the *Paris Convention* and complementing that which was provided under the *Madrid Agreement*.[37] Article 3 of the *Lisbon Agreement* obliges contracting states to ensure protection 'against any usurpation or imitation, even if the true origin of the product is indicated or if the appellation is used in translated form or accompanied by terms such as "kind," "type," "make," "imitation," or the like.'[38] It also facilitates the international protection of appellations of origin

---

30 *Ibid.*, art. 10 *bis* (3)(iii), 10 *ter*.

31 Conrad, *supra* note 6 at 24–25, indicating that at the Lisbon Revision Conference in 1958 the words 'the origin' were deleted from the originally proposed text of Article 10 *bis*.

32 The Madrid Agreement for the Repression of False or Deceptive Indications of Source on Goods of 14 April 1891, last revised at Lisbon on 31 October 1958.

33 See Articles 1–3 of the *Madrid Agreement, ibid.*

34 As expressed by Conrad, *supra* note 6 at 25. See the *Madrid Agreement, ibid.*, art. 4.

35 As at June 2007 only 35 states have acceded to the *Madrid Agreement.*

36 *Supra* note 28.

37 *Ibid.*

38 *Ibid.*, art. 3. This provision encapsulates the protection secured under Article 23(1) of the *TRIPS Agreement.*

by offering the possibility of obtaining their protection in all contracting states (excluding the country of origin) through a single registration.[39]

Appellations of origin would be protected in contracting states as long as they were protected in their respective countries of origin. Consequently, even where appellations became generic in a foreign contracting state, that state would still be required to protect them.[40] Although exacting higher standards of protection, the *Lisbon Agreement* secured fewer accessions than the *Madrid Agreement* thus hampering its effectiveness.[41]

The inadequacies of the three international agreements – the *Paris Convention* with its limited protection and the *Madrid* and *Lisbon Agreements* with their higher standards but low accessions – no doubt made the WTO, which provided a new opportunity for international norm-setting and a robust dispute settlement mechanism, an attractive forum in which 'GI-friendly' countries such as Europe could lobby for the most comprehensive and effective multilateral protection for GIs.

TRIPS-level Protection for GIs

For the purposes of the *TRIPS Agreement*, GIs are defined as 'indications which identify a good[42] as originating in the territory of a Member, or a region or locality in that territory, where a given quality, reputation or other characteristic of the good is essentially attributable to its geographical origin.'[43] Although the definition does not provide any test on what would be considered 'essentially attributable', it has been described as a workable definition enhancing the attractiveness of the *TRIPS Agreement* to several countries as the preferred forum of protection of GIs.[44] It is noticeably not as stringent as the definition of appellations of origin under the *Lisbon Agreement* which requires that the quality and characteristics of the good denoted by the appellation of origin be

---

39 *Ibid.*, art. 5.

40 This was considered the main reason why the US did not join the *Lisbon Agreement*. See Zou, *supra* note 12 at 1151, citing Roland Knaak, 'The Protection of Geographical Indications According to the TRIPS Agreement' in Friedrich-Karl Beier & Gerhard Schricker, eds, *From GATT to TRIPS – The Agreement on Trade-Related Aspects of Intellectual Property Rights* (Weinheim, Ge.; New York: VCH, 1996) 117 at 119.

41 As at June 2007 the members of the *Lisbon Agreement* stood at 26 countries. See Conrad, *supra* note 6 at 23.

42 A GI can apply to services as well. Article 24 of the *TRIPS Agreement* refers to GIs for goods and services. However the protection under Articles 22 and 23 only extends to GIs in relation to goods.

43 *TRIPS*, *supra* note 7, Article 22(1).

44 Conrad, *supra* note 6 at 31.

due exclusively or essentially to the geographical environment, including natural and human factors and that the product's reputation must be due to that origin.[45] Accordingly, whereas the *TRIPS* definition encompasses all appellations of origin, the *Lisbon* definition would exclude some GIs.

Section 3 of the *TRIPS Agreement* establishes two tiers of protection, one applicable to GIs for all kinds of goods as outlined in Article 22 and a higher level applicable only to wines and spirits as outlined in Article 23. In Article 24, it prescribes exceptions to such protection.

Article 22 protection

Under Article 22, which relates to all GIs as defined by the *TRIPS Agreement*, members are required to provide the legal means for interested parties to prevent:

- the use in the designation or presentation of a good which indicates or suggests that it originates in a particular place which is not the true place of origin in a manner that misleads the public as to the true geographical origin[46]
- any use which amounts to an act of unfair competition within the meaning of Article 10 *bis* of the Paris Convention (1967).[47]

These provisions go beyond the level of protection afforded under the *Paris Convention* and incorporate aspects of the protection afforded by the *Madrid Agreement*, by specifically protecting GIs from both false and misleading uses, including misrepresentations about origin.[48]

By virtue of Article 22 an application for registration of a trademark incorporating a GI may be refused or the registration revoked either by virtue of a Member's legislation or at an interested party's request where the use of the GI in the trademark is misleading as to the true place of origin.[49]

Members may however apply a five-year limitation period on the availability of this remedy[50] and shall apply an exception where the trademark has been applied for or registered in good faith or rights in it have been acquired

---

45 The *Lisbon Agreement*, *supra* note 28 art. 2. *TRIPS* omits reference to natural and human factors. However it has been argued that its wording is flexible enough to include non-agricultural goods. See Zou, *supra* note 12 at 1154.

46 *TRIPS*, *supra* note 7, Article 22(2)(a).

47 *Ibid.*, Article 22(2)(b).

48 Even though no specific reference is made to the Article 10 *ter* of the *Paris Convention* those obligations are incorporated by virtue of Articles 1 and 3 of the *TRIPS Agreement*.

49 *TRIPS*, *supra* note 7, Article 22(3).

50 *Ibid.*, Article 24(7).

through *bona fide* use before the *TRIPS* provisions came into operation in the relevant member country or before the particular GI is protected in its country of origin.[51]

Even where a GI indicates the actual origin of the goods in question, for example 'Canadian Swiss Cheese', if it falsely represents that the goods originate elsewhere, interested parties would still be entitled to prevent such a use as well as to request the refusal of application or invalidation of registration of a trademark incorporating the GI subject to the relevant exceptions.[52]

Article 23 protection

Article 23 provides additional protection in relation only to GIs for wines and spirits by virtue of which members are required to provide the legal means for interested parties to prevent:

- use of GIs for wines and spirits that do not actually originate in the place indicated by the GI even where the true place of origin is indicated by the GI in question
- use of GIs for wines and spirits that do not actually originate in the place indicated by the GI even where the true place of origin is indicated and even where used in conjunction with 'kind' 'style' 'imitation'.[53]

This provision incorporates the level of protection granted to GIs under Article 3 of the *Lisbon Agreement*.[54]

Article 23(2) provides that an application for registration of a trademark incorporating a GI for wines and spirits may be refused or the registration revoked either by virtue of a member's legislation or at an interested party's request where the trademark identifies wines or spirits as being of the origin denoted by the GI when it is not the true place of origin.[55] A five-year limitation period may be applicable.[56] Exceptions apply where a trademark has been applied for or registered in good faith or rights in it have been acquired through *bona fide* use before the *TRIPS* provisions came into operation in the

---

[51] This applies in relation to ordinary GIs and GIs for wines and spirits. *Ibid.*, Article 24(5).

[52] *Ibid.*, art. 22(4).

[53] *Ibid.*, art. 23(1). Members may enforce this protection through administrative action. See footnote 4 of Article 23(1).

[54] Article 3 of the *Lisbon Agreement*, *supra* note 28, states that 'Protection shall be ensured against any usurpation or imitation, even if the true origin of the product is indicated or if the appellation is used in translated form or accompanied by terms such as "kind," "type," "make,"' "imitation," or the like.'

[55] *TRIPS*, *supra* note 7, Article 23(2).

[56] *Ibid.*, Article 24(7).

relevant member country or before the GI is protected in its country of origin.[57]

Protection is also to be afforded to homonymous GIs such as 'Rioja' from Spain and 'Rioja' from Argentina which may be allowed to co-exist provided each can be differentiated so as to ensure that the respective producers are not prejudiced and consumers are not misled.[58]

Article 23(4) makes provision for the future establishment of a multilateral system of notification and registration of GI for wines in the context of negotiations to be undertaken in the *TRIPS* Council.[59]

Article 24

Article 24 outlines the mechanism for and scope of future negotiations[60] and establishes exceptions and limitations relating to GI protection.[61] It provides that no member country can reduce the level of protection it afforded to GIs prior to the entry into force of the WTO Agreement.[62] Exceptions which apply to the protection granted to all GIs under Article 22 as well as the additional protection for GIs for wines and spirits under Article 23 concern (i) prior continuous and *bona fide* uses of a GI (ii) conflicting GIs and trademarks (iii) generic GIs and (iv) a person's right to use his/her name or business name.

With regard to personal names, only misleading uses by a person of his/her own name in the course of trade or the name of that person's predecessor in business are prohibited under the *TRIPS* provisions.[63]

In connection with prior continuous use, nothing in the Agreement is to prevent the continued use of GIs identifying wines and spirits that have been continuously used in connection with goods or services produced in a member country for at least 10 years prior to 15 April 1994 or in good faith any time before that date.[64]

In relation to conflicting GIs and trademarks, the remedies of refusal or invalidation, as the case may be, do not apply to trademarks that have been acquired or registered in good faith prior to the date the member country becomes bound by the *TRIPS Agreement* or before the GI is protected in its country of origin.[65]

---

57 *Ibid.*, Article 24(5).

58 *Ibid.*, Article 23(3). See also Calboli, *supra* note 6 at 192.

59 See discussion below under Part III on Canada's stance in the GIs extension debate.

60 *TRIPS*, *supra* note 7, Article 24(1) & (2).

61 *Ibid.*, Article 24(4)–(9).

62 *Ibid.*, Article 24(3).

63 *Ibid.*, Article 24(8).

64 Hence the status quo is maintained. *Ibid.*, Article 24(4).

65 *Ibid.*, Article 24(5).

Article 24(6) provides that, where a GI of one member is identical with a term that has been in customary usage in another member (for example, Canada) or used as the common name for particular goods or services in Canada or is identical with the customary name of a grape variety existing in Canada as at 1 January 1995, nothing in the *TRIPS Agreement* requires Canada to apply protection in respect of the other member's GI.[66] These exceptions effectively bar from protection GIs that have become generic terms in certain countries. This is the most delicate set of exceptions in the context of negotiations of section 3 of *TRIPS* and represents 'a clear compromise between "old" and "new" worlds'.[67]

Finally, no member is obliged to accord the *TRIPS* level protection to GIs of other member countries which have fallen into disuse in that country or are not or have ceased to be protected in their country of origin.[68]

II CANADA'S APPROACH TO GI PROTECTION

GIs are protected in Canada primarily through the trademarks system with a fall-back to the common law tort of passing off.[69] Additional national protection is provided through the Québec Civil Code, the *Competition Act*[70] and the *Food and Drugs Act.*[71] At the multilateral level, protection is afforded by virtue of Canada's participation in the *North American Free Trade Agreement* (*NAFTA*),[72] the *Paris Convention*,[73] the *TRIPS Agreement* and most recently the *Canada–European Community Wine and Spirits Agreement.*[74]

---

66 *Ibid.*, Article 24(6).

67 Calboli, *supra* note 6 at 194.

68 *TRIPS*, *supra* note 7, Article 24(9).

69 See, OECD, Working Party on Agricultural Policies and Markets of the Committee for Agriculture Joint Working Party of the Committee for Agriculture and the Trade Committee, *Appellations of Origin and Geographical Indications In OECD Member Countries: Economic and Legal Implications*, Doc. No. COM/AGR/APM/TD/WP(2000)15/FINAL (2000) at 38-39 [*OECD Document*]. See also discussion on protection at Common Law, below.

70 R.S.C. 1985, c. C-34.

71 R.S.C. 1985, c F-27.

72 The *North American Free Trade Agreement Between the Government of Canada, the Government of Mexico and the Government of the United States*, 17 December 1992, Can. T.S. 1994 No 2, 32 I.L.M. 289 (entered into force 1 January 1994) [*NAFTA*]. Although *NAFTA* obliged parties to protect GIs it only required the *TRIPS* Article 22 level of protection.

73 Canada acceded to Articles 13–30 of the *Paris Convention* (Stockholm) 1967 on 26 March 1970 which entered into force on 7 July 1970 and acceded to Articles 1–12 on 23 February 1996 which subsequently entered into force on 26 May 1996.

74 *Agreement between the European Community and Canada on trade in wines*

Canada has taken steps to comply with its Article 23 *TRIPS* obligations by providing protection to GIs for wines and spirits under amendments to its trademark legislation in 1996.[75] No special provision was enacted in Canada to implement the Article 22 level of protection applicable to all types of GIs as this protection is considered to be already afforded through the certification mark system and at common law.[76]

Article 23 Protection

Protection is afforded to GIs for wines and spirits under special provisions of Canada's *Trade-marks Act*.[77] The Act adopts the *TRIPS Agreement* definition of a GI solely in relation to wines and spirits. Under s. 2 of the Act a 'geographical indication' means in respect of a wine or spirit, an indication that:

(a) identifies the wine or spirit as originating in the territory of a WTO Member, or a region or locality of that territory, where a quality, reputation or other characteristic of the wine or spirit is essentially attributable to its geographical origin, and
(b) except in the case of an indication identifying a wine or spirit originating in Canada, is protected by the laws applicable to that WTO Member. [78]

The application process

In order for a geographical indication to be protected in Canada, it must be proposed by the Minister of Industry, published in the *Canada Gazette* giving three months for objections and, if no or no successful objections, be placed on the list of geographical indications kept by the Registrar of Trademarks by virtue of s. 11.12(1) of the Act. The Minister's proposal must be comprised in a statement setting out the following:

1. the proposal that the indication be entered on the said list
2. that the indication identifies a wine or a spirit
3. the originating territory, region or locality of the wine or the spirit

---

and spirit drinks, 16 September 2003, [2004] O.J. L.35/3 (entered into force on 1 June 2004) [*Canada-EU Agreement*].

[75] The *World Trade Organization Agreement Implementation Act*, S.C. 1994, c. 47, resulted in amendments to the *Trade-marks Act*, R.S.C. 1985, c. T-13 which came into force 1 January 1996.

[76] As discussed below.

[77] *Supra* note 75, ss. 2, 11 and 12(1).

[78] *Ibid.*, s. 2.

4. the quality, reputation or other characteristic of the wine or the spirit that, in the Minister's opinion, qualifies the geographical indication for protection.[79]

The statement must also provide the name and address of the authority to which objections may be directed which should be a person, firm or other entity with sufficient knowledge of, or connection with, the particular GI being proposed by the Minister, the so called 'responsible authority'.[80]

If after publication in the *Canada Gazette* no objection has been filed or served on the responsible authority within the given timeframe, the GI is entered on the list. The only ground on which an objection can be raised is that the indication is not a geographical indication.[81] GIs can also be removed from the list on a statement by the Minister to that effect.[82]

The selection of a GI to be protected under the *Trade-marks Act* falls under the remit of the Minister of Industry with administrative input from the Department of Agriculture and Agri-Food Canada (AAFC) and appears to be more a political rather than a purely administrative matter. [83] The Minister's proposal usually emanates from an application or request by a third party for the GI to be so protected.[84] The application is submitted to and first examined by AAFC which then recommends to the Minister of Industry whether the GI should be published as such.[85]

The applications are assessed on the basis of the GI being a legitimate GI protected in its country of origin and must contain a description of the GI in question and provide virtually all the information required to be set out in the

---

79 *Ibid.*, s. 11.12(3).

80 *Ibid.*

81 *Ibid.*, s. 11.13(2). See Daniel R. Bereskin, 'Legal Protection of Geographical Indications in Canada' (Paper presented to the Intellectual Property Institute of Canada, Nova Scotia, 18 September 2003) at 17, online: <http://www.bereskinparr.com/English/publications/pdf/TM-Geographic-Bereskin.pdf>.

82 *Trade-marks Act, supra* note 75, s. 11.12(4).

83 For an outline of the process see Hugues G. Richard *et al.*, eds., *Canadian Trade-Marks Act Annotated*, looseleaf (Toronto: Carswell, 2004) at 11.1-18. See also Industry Canada, Marketplace Framework Policy Branch, *Consultation Paper on Possible Phase-out of Generic Names for Wines and Spirits (Geographical Indications)*, (4 October 2002) at 4 [*Consultation Paper*].

84 A 'Request for Protection of a Geographical Indication for a Wine or Spirit' form provided by AAFC may be used but is not required. See Agriculture and Agri-food Canada, *Process to Request Geographical Indications for Wines and Spirits to be Entered on Canada's List of Protected GIs*, online: <http://www.agr.gc.ca/itpd-dpci/english/topics/spirits_e.htm>.

85 *Ibid.*

Minister's statement under s. 11.12(1) of the Act.[86] Each application must also specify the law(s) which protect the indication in the WTO Member Territory and describe the quality, reputation or other characteristic of the wine or spirit that is essentially attributable to its geographical origin.[87] The Canadian Intellectual Property Office (CIPO) also examines the application and further information may be required of the responsible authority for the purposes of the evaluation.[88] The system implemented by AAFC allows a response time of six months during which rejected applications can be defended by the applicant.

GIs which have made it to the 'protected list' include Canadian Rye Whisky; Canadian Whisky; Chilean Pisco; Fraser Valley; Lake Erie North Shore; Niagara Peninsula; Okanagan Valley; Pelee Island; Pisco Chilien; Scotch Whisky; Similkameen Valley; and Vancouver Island.[89]

Protection

Protection of a GI on the list is afforded by way of prohibitions on the use and adoption, in connection with a business as a trademark or otherwise, of the geographical indication for wines or spirits not originating in the territory indicated by the protected geographical indication.[90] The prohibitions extend to a translation in any language of the geographical indication in respect of the wine or the spirit in question.[91] In accordance with Article 23(2) of *TRIPS*, trademarks which wholly or partly incorporate a GI in respect of a wine or spirit are excluded from registration where they do not in fact originate in the territory designated by the GI.[92]

Where the product is neither a wine nor a spirit, the registration of a trademark which in part or wholly comprises a GI is not precluded by the Act. For example, a trademark for 'the Champagne of Ginger-ales'[93] would

---

86 *Trade-marks Act*, *supra* note 75.

87 *Ibid.* Each request must be accompanied by a prescribed fee and can relate to only one GI. See *supra* note 84.

88 For example, expert information on the quality or reputation of a wine or spirit may be requested during the review process.

89 See Canadian Intellectual Property Office, *List of Geographical Indications for Wines and Spirits* (January 2007), online: <http://napoleon.ic.gc.ca/cipo/listgiws.nsf/gitoc-e>.

90 *Trade-marks Act*, *supra* note 75, ss. 11.14 and 11.15.

91 *Ibid.*, ss. 11.14(1)(b), (2)(b), 11.15(1)(b) and (2)(b).

92 Paragraph 12(1) of the *Trade-marks Act*, *ibid.*, outlines the criteria for the registration of a trademark by listing what would make the trademark ineligible for registration.

93 '[O]r "North Pole" for bananas, since no one would expect bananas to come from there': Canadian Intellectual Property Office, *A Guide to Trademarks* (June

not be barred from registration by virtue of para. 12 of the Act. It may however be precluded by other provisions such as where it is deceptively misleading.[94]

Exceptions

The exceptions to protection for GIs outlined in the Act generally comply with those mandated by *TRIPS* in Article 24. As such, GI protection does not apply to non-misleading uses of personal names or to GIs which have been used continuously in good faith before the date the *TRIPS Agreement* was concluded or used continuously for at least ten years prior to *TRIPS*.[95] The prohibitions do not apply to the use of a protected GI in comparative advertising pertaining to a wine or spirit, but this exception does not extend to comparative advertising on labels or packaging associated with a wine or spirit.[96]

Further, in compliance with Article 24(7) of *TRIPS*, if proceedings are not taken to enforce these prohibitions within five years after use by a person or that person's predecessor-in-title, the offending trademark has become generally known in Canada or the said trademark has been registered by that person in Canada, the provisions will not be enforceable unless it is established that the trademark was first used or adopted with the knowledge that such use or adoption was contrary to the relevant provisions.[97]

In relation to proceedings for the refusal or invalidation of a trademark comprising a GI by virtue of para. 12(1) (g) or (h) of the Act, the five-year limitation period will not bar the expunging or invalidation of a registered trademark where the applicant for registration applied with knowledge that the trademark was in whole or in part a protected geographical indication.[98] This complies with Articles 22(3) and 24(7) of *TRIPS*.

As permitted under Article 24(5) of *TRIPS*, the Act contains transitional provisions which allow the continuance without prejudice of good faith applications, registrations and the use of a trademark which is identical or similar to GIs for a wine or spirit protected in another WTO Member, made or

---

2005), online: <http://strategis.ic.gc.ca/sc_mrksv/cipo/tm/tm_gd_main-e.html>. The Champagne of Ginger-ales example was given in *Consultation Paper*, *supra* note 83 at 4-5.

94 A similar exclusion was only introduced into the *Trade Marks Act 1994* (U.K.), 1994, c. 26. An equivalent provision is found in s. 11(1)(c) of the *Trade Marks Act No. 32 of 1999* and *Act No. 25 of 2001* (Jamaica) [together hereinafter referred to as the *Trade Marks Act 1999*].

95 *TRIPS Agreement*, *supra* note 7, Article 24(4), (8). *Trade-marks Act*, *supra* note 75, ss. 11.16 and 11.17.

96 *Trade-marks Act*, *ibid.*, s. 11.16(2) and (3).

97 *Ibid.*, s. 11.19(1).

98 *Ibid.*, s. 11.19(2).

acquired prior to the coming into force of the s. 11 provisions and prior to when the GIs are protected in that WTO Member.[99]

Canada-EU Agreement

Perhaps the most controversial exception to GI protection, which accords with Article 24(6) of *TRIPS*, is that GIs which have fallen into disuse in the country of origin or which have become a customary term or synonymous with the customary name of a grape variety in Canada do not qualify for protection under the *Trade-marks Act.*[100] This exception effectively bars GIs from protection in the country where they have degenerated into generic terms.

Canada took the bold step, upon implementing this exception, of actually listing several world-famous GIs in respect of which GI protection would not apply. In effect, anyone in Canada could adopt, use or register any of the listed names as a trademark in connection with a business without contravening the GI provisions under the *Trade-marks Act.*[101] To the chagrin of the EU, the so-called 'generic'names on the lists in their original form included several well-known and highly valued GIs such as Champagne and Bordeaux in respect of which special protection is still valid and in force in their respective countries of origin and regionally.

This triggered a number of complaints before the EC alleging, in summary, that 'the amendment to the Canadian Trade-Marks Act violates Articles 23.1 and 2 as well as Article 24.3 (the so-called standstill clause) of the WTO *Agreement on Trade-Related Aspects of Intellectual Property Rights* (TRIPS) and that such infringements cannot be justified on the basis of the exception under Article 24.6 of TRIPS.'[102] Complaints related to famous GIs such as Bordeaux, Médoc and Parma (for ham from Parma, Italy) which were deemed to have fallen into generic and semi-generic usage.[103] The investigations into the complaint in respect of Bordeaux and Médoc, which was made in June

---

[99] *Ibid.*, s. 11.20.

[100] *TRIPS Agreement*, *supra* note 7, Article 24(6). *Trade-marks Act*, *supra* note 75., s. 11.18. See also Conrad, *supra* note 6 at 38–40.

[101] *Trade-marks Act*, *ibid.*, s. 11.18(3) and (4).

[102] EC, Commission, *Complaint : Canada : Lack of protection of the wines with geographical indication "Bordeaux" and Médoc'*, online: <http://ec.europa.eu/trade/issues/respectrules/tbr/cases/can_bor.htm> [*CIVB Complaint*]. The complaint was brought by Conseil Interprofessionnel du Vin de Bordeaux (CIVB).

[103] A complaint was brought by Consorzio del Prosciutto di Parma (Association of 201 Prosciutto di Parma producers) against Canada's lack of protection of the GI 'Prosciutto di Parma' and the lack of 'appropriate legal remedies to effectively redress the unfair competition generated by the use of the trademark "Parma" by Canadian producers'. See discussions below.

2002, were delayed pending the outcome of bilateral negotiations which were then in progress between Canada and the EU. The outcome of the negotiations was the removal of the so-called generic GIs from Canada's GI 'black lists' with a promise of *quid pro quo* recognition of some of Canada's protected GIs for wines and spirits in Europe.[104]

After almost four years of negotiations culminating in the signing of the *Canada-European Community Wines and Spirits Agreement*, the 'black list-s'were amended.[105] Under the said bilateral agreement, Canada agreed to remove the GIs from the lists in three phases. Upon the entry into force of the bilateral agreement the following GIs for wines were deleted from the list: Claret, Bordeaux, Chianti, Madeira, Malaga, Marsala, Medoc, Médoc, Moselle, Mosel and Tokay. In the second and third phases, by 31 December 2008, Chablis, Burgundy, Bourgogne, Rhine, Rhin, Sauterne and Sauternes will be removed from the list and Champagne, Port, Porto and Sherry will be deleted by 31 December 2013. Grappa, Marc and Ouzo were to be deleted from the list within two years.[106]

The removal of the so-called generic GIs from the lists appeared to be a significant about face turn for Canada, who had seemed to be standing firm against the EU's quest to 'claw back' generic GIs and have them protected, defeating the object of the fought-over *TRIPS* Article 24(6) exception. It is now clear that whereas *TRIPS*, by including such exceptions, did not attempt to and does not reverse past developments in the field, the EU through bilateral negotiations has effectively done just that.[107]

Undoubtedly, this change in position was dictated largely by Canada's commercial interests and is considered to be in the best interest of its local wines and spirits industry. With exports of wine estimated at $1.5 million in 2005, it was anticipated that Canadian exports would pull in $5 million from Europe under the *Canada-EU Agreement*.[108] Additionally, a number of

---

104 *CIVB Complaint*, *supra* note 102. See also the *Canada-EU Agreement*, *supra* note 74.

105 The lists can be amended by the Governor in Council: *Trade-marks Act*, *supra* note 75, s. 11.18(5).

106 The following wines remain on the list under s. 11.18(3) of the Act: Champagne; Port; Porto; Sherry; Chablis; Burgundy; Bourgogne; Rhine; Rhin; Sauterne and Sauternes. The following spirits remain on the list in s. 11.18(4) of the Act: Sambuca; Geneva Gin; Genièvre; Hollands Gin; London Gin; Schnapps; Malt Whiskey; Eau-de-vie; Bitters; Anisette; Curacao and Curaçao.

107 See Conrad, *supra* note 6 at 43.

108 This, Parliamentary Secretary to the Minister of Agriculture and Agri-Food (Rural Development) Hon. Wayne Easter, told the Standing Committee on Agriculture and Agri-Food in the House of Commons, Canada on 27 October 2005. See Canada, Standing Committee on Agriculture and Agri-Food, AGRI 060 (27 October 2005) at 8,

Canadian wines and spirits protected as GIs under the *Trade-marks Act* would be recognized in the EU by virtue of the *Agreement*.[109]

Perhaps anticipating a positive outcome like Australia, which subsequent to its bilateral agreement with the EU in 1994 experienced a boom in its wine industry,[110] with support from the distillers association, the vintners association and the provinces and the Société des alcools du Québec, Canada regarded the *Canada-EU Agreement* as a 'win win'and a resolution of 'past irritants in the wine and spirits sectors' solidifying Canada's market access to the EU.[111] As Parliamentary Secretary to the Minister of Agriculture and Agri-Food in discussions on Bill S-38, the final chapter of Canada's implementation of the *Canada-EU Agreement*, stated:

> The benefits to Canada's wines and spirits sector are substantial, mainly because of the other provisions in the agreement . . . Canada will be able to continue provincial liquor board practices that do favour Canadian producers. As well, the agreement allows for a simplified certification process for Canadian wine exports and it protects Canadian and European wines and spirit drink geographical indicators in the EU market.[112]

Still yet, with all the accolades, worrying concerns expressed by some on the *Canada-EU Agreement* are finding validity in the context of the continuing quest by the EU to extend the level of protection granted under the *TRIPS Agreement* to GIs for wines and spirits to other types of agricultural products.[113] As stated by Ted Menzies in the discussions on Bill S-38, who

---

online: <http://cmte.parl.gc.ca/Content/HOC/Committee/381/AGRI/Evidence/EV2065153/AGRIEV60-E.PDF> [*Standing Committee report*].

109 These include Canadian Rye Whisky and wines originating in the Okanagan Valley, Niagara Peninsula, and Vancouver Island.

110 See Calboli, *supra* note 6 at 200–201 and 'Europe's Trademarks: Protecting names', *Economist* (2 August 2003) 49.

111 'Bill S-38 is truly a good-news story'. It is 'a win for Canada, and it's a win for the European Union'...In short Bill S-38 is an example of how the system can work for the benefit of Canadian producers and consumers': Hon. Wayne Easter, *Standing Committee report*, *supra* note 108 at 1. See also AAFC's website: <http://www.agr.gc.ca/itpd-dpci/english/trade_agr/spirits.htm> and Canadian Vintners Association, press release, 'Canada Makes Inroads in Europe for Wines and Spirits Industry' (16 September 2003), online: <http://www.canadianvintners.com/news/ 20030916_govnews.htm> and 'Inroads in Europe for Canadian Wines and Spirits' (September 2003) 3:3 Growing Tomorrow 1 at 1-2, online: <http://www.iafbc.ca/publications_and_resources/documents/2003-Fall.pdf>.

112 *Standing Committee report*, *ibid.*. Bill S-38 which sought to implement the obligations under the *Canada-EU Agreement* in relation to spirits also had the object of covering obligations under *NAFTA* to protect Tequila from Mexico and Bourbon Whisky from the US.

113 See discussion at Part III, below.

expressed concerns that the *Canada-EU Agreement* might set a bad precedent that would give the EU a strong basis on which to come back at Canada, '. . . I'm concerned for Quebec, for producers of parmesan cheese. If the EU has its way, parmesan cheese will only come from Parma, Italy. It'll be the same with Roquefort. We have a lot of producers and manufacturing plants in Canada making bologna. If they have their way, it will only be made in Bologna, Italy.'[114]

Article 22 Protection

Certification marks

It is Canada's position that certification marks under the *Trade-marks Act*, provide an effective means of protection for GIs in the context of its obligations under Article 22 of the TRIPS Agreement.[115]

Under the Act a certification mark is defined as:

> a mark that is used for the purpose of distinguishing or so as to distinguish wares or services that are of a defined standard with respect to:
> (a) the character or quality of the wares or services,
> (b) the working conditions under which the wares have been produced or the services performed,
> (c) the class of persons by whom the wares have been produced or the services performed, or
> (d) the area within which the wares have been produced or the services performed,
> from wares or services that are not of that defined standard.[116]

Once registered, subject to some specific provisions, certification marks are afforded the same level of protection granted to any other registered trade-mark.[117] The registered owner of a certification mark can license others to use the mark in association with goods or services that meet the defined standard as well as prevent unlicensed persons from using the mark. [118] The registered

---

[114] *Standing Committee report*, *supra* note 108 at 8.

[115] See Agriculture and Agri-food Canada, 'Agri-food Trade Policy – Geographical Indications Questions and Answers' (September 2006), online: <http://www.agr.gc.ca/itpd-dpci/english/topics/tripsqsas.htm> and Agriculture and Agri-food Canada, 'Agri-food Trade Policy – Means of Protection of Geographical Indications in Canada' (June 2003), online: <http://www.agr.gc.ca/itpd-dpci/english/topics/tripsqsas_protection.htm>. See also Bereskin, *supra* note 81 at 14.

[116] *Trade-marks Act*, *supra* note 75, s. 2.

[117] The definition of a 'trade-mark' under the Act includes a certification mark. *Ibid.*, s. 2.

[118] *Ibid.*, s. 23(2).

owner can also prohibit the use of the mark by licensees in association with any goods or services to which the licence does not extend even where they are covered by the registration.[119] The certification mark can also be transferred to another proprietor.[120]

Certification marks operate with some restrictions which are not applicable to ordinary trademarks. For one, the applicant must not be carrying on business involving the supply of goods or services to be certified.[121] Further, the scope of exclusivity that is granted to owners of a geographically descriptive certification mark is delineated. Certification marks which are descriptive, but not confusing with any registered trademark, are only registrable where 'the applicant is the administrative authority of a country, state, province or municipality including or forming part of the area indicated by the mark, or is a commercial association having an office or representative in that area' and the owner of the mark so registered must 'permit the use of the mark in association with any wares or services produced or performed in the area of which the mark is descriptive.'[122]

In the US and Canada, a number of European GIs, such as Stilton Cheese, Parmigiano Reggiano and Mozzarella di Bufala Campana are protected as certification marks. By not treating GIs as a separate class of intellectual property,[123] the US in its first proposal in the Uruguay Round negotiations of the GATT/*TRIPS Agreement* put forward certification and/or collective marks as ideal means of protection for GIs.[124] This position is in stark contrast with that of many European countries which provide GI protection by way of special provisions separate and apart from certification marks.[125] The divergence of

---

119 *Ibid.*, s. 23(3).

120 *Ibid.*, s. 48(1).

121 *Ibid.*, s. 23(1).

122 *Ibid.*, s. 25.

123 See also Tim Josling, 'What's in a Name? The economics, law and politics of Geographical Indications for foods and beverages' (2005) IIIS Discussion Paper No. 109 at 11.

124 See GATT, *Draft Agreement on the Trade-Related Aspects of Intellectual Property Rights – Communication from the United States*, GATT Doc. MTN.GNG/NG11/W/70, reprinted in (1990) 10 W.I.P.R. 128. Collective marks are trademarks owned by an association for use by its members often in accordance with special requirements laid down by that association. Such a mark may include a GI but the proprietor cannot prevent *bona fide* and honest use by another person entitled to use the GI for a particular product. See Conrad, *supra* note 6 at 21 citing the *Lanham Act* §45, 15 USC §1127 and *State of Florida, Dept. of Citrus v. Real Juices, Inc*, 330 F. Supp. 428 (M.D. Fla. 1971).

125 See the EU Draft proposal embodied in GATT, *Draft Agreement on Trade-Related Aspects of Intellectual Property Rights*, GATT Doc. MTN.GNG/NG11/W/68, reprinted in (1990) 10 W.I.P.R. 108. EU Members now implement a raft of regulations

approaches has generated debate about whether the use of certification marks to protect GIs is conceptually sound.[126]

There are obvious distinctions between trademarks and GIs which may give rise to legitimate concerns about the appropriateness of this form of protection for GIs.[127]

Unlike ordinary trademarks, GIs are classically regarded as collective and not freely transferable.[128] For this reason, some view trademarks as the more attractive and valuable form of intellectual property and criticize the GI system as part of an anti-competitive strategy by certain producer groups and a form of unjustifiable monopoly.[129]

It is the focus on the geographical origin and the peculiarity that origin brings to the product which arguably give GIs a unique place in the economic policies of certain countries which have much at stake when their GIs are not recognized abroad.[130]

Nevertheless, the peculiarities of the certification mark system, which differentiate it from ordinary trademarks, make it a proper mode of protection of GIs albeit as a complement to other modes.[131]

The Canadian definition of a certification mark is wide enough to include GIs as defined by the *TRIPS Agreement*. The elements of a certification mark which are common to a GI are those denoting the character or quality of a particular good and the location where the good has been produced. The elements relating to working conditions and class of persons

---

including the EC, *Council Regulation (EEC) No 509/2006 of 20 March 2006 on agricultural products and foodstuffs as traditional specialities guaranteed*, [2006] O.J. L.93/1 and *Council Regulation (EEC) No. 510/2006 of 20 March 2006 on the protection of geographical indications and designations of origin for agricultural products and foodstuffs*, [2006] O.J. L.93/12. See *OECD Document*, *supra* note 69 at 48–53.

[126] Zou, *supra* note 12 at 1163; Conrad, *supra* note 6 at 20; see generally Burkhart Goebel, 'Geographical Indications and Trademarks: The Road From Doha', WIPO Doc. WIPO/GEO/SFO/03/11.

[127] See generally Stephen Stern, 'Geographical Indications and Trade Marks: Conflicts and Possible Resolutions', WIPO Doc. WIPO/GEO/SFO/03/13 and Jean Rodesch, 'Trademarks and Geographical Indications: Complementary Assets', WIPO Doc. WIPO/GEO/SFO/03/23 Rev.

[128] 'Because geographical indications are inherently collectively owned (all cheese makers in Roquefort region are the actual "owners"), they are an excellent tool for regional or community-based economic development': Kamil Idris, *Intellectual Property: A Power Tool for Economic Growth* (Geneva: WIPO, 2002) at 181.

[129] See IPR Helpdesk, 'Geographical Indications' (July 2006) at 3, online: <http://www.ipr-helpdesk.org>.

[130] The GI Darjeeling has made India the world's largest tea grower. See generally, Naba Kumar Das, 'Protection of Darjeeling Tea', WIPO Doc. WIPO/GEO/SFO/03/8.

[131] See Conrad, *supra* note 6 at 21.

can also furnish the reputation and environmental factors usually present in a GI.[132]

The certification process which underlies the licensing of the certification mark resembles features of the classic GI system which seek to ensure close regulation of the GI and the production of the GI product to the requisite specifications. The delineated scope of exclusivity granted to the owner of a geographically descriptive certification mark fits GIs which are open to use by all traders in a particular geographic location of products emanating from that location.[133]

Further, the bar on use of the certification mark by the actual owner favors the independent regulatory role played by some GI authorities.[134] The restrictions on the transferability of GIs also find a fit in some certification mark systems where any transfer of the mark would be subject to the consent of the Registrar.[135]

In some respects, certification marks have broader commercial application than protection to be afforded to GIs under *TRIPS*, by virtue of the fact that they apply equally to goods and services.[136]

Admittedly, several foreign GIs would not fit well in the classification of a certification mark if only for the reason that a GI which exclusively comprises a place name would normally be barred from trademark registration unless the mark has acquired distinctiveness through use in the territory where protection is sought.[137] It is therefore not surprising that the certification mark approach has not gained wide acceptance as being sufficient for GIs and has been used in the absence of special protection for GIs rather than as an ideal forum for it.

---

[132] The Lisbon definition of an appellation of origin makes express reference to geographical environment including human factors: *Lisbon Agreement*, *supra* note 28.

[133] Where certification marks comprise a geographical indication the proprietor is not able to prevent *bona fide* and honest uses of the geographical name by other persons who are entitled to use the name. In these instances the mark is usually registered subject to a disclaimer of the geographical name.

[134] Collective marks are less restrictive in that the owner of the marks can use or trade under the marks however a similar disclaimer of the geographical name may be required.

[135] Under the *Trade Marks Act 1999* (Jamaica), *supra* note 94, a certification mark can only be transferred with the consent of the Registrar: see Second Schedule, s. 10 of the Act.

[136] It could be said that Canada, like several other countries, extends a level of protection to GIs for services which it is not actually obliged to do under the *TRIPS Agreement*.

[137] See ss. 11(1)(c) and 11(2) of the *Trade Marks Act 1999* (Jamaica) and the *Trade Marks Act 1994* (U.K.), *supra* note 94. See Conrad, *supra* note 6 at 40.

In fact, registration of GIs as certification marks has had to suffice for some countries where no *sui generis* protection has been available.[138] This was the case in the UK prior to changes to English law which were made pursuant to new regulations on GIs in the EU.[139] In former British colonies, including Jamaica, protection for GIs by way of certification marks has now been augmented by more comprehensive protection under special laws and regulations.[140]

It is clear that the certification marks system is not an ideal substitute for *sui generis* protection for GIs as a number of foreign GIs would have the challenge of fitting into a mold which was not originally designed for them.[141] However, these hurdles are not insurmountable and certification mark systems do provide a mode of protection for GIs that can be effectively employed along with other avenues of protection. As has been said, '[t]he road to protection for geographical indications is not a single road but a number of parallel roads.'[142]

The common law element

Canada also implements its Article 22 protection through other statutes[143] and at common law. In fact, prior to the C-57 Amendment to the *Trade-marks Act*,[144] GI protection in Canada was primarily based on common law in all provinces except Quebec, where the protection was granted by Article 1457 of

---

138 Notably in the English-speaking Commonwealth Caribbean countries.

139 See David Kitchin *et al.*, *Kerly's Law of Trade Marks and Trade Names*, 14th ed. (London: Thompson, Sweet & Maxwell, 2005) at paras. 11-003, 321–2, 11-004–11-042. The EU Regulations protect Designations of Origin and GIs, *supra* note 125.

140 In Jamaica 'Jamaica Blue Mountain Coffee' is a registered certification mark owned by the Coffee Industry Board. The *Protection of Geographical Indications Act No. 5* of 2004 was enacted to implement Section 3 of *TRIPS* in Jamaica. This Act augments the Article 22 protection already available to GIs through trademarks and at common law and gives special protection to GIs for wines and spirits in accordance with Article 23 of *TRIPS*. See also Carlos M. Correa, 'Protection of Geographical Indications in CARICOM Countries' (September 2002), online: <http://www.crnm.org/documents/studies/Geographical%20Indications%20-%20Correa.pdf>.

141 Some foreign GI authorities would have to establish a presence in the country where protection is sought in order to monitor the use of the certification mark. Some would need to ensure that they do not run afoul of the restriction which bars them from using the mark themselves. In this regard, a collective mark system may better suit some GIs.

142 Conrad, *supra* note 6 at 22 quoting M. G. Coerper.

143 Reference is also made to the *Food and Drugs Act*, *supra* note 71, under which regulations outline certain GIs for wines and spirits which cannot be used unless coming from the country of origin. Reference is also made to the *Unfair Competition Act*, R.S.C. 1952, c. 274.

144 *Supra* note 75.

the Civil Code.[145] Similar to other countries having a common law tradition, a GI can be protected in Canada from false and misleading uses and unfair competition under the tort of passing off, but a number of elements have to be proved to guarantee a successful outcome.[146]

In its early development, the tort of passing off seemed aptly suited to address the core elements of GI protection, namely, protecting consumers from misleading product description and association and traders from acts of unfair competition preserving their goodwill as a consequence.[147] However, the failed attempts at protection in Canada via this route by European GI authorities illustrate the inherent complexities in the tort of passing off when applied to GIs and the apparent redundancy of this form of protection.[148]

The famous GI-type cases of *Spanish Champagne*,[149] *Sherry*[150] and *Advocaat*[151] apply an extended form of the tort as elucidated by Lord Diplock in the *Advocaat* case. Therein his Lordship identified the five essential ingredients of the tort. In essence, there must be (1) a misrepresentation, (2) made by a trader in the course of trade, (3) to prospective or ultimate customers of goods or services supplied by him, (4) which is calculated to, or may in a reasonably foreseeable way, injure the business or goodwill of another trader and (5) which causes or may probably cause, actual damage to a business or goodwill of the trader by whom the action is brought.[152]

Canada, in applying the tort appears to favor the condensed three-step test outlined by Lord Oliver in the *Jif Lemon Case*[153] namely, (1) goodwill (2) misrepresentation/deception and (3) damage.[154] In the case of *Ciba-*

---

145 Infringement of a GI must adjust to the general criteria outlined in the Code.

146 See Conrad, *supra* note 6 at 20 on the common law and the US approach and at 17, with respect to unfair competition (the problem arises when this type of protection is sought internationally as GIs often lose their goods-place association in foreign territories as they are less well-known there).

147 See generally Bereskin, *supra* note 81. Early cases in which the tort applied include *Seixo v. Provezende* (1866), L.R. 1 Ch. App. 192 and *Manchester Brewery Company, Limited v. North Cheshire and Manchester Brewery Company, Limited*, [1898] 1 Ch. 539.

148 See discussion on the 'INAO' cases below.

149 *Bollinger v. Costa Brava Wine Co.*, [1961] R.P.C. 116, [1961] 1 All E.R. 561 (Ch.D.) [*Spanish Champagne*].

150 *Vine Products v. Mackenzie*, [1969] R.P.C. 1 [*Sherry*].

151 *Erven Warnink B.V. v. J. Townend & Sons (Hull) Ltd.*, [1979] A.C. 731, [1980] R.P.C. 31 (H.L.) [*Advocaat*].

152 Lord Diplock's statement slightly paraphrased, *ibid.* at 93.

153 *Reckitt & Colman Products Ltd. v. Borden Inc.*, [1990] 1 All E.R. 873 at 880 (H.L.) [*Jif Lemon*].

154 For more on the tort of passing off and its application in Canada see R. Scott Joliffe, 'The Common Law Doctrine of Passing Off' in Gordon F. Henderson., ed., *Trademarks Law of Canada* (Scarborough, Ont.: Carswell, 1993) 197.

Geigy,[155] the Canadian court adopted the tort as restated by Lord Oliver where it found passing off in relation to the get-up of a prescription drug. Gonthier J. stated as follows:

> The three necessary components of a passing-off action are thus: the existence of goodwill, deception of the public due to a misrepresentation and actual or potential damage to the plaintiff.[156]

Subsequent cases have applied this test such as the *Lego* case[157] wherein LeBel J. stated that:

> [t]he first component is goodwill or reputation. The claimant must establish goodwill in respect of the distinctiveness of the product. Evidence of goodwill solely attached to the techniques and processes which create the product will not do. The doctrine of passing off did not develop to protect monopolies in respect of products but of guises, get-ups, names and symbols which identify the distinctiveness of a source.[158]

It is quite well established that the common law does not recognize a property right in the name itself.[159] Hence, to succeed in an action for passing off, reliance must be placed on the existence of goodwill in the particular class of traded goods or services in the territory where the action is being enforced, by association with the get-up which can include a name, label or packaging. The *Pillsbury*[160] case illustrated that the name must have acquired a secondary meaning in the mind of the public as being goods or services of the plaintiff having certain qualities or characteristics.[161]

The final hurdle is that the plaintiff's goodwill must be affected or likely to be affected as a result of the defendant's misrepresentation. In relation to the element of misrepresentation leading to confusion in the marketplace, according to *Ciba-Geigy* the confusion need not arise from willful misrepresentation or deceit. The doctrine of passing off also covers negligent or careless misrepresentation by the trader.[162]

---

155 *Ciba-Geigy Canada Ltd. v. Apotex Inc.*, [1992] 3 S.C.R. 120 [*Ciba-Geigy*].

156 *Ibid.*

157 *Kirkbi AG v. Ritvik Holdings Inc.*, [2005] 3 S.C.R. 302, 2005 SCC 65 [*Kirkbi*].

158 *Ibid.* See also *Oxford Pendaflex Canada Ltd. v. Korr Marketing Ltd.*, [1982] 1 S.C.R. 494 at 504 and 507, Estey J.

159 See *A.G. Spalding & Bros. v. A. W. Gamage* (1915), 32 R.P.C. 273 at 284, [1914–1915] All E.R. 147 (H.L.), Lord Parker.

160 *Pillsbury-Washburn Flour Mills Co. v. Eagle*, 86 F. 608 (7th Cir. 1898).

161 See Bereskin, *supra* note 81 at 5.

162 *Ciba-Geigy, supra* note 155 at 133. See also *Kirkbi*, *supra* note 157 at para. 68 and *Consumers Distributing Co. v. Seiko Time Canada Ltd.*, [1984] 1 S.C.R. 583 at 601, Estey J.

The House of Lords in the *Advocaat* case held that the defendants were engaging in passing off as they deliberately induced members of the public to believe that in buying the defendants' 'Old English Advocaat', they were in fact buying the 'Advocaat' drink sold by the plaintiffs. However, the protection granted under the law of passing off had less to do with geographical location and more to do with the goodwill in respect of the particular class of goods. As stated by Lord Fraser: 'How can it matter whether the name by which the genuine product is known has geographical origin or has no natural connection with the product [...] provided that it is distinctive of a particular class of goods?'[163]

The House of Lords contrasted the *Advocaat* case with that of the *Spanish Champagne* case[164] which established that a passing off action could be initiated by a group of owners and that proof of damage to the plaintiff's goodwill occasioned by a false trade description would suffice.[165]

There can be instances where a GI, while originating from and bearing characteristics attributable to a particular location, has not acquired goodwill or a reputation in the country where protection or enforcement is being sought. In such an instance, it is hardly likely that the tort of passing off, which requires that the name or description for which protection is claimed must 'genuinely indicate...that [the product] has gained a reputation and goodwill',[166] will provide sufficient protection.

It is instructive that GIs such as Champagne and Parma ham have not found protection in Canada and the tort of passing off has offered little assistance. In the *Andres* case,[167] the Institut National des Appellations d'Origine des Vins et Eaux-de-Vie (INAO) unsuccessfully claimed passing off against Andres Wines Limited and others regarding the use of the GI 'Champagne' in the take-off 'Canadian Champagne'. INAO failed to prove essential criteria of passing off: evidence that consumers were or would have been misled or confused and interference with the goodwill or reputation of the INAO. In fact, the court actually found that the defendants'product had acquired its own distinct goodwill in Canada.

The INAO met with mixed success in the *Cognac* case[168] when it opposed an application for a mark for beer. While the INAO succeeded in its claim that

---

[163] *Advocaat*, *supra* note 151 at 104.

[164] *Spanish Champagne*, *supra* note 149.

[165] See Bereskin, *supra* note 81 at 6.

[166] Per Goulding J. in the *Advocaat* case, *supra* note 151 at 46.

[167] *Institut National des Appellations d'Origine des Vins et Eaux-de-Vie ['INAO'] et al. v. Andres Wines Ltd. et al.* (1987), 16 C.P.R. (3d) 385 (Ont. H.C.J.), aff'd (1990), 30 C.P.R. (3d) 279 (Ont. C.A.) [*Andres*].

[168] *INAO v. Brick Brewing Co. Ltd.* (1995), 66 C.P.R. (3d) 351 (T.M.O.B.) [*Cognac*].

the applicant violated s. 5(2) of the *Food and Drugs Act*,[169] it failed to prove that the average consumer would be misled into thinking that the applicant's mark was associated with 'Cognac' from France. The INAO had a similar outcome when arguing that consumers would be misled by the use of 'Bordeaux' for cookies.[170] The law of passing off however was not the determining forum in either case.

In the case of *Beatrice/Hunt-Wesson Inc. v. Chocosuisse, Union des Fabricants Suisses de Chocolat*,[171] the principles of passing off were applied in protecting the 'Swiss' GI. However, more than the use of the name 'Swiss', it was the imitation of the authentic packaging of the claimant's goods by the defendants that was held to misrepresent the products to consumers.

It is clear that the law of passing off has not been extended to provide better protection for GIs, but some GIs have been fortunate to find a 'safety net' of sorts inside the well established parameters of the tort.

III CANADA'S STANCE IN THE GIs EXTENSION DEBATE

Canada has adopted a minimalist approach to the implementation of the *TRIPS Agreement* by maintaining the dichotomy of protection between GIs for wines and spirits and other products. Canada's refusal to grant protection for GIs other than wines and spirits beyond the current *TRIPS* requirements is no doubt influenced by Canadian local industry, foreign trade interests and existing obligations under agreements such as *NAFTA*.[172] This position is consistent with Canada's alignment with WTO Members holding the view that the Article 23 level of protection is exceptional and that any multilateral system of registration and notification of GIs should be voluntary and legally non-binding.

This stance by Canada should not be surprising as, despite being a member of the *Paris Convention* since 1970, Canada has not participated in the two international agreements which have offered substantive levels of protection to GIs.[173] Further, in the GATT/TRIPS negotiation, Canada aligned itself with the US which was resistant to the concept of special protection for GIs.

The questions of extension of protection and establishment of a global GI registry are in essence the issues which have fuelled tensions among WTO

169 *Food and Drugs Act*, *supra* note 71, s. 5(2).
170 *INAO v. Pepperidge Farm, Inc.* (1997), 84 C.P.R. (3d) 540 (T.M.O.B.).
171 (1992), 45 C.P.R. (3d) 268 (T.M.O.B.).
172 *Supra* note 72.
173 See discussion in Part I, above, on the *Madrid* and *Lisbon Agreements*.

member countries and the point has been aptly made that 'the same ideological divide as to GIs protection that characterized pre-*TRIPs* negotiations has continued to affect the post-*TRIPs* debates.'[174]

Article 23(4) of the *TRIPS Agreement* makes provision for 'negotiations to be undertaken in the Council for TRIPS regarding the establishment of a multilateral system of notification and registration of geographical indications for wines which are eligible for protection in Member countries participating in the system with a view to facilitating GI protection for wines.'[175] There is also provision for international negotiations aimed at increasing the protection of individual GIs under Article 23, arguably only for wines and spirits, and for the timely review by the Council for *TRIPS* of the provisions under that section.[176]

At the WTO Ministerial Conference in Doha in November 2001, Members agreed on a work programme to address 'implementation-related issues and concerns' and trade-related aspects of intellectual property rights.[177] Paragraph 18 of the Ministerial Declaration adopted at the Doha Round provided the mandate in relation to the implementation of the multilateral system of notification and registration of GIs.

The opposition centers around the proposed nature of the system and its legal effect on members. The EU recommends a compulsory regime for the notification and registration of GIs which would have a legally binding effect on decisions by members to protect GIs in their respective territories.[178] Such a system would necessitate an amendment to Article 23(4) of the *TRIPS Agreement*.[179] The presence of a GI on the international register would create

---

174 Calboli, *supra* note 6 at 194. See generally, Hughes, *supra* note 8, Zou, *supra* note 12, Steven Bowers 'Location, Location, Location: The Case against Extending Geographical Indication Protection under the TRIPS Agreement', (2003) 31 AIPLA Quarterly Journal 129. Tunisia L. Staten, 'Geographical Indications Protection under the TRIPS Agreement: Uniformity Not Extension' (2005) 87 J. Pat. & Trademark Off. Soc'y 221, Frances G. Zacher, 'Pass the Parmesan: Geographic Indications in the United States and the European Union – Can There be Compromise?' (2005) Emory Int'l L. Rev. 427, Jose Manuel Cortes Martin, 'The WTO TRIPS Agreement – The Battle between the Old and the New World over the Protection of Geographical Indications' (2004) 7:3 J. of World Int. Prop. 287-326.

175 *TRIPS Agreement*, *supra* note 7, Article 23(4).

176 *Ibid.*, Article 24(1), (2).

177 WTO, *Ministerial Declaration Adopted on 14 November 2001*, WTO Doc. WT/MIN(01)/DEC/1 (20 November 2001), online: <http://docsonline.wto.org> [Doha Declaration].

178 The EU Proposal is embodied in WTO, *Communication from the European Communities*, WTO Doc. TN/IP/W/11 (14 June 2005), online: <http://docsonline.wto.org> [*EU Proposal*].

179 *Ibid.*

a rebuttable presumption that the GI should be protected in the country where protection is being sought. The EU proposal also makes provision for reservations to be lodged against the GI on certain grounds including that the GI has become a generic term or that the so-called GI is not in fact a GI.[180]

Canada, on the other hand, supported a joint proposal which recommended that a voluntary system of notification and registrations be adopted.[181] The group of opponents to the EU proposal comprises a combination of developing countries of Latin America and few developed countries, resembling the so called 'JUSCANZ+'[182] which was obviously drawn together by the market realities of their affected industries.[183] Under their proposed system, non-participating countries would not be obliged to consult the multilateral database of GIs nor would any member be bound by the system; however, wide participation would be encouraged.[184]

The negotiations on the issue of extension of protection are very heated and particularly worrisome for countries seeking the extension as the very premise for treating it as a negotiation item has been brought into question by those members that oppose it. The EU maintains that the 'extension of the protection' was an implementation issue, as well as a developmental one, which the General Council and Trade Negotiations Committee should consider favourably.[185] However, opposing Members have argued that 'paras. 12 and 18 of the Doha Declaration did not constitute a commitment to negotiate on GI extension and that treating the matter as a development issue was inappropriate given that the differences on this matter were not between developed and developing countries.'[186] They argue further that *TRIPS* contains no provisions in relation to the extension of Article 23 level protection to products other than wines and spirits or any mandate to negotiate on this issue.[187]

---

180 *Ibid.* Failure on the part of a member to object to a generic GI would operate as a bar to future objections in relation to the GI in question.

181 The joint proposal is embodied in WTO, *Proposed Draft TRIPS Council Decision On The Establishment of a Multilateral System of Notification and Registration of Geographical Indications for Wines and Spirits*, WTO Doc. TN/IP/W/10 (1 April 2005), online: <http://docsonline.wto.org> [*Joint Proposal*].

182 These are US, Australia and New Zealand minus Japan. See Hughes, *supra* note 8 at 321.

183 The other countries are Argentina, Australia, Chile, Colombia, the Dominican Republic, Ecuador, El Salvador, Guatemala, Honduras, Panama, Paraguay, the Philippines and Chinese Taipei.

184 *Joint Proposal*, *supra* note 181.

185 *Ibid.*, at para. 46.

186 The views as outlined in *Issues Related to the Extension of the Protection of Geographical Indications*, *supra* note 19, which is a compilation of issues raised and view expressed and compiled by the Secretariat.

187 *Ibid.* This view is also supported by Hughes, *supra* note 8 at 321–31.

The EU has gained a number of GI-friendly allies in its quest for the extension of the higher level of protection to other products. To some developing countries, the EU proposal highlighted the benefit of the ability to protect agricultural and food products such as coffee, rice and tea at the Article 23 level which would enable them to prevent wrongful though non-misleading uses of these GIs in other members.[188] The EU GI-friendly allies include developing countries such as Jamaica,[189] India,[190] Pakistan and some African countries.[191] Some of the arguments in support of the extension stem from accusations of 'usurpation'and 'free-riding' of various GIs by some countries.[192] Canada, together with other opponents to the extension, maintains that the current level of protection afforded by *TRIPS* is adequate and that nothing has been put forward by the proponents to establish otherwise.[193] Furthermore, it is argued that there are several commercial and legal implications, such as consumer confusion and the effects on trademarks owners, that have been overlooked. An equal level of protection for GIs on all products is viewed therefore as potentially disruptive to global trade in goods.

Fuelling the debate are the attempts by the EU in the forum of the WTO negotiating group on agriculture to 'claw-back' European GIs that have been deemed generic by other members, a move that clearly runs counter to the exceptions on generic GIs under Article 24 of the *TRIPS Agreement*.

The claw-back is also evident in the *Canada-EU Agreement* with the phased-out removal of practically all the generic GIs from the lists which, interestingly, was viewed positively in the context of the wine and spirits industry in Canada.[194] In a press release on the signing of the *Canada-EU Agreement*, Franz Fischler, Commissioner for Agriculture, Rural Affairs and Fisheries, said: 'This agreement is a great achievement for EC-Canada rela-

---

188 *EU Proposal*, *supra* note 178.

189 Jamaican Blue Mountain Coffee, one of the most expensive and sought-after coffees in the world, is also a PDO in the EU. The Jamaica GI 'Appleton', reportedly the leading imported rum in Canada and Mexico, was awarded the 'Grand Gold' Medal by the Monde Selection International Institute for Quality Selections of Spirits and Liqueurs for 2007. See 'Appleton Estate Jamaica Rum takes double "Gold" ', *The Sunday Observer* [of Jamaica] (24 June 2007) p. 9, online: <http://www.jamaicaobserver.com>.

190 In India, Darjeeling is protected as a certification mark as well as through a system established by the *Tea Act* of 1953.

191 The other countries are Bulgaria, Guinea, Kenya, Madagascar, Mauritius, Morocco, Pakistan, Romania, Sri Lanka, Switzerland, Thailand, Tunisia and Turkey.

192 Opposing countries raised strong objections to the use of such language. See *Issues Related to the Extension of the Protection of Geographical Indications*, *supra* note 19.

193 *Joint Proposal*, *supra* note 181.

194 See discussion on the Canada-EU Bilateral, above.

tions...However you look at it, there is something not genuine about using a European name to describe a New World wine. Renouncing these names is a decision Canada's winemakers will not regret.'[195]

However, in the context of the extension debate, Canada remains adamant in its resistance to the prospects of EU claw-backs in relation to other products. Coupled with a possible extension of the higher level protection to foods, the claw-backs would mean that several GIs now being used in Canada either generically (for example, gorgonzola) or semi-generically (for example, Parma ham) as part of other trademarks that have acquired their own distinctiveness, would no longer be available to Canadian traders and producers who have used these GIs for decades. This would result in untold losses not only to traders and producers but also to consumers. Accordingly, Canada's intransigent position in this perspective is most understandable.

As the WTO Members continue to debate it remains to be seen which stance gains acceptance as being reflective of the commitments of members under the *TRIPS* accord.

CONCLUSION

Canada's defiance to the protection of GIs in the context of global trade liberalization and competition is aptly reflected in the words of Sergio Marchi, Canada's Ambassador to the WTO, who stabbed at the very heart of the protection afforded by geographical indications by stating that the concept ran 'contrary to the whole liberalization that underscores the whole Doha round'.[196]

Minimally *TRIPS* compliant, Canada's approach to protection of GIs falls well short of the protection being afforded in the EU and other GI friendly countries. Notwithstanding this, Canada's compliance ought not to be measured against the maximalist approach adopted by the EU.

The protection afforded by Canada through the certification mark system may be regarded as a 'by default' regime which is of necessity limited by practical and fundamental distinctions between a GI and a trademark. Indeed, while many WTO Members afford protection to GIs through certification marks, it is done complementarily and not as a substitute for special GI protection. Even the US employs collective marks together with certification marks, hence offering foreign GI authorities more avenues of protection.

---

[195] Delegation of the European Commission to Canada, Press Release, 'Fischler hails signature of wine and spirits accord as "*great achievement for EC-Canada trade relations*"' (16 September 2003), online:http://www.delcan.cec.eu.int>.

[196] Bereskin, *supra* note 81 and 21.

The fall-back to the common law tort of passing off is itself also riddled with obstacles and can only be used very selectively by GI authorities when all the criteria for establishing the cause of action are present. The Canadian experience where producers have established their own goodwill in relation to foreign GIs, which now must suffer the fate of genericism, has demonstrated that the criteria can hardly ever be met.

The protection Canada affords to wines and spirits and the relatively swift pace at which she moved to have the system working must be construed as indicative of Canada's willingness to consider the global impact of those kinds of geographical indications and her endorsement of the merits of protecting them. This attitude is tempered by perhaps the greatest show of defiance on Canada's part in citing the world famous GIs on the 'black lists'. This stance forced the EU to come to the table with some *quid pro quos* of mutual recognition.

While some may question whether a bad precedent might have been set and whether the long term impact of the EU's claw-backs under the *Canada-EU Agreement* will outweigh what is being offered to Canada in return, Canada's commitment to the bilateral process and her firm stance in the multilateral process displays her formidable ability to effectively navigate perhaps the most turbulent waters of the global intellectual property rights regime in the twenty-first century.

4. From Pasteur to *Monsanto*: approaches to patenting life in Canada

Mark Perry[1]

BACKGROUND

Few would dispute that one of the main rationales of all patent regimes is to encourage the development of new 'inventions', to promote innovation by direct reward (the grant of the monopoly from the state), and to ensure the dissemination of information required to stimulate further invention.[2] It is usually stated from the utilitarian perspective by the courts:[3]

> There is no doubt that two of the central objects of the Patent Act are 'to advance research and development and to encourage broader economic activity'.

It is notable that the Canadian courts are recently giving recognition to the wider theoretical basis for the state granting Intellectual Property rights to inventors, authors, and traders, in particular the sense that there are balancing 'user rights' for the consumers and the users of the material protected by intellectual property rights.[4] In the realm of biotechnology, however, there have been some problems in the application of these tenets, whether the new or the old. The objective of promoting innovation has been met with the denial of

---

[1] Many thanks to Stephanie Sutherland (Law Class of 2008) and Jennifer Hoffman (Law Class of 2009) for their diligent assistance, and to the Law Foundation for their support. However, all errors and omissions are my own.

[2] Graeme W. Austin, 'Copyright's Modest Ontology – Theory and Pragmatism in *Eldred v. Ashcroft*' (2003) 16:2 Canadian Journal of Law and Jurisprudence 163.

[3] *Free World Trust v. Électro Santé Inc.*, [2000] 2 S.C.R. 1024, 2000 SCC 35, Bastarache J.

[4] Recent cases include: in copyright, *Théberge v. Galerie d'Art du Petit Champlain Inc.*, [2002] 2 S.C.R. 336, 2002 SCC 34 and *CCH Canadian Ltd. v. Law Society of Upper Canada*, [2004] 1 S.C.R. 339, 2004 SCC 13; in trademark, *Mattel Inc. v. 3894207 Canada Inc.*, [2006] 1 S.C.R. 772; in patents, *Whirlpool Corp. v. Camco Inc.*, [2000] 2 S.C.R. 1067, 2000 SCC 67, *Bristol Myers Squibb Co. v. Canada (Attorney General)*, [2005] 1 S.C.R. 533, 2005 SCC 26, and *Astrazeneca Canada Inc. v. Canada (Minister of Health)*, [2006] 2 S.C.R. 560.

patents on 'higher lifeforms', and user rights restrained by a broad interpretation of 'use'. The last few decades have seen the discussion of transgenic lifeforms come to the fore, in the media,[5] a Canadian Government advisory committee,[6] and not least in the courts.[7] In *Harvard*, the Supreme Court of Canada denied a patent on a transgenic mouse that was undoubtedly an innovation, and in *Monsanto*, the same court found infringement in the use of a transgenic cell in a plant.[8]

The use of biological sciences has led to forms of life that have not been encountered in nature. Although some new variants of lifeforms have been created over the millennia using 'traditional breeding', or over the last century by techniques such as mutation-induced breeding, recent advances in biotechnology have allowed the controlled creation of altered lifeforms that display hitherto novel traits (referred herein as new lifeforms) in a relatively short timeframe. Undoubtedly these innovations have utility, in addition to being novel, but in Canada there has been much debate on the applicability of patents to such new lifeforms. In the last two decades the Canadian Supreme Court has been challenged with life patent scenarios, most recently with two cases based on transgenic engineering. The 5–4 split decisions in these two cases have led to what is arguably a legally coherent but illogical outcome. The Canadian approach to patent claims that are based on new forms of life has been to distinguish 'higher' lifeforms from other lifeforms, denying patents on the former. The first Canadian *Patent Act* 1886 after confederation was a break from the patent model of the United Kingdom with its adoption of a United States stance on this form of protection.

A description of the techniques required for creating a transgenic animal or plant is often missing from discussions on the patentability of higher lifeforms, even the oncomouse of the type referenced in the *Harvard* patents. Although a full description of the techniques may be beyond the scope of this paper,

---

5 For example, Christine Gorman, 'A Mouse that Roared' *Time* (25 April 1988) 53.

6 The now defunct, but hopefully superseded, Canadian Biotechnology Advisory Committee recommended the patenting of higher lifeforms, but only with protection of a 'farmers privilege', innocent bystanders and research and experimental use: *Patenting of Higher Life Forms and Related Issues* (Ottawa: Canadian Biotechnology Advisory Committee, 2002), online: <http://www.cbac-cccb.ca/epic/site/cbac-cccb.nsf/en/ah00188e.html>.

7 *Diamond, Commissioner of Patents and Trademark v. Chakrabarty* (1980), 447 U.S. 303, 206 U.S.P.Q. 193 [*Chakrabarty*]; *Pioneer Hi-Bred Ltd. v. Canada (Commissioner of Patents)*, [1989] 1 S.C.R. 1623 [*Pioneer Hi-Bred*]; *Harvard College v. Canada (Commissioner of Patents)*, [2002] 4 S.C.R. 45, (2002), 219 D.L.R. (4th) 577 [*Harvard*]; and *Monsanto Canada Inc. v. Schmeiser*, [2004] 1 S.C.R. 902, 2004 SCC 34, [*Monsanto*] discussed below.

8 *Harvard, Monsanto, ibid.*

some basic idea of the science involved sets the scientific background to the case law. The creation of a transgenic animal is illustrated by the transgenic oncomouse, the subject of the *Harvard* patent. This is a mouse whose germ (reproductive) cells and somatic (other) cells contain an activated oncogene (a cancer-inducing gene) that is introduced at an embryonic stage (preferably the one-cell stage) of the animal. The introduced oncogene sequence was integrated at random sites in the chromosome of the injected embryo, although it is possible today to target the gene by homologous recombination at a particular site. As cell division and differentiation ensue during the development of the embryo, each of the resulting germ and somatic cells of the transgenic 'founder' mouse (the primary mouse that acquires the transgene by human manipulation) end up with a complement of chromosomes, including the integrated oncogene sequence. The presence of an oncogene sequence in the cells of the animal increases the probability of the development of cancer in the animal, hence the term oncomouse. This type of development is a vital tool for the testing of both carcinogenic materials and the properties of cancer treatment drugs. As such techniques (for example, transgenic mouse technology) become commonplace, in jurisdictions that grant patents on lifeforms the novelty aspect turns on the particular DNA constructs introduced into embryonic cells, and the traits conferred on the organism by the introduced genetic material, rather than the techniques as such.

Similarly, the creation of new types of transgenic plants using recombinant DNA techniques, such as the Glyphosate-tolerant canola at issue in the *Monsanto*[9] case, is relatively new to the world. The transgenic plants/animals are often referred to as Genetically Modified Organisms (GMOs) – something of a misnomer, as most crop plants and domesticated animals have been genetically modified by traditional breeding, or by other more drastic mutagenesis approaches, and a subset of these types are known as transgenics, where genes are taken from a different organism. The introduction of foreign genes into plants is effected by bombardment of plant cells with tiny gold particles carrying the new genes, by using *Agrobacterium*, or by other means.[10]

---

9 *Monsanto*, *supra* note 7.

10 For a good review of plant techniques, see Philippe Vain, 'Thirty years of plant transformation technology development' (2007) 5 Plant Biotechnology Journal 221.

THE LAW

Today, the *Patent Act* provides for patents to be granted for inventions, defined as:

> [A]ny new and useful art, process, machine, manufacture or composition of matter, or any new and useful improvement in any art, process, machine, manufacture or composition of matter.[11]

Thus, a new lifeform may have the potential to satisfy the requirements of the definition, provided that it is within the subject matter (art, process, machine, manufacture or composition of matter), and it can satisfy the requirement for novelty (that is, no prior disclosure) and utility.[12] This has not been possible in Canada where the Supreme Court has decided that 'higher' lifeforms are not patentable subject matter, as they are neither a 'manufacture' nor 'compositions of matter'.

The *Patent Act* is silent on the types of inventions that may or may not be patented. Unlike some jurisdictions,[13] Canada has specifically excluded 'any mere scientific principle or abstract theorem'[14] from patentability, but there are no specific exclusions in the Act for plants and animals, nor for *ordre public* exceptions as permitted under Article 27(2) & (3) *TRIPS* [emphasis added]:[15]

> 2. Members **may exclude** from patentability **inventions**, the prevention within their territory of the commercial exploitation of which **is necessary to protect ordre public or morality**, including to protect human, animal or plant life or health or to avoid serious prejudice to the environment, provided that such exclusion is not made merely because the exploitation is prohibited by their law.
> 3. Members **may also exclude** from patentability:
>
> … (b) **plants and animals other than micro-organisms**, and essentially biological processes for the production of plants or animals other than non-biological and microbiological processes. However, Members shall provide for the protection of plant varieties either by patents or by an

---

11 R.S.C. 1985, c. P-4, s. 2.

12 *AB Hassle v. Apotex Inc.*, [2006] 4 F.C.R. 513 (F.C.A.), 2006 FCA 51; *Monsanto*, *supra* note 7; *Chakrabarty*, *supra* note 7, *Patent Act*, *ibid.*

13 For example, the Andean Group (currently Bolivia, Colombia, Ecuador, Peru and Venezuela) excludes all substances that exist in nature. Brazil excludes plants and animals and their parts, as does India's *The Patents (Amendment) Act*, No. 38 of 2002, s. 3(j), online: <http://www.patentoffice.nic.in/ipr/patent/patentg.pdf>.

14 *Patent Act*, *supra* note 11, s. 27(8).

15 *Agreement on Trade-Related Aspects of Intellectual Property Rights*, 15 April 1994, 1860 U.N.T.S. 299, 33 I.L.M. 1197 [*TRIPS*].

> effective *sui generis* system or by any combination thereof. The provisions of this subparagraph shall be reviewed four years after the date of entry into force of the WTO Agreement.

Some countries specifically exclude the granting of patents on animals and seeds,[16] as envisioned by *TRIPS*, and largely following the *TRIPS* formulation. For example, in India it is not possible to get a patent on plant or animals (although the methods for transgenics are protectable):

> 3(j) Plants and animals in whole or any part thereof other than microorganisms but including seeds, varieties and species and essentially biological processes for production or propagation of plants and animals;
> Example: Clones and new variety of plants are not patentable. But process/method of preparing Genetically Modified Organisms are patentable subject matter.[17]

In Europe, the inclusion of the *ordre public* exception enabled challenges at the European Patent Office to the patenting of transgenic lifeforms, including the Harvard mouse, although that particular challenge failed ultimately.[18]

In the past the creation of new lifeforms has been rewarded with patents, such as the patent issued in 1871 in France to Pasteur for improvements in the manufacture of beer and yeast, and also issued in the United States two years later. A key part of the patent was claimed for 'pure yeast, free from pernicious germs'.[19] In Germany, the *Rote Taube*[20] decision (1969) set the standard for biotech patent grants in that jurisdiction. This case concerned a claim of a method of cross breeding to achieve a red dove, and concluded that 'a patentable invention is a teaching for plan-conformant action utilising controllable forces of nature for

---

16 The WIPO survey at Intergovernmental Committee on Intellectual Property and Genetic Resources, Traditional Knowledge and Folklore, *Information Provided by WIPO Member States Concerning Practices Related to the Protection of Biotechnological Inventions*, WIPO Doc. WIPO/GRTKF/IC/1/6 (6 April 2001), online: <http://www.wipo.int/meetings/en/doc_details.jsp?doc_id=1681>, shows eight nations that do not permit plant patents at all.

17 See *supra* note 13, and Indian *Patents (Amendment) Act*, *supra* note 13, s. 3(j).

18 *The President and Fellows of Harvard College v. British Union for the Abolition of Vivisection et al.* (6 July 2004), Boards of Appeal of the European Patent Office Decision T-0315/03, online: <http://legal.european-patent-office.org/dg3/pdf/t030315ex1.pdf>. Discussion of the European perspective can be found in Mark Perry, 'Lifeform Patents: the high and the low' (2004) 1 J.I.B.L. 25.

19 This is quoted from the United States patent issued in 1873, Letters Patent Number 141,072. There were also several 'Yeast' patents issued in Canada prior to 1900, although most of these relate to the preparation of dried yeast.

20 Bundesgerichtshof, 27 March 1969 (German Federal Supreme Court), English version available in (1970) 1 I.I.C. 136 (*Rote Taube*).

achieving a causally overseeable result'.[21] The patent was refused on the grounds of lack of repeatability (perhaps the doves used were not described in enough detail, a theme which is echoed in *Pioneer*), but this case opened up the concept of modifications to life being considered as patentable.

In *Diamond v. Chakrabarty*, the United States Supreme Court held (with a 5–4 majority) that a genetically engineered bacterium used to degrade crude oil was patentable. This case was key in the development of broad patentability in the United States. The majority of the court said that the proper question is not whether invention is animate or inanimate – but rather whether it is made by a person or is naturally occurring. In this case, the bacterium in question was constructed by human intervention. The majority also noted that the subsequent passage of the special *Plant Variety Protection Act* (PVPA) in 1970 did not alter the fact that the invention was patentable under the *Patent Act* itself. The minority view was that the *PVPA* was passed to allow a type of 'patentability' which did not exist before. The *Chakrabarty* approach was adopted in the consideration of an oyster in *Ex Parte Allen*, deciding on the facts (due to obviousness) that the oyster in question was not patentable, but made it clear that non-humans could be patented.[22] The Patent Commissioner announced after this case that animals would be considered for patentability.

In *Re Application of Abitibi Co.*,[23] the Patent Appeal Board had to consider whether a yeast culture that could be used to digest a pulp mill waste product (spent sulfite liquor) was patentable. Although the yeasts were naturally occurring, there was the need for human intervention in order to get them to work on the spent sulphite waste materials. The yeast had to be acclimatized and treated in order to function. The Board determined that a yeast culture that could be used to digest spent sulfite liquor was patentable: the yeasts were based on naturally occurring varieties, but they had been treated to develop sulphur resistance and were thus significantly different to the naturally occurring varieties. The invention applied the yeast to the spent sulfite liquor, such as that produced by paper mills. The Board noted the 'ability to reproduce the yeast uniformly' – but expressed doubt as to whether such uniformity would hold in cases of higher lifeforms due to natural variations. Nevertheless, in

---

21 Bundesgerichtshof, 22 June 1976 (German Federal Supreme Court), English version online ('teaching for plan-conformant action' means that disclosure is meant to provide the 'plan' for repeating the invention): <http://eupat.ffii.org/papers/bgh-dispo76/index.en.html> (*Dispositionsprogramm*).

22 *Ex Parte Allen*, 2 U.S.P.Q.2d 1425 at 1426-27 (B.P.A.I. 1987). Here it was established that multicellular organisms such as polyploid oyster are patentable. Although there was human intervention, the patent was denied on the grounds of obviousness.

23 (1982), 62 C.P.R. (2d) 81 (P.A.B) [*Abitibi*].

allowing this patent, the Board recognized that it would extend the scope of patents:

> Certainly this decision will extend to all microorganisms, yeasts, moulds, fungi, bacteria, actinomycetes, unicellular algae, cell lines, viruses or protozoa; in fact to all new life forms which are produced *en masse* as chemical compounds are prepared, and are formed in such large numbers that any measurable quantity will possess uniform properties and characteristics ... Whether it reaches up to higher life forms - Plants ... or animals – is more debatable ...[24]

In *Pioneer Hi-Bred*, Pioneer sought a patent for a new soybean variety obtained from crossing three varieties of soybean over many iterations, using traditional hybridization techniques. The Commissioner of Patents held that a variety of naturally grown plant derived by artificial crossbreeding is not an invention within the meaning of s. 2 of the Act. In the Federal Court of Appeal the majority opined that Canadian patent legislation does not expressly exclude living organisms from patentability.[25] However, the focus of the FCA in upholding the Commissioner was on the common meaning of the terms 'manufacture' and 'composition of matter' used in the legislation. Pratte J. concurred, adding that the alleged invention is incapable of being described (that is, full disclosure as required by s. 36) as required by the Act, since a 'degree of luck' was involved (and the depositing of seed was not an adequate substitute as was permitted in *Abitibi*). The Supreme Court noted that it was unwilling to stretch the scope of patent protection beyond the Act, and since the Act is silent on new lifeforms, traditional standards apply. The court however avoided a decision on whether hybrid seeds could be considered an invention within the meaning of s. 2 of the Act, deciding that the patent failed for lack of sufficient disclosure.

This case is of interest on many fronts. In addition to demonstrating the unwillingness of the court to go into the 'life-form patent' discussion, it also distinguished between two types of genetic engineering: (1) crossing different varieties through hybridization, whereby there is human intervention in the reproductive cycle, but the actual rules of reproduction continue to obey laws of nature (as in Pioneer's soybean application in the case), and (2) involving recombinant DNA techniques:

> [The second] type of genetic engineering, which requires a change in the genetic material – an alteration of the genetic code affecting all the hereditary material – since in the latter case the intervention occurs inside the gene itself. The change

---

24 *Ibid.* at paras. 21 and 22.

25 *Pioneer Hi-Bred Ltd. v. Canada (Commissioner of Patents)*, [1987] 3 F.C. 8 at para. 10, 77 N.R. 137 (F.C.A).

> made is thus a molecular one and the 'new' gene is thus ultimately the result of a chemical reaction, which will in due course lead to a change in the trait controlled by the gene. While the first method implies an evolution based strictly on heredity and Mendelian principles, the second also employs a sharp and permanent alteration of hereditary traits by a change in the quality of the genes.[26]

What the court outlines as the 'second type' of genetic engineering is somewhat unclear, but can be interpreted to be referring to recombinant DNA engineering techniques that directly insert new genetic material into the lifeform (whether plant, animal or microbe), to produce transgenic plants and animals of the kind that came before the court in *Harvard* and *Monsanto*.

With this background it is perhaps difficult to see how the court in *Harvard*[27] came to the conclusion that a transgenic mouse was not patentable subject matter. The experimental oncomouse (the mouse in question in *Harvard*) was well characterized at the molecular level before it was used, making it a good tool in cancer research.[28] The *myc* gene used for the mouse is an oncogene that can be activated. The mouse mammary tumour virus long terminal repeat ('MMTV LTR') sequences contain a steroid-regulatable promoter. The promoter is a kind of switch; it is a sequence that controls the expression of a gene at the level of transcript synthesis. The DNA constructs for the oncomouse were made by the Harvard team, and these carried either the full *myc* gene or portions of it fused to the MMTV promoter. Similarly, another DNA construct containing the Rous Sarcoma Virus promoter fused to the *myc* gene was also constructed by the Harvard team. These were new constructs. In both cases, the *myc* gene was placed under the control of a viral promoter sequence with the aim of expressing the gene to levels higher than usual. It is possible for the oncogene and the promoter to vary somewhat from the DNA constructs described in the original Harvard patent application in the United States. However, it was these constructs that were injected into fertilized mouse eggs, which were then transferred to pseudo-pregnant foster female mice and allowed to develop to term. The presence of the injected oncogene, the pattern of its insertion into the chromosome, its expression in different tissues and organs, as well as inheritance, can all be examined in the transgenic animal. DNA was extracted from the tails of the mice pups born, and was analyzed by molecular techniques for the presence of the injected sequences. The progeny of the mice that retained the oncogene sequence were

---

26 *Pioneer Hi-Bred*, *supra* note 7.

27 For discussion on the FCA ruling on this, see Mark Perry & Priti Krishna, 'Making sense of mouse tales: Canada lifeform patents topsy-turvy' (2001) 23 E.I.P.R. 196.

28 The description of this process is taken and modified from Perry & Krishna, *ibid*.

then tested for the expression of the *myc* gene, that is, the levels of the *myc* mRNA, in major tissues and organs of these animals. Only some organs showed enhanced *myc* expression. Furthermore, considerable variation was observed in *myc* expression in different transgenic lines. The variables associated with transgenic mice do not pose any major problems in the experimental environment.

In June 1985, a patent application was filed for the oncomouse invention entitled 'Transgenic Animals' by assignee Harvard. In 1988 the United States Patent and Trademark Office issued a patent to Harvard for 'A transgenic non-human mammal all of whose germ cells and somatic cells contain a recombinant activated oncogene sequence introduced into said mammal...',[29] (as the animal used was a mouse, it became known as the 'Harvard Mouse' or 'oncomouse' although the same techniques could be used with other mammals). In March 1993 the Canadian Patent Examiner refused the application for the oncomouse. Claims 1–12 were directed to a transgenic non-human mammal, but were rejected as being directed to non-statutory subject matter. In 1995, the Commissioner at the hearing before the Patent Appeal Board upheld the refusal to grant claims 1–12. On appeal, the FCTD maintained the Commissioner's decision, continuing to allow Claims 13 to 26 to be patentable. These were for: methods for the production of transgenic non-human mammals or transgenic cell cultures, methods for using transgenic non-human mammals, methods of testing materials suspected of being carcinogens using transgenic non-human mammals, and various plasmids and somatic cell cultures. In 2000, the Federal Court of Appeal reversed the earlier decision and took a US approach to life-form patents. The majority of the FCA found that the lower courts had erred on a number of points, in particular by relying on the minority in *Chakrabarty*, and finding that the complex lifeforms were not within the parameters of the Act. They noted that such policy arguments are for Parliament, not the courts (ironic given that the SCC used the same argument when reversing the decision).

The Supreme Court of Canada ruled on their hearing of the case in 2002. Again, this was a majority decision (5–4), with Justices Bastarache, L'Heureux-Dubé, Gonthier, Iacobucci, and LeBel deciding against the patent for the animal, making a number of points:

- The choice of an exhaustive definition signals a clear intention to exclude certain subject matter as being outside the confines of the Act.
- While the definition is broad, Parliament did not define 'invention' as

[29] P. Leder & T.A. Stewart, *Transgenic non-human mammals,* U.S. Patent 4736866 (1988).

anything new and useful made by man' (that is, not the *Chakrabarty* approach).

- Just because all inventions are unanticipated and unforeseeable, it does not necessarily follow that they are all patentable: for example they could be discoveries.
- While a fertilized egg injected with an oncogene may be a mixture of various ingredients, the body of a mouse does not consist of ingredients or substances that have been combined or mixed together by a person.
- It is a highly contentious matter, raising complex issues and requiring clear legislation.
- The term 'manufacture', in the context of the Act, is understood to denote a non-living mechanistic product or process, not a higher life-form.
- Higher lifeforms cannot be conceptualized as mere 'compositions of matter' within the context of the *Patent Act*. The term 'composition of matter' does not include a higher life form. These latter two points were described as the crux of the case, although the route to their majority adoption is opaque. This of course raises the question 'what is a higher lifeform?'

The court did not satisfactorily answer the latter question, but merely noted:

> [patentability of lower life forms is not at issue in this case,] but it is easier to conceptualize a lower life form as a 'composition of matter' or 'manufacture' than it is to conceptualize a higher life form in these terms.[30]

Though it has been suggested that the Parliament responded to *Pioneer Hi-Bred* by enacting *sui generis* legislation *Plant Breeders' Rights Act*[31] [*PBRA*], for plant breeders, it is more likely that the pressure to comply with the UPOV convention,[32] especially with the upcoming, at that time, discussions of *TRIPS*, had considerable influence. The *PBRA*, of course, did not address other lifeforms. It was also argued that as the position of the Patent Commissioner was that higher lifeforms were not patentable, had Parliament intended to extend patentability to higher lifeforms other than crossbred plants, it would likely have done so at that time. This is peculiar as the *PBRA* is much more limited than patents and, in many jurisdictions including the US, not mutually

---

30 *Harvard*, *supra* note 7 at para 201.

31 *Plant Breeders' Rights Act*, S.C. 1990, c. 20 [*PBRA*].

32 *International Convention for the Protection of New Varieties of Plants*, 2 December 1961, revised in 1972, 1978 and 1991 (known by the French acronym, UPOV).

exclusive. A *sui generis* plant act can coexist with plant patents. The *Harvard* majority went on to say:

> The passage of the Plant Breeders'Rights Act demonstrates that mechanisms other than the Patent Act may be used to encourage inventors to undertake innovative activity in the field of biotechnology.
>
> If a special legislative scheme were needed to protect plant varieties, a similar scheme may also be necessary to deal with the patenting of higher life forms in general.
>
> Only Parliament is in the position to respond to the concerns associated with the patenting of all higher life forms, should it wish to do so, by creating a complex legislative scheme – it's beyond the competence of this Court. [33]

On the other hand, the minority of the court, McLachlin C.J., and Major, Binnie and Arbour JJ., thought that there was no statutory authority in the Act for drawing a line between 'higher' and other lifeforms, and that the term 'composition of matter' was an open-ended expression not confined to the inanimate. Furthermore, whether there should be carved out from the subject-matter realm an exception for 'higher' lifeforms, and how higher lifeform is to be defined, is a policy matter for Parliament, and neither the Commissioner nor the courts have the authority to declare a moratorium on higher life patents until Parliament chooses to act. Most damningly the minority noted that the court failed to show what is meant by a 'higher lifeform'.

While *Harvard* was wending its way through the court system, a transgenic canola based case was growing in Saskatchewan. Canola is a major Canadian crop, contributing to 15 per cent of the world oil market, and its production is expected to increase.[34] Monsanto, a large agricultural company, created Roundup Ready Canola that was first on the market in 1997 – this canola has a genetic insert that gives it a high level of resistance to the herbicide glyphosate.[35] Note that a farmer who wishes to grow Roundup Ready Canola must enter into a licensing agreement called a Technology Use Agreement (TUA) and must pay a licensing fee for each acre planted with Roundup Ready Canola. Percy Schmeiser is a Saskatchewan farmer who has been growing canola since the 1950s, but never purchased Roundup Ready Canola and never signed the Monsanto TUA. In 1996 a neighbour grew Roundup Ready Canola on a field diagonally adjacent to Schmeiser's field. In 1997 Schmeiser noticed that a large number of canola plants from seeds saved from the field survived

---

33 *Harvard*, *supra* note 7.

34 Agriculture and Agri-Food Canada, *Bi-weekly Bulletin* 20:7 (4 May 2007), online: <http://www.canola-council.org/PDF/bulletin_20_7_2007-05-04_e.pdf>.

35 There are a number of 'varieties' of Roundup Ready Canola. More information at <http://www.monsanto.com/>.

his normal spraying with Roundup for weed control along road allowances. He tested a section of the field by spraying it with Roundup, and 60 per cent of the plants survived. Seeds from that crop were used to plant all of his fields in 1998.

The major issues were whether Schmeiser infringed the patent despite the fact that he did not use Roundup in the 1998 crop, and whether it mattered how the Monsanto gene came to be in Schmeiser's crop. There were a number of outcomes of this case that potentially will have a large influence in the development of interpretation of patent enforcement in Canada if there is no clarification by legislation. It has been clear for some time that possession, at least in commercial circumstances, raises a rebuttable presumption of 'use' of a patented 'part'. Even possession of an object incorporating a patented feature may constitute 'use' of the object's *stand-by* or *insurance* utility and thus infringe the patent. The court observed that saving and planting seeds, then harvesting and selling plants that contained the patented cells and genes, constituted such use and utilization of the patent. By cultivating a plant containing the patented gene and composed of the patented cells without license, the appellants deprived the respondents of the full enjoyment of the monopoly. The appellants' involvement with the disputed canola was also clearly commercial in nature. Schmeiser was held to have infringed Monsanto's patent rights, and it was found that the source of the seed for the crop was irrelevant.

These results in *Monsanto* raise a number of questions, but solve few potential issues, not so much on the facts of this particular case but on the question of patenting in this area. What of the situation where there are truly volunteer plants (containing the patented gene and composed of the patented cells);[36] would their 'use' infringe the Monsanto patent?

> While intention is generally irrelevant to determining whether there has been 'use' and hence infringement, the absence of intention to employ or gain any advantage from the invention may be relevant to rebutting the presumption of use raised by possession.[37]

The court took a 'but-for benefit' approach to their award on accounting for profits. Since there was no evidence that Schmeiser had used Roundup on the crop, he had not profited from the patent infringement.

---

[36] I.e. plants that have arrived at their destination without deliberate action to put it at that destination by the 'user'. There could be volunteer animals as well.

[37] *Monsanto*, *supra* note 7.

CONCLUSION

There is little objective standard to determine what is a *higher* lifeform, nor are there any rational means of discriminating even between the developmental stages in the same lifeform. Despite the lack of a legal definition of 'higher lifeform' in Canada, according to a 2005 version of the *Manual of Patent Office Practice* (*MOPOP*), higher lifeforms include animals, plants, seeds, and mushrooms as they are 'multi-cellular differentiated organisms (plants, seeds and animals)'.[38] The latest version has dropped the 'multi-cellular differentiated organisms' phrase, but kept the categories of animals, plants, and seeds.[39]

One cell is patentable subject matter, but at what stage does the blastocyst/embryo fall out of the realm of being within patentable subject matter: when the cells start to differentiate? This can be hard to determine. What of various lifeforms that do not fit neatly within the 'non-definition' of higher, truly artificial lifeforms, and those that are not easily categorized? Even the term 'seed' is ambiguous, as this would not, presumably, include a mouse egg or sperm. What of a stem cell line (patentable), that has been treated to differentiate (not patentable)? How to deal with volunteer plants and unwanted transgene contamination? There are many more questions that need addressing at a policy level than simply that of patents, but it is clearly an area that needs addressing by legislation to clarify the policy that Canada wishes to adopt. The current divisions are not only arbitrary (though in law we are used to this) but also incoherent. The vague nature of 'higher lifeform' is not useful in an area where the stakeholders require certainty. There are a number of such questions that require clarification, not just in Canada, but worldwide, when the issue is of lifeform patents. The WTO *Review of the Provisions of Article 27.3(B)*:

> Life-forms in their natural state would not satisfy the criteria for patentability in the TRIPS Agreement. It has been elaborated that if, however, naturally occurring things, such as chemical substances or micro-organisms, have been first isolated artificially from their surroundings in nature they are capable of constituting an invention. It has also been said that the subject-matter of a patent has involved sufficient human intervention, such as isolation or purification, and if the isolated or purified subject-matter is not of a previously recognized existence, then it is considered an invention. Plants, animals or micro-organisms and other genetic resources would have to be altered by the hand of man or produced by means of a technical process to satisfy the criteria of patentability.[40]

---

38 Canada, Canadian Intellectual Property Office, *Manual of Patent Office Practice* (Ottawa-Gatineau: Patent Office, 1998, updated April 2006) at c. 12, s. 12.04.01 '*Living Matter*' and s. 12.05 '*Examples of Non-Statutory Subject-Matter*'.

39 '*Living Matter*', *ibid.*

40 WTO, *Review of the Provisions of Article 27.3(B) – Summary of Issues Raised*

Indeed, there is a good deal of debate about what is meant by a 'lifeform', especially as the likelihood of entirely artificial life created from human-assembled DNA becomes likely[41] on the filing of a minimal set of genes required to create a free-living organism.[42] Although the current claimed invention in the US deals with bacteria, 'higher' lifeforms will not be long behind. Are designed beings, from the DNA base-pairs up, not to be considered lifeforms but patentable, or patentable but not lifeforms? Canada has adopted a patent stance on biology that is inconsistent with its US patent law roots, but without the issues having been addressed directly by the legislature. The pressure of science on the legal system, particularly in cutting edge areas such as biotechnology patents, requires legislation for patents that is clear and 'technologically neutral' (as policymakers often claim of proposed legislation), and in accordance with our international obligations, which themselves are under tension to clarify. Most stakeholders would be happier with a broader inclusion in subject matter of the *Canadian Patent Act*, or at least with greater clarity in the definitions. However, it is unlikely that this level of patent reform will be addressed any time soon in Canada, despite pressure from the biotech sector and recommendations of advisory committees.

---

and Points Made Revision, WTO Doc. IP/C/W/369/Rev.1 (9 March 2006) at para. 37, online: <http://docsonline.wto.org> [citations omitted]. At the time of writing this, the Canadian Intellectual Property Office is rewriting Chapter 12 of the *Manual of Patent Office Practice*, and is soliciting comments by December 2007. See <http://strategis.ic.gc.ca/sc_mrksv/cipo/patents/mopop/mopop_dnld-e.html>.

[41] Philip Ball, 'The patent threat to designer biology' *Nature News* (22 June 2007), online: <http://www.nature.com/news/2007/070618/full/070618-17.html>.

[42] US Patent Application 20070122826. The Abstract for Minimal bacterial genome: 'The present invention relates, e.g., to a minimal set of protein-coding genes which provides the information required for replication of a free-living organism in a rich bacterial culture medium, wherein (1) the gene set does not comprise the 101 genes listed in Table 2; and/or wherein (2) the gene set comprises the 381 protein-coding genes listed in Table 3 and, optionally, one or more of: a set of three genes encoding ABC transporters for phosphate import (genes MG410, MG411 and MG412; or genes MG289, MG290 and MG291); the lipoprotein-encoding gene MG185 or MG260; and/or the glycerophosphoryl diester phosphodiesterase gene MG293 or MG385.'

5. Canadian pharmaceutical patent policy: international constraints and domestic priorities[1]

Mélanie Bourassa Forcier and Jean-Frédéric Morin[2]

INTRODUCTION

This chapter addresses the Canadian pharmaceutical patent policy (hereinafter 'patent policy') and underscores the aspects of this policy that demonstrate Canada's continuing effort to promote pharmaceutical R&D and consumer access to new medicines.

In order to ensure that our study has worldwide appeal, we have adopted a comparative approach towards Canadian patent policy and policies of other countries. It is often believed that Canada is in a delicate position for adopting a strongly different patent policy from the United States ('US'). It is true that the Canadian economy is greatly dependent on its southern neighbor. In 2005, 84 per cent of Canadian exports were destined for the US market and 64 per cent of foreign direct investment stock in Canada was owned by American investors.[3] Additionally, the Canadian government intentionally strengthened these economic and industrial ties by signing a free trade agreement in 1988,[4] followed by the North American Free Trade Agreement[5] in 1992.

[1] The authors wish to thank Rhonda Grintuch for her assistance and the anonymous reviewer for his/her helpful comments.

[2] Mélanie Bourassa Forcier is researcher at the Centre for Intellectual Property Policy at McGill University. Jean-Frédéric Morin is professor at the Université libre de Bruxelles, Science Po. melanie.bourassaforcier@mcgill.ca; jmorin@ulb.ac.be.

[3] Office of the Chief Economist of Foreign Affairs and International Trade Canada, *Seventh Annual Report on Canada's State of Trade* (Canada: Minister of Public Works and Government Services, June 2006), online: <http://www.international.gc.ca/eet/trade/sot_2006/sot-2006-en.asp#aiv1>.

[4] *Free Trade Agreement between the Government of Canada and the Government of the United States of America*, 2 January 1988, Can. T. S. 1989 No. 3.

[5] *North American Free Trade Agreement Between the Government of Canada, the Government of Mexico and the Government of the United States*, 17 December 1992, Can. T.S. 1994 No. 2, 32 I.L.M. 289 (entered into force 1 January 1994) [*NAFTA*].

Nevertheless, our study reveals that during the last century Canada did not hesitate to depart from the US model to design a unique patent policy for pharmaceutical products. While the US patent policy mostly reflects libertarian values, the history of the Canadian patent policy, although increasingly imprinted by US influences, reveals a Canadian philosophy for justice in access to health care services. One could even argue that universal access to health services is an integral component of the Canadian identity and a source of national pride. In 2004, Tommy Douglas, a politician known as Canada's father of Medicare, was named the Greatest Canadian of all time in a nationwide contest casting over 1.2 million votes.

Although the federal government consistently took into account the objective of providing fair access to pharmaceutical products in its patent policy, the *Constitution Act*[6] of 1867, s. 92(7), provides the provinces and territories with the exclusive power to deliver health care services. While the federal government has jurisdiction over patents and the initial approval of prescription drugs, it is the provincial governments that pay for drugs dispensed in facilities providing hospital care and administer public drug insurances.[7] Interestingly enough, a province can use its purchasing power and capacity to pay higher prices as policy tools, in combination with fiscal policies, to attract pharmaceutical investments. The end result is a sharp asymmetry in the geographical distribution of the pharmaceutical industry. While most generic companies, including Apotex, the largest Canadian-owned pharmaceutical company, are headquartered in the province of Ontario, many transnational innovative companies established their Canadian operations in the province of Quebec.

This continuous concern to provide access to pharmaceutical products, and the capacity to create incentives for investments in R&D by other means, contribute to the uniqueness of the Canadian patent policy. In many ways, this Canadian experience could be of interest to large developing countries with significant generic manufacturing capacities, foreign investment in the pharmaceutical sector, and numerous international IP obligations. These countries should nevertheless find in this study a sign that, even in presence of international trade agreements, there is always room to make medicines more accessible.

Each of the six following sub-sections presents past or present distinctive features of the Canadian patent policy, following a roughly chronological order. To begin, we provide an overview of the history of compulsory licence

---

6 *Constitutional Act, 1867* (U.K.), 30 & 31 Vict., c. 3, reprinted in R.S.C. 1985, App. II, No. 5.

7 Aslam H. Anis, 'Pharmaceutical Policies in Canada: Another Example of Federal-Provincial Discord' (2000) 162:4 Canadian Medical Association Journal 523 at 523.

rights in Canada. For a length of time, compulsory licences were considered an essential tool for containing drug expenditures in Canada. In the third section, we describe the uniqueness of the Canadian price regulations scheme and focus on the role of the Patented Medicine Prices Review Board (PMPRB), a federal organization exclusively created to control patented drug prices. Following this analysis, we highlight the 'early working' and 'stockpiling' exceptions introduced to limit the negative impact of restricted compulsory licence rights on the access to medicines. In the fifth section, we draw attention to the Canadian Notice of Compliance Regulations. These regulations, sometimes qualified as 'automatic injunction tools' available to the pharmaceutical industry, were, in turn, created in response to the early working and stockpiling exceptions in an effort to keep the balance of the Canadian patent policy. The sixth section of this chapter provides a review of the history of the different patent terms that have existed in Canada. In contrast to its American and European counterparts, Canada has not provided the industry with a patent term restoration to compensate delays in drugs' approval. However, as explained in the following section, the Canadian government has recently granted the industry an 8-year clinical data protection. This chapter ends as it started, with a review of the Canadian compulsory licences policy. While the earlier regime was abandoned to comply with NAFTA requirements, the federal government amended its patent law in 2004, following a WTO decision authorizing compulsory licensing to provide countries with insufficient manufacturing capacities.

A SPECIAL REGIME OF COMPULSORY LICENCES

Past and present Canadian policies regarding compulsory licences are often provided as an example to (or not to) follow. Jerome Reichman and Catherine Hasenzahl from Duke University suggest that Canada's historical use of compulsory licences could inspire policy makers in developing countries.[8] From another perspective, Harvey Bale, of the International Federation of Pharmaceutical Manufacturers Association, used the Canadian example to demonstrate that the abandonment of a generous compulsory licensing system could foster local investment in R&D.[9] Although it is difficult to establish

---

8 Jerome H. Reichman & Catherine Hasenzahl, 'Non-voluntary Licensing of Patented Inventions: The Canadian Experience' (2002), online: <http://www.iprsonline.org/unctadictsd/docs/reichman_hasenzahl_Canada.pdf>.

9 Dr. Harvey E. Bale Jr., 'The Impact of the Patent System on Research Investment for Developing Countries' (Presentation at the Conference on the International Patent System, Geneva, 2002), online: <http://www.wipo.int/patentagenda/en/meetings/2002/presentations/bale.pdf>.

which policies are best for developing countries, it is undisputable that the Canadian legal history of compulsory licensing is unique, having undergone radical changes in the early 1990s, announcing broader shifts at the international level.

During most of the twentieth century, Canada had few international obligations with respect to compulsory licensing. The only restriction prescribed by the *Paris Convention* was a minimum period of time before a compulsory licence could be applied for.[10] Since no international treaty prohibited discrimination in the field of technology, Canada could develop an aggressive policy for compulsory licences on pharmaceutical products. The initial conceptualization of this policy dates back to 1923 when the Parliament adopted a bill, modeled on British patent law, to keep the price of medicines reasonably low and encourage the domestic generic drug industry. Under the regime of the *Patent Act*, any person with an interest in exploiting a patent on foods and medicines was virtually entitled to a 'licence of right' for manufacturing purposes. To obtain a compulsory licence, it was not necessary to demonstrate any abuses of the patentee's rights, failures to work locally, or anticompetitive practices. The only requirement was to manufacture the chemical ingredients in Canada.[11] This single requirement was, in fact, a major impediment and contributed to the modest results of the regime. Since the Canadian market was relatively small, the generic producers had neither the capacity nor the willingness to manufacture the chemical ingredients in Canada.[12] In consequence, until 1969, only 49 applications were submitted, of which 22 were granted.[13] Some innovative companies even took advantage of their favorable position and prices of patented medicines became significantly higher in Canada than in other industrialized countries. This failure of the Canadian regime became a major public crisis in the 1960s when Canadian provinces were nationalizing their medical services and beginning to pay for pharma-

---

[10] *Paris Convention for the Protection of Industrial Property*, 20 March 1883, art. 5A.

[11] Thierry Orlhac, 'The New Canadian Pharmaceutical Compulsory Licensing Provisions or How to Jump Out of the Frying Pan and Into the Fire' (1990), online <http://www.robic.com/publications/Pdf/167E-TO.pdf> at 3 (published in French in (1990) 6 C.I.P.R. 276).

[12] Donald G. McFetridge, 'Intellectual Property, Technology, Diffusion, and Growth in the Canadian Economy' in Robert D. Anderson & Nancy T. Gallini, eds, *Competition Policy and Intellectual Property Rights in the Knowledge-Based Economy* (Calgary: University of Calgary Press, 1998) 65 at 81–2.

[13] Canada, Minister of Supply and Services, Commission of Inquiry on the Pharmaceutical Industry, *The Report of the Commission of Inquiry on the Pharmaceutical Industry* (Ottawa: Queen's Printer, 1985) at 14–15 [*Commission of Inquiry on the Pharmaceutical Industry*].

ceuticals. A Royal Commission established by the government and a special Parliamentary committee investigated the issue and concluded that the regime needed to be reformed.[14]

This reform occurred in 1969 when the Canadian Parliament amended its *Patent Act*. According to the amendment,[15] any person could apply for a compulsory licence to import medicines or bulk active ingredients produced with patented processes. The Commissioner of Patents was required to grant the licence unless he saw 'good reasons' not to, with the result that most licence applications filed and not abandoned were granted.

The reform had immediate consequences. In the two decades following the enactment of these provisions, 1030 applications were filed and 613 licences were granted.[16] The generic industry significantly increased its market share and drug prices decreased substantially. According to the report of the Eastman Commission of Inquiry on the Pharmaceutical Industry, Canadians saved more than 210 million dollars per year as a result of the 1969 amendment.[17] More surprisingly, investments in R&D in the pharmaceutical sector did not experience major fluctuations.[18]

Despite these positive results, Canada was under diplomatic pressure to move away from its policy. At the end of the 1980s, while a bilateral free trade agreement with the US was under negotiation, the Reagan Administration used the access to the large American market to pressure the Canadian government.[19] It also threatened the Canadian government with trade sanctions by adding the Canadian compulsory licensing regime for pharmaceutical products to the Special 301 Watch List. Consequently, Bill C-22, amending the

---

14 Canada, Department of Justice, Restrictive Trade and Practices Commission, *Report Concerning the Manufacture, Distribution and Sale of Drugs* (Ottawa: Queen's Printer, 1963); Canada, Royal Commission on Health Services, *Report of the Royal Commission on Health Services* (Ottawa: Queen's Printer, 1964); Canada, House of Commons, Special Committee on Drug Costs and Prices, *Report of the Standing Committee on Drug Costs and Prices* (Ottawa: Queen's Printer, 1966).

15 *Act to Amend the Patent Act, the Trade Marks Act and the Food and Drug Act*, S.C. 1968–69, c. 49, s. 41(4).

16 Reichman & Hasenzahl, *supra* note 8 at 38.

17 *Commission of Inquiry on the Pharmaceutical Industry*, *supra* note 13 at xvii.

18 *Ibid.* at 62–63, 230.

19 David J. French, 'Patent Law Reform in Canada' (1987) 4 Canadian Intellectual Property Review 337 at 341–2; Giles Gherson 'Free Trade Flash Points: Lumber, Drugs, Publishing are Prickly Issues' *Financial Post* (21 December 1985) at 1; Christopher Scott Harrison, 'Protection of Pharmaceuticals as Foreign Policy: The Canada-U.S. Trade Agreement and Bill C-22 versus the North American Free Trade Agreement and Bill C-91' (2000–01) 26 North Carolina Journal of International Law and Commercial Regulation 457–528.

Canadian *Patent Act*, was introduced and adopted in 1987.[20] Section 46 of the Bill provided that generic producers could not obtain a compulsory licence until a deferral period of exclusivity had elapsed. On the other hand, it included two discriminatory measures that were heavily condemned by the US government. First, the deferral period varied with whether the generic drugs would be imported or locally manufactured. It could be reduced from ten to seven years if production occurred in Canada. Second, the amendment excluded patented pharmaceutical products invented or developed in Canada from the application under the compulsory licences regime. This 'Made-in-Canada' policy was obviously adopted to encourage local investment more than to alleviate criticism from the US and transnational corporations.

Not surprisingly, 'the Canadian reform of 1987 became emblematic of the type of regime the United States Trade Representative would challenge in the course of regional and international trade negotiations'.[21] Pressure on the Canadian government reached an unprecedented level during the negotiation of *NAFTA*.[22] The US government especially condemned the less favorable treatment given by the Canadian regime to pharmaceutical products, inventions made outside Canada and imported generics. Accordingly, Canada traded a privileged access to US market against a reinforced protection of its intellectual property rights, including a provision that made patents 'available and patent rights enjoyable without discrimination as to the field of technology, the territory of the Party where the invention was made and whether products are imported or locally produced'.[23] This provision forced Canada to abolish its special regime of compulsory licensing for patented medicines, which it did in 1993, through the adoption of the Bill C-91.

NAFTA's rule on non-discrimination was duplicated in the TRIPs Agreement[24] with the consequence that no other WTO member could follow the Canadian experience on compulsory licensing. Nevertheless, another specificity of the Canadian system, the Patented Medicine Prices Review

---

20 *An Act to amend the Patent Act and to provide for certain matters in relation thereto*, S.C. 1987, c. 41.

21 Reichman & Hasenzahl, *supra* note 8 at 42.

22 Joel Lexchin, 'Globalization, Trade Deals and Drugs: Heads, the Industry Wins; Tails, Canada Loses' (November 2001) 2:8 Canadian Centre for Policy Alternatives, Briefing Paper Series: Trade and Investment 1 at 2–3; Maryse Robert, *Negotiating NAFTA: Explaining the Outcome in Culture, Textiles, Autos, and Pharmaceuticals* (Toronto: University of Toronto Press, 2000) at 298.

23 *NAFTA*, *supra* note 5, Article 1703.

24 Agreement on Trade-Related Aspects of Intellectual Property Rights, Annex 1C of the *Marrakesh Agreement establishing the World Trade Organization*, signed in Marrakesh, Morocco on 15 April 1994 (entered into force on 1 January 2005), art. 27(1) [*TRIPs*].

Board (PMPRB), created by the Bill C-22 in 1987 to compensate for the effect of the new restrictions on compulsory licences through price control, is not prohibited by multilateral treaties and can serve as an alternative model for countries wishing to maintain low drug prices.

THE UNIQUENESS OF THE CANADIAN DRUG PRICE REGULATIONS

As mentioned in an OECD report on pharmaceutical pricing policies,[25] all OECD countries use some form of price control regulations in order to contain drug expenditures. What distinguishes Canada from other countries is the federal government's direct price control, which is suppletive to provincial price regulations and exclusive to patented drugs.

Drug price regulations in Canada were originally part of the provincial jurisdiction. Provincial drug price regulations, however, only apply for public drug coverage. Therefore, private insurers could theoretically decide not to follow the different provincial pricing schemes. Each province has a distinct drug coverage policy. Some provinces, such as Quebec, offer comprehensive public drug coverage while others only offer catastrophic drug insurance.[26] Each province determines the criteria for reimbursing (or not) a new drug under the public coverage. For example, British Columbia has created a reference-pricing scheme. In this scheme, drugs with the same therapeutic effects are clustered into different groups. A drug will be fully reimbursed by the province if its price is equal to, or below, the reference price. This reference price is, in British Columbia, that of the most cost-effective drug within each group (a reference price could also be an average price of the lowest price for a drug within a group). Other provinces, such as Ontario or Quebec, have decided not to follow the British Columbia model and have preferred to limit their policy to the reimbursement of generic drugs, once marketed.[27] However, Quebec has additionally created the '15-year rule' as part of its effort to attract R&D investments from the brand-name industry. According to this rule, brand-name drugs can be reimbursed for 15 years after they are marketed in Quebec even if generic drugs are available. This rule is highly criticized by the generic industry and it is not clear whether it effectively helps the province to

---

[25] Valérie Paris & Elizabeth Docteur, *Pharmaceutical Pricing and Reimbursement Policies in Canada,* OECD Health Working Papers, No. 24 (Paris: OECD, 22 December 2006), online: <http://www.oecd.org/dataoecd/21/40/37868186.pdf>.

[26] *Ibid.*

[27] *Ibid.* at 20–1.

attract R&D investments.[28] Finally, most provinces use positive drug reimbursement lists and have established a 'lowest price' policy. According to this policy, a province will not reimburse a drug if its price is not the lowest among all Canadian provinces.

The provincial drug pricing schemes can be compared to the different pricing schemes existing in countries with public drug coverage, such as the PBS pricing scheme in Australia[29] or the reference pricing scheme in Germany.[30] These schemes could be referred to as 'indirect pricing schemes' since they do not directly regulate the pharmaceutical industry but provide a strong incentive for reducing the price of its drugs.

In Canada, in addition to being regulated at the provincial level, patented drug prices are also controlled by a federal, independent and quasi-judicial body, the Patented Medicines Price Review Board (PMPRB). The PMPRB was created by the 1987 amendments to the *Patent Act*, concomitantly to the introduction of limited rights to compulsory licences. Its creation was a clear attempt to limit the negative impact that restrictive compulsory license rights would have had on drug prices, that is, by limiting generic entry.[31]

The PMPRB's mandate is to protect Canadian consumers from excessive prices for patented drugs prior to or after their marketing. When determining whether a drug is being sold or has been sold at an excessive price, the PMPRB takes different factors into consideration. Only off-factory prices are considered (as opposed to retail prices). In the presence of a breakthrough drug, particular attention is given to the median price for this drug in seven comparable countries: France, Germany, Italy, Sweden, Switzerland, the UK and the US. If the drug contains a small improvement to already existing drugs, the Board will first compare its price with one of the drugs in the same therapeutic class. This price comparison system is, in fact, very similar to those used in other countries, such as in France or Spain, when determining what brand-name drug (patented or not, in these cases) can be listed on drug

---

[28] David Bahan *et al.*, *Les impacts économiques de la «règle des 15 ans» appliquée au remboursement des médicaments innovateurs au Québec* (Québec: Direction des communications du ministère des Finances, 2005), online: <http://www.finances.gouv.qc.ca/documents/feuille/fr/2005_002.pdf>.

[29] Ken Harvey, 'The Pharmaceutical Benefits Scheme: History, current status and post-election prognosis' *Australian Review of Public Affairs – Digest* (2 November 2001), online: <http://www.australianreview.net/digest/2001/11/harvey.html>.

[30] Patricia M. Danzon & Jonathan D. Ketcham, *Reference Pricing of Pharmaceuticals for Medicare: Evidence from Germany, The Netherlands and New Zealand* (Cambridge, Mass.: National Bureau of Economic Research, 2003), online: <http://www.nber.org/papers/w10007>.

[31] Paris & Docteur, *supra* note 25 at 12.

formularies. In Canada, patented drug prices cannot, in any case, exceed changes in the Consumer Price Index.

In contrast with other countries, where a drug is not reimbursed if its price exceeds a ceiling price, a Canadian patented drug cannot be marketed if its price is not first approved by the PMPRB. If, once marketed, a drug price becomes excessive in the opinion of the PMPRB, it may either direct the patentee to reduce the price of the drug or any of its marketed drugs in Canada, or order the patentee to compensate the government for the excess in profits having resulted from the sale of the high-priced drug.

It is generally acknowledged that the creation of the PMPRB has been effective in controlling and keeping the price of Canadian patented drugs low. In 1987, before the organization was created, the price of patented drugs was 23 per cent higher than the international median price. After 1987, patented drug prices were reduced considerably and have become, over the last few years, on average, below the international median price.[32]

Although the PMPRB's creation in 1987 was accepted by the pharmaceutical industry, we note a growing pressure from the Pharmaceutical Research and Manufacturers of America (PhRMA) on the Canadian government to eliminate the review board. This growing pressure has emerged following the US consumers' growing interest in cheap Canadian drugs, which can be up to 40 per cent less expensive than in the US. In fact, some Canadian provinces, particularly Manitoba, are now recognized for the success of Internet Pharmacies whose main business is cross-border-trade of drugs between Canada and the US.[33] Even though the pharmaceutical industry has deployed lobbyists in Canada to urge the government to free-up drug prices, the government keeps sending the signal that the PMPRB will survive. However, due to the industry threat that the exportation of drugs may limit the supply in Canada, it is possible that a law be eventually adopted to prevent, or limit, such exportation.

Considering the pharmaceutical industry's general dissatisfaction with restrictive marketing rights, it has occasionally been pointed out that, although effective on controlling drug prices, the PMPRB might have chilled R&D investments in Canada. This argument lacks empirical data due to the difficulty in isolating the specific impact of the 1987 amendments to the *Patent Act* which introduced at the same time (1) the PMPRB and (2) limited compulsory licensing rights. This last amendment was precisely aimed at promoting R&D

---

32 *Ibid.* at 15.

33 Brett J. Skinner, *Price Controls, Patents and Cross-Border Internet Pharmacies, Risks to Canada's Drug Supply and International Trading Relations* (2006) The Fraser Institute: Critical Issues Bulletin at 9, online: <http://www.fraserinstitute.org/commerce.web/publication_details.aspx?pubID=3121>.

in Canada. Considering the dichotomist effects these amendments might have had on R&D, we are confronted with uncertainty as to the impact one or the other has had on R&D. From the PMPRB's annual reports, we note that after 1987, R&D investments have increased. However, we may wonder if these investments would have been higher without the existence of the PMPRB.

EXCEPTIONS TO RIGHTS CONFERRED

When the special regime's compulsory licensing on medicines was completely abolished in 1993 to comply with the *NAFTA* and TRIPS requirements, the Canadian government sought to maintain the equilibrium of its patent system and ensure access to low-cost drugs. The need to find another policy tool to address cost control in the health care system was especially crucial as the expenditures on therapeutic drugs had dramatically risen between 1975 and 1993.[34] With this objective in mind, the Canadian Parliament introduced two new exceptions to rights conferred by a patent.

The first exception authorized the production, use and sale of a patented invention for the purpose of seeking regulatory approval in Canada or any other country (sometimes referred to as the 'early working exception').[35] Since the regulatory approval process needed to demonstrate that a generic drug is equivalent to the brand-name drug takes about 2–3 years, this measure could significantly accelerate the market entry of generic drugs. The second exception, called the stockpiling exception, was a unique Canadian measure, having had no equivalent in European or American law. It allowed generic producers who use the regulatory approval exception to manufacture and store, during the last six months of the patent term, the drugs intended for sale. With these exceptions, generic producers were able to market and sell their products the day after the patent expired.

The regulatory approval and the stockpiling exceptions were, predictably, heavily criticized by innovative pharmaceutical companies.[36] Nevertheless, they did not succeed in convincing the US government to bring the matter

---

[34] Health Canada, Policy and Consultation Branch, *National health expenditures in Canada, 1975–1994* (Ottawa: Supply and Services Canada, 1996).

[35] *Patent Act*, R.S.C., 1985, c. P-4, art. 55.2. This exception is similar to what is known in the US as the Bolar exception, introduced in 1984 by the *Drug Price Competition and Patent Term Restoration Act*, Pub. L. No. 98-417, 98 Stat. 1585 (1984) [*Hatch-Waxman Act*].

[36] United States Trade Representative, *Special 301 Report* (Washington: United States Trade Representative, 2001).

under the WTO dispute settlement mechanism. Drug pricing was a sensitive issue in American politics and the government did not want to put its own Bolar exception at risk.[37] Therefore, European and US companies, through their European branches, turned to the European Commission, which requested the establishment of a WTO panel in 1998.

Canada acknowledged that its exceptions conflicted with the patent rights granted in accordance with Article 28 of the TRIPs Agreement, but it claimed that they were exceptions authorized by Article 30 of the Agreement. Consequently, the main task of the Panel was to determine if the two exceptions fulfilled the triple-test of Article 30. Inspired by Article 9(2) of the Berne Convention,[38] this provision authorizes exceptions to rights conferred as long as they are limited, do not unreasonably conflict with the normal exploitation of the patent, and do not unreasonably prejudice the legitimate interests of the patent owner.

In its report issued in March 2000, the panel concluded that the exception for regulatory approval could be covered by Article 30. It does not need to be compensated by an extension of the patent term in proportion with the duration of delays caused by the regulatory approval process, as the US did with the *Hatch-Waxman Act*. However, the panel found that the stockpiling exception does not fulfil the triple test. It failed to be limited, as evidenced by the first requirement for authorized exceptions: 'With no limitations at all upon the quantity of production, the stockpiling exception removes that protection [on making and using] entirely during the last six months of the patent term, without regard to what other, subsequent, consequences it might have.'[39] The panel dismissed Canada's argument that the curtailment was limited because it preserved the exclusive right to sell, it could only be used by those having utilized the regulatory approval exception, and it only applied for six months. It agreed with the European Community (EC) that 'six months was a commercially significant period of time, especially since there were no limits at all on the volume of production allowed, or the market destination of such production.'[40]

Canada did not refer the dispute to the Appellate Body, complied with the Panel report, and amended its *Patent Act*. Since the stockpiling exception was

---

[37] Duncan Matthews, *Globalising Intellectual Property Rights: The TRIPs Agreement* (New York: Routledge, 2002) at 101.

[38] *Berne Convention for the Protection of Literary and Artistic Works*, 9 September 1886.

[39] *Canada – Patent Protection of Pharmaceutical Products (Complaint by the European Communities and their Member States)* (2000), WTO Doc. WT/DS114/R at para. 7.34 (Panel Report), online: <http://docsonline.wto.org>.

[40] *Ibid.* at para. 7.37.

introduced to compensate for the abandonment of its compulsory licensing regime for drugs, with its abrogation, Canada once again faced the prospect of an unbalanced patent system. This was even more the case if one considers the parallel maintenance of the *Patented Medicines (Notice of Compliance) Regulations*,[41] initially adopted to limit the effect of the regulatory approval and the stockpiling exceptions.

NOTICE OF COMPLIANCE (NOC) REGULATIONS

The NOC Regulations were adopted in 1993 in order to limit the likelihood of patent infringements by generic companies facilitated by the newly introduced early working and stockpiling exceptions.[42] The NOC Regulations are, from time to time, referred to as linkage regulations because they now require the Minister of Health ('Minister') to take into consideration the existing registered patents before issuing a Notice of Compliance (NOC) to a generic drug company after it has filed an Abbreviated New Drug Submission (ANDS). By filing an ANDS a generic drug company can only demonstrate the bioequivalence of its product with the brand-name drug. The company is thus exempted from undertaking the complete clinical trial process required to prove the safety and efficacy of a new drug.

Until recently, linkage regulations only existed in the US and Canada. This situation has now changed since different countries have entered into bilateral agreements with the US, where the US has made linkage regulations a component of these agreements. In consequence, Australia and different co-contracting developing countries have recently introduced linkage regulations into their national laws.[43]

According to the Regulations, when a brand-name company submits a NOC application or a supplement to its NOC application, it can join a list of patents to be registered on the patent registry. When a generic company files an ANDS it must inform the Health Minister of the existing registered patents, if any, pertaining to the brand-name drug to be copied. When the brand-name drug is still under patent, the generic company must either state that it is willing to wait until the patent expires before a NOC is issued for the generic drug or allege ('Notice of Allegation') that the registered patent has expired, is invalid or will not be infringed by the NOC's delivery.

---

41 SOR/93-133 [NOC Regulations].

42 *Regulatory Impact Analysis Statement*, Canada Gazette 2006.I.1611.

43 Judit Rius Sanjuan, 'Patent-Registration Linkage' (2006) Consumer Project on Technology, online: <http://www.cptech.org/publications/CPTechDPNo2Linkage.pdf>.

Once the brand-name drug company is informed of this allegation, it can ask the Court for an order prohibiting the Minister from issuing a Notice of Compliance until after the expiration of the patent that is the subject of the Notice of Allegation. This prohibition would however not apply if the generic company has filed a full NOC application rather than an ANDS. In such case, the Minister would thus not be tied up by the existence of patents applying to the brand-name product.[44]

The simple deposit of this request by the brand-name company triggers a 24-month delay before an NOC can be issued to the generic drug company except if, during that time, the patent expires or the Court renders its order. We underline here that, in this order, the Court is not allowed to assess the validity of patent(s) as it would do in patent infringement proceedings.[45] Consequently, it is possible that, following this order, a generic company be allowed to market its product and, afterward, be judged by another court to infringe an existing patent or, *vice versa*, a generic company could be prevented from marketing its product by this order but another court could conclude that the existing patents are invalid. The likelihood of such contradictory judgments provides high incentives for pharmaceutical companies to occupy the judicial system in Canada.[46]

Because the brand-name company's request to prevent the Minister from issuing a NOC to the generic company triggers a 24-month stay, its effect can be compared to that of an automatic interlocutory injunction. This makes the Canadian patent policy particularly favorable to brand-name companies, considering that it is generally acknowledged that interlocutory injunctions are rarely granted to pharmaceutical companies in Canada. Effectively, in contrast to European courts, Canadian courts do not generally consider a loss of profit to be a criterion for granting an interlocutory injunction.[47] Nevertheless, during this suspension period, the Minister will examine the generic company's ANDS. This factor is crucial because it allows the generic company to obtain an NOC as soon as the 24-month delay elapses.

Since their creation, the regulations have been highly criticized due to the existence of important pitfalls leading to evergreening practices by brand-name drug companies. Rapidly, as also happened in the US, the industry

---

44 *Bristol-Myers Squibb Co. v. Canada (Attorney General)*, [2005] 1 S.C.R. 533, 2005 SCC 26.

45 *Merck Frosst Canada Inc. v. Canada (Minister of National Health and Welfare)* (1994), 55 C.P.R. (3d) 302 (F.C.A.).

46 *Janssen-Ortho inc. v. Novopharm Ltd.* (2006), 57 C.P.R. (4th) 6, 2006 FC 1234.

47 *American Cyanamid v. Ethicon*, [1975] A.C. 396 (H.L.); *Centre Ice Ltd. v. National Hockey League* (1994), 53 C.P.R. (3d) 34 (F.C.A.).

developed different strategies for registering additional patents for marketed drugs or abuses of the opposition process to prevent generic companies from obtaining an NOC approval. With this regard, the case *Ferring Inc. v. Canada*[48] provides a good illustration of the tactics used by the brand-name industry to extend its monopoly. In this case, Ferring tried to extend its monopoly by filing, on a strategic date, a supplement to its NOC for a change in the name of its product. This strategy was used to file, at the same time, a new patent list in order to remediate to the company's fault to file on time an additional patent to its product. Fortunately, this practice has been rejected by the Federal Court of Appeal which stated:

> [15] Against this background, it is apparent that the only conclusion that can be drawn is that, as in BMS, the change in trade name was part of a strategy designed to overcome the time limitation within which a first person must file its patent list under section 4 of the *Patent Regulations*. As was pointed out in BMS, this strategy, if sanctioned by the Court, would render the time requirements embodied in section 4 meaningless.

In order to rebalance the Canadian patent policy, the government was thus forced to amend its regulations several times after their initial implementation. The first amendments were a response to the 1997 Report of the House of Commons Committee on Industry which recommended a regulatory reform to prevent abuses by the brand-name industry. After their introduction in 1998, the proportion of court orders prohibiting the Minister of Health from issuing an NOC to a generic company fell from 26 per cent to 9 per cent.[49] Among others, one of these amendments was aimed at shortening the suspension period, which was at that time 30 months, to 24 months.[50] In 2002, the Commission on the Future of Health Care in Canada[51] reported persisting concerns about still existing evergreening practices from the pharmaceutical industry. Also, due to the lack of clarity of the NOC Regulations, Canada was faced with different judicial interpretations of the regulations.[52] In 2003, after

---

48 *Ferring Inc.* v. *Canada (Attorney General)* (2003), 26 C.P.R. (4th) 155, 2003 FCA 274.

49 Dominique Valiquet, *The Patented Medicines (Notice of Compliance) Regulations* (Canada: Parliamentary Information and Research Service, Law and Government Division, 4 May 2006) at 10.

50 *Regulations Amending the Patented Medicines (Notice of Compliance) Regulations*, Canada Gazette 1998.II.1051.

51 Commission on the Future of Health Care in Canada, *Building on Values – The Future of Health Care in Canada* (2002), online: <http://www.hc-sc.gc.ca/english/care/romanow/index1.html> (Commissioner: Roy J. Romanow, Q.C.).

52 Federal Trade Commission, *Generic Drug Entry Prior to Patent Expiration: An FTC Study* (Washington: Federal Trade Commission, July 2002) at i, online: <http://www.ftc.gov/os/2002/07/genericdrugstudy.pdf>.

the US proposed a modification to its own regulations, the House of Commons Standing Committee on Industry, Science and Technology entered into another reviewing process of the NOC Regulations. It was in October 2006, both after a long negotiating process with industry stakeholders and the submission of proposals for modifications in 2004, that the government finally introduced important clarifications to the regulations.[53]

In particular, it is now clear that to be listed on the patent registry, the patent list submitted by the patentee must be linked to the drug subject to the NOC application. Previously, it was unclear whether a company could submit a new list of patents when it filed a supplementary drug application for cosmetic changes to the drug, name change, or changes in manufacturing facilities.[54] Some companies benefited from this lack of clarity to continuously file new patents and thus, prevented generic drug companies from obtaining a NOC.[55] The new amendments also limit the type of patents that can be included in the registry. Since 2006, the patent must relate to: (1) a claim for the approved medicinal ingredient, (2) a claim for the approved formulation containing that medicinal ingredient, (3) a claim for the approved dosage form, or (4) a claim for an approved use of the medicinal ingredient.[56] The delay for registering new patents on the registry is also limited to 30 days after the patent is issued if the patent application was submitted to the patent office before the NOC application.[57] This time limit was introduced in order to prevent brand-name companies, who had forgotten to register the patents attached to their drug at the time they had filed their NOC, from adding these patents to the registry. Finally, to limit the number of Notice of Allegation's requirement for generic companies, the amendments provide that the register will be 'frozen' from the time a generic drug company files an ANDS. Consequently, this modification impedes brand-name companies from submitting new patents after the generic drug company's ANDS to force it to constantly send new Notices of Allegation.[58]

By clarifying the NOC Regulations, it is the Canadian government's hope that they will finally reach their objective of creating a balance between the promotion of R&D in the pharmaceutical industry, through a strong IP

[53] *Regulations Amending the Patented Medicines (Notice of Compliance) Regulations*, Canada Gazette 2006.I.1611.

[54] *Ferring Inc. v. Canada, supra* note 48; *Hoffmann-La Roche Ltd. v. Canada (Minister of Health)* (2005), 40 C.P.R. (4th) 108, 2005 FCA 140.

[55] *Ferring Inc. v. Canada, ibid.*; *Hoffmann-La Roche Ltd. v. Canada, ibid.*

[56] *Regulations Amending the Patented Medicines (Notice of Compliance) Regulations, supra* note 53, s. 4(2).

[57] *Ibid.*, s. 4(6).

[58] *Ibid.*, s. 5(4).

protection, and access to generic and affordable drugs. Only the future can tell whether or not this will occur. For now, it can be noted that discrepancies still exist within the regulations. In particular, nowhere in the regulations is the Minister granted the power to withdraw a patent from the registry if it is qualified as invalid by the Court. Consequently, this forces generic companies to file a Notice of Allegation for the drug, although the patent registered for it has been judged as invalid in a previous opposition process.

If the future reveals the Canadian government's failure to reach its objective, it would probably be the time to consider different avenues for balancing the Canadian patent policy. Considering the US trade pressures on countries for implementing linkage regulations, it would, however, be surprising if Canada would abrogate its NOC Regulations. However, different options could be offered. For example, Canada could follow the US example where brand-name companies only benefit from a single 30-month waiting period for each new drug subject to a new drug application.[59] The 24-month delay in Canada could be shortened to the average generic approval time in Canada, which is about 17 months.[60] On the contrary, the future could theoretically reveal abuses by generic companies. This last aspect is seldom mentioned in discussions about linkage regulations. It must not be forgotten that these regulations aim at limiting patent infringements. If they accomplish their role without strengthening the brand-name industry's monopoly, they should be considered a good tool to free up the judicial system.

TERM OF PROTECTION

Members of the Paris Union are free to determine the term of protection. In the 1980s, the duration varied extensively from one country to another, and sometimes between fields of technology, ranging from 3 to 20 years and calculated either from the filing date of the application or the date of the grant. Canada and its southern neighbour had offered a protection of 17 years, calculated from the grant of the patent in any field of technology. But the Canadian legislation was amended twice to modify this term of protection.

The first and most important amendment entered into force in 1989. It moved to a term of protection of 20 years from the filing date for patents filed

---

[59] *Federal Food, Drug, and Cosmetic Act*, 21 U.S.C.S. § 355 (2005), (j)(5)(B)(iii).

[60] Health Canada, *Therapeutic Products Directorate (TPD) – 2004 Annual Drug Submission Performance Report – Part I* (24 April 2005) at 31, online: <http://www.hc-sc.gc.ca/dhp-mps/prodpharma/applic-demande/docs/perform-rendement/ar-ra/tpd_dpt_annual_annuel_04_e.html>.

after 1 October 1989. In other words, these 'New Act patents' could benefit from a longer effective term of protection if the period between the filing and the granting was less than three years. For 'Old Act patents', filed before 1 October, the term remained unchanged.

Contrary to most legislative amendments to the Canadian *Patent Act*, this change in term of protection was not externally dictated. Even *NAFTA*, signed in 1992, left some flexibility to its signatories by providing that the term of protection should be 'at least 20 years from the date of filing or 17 years from the date of grant'.[61] The US took advantage of this flexibility and adopted the 20-year standard only in 1995, to comply with the TRIPS Agreement. In fact, the 1989 change in the term of protection was adopted, together with the first-to-file principle, early publication of applications, and deferred examination, to simplify administrative procedures and increase the predictability of the patent system.

The Canadian term of protection came under the international spotlight in 1999 when the US filed a complaint with the WTO dispute settlement mechanism. The US claimed that the term of protection available for the 'Old Act patent' did not comply with Article 33 of the TRIPs Agreement, which requires that 'the term of protection available shall not end before the expiration of a period of twenty years counted from the filing date.' It argued that Canada should protect patents filed before 1 October 1989 for a duration of 20 years from the filing date or 17 years from the grant date, whichever is longer. It estimated that over 66,000 'Old Act patents', including 33,000 from US applicants, would expire sooner than would be the case if Canada had provided a term of 20 years from filing.[62] Despite these impressive numbers, the real issue under this dispute was related to some 30 commercially significant drugs.[63]

Canada's main argument was that an 'effective' term of protection of 17 years is equivalent to a nominal term of 20 years and, therefore, consistent in substance with Article 33. Canada made this assertion based on the fact that the administrative procedures between the filing date and the issuance date could exceed three years, making a term of 20 years 'available' to patent holders. The Panel and Appellate Body dismissed Canada's arguments, stating that the notion of an 'effective' term of protection was not supported by Article 33, and

---

61 *NAFTA*, *supra* note 23, Article 1709(12).

62 *Canada – Term of Patent Protection* (2000), WTO Doc. WT/DS170/R at para 6.60 (Panel Report).

63 Industry Canada, News Release, 'Government Tables Amendments to Bring Patent Act Into Conformity with WTO Agreement' (20 February 2001), online: <http://www.ic.gc.ca/cmb/welcomeic.nsf/ffc979db07de58e6852564e400603639/85256779007b82f4852569f9006a56c7!OpenDocument>.

that making a term of protection 'available' is a matter of legal right and certainty.[64] They concluded that the term of protection for 'Old Act patents' is inconsistent with Article 33 of the TRIPs Agreement. In 2001, Canada complied with the Appellate Body's recommendations and amended its *Patent Act* to entitle 'Old Act patents' to the longer term of 17 years from the date of the grant or 20 years from the date of filing.

Since the time-period between the filing date and the granting date is sometimes longer than three years, especially in Canada, the effective patent term could be shorter than it would have been prior to the 1989 amendment.[65] To avoid this problem, the US adopted the *Patent Term Guarantee Act*[66] in 1999 and extended the term of protection in the event that issuance was delayed due to a secrecy order, interference, or successful appellate review. This measure has the effect of ensuring a term 17 years from the granting of the application, even though the US has formally converted to a standard of 20 years from the application's filing. Although Canada did not follow this model and does not compensate any delays in examination, it followed and even surpassed the US model on data protection.

DATA PROTECTION

Data protection in Canada was intended to implement Canada's *NAFTA* obligations, which require signatories to provide a minimum of a 5-year protection against the unfair commercial use of undisclosed tests or other data submitted by a pharmaceutical company in order to obtain a NOC approval.[67] The main objective of this protection is to grant a protection to the company of the investments made in the development of the product by allowing a period of market exclusivity. This market exclusivity must be distinguished from the one resulting from patent rights. The result of such protection is to prevent generic drug companies from obtaining a NOC until the period of protection expires. The underlying reasoning is that, to prove the bioequivalence of its product with the brand-name one, a generic company must refer to the data submitted by the

---

64 *Canada – Term of Patent Protection* (2000), WTO Doc. WT/DS170/AB/R at paras. 80–101 (Appellate Body Report).

65 *Biotechnological Intellectual Property and the Patenting of Higher Life Forms*, Consultation Document (Ottawa: Canadian Biotechnology Advisory Committee, 2001) at 16, online: <http://cbac-cccb.ca/epic/site/cbac-cccb.nsf/vwapj/Consultation_IP_e.pdf/$FILE/Consultation_IP_e.pdf>.

66 *Patent Term Guarantee Act of 1999*, Pub. L. No. 106-113, § 4401-4405, 113 Stat. 1501.

67 *NAFTA*, *supra* note 23, Article 1711(5)–(6).

brand-name company in its NOC application (these data demonstrate the safety and efficacy of the new drug). Therefore, until the data protection expires, this comparison is impossible.

Before 2006, Canada granted a 5-year data protection to brand-name companies from the date of their first NOC. This protection was, however, considered ineffective due to the interpretation given to the protection in *Bayer Inc. v. Canada (Attorney General).*[68] In this case, it was held that the protection is not triggered if the generic drug company can demonstrate the bioequivalence of its product without requiring the Minister to consult the data submitted by the brand-name company. Since this situation was common, the protection was seldom applied.

At the end of 2006, following pressures from the pharmaceutical industry and allegations that Canada was not following its international obligations[69] the government modified its regulations and introduced an 8-year data protection with the possibility for generic companies to file an ANDS two years before the expiration of the protection.[70] In the case of pediatric drugs, the protection is prolonged for 6 months. The possibility for a generic drug company to file an ANDS two years before the protection ends reflects the Canadian government's effort to facilitate generic entry. During these two years, it is possible for the Minister to review the ANDS application, thus making possible the marketing of the generic drug immediately after the data protection expires.

The Canadian data protection model is somewhat peculiar. It is difficult to trace the impetus of the choice to grant an 8-year data protection, when *NAFTA* requires a minimum of 5 years (and it is still unclear whether the previous existing 5-year data protection in Canada, as applied by the *Bayer* decision, effectively contradicted *NAFTA*). Actually, the Canadian data protection seems to result from somewhat of an average of the data protection periods existing in the US and in European countries. The former offers a 5-year data protection to its industry, while the latter offers ten years.[71] It would have been interesting to compare cost-benefit analyses demonstrating the positive

---

[68] *Bayer Inc.* v. *Canada (Attorney General)* (1998), 84 C.P.R. (3d) 129, [1999] 1 F.C. 553 (F.C.T.D) [*Bayer*].

[69] Pharmaceutical Research and Manufacturers of America (PhRMA), *Special 301 Submission* (2003).

[70] *Regulations Amending the Food and Drug Regulations (Data Protection)*, Canada Gazette 2006.I.1598.

[71] *Drug Price Competition and Patent Term Restoration Act of 1984*, Pub. L. No. 98-417, 98 Stat. 1585 (codified as amended 21 U.S.C. §355 (1994)) and EC, *Council Regulation (EEC) No 1768/92 of 18 June 1992 concerning the creation of a supplementary protection certificate for medicinal products*, [1992] O.J.L. 182/1.

impact of an 8-year data protection, versus 5 years, on R&D investments in Canada. If these analyses exist, the government has not published them.

Fortunately, the impact of data protection in terms of access to medicines is still fairly limited. The protection only grants a period of market exclusivity for non-patented drugs or for drugs for which the patent expires before the end of the 8-year data protection. However, in the former case, data protection might soon represent a problem due to the emergence of out-of-patent biologic drugs, for which innovative companies increasingly rely on trade secrets.

CANADA'S ACCESS TO MEDICINES REGIME

This chapter begins and ends with an analysis of two different Canadian regimes for compulsory licensing in the pharmaceutical sector. As mentioned earlier, the first regime was intended to improve access to medicines for Canadians and was abolished in 1993 in order to comply with Canada's international obligations. In contrast, the second regime that is described in this section is intended to improve access in developing countries and was established to implement a WTO decision.

The WTO decision that Canada implemented was adopted on 30 August 2003, on the eve of the Cancun Ministerial Conference. Although the TRIPs Agreement allows WTO members to issue compulsory licences, countries with insufficient manufacturing capacities in the pharmaceutical sector cannot make effective use of them. WTO members also face difficulties importing pharmaceutical products manufactured under compulsory licences because Article 31(f) of TRIPs provides that they must be 'authorized predominantly for the supply of the domestic market of the Member authorizing such use.' The August 2003 decision 'waived' under specific conditions, this restriction on exports to countries that cannot manufacture the pharmaceuticals themselves.

On 26 September 2003, the Canadian government was the first WTO member to announce its intention to implement the 2003 WTO decision. This announcement was partly the result of pressure from the Canadian Generic Pharmaceutical Association and Canadian activists, including Stephen Lewis, the UN Special Ambassador for HIV/AIDs. It was above all the result of a few individual leaders inside the Jean Chrétien government which, in the last months of its 10-year reign, wanted to leave a positive legacy, including assistance for African countries. The government promptly drafted a bill, sought advice from the industry and selected NGOs, and made sure that the Bill C-9, oddly named the *Jean Chrétien Pledge to Africa*, would be enacted prior to the 2004 general elections.

The Canadian government had little flexibility in the drafting of its bill since it was bound by the numerous conditions already negotiated in the 2003 WTO decision. Nevertheless, the Canadian legislation clarified some ambiguities and included additional restrictions.[72] With the objective of improving access to medicines in developing countries, the royalty rate is linked to the ranking of the importing country on the UNDP Development Index; the requisite negotiations over a possible voluntary licence between the generic producer and the patent holder are limited to 30 days; the regime is open to least-developed countries and other developing countries that are not WTO members; and NGOs authorized by the government of the importing country are considered eligible purchasers. On the other hand, to maintain the integrity of its patent system, pharmaceutical products that can be manufactured and exported under this regime are restricted to a specific list; the term of compulsory licences is limited to a 2-year cap with the possibility of one easily obtained renewal; and patent holders may apply for a court order terminating a compulsory licence or ordering a higher royalty on the grounds that a generic company's contract with a purchaser is commercial in nature. Another controversial provision of the Canadian legislation is the requirement that a drug manufactured solely for export undergo a Canadian regulatory approval process. These features are the most significant aspects that do not typically appear in legislations of other WTO members who implemented the August 2003 Decision, including Norway, India, Korea, China, and the European Union.

Although legislations implementing the August 2003 decision are slightly different, none of them were used at the time of writing this chapter.[73] This lack of effectiveness brought Canada's Access to Medicines Regime from initial warm reactions to criticism, especially from the NGO community. Among the explanations frequently mentioned for its ineffectiveness are the procedural burdens that dissuade generic producers, the lack of capacity and information in potential importing countries, and the competition from other

---

[72] Richard Elliott, 'Pledge and Pitfalls: Canada's Legislation on Compulsory Licensing of Pharmaceuticals of Export' (2006) 1:1 International Journal of Intellectual Property Management 94; Matthew Rimmer, 'The Jean Chrétien Pledge to Africa Act: Patent Law and Humanitarian Aid' (2005) 15:7 Expert Opinion on Therapeutic Patents at 889.

[73] Between the time this chapter was written and published, the Federal Commissioner of Patents did issue a compulsory licence for ApoTriAvir (a drug to address HIV/AIDS), thus allowing Apotex to export its product to Rwanda. Nevertheless, considering the long negation time taken to reach this outcome, the Canadian policy is still considered as highly ineffective. See Matthew Rimmer, 'Race Against Time: The Export of Essential Medicines to Rwanda' (2008) 1:2 Public Health Ethics 89–103.

exporting countries, including India and China. These issues and potential amendments are currently under discussion by the government and the Canadian Parliament, since the law is under review. Although Canada's Access to Medicines Regime is one of the last innovations of the Canadian patent system, it may well be the target of the next amendment to the *Patent Act*.

CONCLUSIONS

To conclude, the Canadian patent policy history is rich with examples demonstrating the Canadian government's efforts in promoting the equilibrium between R&D investments and consumers' access to medicines. Limits to compulsory licences rights, NOC Regulations and data protection are all different components of the Canadian patent policy aimed at promoting the interest of the pharmaceutical industry with, as justification, positive effects on R&D investments. On the other hand, other components of the policy, such as the PMPRB; the Canadian refusal for adopting a patent term restoration; the possibility for a generic company to file an ANDS two years before the end of the data protection; and the early working exception all exist to promote access to medicines in Canada.

Our study, being law oriented, does not provide empirical data for assessing the effectiveness of each of the Canadian patent policy aspects in reaching the Canadian government's equilibrium goal. However, the fact that R&D in Canada is increasingly focused on clinical trials, combined with the relatively small size of the Canadian market,[74] leaves us questioning whether the patent policy could ever, in practice, represent an effective tool for promoting R&D. However, it certainly contributed to promote access to pharmaceutical drugs. Canadian prices for patented medicines consistently decreased from 1987 to 1994, when prices stabilized up to 10 per cent below the median in seven comparative countries.[75] Simultaneously, the generic industry flourished and increased the export of its products to the US.[76]

Given the priorities of the Canadian society for access to pharmaceutical products, the modest amount of investments in pharmaceutical R&D, and the trading perspectives for generic industry, it appears that Canada shares significant characteristics with large developing countries. Like most of them, the Canadian government had a defensive approach at the WTO and strengthened its patent system to comply with international trade treaties.

---

74 Paris & Docteur, *supra* note 25.

75 *Ibid.* at 15.

76 *Ibid.* at 69.

Nevertheless, some new characteristics of the Canadian regime are puzzling. In that respect, we recommend the undertaking of an in-depth economic analysis of the usefulness of the NOC Regulations and of the 8-year data protection, particularly in the context where the government is not compelled by any agreements to have these regulations as part of its patent policy. In addition, considering the new emergence of biomedicines, where it is recognized that the 'product is the process', we are worried that the PMPRB's role might become limited in the next few years. These products, often out-of-patents, would not be subject to PMPRB and thus would represent a real threat to consumers' access to affordable medicines. As for the success of the Canadian policy in making generic drugs accessible to developing countries, our doubts are now certitudes. A parliamentary review is currently investigating the reasons behind this failure, which might well lie in the 2003 WTO decision itself.

PART 2

Copyright

6. Canadian colonial copyright: the colony strikes back

Pierre-Emmanuel Moyse

The study of Canada's colonial copyright offers a formidable *vivarium* of legal manifestations that have been largely underexploited until this day. It abounds with instructive data of economic and social importance regarding the development of the early international trade of books. It is naturally enriched with past legal experiences. Colonial copyright is a unique laboratory allowing us to understand the legal normative response to social changes in matters of cultural dimensions, national sovereignty and identity. It is our opinion that the topic deserves closer attention, from the purely academic standpoint certainly, but also for the purpose of policy formation. In a time of continuous reforms, we should redirect our reflections towards lessons of the past and, perhaps, resist the immediate magnetism of technological issues. It might be beneficial to start our reflections anew from fixed anchors. The colonial episodes concerned with the present article takes root in 1832,[1] the date of the first Canadian copyright legislation passed in what would become in 1840 the Province of Canada,[2] and ends with the passing of the 1911 Imperial legislation empowering colonial Parliaments to extend its provisions and adopt them as their own.[3] Canada did not elect to implement the British statute, but rather passed its own 1921 Act which came into force in 1924.[4] This latter decision was a gesture of obvious significance, since it closes a sore chapter of tumultuous negotiations between the Colony and the Imperial Government.

Colonial copyright is one of the most important questions of nineteenth century intellectual property debates, together with the collateral question of international copyright which, in American legal literature, refers generally to

1 *An Act for the protection of Copy Rights, 1832* (Can.), 2 Will. IV, c. 53.

2 *An Act to reunite the Provinces of Upper and Lower Canada, and for the Government of Canada, 1840* (UK), 3 & 4 Vict., c. 35 [*Union Act*]. One year later, the Statute of 1832 would be reenacted under the title *An Act for the protection of Copy Rights in this Province, 1841* (Can.), 4 & 5 Vict., c. 60–1.

3 *Copyright Act, 1911* (UK), 1 & 2 Geo. V, c. 46, s. 26.

4 *Copyright Act, 1921* (Can.), 11 & 12 Geo. V, c. 24.

foreign rights of Americans and the American rights of foreigners.[5] It constitutes a fascinating account of declining colonialism and a unique testimony about the emerging society of Canada. The colonial system proved itself inept at answering the need for affordable books in the colonies, especially for those that were largely dependent on European supplies for literature. Such was the case for Canada. The passing of the 1842 Imperial *Copyright Act*[6] generated immediate grievances for Canadians – and, consequently, became *infamous*, since it had the effect of prohibiting the importation and sale of reprints of British copyrighted books which were manufactured in foreign countries. Until then, Canada largely benefited from its geographical position and imported its literature from America. The United States was the fertile soil from which Canadian readers and booksellers drew their intellectual food. The *1842 Copyright Act* prevented Canadian merchants from carrying on such commerce, and forced the latter to import, at great cost, books which were sold on the British market at a price which was unattainable for most colonial readers. Combined with the systematic refusal by British publishers to grant licenses to reprint their authors' works, the legislation in operation triggered an unexpected and vehement resistance from the colonial Government and challenged the question of Canadian self-governance. The Canadian *Maquis* grew in strength and defied the Imperial ruling. The issue reached an unexpected climax when Canada threatened to withdraw from the Berne Convention.[7]

It is our belief that colonial history will provide invaluable guidance in further understanding the impact of intellectual property legislation on the distribution of knowledge and the sharing of wealth. In particular, it should serve as a reminder to state members of the G8 countries that have experienced, in different contexts, situations in which a dominant country imposed its rules on satellite countries that were former colonies. In fact, colonial history shaped 100 years of copyright reforms and legislation. Innovatively, as it will be shown, it implemented the first modern licensing scheme for the distribution of works. It was also a very productive period marked by acrimonious correspondence and continuous dissension between the Imperial and the colonial powers. Between 1832 and 1921, the Canadian legislature passed

---

[5] Stanley Rothenberg, *Legal Protection of Literature, Art, and Music* (New York: Clark Boardman, 1960) at 140. Foreign authors were not eligible to legal protection under American law until 1891, the year in which the *Chace Act* was passed (*An act to amend title sixty, chapter three, of the Revised Statutes of the United States, relating to copyrights*, ch. 565, 26 Stat. 1106 (1891)).

[6] *An Act to Amend the Law of Copyright, 1842* (UK), 5 & 6 Vict., c. 45.

[7] *Correspondence on the Subject of the Law of Copyright in Canada* (London: Eyre and Spottiswoode, 1895) no. 26 at 38 and G. H. Putnam, *The Question of Copyright*, 2nd ed. (New York: Putnam, 1896) at 466–7.

several bills directly related to copyright matters. Some met with strong opposition in London, such as the *Copyright Act* of 1872 or the *Copyright Act* of 1889 for which the Royal Assent was finally withheld.[8]

Colonial history is more vocal than one would expect about the development of copyright law and its inherent policy implications both at the national and international levels. In many ways, colonial preoccupations anticipate modern geopolitical concerns that are slowly being taken into account in international diplomatic rounds held under the auspices of WIPO or WTO. As a contemporary observer wrote recently, the analogy between early nineteenth century and contemporary copyright is not only possible, but may also be fruitful as long as we recall that developing countries of the nineteenth century were in need of cheap literature:

> There are a number of similarities and contrasts between copyright in the 19th century United States and late 20th century China. A principal commonality is the use of material copyrighted in other nations without the permission of, or compensation paid to, holders of copyrights. [...] A factor which should be emphasized, and which forms one rationale for this paper, is the disturbing lack of historical consciousness in current discussions of intellectual property relations between the United States and China. The general lack of references to the United States as a copyright haven in these discussions, combined with a rather moralistic tone, does give the impression of a collective forgetting or repression.[9]

Few scholars have ventured into the field of study of colonial intellectual property, as the phenomenon of technology has diverted their attention towards its glittering novelty and technological promises. A recent publication broke the spell in 2006: in her second book *The Internationalisation of Copyright*,[10] Professor Catherine Seville devotes many pages to the colonial challenges – largely based on the Canadian experience, a contribution that will, without a doubt, revive interest in this field. This aside, modern legal literature on the topic is scarce. The first edition of *Fox on Copyright*, issued in 1944, devotes very few pages to Canadian legal history and remains silent on the colonial controversy. Indeed, legal scholars are indebted to historians,

---

8 Respectively, *Sessional Papers of the Dominion of Canada* (1875) vol. viii; No. 28 and *Correspondence on the Subject of the Law of Copyright in Canada*, *supra* note 7 No. 6 at 13.

9 Julian Warner, 'Information Society or Cash Nexus? A Study of the United States as a Copyright Haven' (1999) 50 J. of the American Soc. for Information Science 461 at 462.

10 Catherine Seville, *The Internationalisation of Copyright* (Cambridge: Cambridge University Press, 2006) at 78–145; see also Pierre-Emmanuel Moyse, *Le droit de distribution – Analyse historique et comparative en droit d'auteur* (Montreal: Yvon Blais, 2007).

librarians and political scientists for having partially unveiled the story, at least in retrieving, archiving and organising historical facts that include or surround legislative activities. In particular, credit must be given to the monumental work accomplished since 2000 by the History of the Book in Canada/*Histoire du livre et de l'imprimé au Canada* Project Group who have produced, under the direction of Professors Lamonde, Fleming and Gallichan, an unprecedented collection of articles dealing with the history of the book in Canada. This work is comprised of three volumes, with Volumes I and II covering the colonial period in which we are interested.[11] We should also mention the excellent work of Professor George Parker, who has successfully captured the legal dimension of the commercial situation of Canada in his 1985 book on the beginning of the book trade in Canada.[12] His study shows to what extent topics of copyright and book trade are interwoven and complementary. For at least the first half of the nineteenth century, copyright history is affiliated with, if not a product of, early commercial developments following the introduction of the printing press in Canada in the late eighteenth century. The aforementioned remarkable studies, however, cannot replace a proper legal analysis. They do not, by any means, exhaust or fully embrace the entire copyright issue. We hope that this brief overview of Canadian history will ignite in other former colonies enterprises such as the one we have undertaken.

In Part I of this study, we will present the origins of Canadian copyright law (I). The second part will more specifically address the Canadian problem in regard to its subordinate position vis-à-vis Great Britain (II).

I THE ORIGINS OF CANADIAN LAW

In this part, we will successively visit (1) the first colonial statutes, (2) the first Canadian doctrine and (3) early Canadian cases. This journey into early developments aims simply to present the reader with important milestones in Canadian copyright legal history.

The First Colonial Statutes

In 1832, the Parliament of the Province of Lower Canada voted the first colonial statute on copyright entitled 'An Act for the Protection of Copy Rights',[13]

---

11 Patricia Lockhart Fleming, Gilles Gallichan & Yvan Lamonde, eds., *History of the Book in Canada* (Toronto: University of Toronto Press, 2007) vol. 1–3.

12 George L. Parker, *The Beginnings of the Book Trade in Canada* (Toronto: University of Toronto Press, 1985).

13 *Supra* note 1.

an act granting copyright to residents of the Province. British subjects benefited from the set of prerogatives provided by the Imperial laws which were applicable throughout the British territories. Although some doubts may have existed in this regard – early British enactments, beginning with the *Statute of Anne 1709*,[14] are unclear as to their application to the colonies and failed to address the Colonial question – the provisions of the 1842 *Copyright Act* expressly applied to 'all Parts of the United Kingdom of Great Britain and Ireland, the Islands of Jersey and Guernsey, all Parts of the East and West Indies, and all the Colonies, Settlements, and Possessions of the Crown which now are or hereafter may be acquired'.[15] An author publishing works in London was thus granted an extended privilege in an Empire on which the sun never set. In 1832, Canada was a young British colony ceded by France in 1763 with the signing of the Treaty of Paris. During this era and in a country which had yet to be settled, we are far from the learned debates on the nature of copyright, which would become the favourite topic of nineteenth century scholars.[16] Such debates would later find some resonance in the works of the first Canadian doctrine. The rather succinct text of 1832 simply conveys the ambitions of the legislator for encouraging the birth of a literary and artistic nation, providing it with the means for its education and its cultural achievements in promoting literature, bookshops and the local press. The ink of the first printing presses was still fresh. The Canadian *Copyright Act* of 1832 was voted for a period of eight years and its duration coincided with the reunification in 1840 of the Provinces of Upper and Lower Canada (today, respectively, Ontario and Québec), forming thus the Province of Canada.[17] The law was repealed and replaced in 1841 by *An Act for the Protection of Copy Rights in this Province* recalling for the most part the text of 1832.[18]

The registration of a copy of a book with the Canadian authorities was a prerequisite to copyright protection. As of 1832, the law on this point was very

---

[14] *An Act for the Encouragement of Learning by Vesting the Copies of Printed Books in the Authors or Purchasers of such Copies, During the Times therein Mentioned, 1710* (UK), 8 Anne, c. 19. The Copyright Act 1801, for instance, applied 'in the United Kingdom of Great Britain and Ireland', *An Act for the further Encouragement of Learning, in the United Kingdom of Great Britain and Ireland, by Securing the Copies and Copyright of printed Books, to the Authors of such Books, or their Assigns for the Time herein mentioned, 1801* (UK), 41 Geo. III, c. 107.

[15] *Copyright Act, 1842* (UK), *supra* note 6, ss. 2, 29.

[16] Pierre-Emmanuel Moyse, 'La nature du droit d'auteur: droit de propriété ou monopole?' (1998) 43:3 McGill L.J. 507.

[17] *Supra* note 2. On 30 March of the previous year, Nova Scotia passed *An Act for Securing Copy Rights, 1839*, 2 Vict., c. 36. Nova Scotia joined the Canadian Confederation in 1867 together with New Brunswick.

[18] *Supra* note 2.

clear: '[...] no person shall be entitled to the benefit of this Act unless he shall, before publication, deposite a printed copy of such book or books, map, chart, musical composition, print, cut, or engraving, in the Office of the registrar of the Province.'[19] Furthermore, to be eligible under this law, the authors had to reside in the Province.[20] The text is less clear with regard to the requirement to first publish or print the book in Canada. Since the objective of colonial law was undoubtedly to promote the local cultural industry, one should assume that the legislator prioritized the manufacturing of books in Canada. However, the Canadian legislator was cautious not to make too explicit its intent on this point. The law thus remains understandably vague, since a provision calling for the publication in Canada would have conflicted with the Imperial legislation. For this very reason and out of fear of the establishment of a distinct colonial system (which would exclude British authors), Great Britain vigorously demanded guarantees that subjects of Great Britain and Ireland be eligible for protection under Canadian law in the same manner as the colony's residents. Anticipating an autonomy which would be detrimental to the interests of the home country, in 1842 the British Parliament adopted the *Talfourd Bill*,[21] a British statute commercially annexing Canadian territory to that of Great Britain. This Imperial statute was a law designed to protect English publishers, and applied to the Colonies *mutatis mutandis*. It was an exceptional measure in the sense that Westminster had progressively refrained from interfering with colonial governance. In 1847, Canada passed *An Act to extend the Provincial Copyright Act to Persons Resident in the United Kingdom*,[22] which confirmed the fears of the Home Government. British authors residing in Great Britain and Ireland would not be entitled to protection unless their works were printed and published in the Province of Canada. The printing and publishing of works in Canada was made compulsory, with the text further specifying that the work must mention the author's name and place of abode or business in the Province, as well as the name of the printer and publisher.[23] The statutes of 1841 and 1847 were eventually revised with minor modifications in 1859.[24] Buried in the text, the requirement of a Canadian printing

---

19 *Copyright Act, 1841* (Can.), *supra* note 2, s. 5. Section 4 of the *Copyright Act*, 1832 (Can.), *supra* note 1 identified the Superior Court as the place of deposit.

20 *Copyright Act, 1832* (Can.), *ibid*., s. 1 and *Copyright Act, 1841* (Can.), *ibid*., s. 1.

21 Catherine Seville, 'Talfourd and His Contemporaries: The Making of the 1842 Copyright Act' in A. Firth, ed., *The Prehistory and Development of Intellectual Property Systems* (London: Sweet & Maxwell Limited, 1997).

22 *An Act Respecting Copyrights, 1859* (Can.), 22 Vict., c. 81.

23 *Ibid.*

24 *Ibid.*

initially passed unnoticed, but was subsequently denounced by the Imperial Government, since it effectively created an exclusive Canadian market.[25]

The *British North America Act* of 1867 provided Canada with its first constitution. The text grants powers to the Federal Parliament in matters such as copyright and patents.[26] This allocation of power was perceived in Canada as a new deal. From the Canadian perspective, it meant the Canadian Parliament should have the exclusive power to legislate in copyright and related matters. Based on this contention, the honourable Pierre-Basile Mignault concluded that 'in this country, we can freely enact laws regarding literary property'.[27] The adjective 'freely' is certainly deceptive since, in fact, the Act of 1867 aimed at organising the respective powers of Federal and Provincial legislatures within the Federation and was not deemed to take away the Imperial jurisdiction.[28] Case law issued by both English and Canadian courts confirmed this interpretation.

Nonetheless, one year later, the Canadian Federal Parliament hastened to pass *An Act respecting Copyrights*,[29] an act that re-established the formalities and the publication requirement expressly introduced in 1847. Notably, s. 9 of the Act of 1868 imposed the obligation on British authors to print and publish in the Dominion and to indicate 'the place of abode or business in Canada of the printer and publisher thereof'. The Bill was reserved by the Imperial Government, since doubts had arisen as to whether or not it was repugnant to an Order in Council adopted the same year regarding the protection granted to British authors with respect to the importation of reprints of their work in Canada.[30] However, the Imperial Government

---

25 *An Act to extend the Provincial Copyright Act to persons resident in the United Kingdom, on certain conditions, 1847* (Can.), 10 & 11 Vict., c. 28.

26 *British North America Act, 1867* (UK), 30 & 31 Vict., c. 3., s. 91(23):

> [...] the exclusive Legislative Authority of the Parliament of Canada extends to all Matters coming within the Classes of Subjects next hereinafter enumerated; that is to say, –
> 22. Patents of Invention and Discovery.
> 23. Copyrights.
> [...].

27 P. B. Mignault, 'La propriété littéraire' (1880) 2 *La Thémis* 367 at 368 [2nd article].

28 Confirming this interpretation, see *Routledge v. Low* (1868), L.R. 3 (H.L.) 100; *Hubert v. Mary* (1906), 15 B.R. 381 (Que. C.A.); *Black v. The Imperial Book Company* (1904), 8 Ont. L. R. 9 (Ont. C.A.); *Joubert v. Geracimo* (1916), 26 B.R. 97, 35 D.L.R. 683 (Que. K. B.).

29 *An Act respecting Copyrights, 1868* (Can.), 31 Vict., c. 54.

30 This issue is explicitly referred to in the Preamble of the Imperial Act of 1875, *An Act to give effect to an Act of the Parliament of the Dominion of Canada respecting*

remained unyielding, calling on Canada to revise its 1868 statute in order to leave Imperial law intact.

Ultimately, the forced coexistence of two jurisdictional orders would embroil the Imperial and Federal Governments in an unprecedented quarrel. Ottawa insisted on drafting a bill that would encourage the local production of books produced under British license or, if necessary, under a legal licensing scheme. The future of the publishing industry in Canada was at stake. In 1872, in a provocative move to reclaim its control, Canada adopted a Bill which introduced the projected licensing scheme, a legal mechanism which subjected the reprint of foreign books to a fixed royalty.[31] The Home Government opposed this measure and it never received Royal Assent. Canadian industry had suffered far too long from the London publishers' monopoly, with Canadians being forced to revert to the practice of first publication in London and British publishers failing to grant licenses to Canadian publishers, thereby preventing the production of copyrighted books in Canada. By stark contrast, the London publishing industry enjoyed the state of copyright affairs, attracting most of the authors from the colonies. Naturally, registration in Canada gave very little incentive since protection was limited to Canada.

Under these circumstances and in order to encourage the local publishing industry, the Canadian government concentrated its legislative and diplomatic efforts on attenuating the effects of the British *Copyright Law* of 1842. In all certainty, Canada could not obtain the requirement of first publishing without the assent of the British Parliament. Therefore, as a compromise, a new Canadian statute was voted in 1875 providing for the protection of British authors to the extent that they *reprint* or *republish* their works in Canada: '. . . works of which the copyright has been granted and is subsisting in the United Kingdom, and copyright of which is not secured or subsisting in Canada, under any Canadian or Provincial Act shall, upon being printed and published, or reprinted and republished in Canada, be entitled to copyright under this Act.'[32] The Statute of 1875 was approved the same year,[33] renewed with amendments in 1886 mirroring the Imperial Act of 1886 on international copyright.[34] In

---

Copyright, 1875 (UK), 38-39 Vict., c. 53. This Act of 1875 was adopted to remove any doubts as to the validity of the Colonial legislation of 1875, hence avoiding the speculations which followed the enactment of the previous statute.

[31] Harold G. Fox, *The Canadian Law of Copyright*, 1st ed. (Toronto: The University of Toronto Press, 1944) at 24.

[32] *An Act Respecting Copyrights, 1875* (Can.), 38 Vict., c. 88, s. 15. On this point, see P. B. Mignault, 'La propriété littéraire' (1881) 3 *La Thémis* 1 at 6.

[33] *An Act to give effect to an Act of the Parliament of the Dominion of Canada respecting Copyright, 1875* (UK) 38–39 Vict., c. 53.

[34] *An Act to amend the Law respecting International and Colonial Copyright, 1886* (UK), 49–50 Vict., c. 33.

addition, having undergone minor modifications in 1889, 1890, 1891, 1895 and 1900, the Statute was revised in 1906 and maintained the 1875 provision as to the republication and reprinting conditions.[35] It was repealed and replaced by the 1921 Act, an Act that would close the colonial chapter removing copyright from the control of the British Parliament.[36]

The British Act of 1842 provoked a cascade of diplomatic and legislative events, characterized by a dramatic colonial tango to the Canadian national identity's tune.

Emergence of a Canadian Copyright Doctrine: Mignault, Dawson and Perrault

In the preface to the first edition of his treatise *The Canadian Law of Copyright* (1944), Harold Fox contends that no other literature prior to his own was interested in copyright: 'Despite the fact that the first statute dealing with copyright in this country was enacted over a century ago no work has, up to the present, been written which has dealt with the Canadian law of copyright.'[37] This statement overlooks the works of other Canadian writers and notably those of three prominent jurists: Pierre-Basile Mignault (1854–1945), Samuel Edward Dawson (1833–1916) and Antonio Perrault (1880–1955), all three from Lower Canada, the former and the latter both well-known attorneys and Dawson an eminent writer, publisher and bookseller. They certainly preceded Fox and could lay claim to his self-bestowed crown of laurels. It is true that the writings of Mignault and Dawson are prior to the first proclaimed *modern* Canadian *Copyright Act* of 1921 – a title that is certainly deceiving, since it is difficult to isolate modern legislation from its historical continuum – and they do not have the format of a treatise, nor the widespread distribution of Fox's work. However, this should not cast shade on their contributions. This section is dedicated to the early Canadian doctrine, a doctrine that is worth reviving.

In 1880, Mignault published a series of articles on literary property in the Quebec journal *La Thémis* (1879).[38] His first article, appearing in November

---

35 *An Act Respecting Copyright, 1886* (Can.), 49 Vict., c. 62; *An Act to amend 'The Copyright Act', Chapter Sixty-two of the Revised Statutes, 1889* (Can.), 52 Vict., c. 29; *An Act to amend 'The Copyright Act', 1889* (Can.), 53 Vict., c. 12; *An Act to amend the Copyright Act, 1891* (Can.), 54–5 Vict., c. 34; *An Act to amend the Copyright Act, 1895* (Can.), 58–9 Vict., c. 37; *An Act to amend the Copyright Act, 1900* (Can.), 63–4 Vict., c. 25.

36 *Copyright Act, 1921* (Can.), 11–12 Geo. V, c. 24.

37 Fox, *supra* note 31, Preface.

38 Pierre Basile Mignault, 'La propriété littéraire', (1880) 2 *La Thémis* 289 [1st article]; (1880) 2 *La Thémis* 367 [2nd article] and (1881) 3 *La Thémis* 1; (1881) 3 *La Thémis* 11 [3rd article] and (1881) 3 *La Thémis* 43; (1881) 3 *La Thémis* 49 [4th article]

1880, deals with the nature of copyright. He reviews the set of traditional themes developed in Continental Europe on the nature of literary property. His sources are diverse and he draws from the works to which he has access, mainly those from British jurisprudence and doctrine (namely Shortt).[39] However, with a grand show of open-mindedness, he cites in equal measure Renouard[40] and Drone.[41] Since he cannot support his writings with any contemporary Canadian doctrine, his work is that of a pioneer. Mignault's talent shows in the difficult comparative exercise to which he has subjected himself. Educated in civil law, Mignault ventures for the first time into a new and complex field of law which is deeply rooted in the *common law* tradition. Savvy in the latter, he makes frequent references to *civil law concepts*. Mignault's views elevate the discussion to a trans-systemic and comparative level. He finds himself immediately confronted by the linguistic dimension of his exercise: 'And, first of all, how is one to understand literary property, author's rights, copyright, as I would use all three of these expressions indistinctly during the course of this work?'[42] He outright expresses his preference for the more concise civil law legislative approach, longing for 'a law as clear and concise such as that of July 19th, 1793, which still governs literary property in France'.[43] Mignault develops the comparison between literary property and ownership as defined under Article 406 of the *Civil Code of Lower Canada*,[44] but refuses any assimilation. If the manuscript can be the object of such property, the ideas embedded therein are not susceptible to appropriation. For Mignault, the author is a collaborator for society, who draws his raw material from a common heritage to which he is indebted. The property right which is vested in him must be strictly organized with the main purpose of rewarding him for his contribution. The idea of an exclusive and temporary right, resulting from a state concession, dominates Mignault's reflections. He provides the following definition: '... it is the exclusive right, granted for a certain period to the author or his assignees, to reproduce, for public dissemination, literary, scientific or artistic works'.[45] He argues that if copyright were to be conceived, and understood, as a kind of real property, copyright would

---

and (1881) 3 *La Thémis* 65; (1881) 3 *La Thémis* 97 [5th article]; (1881) 3 *La Thémis* 161 [6th article].

[39] Mignault, '3rd article', *ibid.* at 4.

[40] Mignault, '1st article', *supra* note 38 at 298.

[41] Mignault, '2nd article', *supra* note 38 at 374.

[42] Mignault, '1st article', *supra* note 38 at 291 [our translation].

[43] Mignault, '2nd article', *supra* note 38 at 370 [our translation].

[44] Article 406 C.C.L.C.: 'Ownership is the right of enjoying and of disposing of things in the most absolute manner, provided that no use be made of them which is prohibited by law or by regulations.'

[45] Mignault, '1st article', *supra* note 38 at 291 [our translation].

arguably be absolute and perpetual – a construction which he is not ready to embrace. Mignault understands how damaging the idea of perpetuity can be when associated with intellectual productions: '[I]f copyright constituted a real property, it most certainly would be perpetual. However, it is contrary to its essence, and as in all modern legislation, lasts solely for a limited amount of time. Hence, the author does not have an ordinary property right in his works'.[46] His position is better understood when one considers the dependent situation of Canada concerning foreign literary and artistic literature. Access to foreign books is essential, as it conditions education in this country. Mignault appears to be particularly sensitive to the role copyright legislation plays in the promotion of social interests and the encouragement of the humanities. He opposes the idea of an all-powerful private right.[47]

Mignault certainly provides us with little material on the state of his society, focusing as he did, on the academic discussion. He takes note of the awakening of the community to the question of copyright, a right which, he anticipates, will receive increasing attention: 'This study, I hope, is not without its usefulness to the public, as nowadays the literary movement is accentuated more and more in our Canadian society, and we should anticipate frequent discussions on the matter'.[48] Mignault shies away from the thorniest political debate which would bring his country to withdraw from the Berne Convention a few years later. Only in passing does he invoke the injustice of the colonial situation which favours authors from the home country, commenting that 'the lowliest English scribbler was protected in every corner of the British Empire'.[49]

In 1918, Mignault is named judge of the Supreme Court. Expert in civil law, conscious of the British legacy, he proposes an analysis of copyright as a creature of the law, and therefore a very legalist one.

Dawson holds a 'special' place in our study. He was the author of historical and geographic works – *The Saint Lawrence, Its Basin and Border-lands: The Story of Their Discovery, Exploration and Occupation*,[50] *The Voyages of the Cabots: Latest Phases of the Controversy*,[51] and member of the prestigious Royal Society of Canada. In 1882, he publishes a lecture given that same year at the law faculty of Bishop's University in Sherbrooke, Québec. Although he professes to be a layman, his opinion on the subject of copyright is articulated with expertise and his views are guided by years of practice as a publisher. He

46 *Ibid.* at 293 [our translation].
47 *Ibid.* at 291.
48 *Ibid.* [our translation].
49 Mignault, '2nd article', *supra* note 38 at 367 [our translation].
50 (New York: Frederick A. Stokes Company, 1905).
51 (Ottawa: Transactions of the Royal Society of Canada, 1897).

removes the discussion on the nature of copyright from what he would have called sterile academic debates and sets aside the discussion on natural law:

> Copyright, the right to copy, or simply 'copy' [...] is asserted by some to be a natural right founded on a law of Nature. It is, they say, a Title in perpetuity [...]. It may be because I am a layman, but I must confess that I find it difficult to attach any precise meaning to the expression Natural Law.[52]

Although Dawson was not educated in law, his analysis of Canadian law is exemplary. *Copyright in Books* provides an incisive description of the situation of colonial Canada and contains particularly stinging remarks regarding colonial policy in matters of publishing. Dawson denounces the encroachment of Imperial power and the partiality of laws which it intended to apply in its colonies. The Imperial *Copyright Law* of 1842 confiscated control of the Canadian publishing and printing market: 'The object of the Imperial act is to induce foreigners and others to publish in Great Britain (*Low v. Routledge*). And yet so selfish were the framers of that measure, so reckless of the interests of all but English manufacturers, that they made it extend over the whole Empire. They were determined to centre the printing trade in the British Isles,'[53] and further: 'The absurdities of the English book-trade are, owing to this system, almost incredible, and establish the truth of Lord Macaulay's words that copyright is monopoly.'[54] Dawson provides supporting evidence. He notes the prohibitive pricing practiced by British publishers who refuse to authorize reprints of books in Canada, who systematically oppose American imports and who practice discriminatory pricing: 'For instance, a leading historical work is published in Paris with profit to the author at 9 francs. The French copyright edition is sold in London at 9s. Sterling, but the translation under the International Treaty is sold at 16s. Such was the system which the Act of 1842 sought to impose on the colonies.'[55] The monumental work of Macaulay, *History of England*, Dawson further notes, is sold on the American market for 75 cents per volume, while it is offered through import from the British publishers at the price of 5 dollars. Without mincing words, Dawson further denounces the arrogance of British civil servants who were stationed at Canadian borders until 1850 and who blindly applied British law, to the

---

52 S. E. Dawson, 'Copyright in Books, An Inquiry into its Origin, And an Account of The Present State of The Law In Canada' (A Lecture Delivered Before The Law School of Bishop's College, at Sherbrooke, P.Q., Thursday, January 26th 1882) (Montreal: Dawson Brothers Publishers, 1882) at 6 [Dawson, 'Copyright in Books'].

53 *Ibid.* at 18.

54 *Ibid.* at 16.

55 *Ibid.*

extent of burning books imported from the United States.[56] His personal views are as precious as his more technical analysis of the law of 1875. Dawson highlights particular noteworthy mechanisms adopted by the Canadian legislature. He points out a remarkable exception embodied in the *Copyright Act* of 1875 which neutralizes the right of a British author to forbid the importation into Canada of works printed with his consent in the United Kingdom. Given that the benefit of the law of 1875 is granted to one who prints or reprints his work in Canada, regardless of the quality of the printing, the Canadian legislature apparently reserved its prerogative to access original editions which were of reputedly better quality:[57] 'The object of this proviso is to prevent a Canadian publisher issuing cheap and poor editions of a book, and shutting out of the country the superior and authentic original editions. It was enacted in the interest of the reading public.'[58]

Several years later, navigating in less troubled waters, the eminent Perrault released his contribution to Canadian doctrine. His work was published in 1924 in the *La Revue du droit*[59] – a legal journal published between 1922 and 1939[60] – and therefore coinciding with the coming into force in 1924 of the Canadian law of 1921. The law of 1921 confirms the legislative independence of Canada, Westminster's Parliament having left all latitude to the colonies to legislate in copyright matters. This political context explains why the writings of Perrault appear to be more assertive than those of Mignault, but definitely less committed than those of Dawson. Reflecting on decades of dissension, Perrault explains: 'Withdrawing Canada from the application of English laws and making it adhere to the Berne Convention, pushes it towards autonomy.

56 *Ibid.* at 17: 'Where a whole community is determined to disobey any given law, the repeal of that law must soon come about, and in this case the antagonism was heightened by the arrogance of the Imperial officers. The Canadian Government in one or two cases issued permission to return some books which had been seized, to the United States; but the English officer refused to give them up and burned them.'

57 *An Act Respecting Copyrights*, 1875 (Can.), *supra* note 32, s. 15: 'Works of which the copyright has been granted and is subsisting in the United Kingdom, and copyright of which is not secured or subsisting in Canada, under any Canadian or Provincial Act, shall, upon being printed and published, or reprinted and republished in Canada, be entitled to copyright under this Act; but nothing in this Act shall be held to prohibit the importation from the United Kingdom of copies of such works legally printed there.'

58 Dawson, 'Copyright in Books', *supra* note 52 at 24.

59 Antonio Perrault, 'La propriété des oeuvres intellectuelles' (1924) 3 La Revue du droit 49 [Perrault, 'Part one'] & (1924) 3 La Revue du droit 107 [Perrault, 'Part two'].

60 A journal with partisan and religious inclinations. See Jean-Guy Belley, 'Une croisade intégriste chez les avocats du Québec: La Revue du droit (1922-1939)' (1993) 34 Les Cahiers de Droit 183.

Such achievements, it is true, are not obtained without the consent of the masters in London – we do not drop the ties that bind unless they judge it suitable'.[61] Perrault revisits, as others before him, the debates on the nature and justification of copyright: 'Is property law founded on "natural law", on the basic premise of occupation, or on civil law?'[62] Less hesitant in this regard than Mignault, Perrault has no difficulty in accepting a *lato sensu* property right, which basis is to be found entirely in natural law. This concession, he believes, does not hinder or take away the force of statutory law which prevails and sets the conditions and limits of copyright.[63] Perrault's analysis can be characterized as positivist, and supports the view that the natural right of authors end upon publication of the work with the consent of the author.[64]

For Perrault, the intellectual production is susceptible to appropriation, even in the absence of actual possession or physical control. 'The products of our intelligence', he writes, 'are also matters of property rights.'[65] This idea of intellectual property thus transcends the distinction between the possession of a manuscript and its delivery to the public resulting from its publication. It is logically inferred that copyright cannot be summed up as a reproduction right, but rather is conceived of as a right to exploit and follow the work through its different uses. Perrault's theory is in many ways avant-garde and precedes many written works on the scope of intellectual property rights once the physical copy has been put into circulation. On the relationship between the control of a physical copy and its content, he wrote:

> Absent any specific provision, in selling a copy, has the author, by virtue of this act, sold the work, abandoned all right to correct and reproduce it? Answering this question in the affirmative would be to abusively interpret the contract of sale between the author and the purchaser of a copy. The sale of hundreds of copies does not change this legal situation. The author retains the right to modify, to dispose of and to reproduce his work. The public is only a group of purchasers. The group does not have any more right than each as individuals.[66]

This is a fascinating reflection which in a few lines anticipates the debate on exhaustion and on the right of an author to control subsequent distribution of copies of his work.[67] Perrault's vision is one that clearly favours rightholders,

---

61 Perrault, 'Part two', *supra* note 59 at 116 [our translation].
62 Perrault, 'Part one', *supra* note 59 at 56 [our translation].
63 *Ibid.* at 56-57 [our translation].
64 *Ibid.* at 61.
65 *Ibid.* [our translation].
66 *Ibid.* at 67–8 [our translation].
67 J. H. Spoor, W. R. Cornish & P. F. Nolan, *Copies in Copyright* (Netherlands: Alphen Aan Den Rijn, Sithoff & Noordhoff, 1980).

since it '...would ruin the basis itself of property not to recognize, under the pretext of public convenience and necessity, the moral right and the pecuniary profit that the work can provide its author'.[68] Perpetual property appears to him to be justifiable from a theoretical point of view, even though he reckons that certain works should return to common heritage because of their utility.[69]

The labours of Perrault are enlightening. As Mignault predicted, they attest to the real and growing interest in this field of law. Prior to the writings of Mignault, Dawson and Perrault, there was no Canadian doctrine in matters of copyright. One had to look elsewhere, to Pouillet or Blackstone for example. Mignault, Dawson and Perrault thus contributed to create Canadian doctrine, which in itself is remarkable. Furthermore, establishing an emerging Canadian model, these authors borrowed elements from both the common and civil law systems to devise solutions. The three authors we have studied cited French doctrine. Dawson goes so far as to affirm in a peremptory tone the importance of French law: 'Canada, and especially this province of Quebec, is not only an English country – it is a French one; and, inasmuch as the foundation of our Civil Law is derived from France, some notice should be taken of the French one. But that is very clear.'[70] One can observe, by virtue of these references, a phenomenon of infiltration of civil law thoughts into Canadian copyright theories. This discrete influence would explain why Canadian law is perhaps more inclined to *jusnaturalistes* or *personnalistes* theories, with the important caveat that it consists of a copyright system. The influence of civil law – even received in small homeopathic doses – on common law is very palpable, and particularizes Canadian copyright law.

Early Canadian Case Law

Although colonial statutes had been in force in the British North American colonies since 1832, Canadian copyright cases falling under the strict application of colonial laws seem to be either nonexistent or at least unreported before 1867. The earliest Canadian cases pertain therefore to the post-Confederation era. This could be explained by a combination of factors such as the limited number of printing businesses in Canada until late in the nineteenth century (the first commercial printing offices appeared in Winnipeg and Victoria in 1858),[71] the institution of a provincial school system initiated during the

68 Perrault, 'Part one', *supra* note 59 at 70 [our translation].

69 *Ibid.* at 71.

70 Dawson, 'Copyright in Books', *supra* note 52 at 10.

71 There were no printing presses in New France. Consequently, the French colony was dependent on the productions from France, '... which, comments François Melançon, followed the mercantilist economic thinking of the royal authorities.' See

1850s, and the slow emergence of a reading public.[72] Indeed, Canadian cases could be regrouped in two categories. First and in predominant proportion, are cases dealing with the protection in Canada of foreign works and which expose the complexity of Canadian copyright law as a result of Imperial interference. They form the *lieu* and expression of all the political dissensions that opposed the two governments for decades. They show law in action and, in our particular case, how actions at law were guided to exclude Canadian publishers from their small but growing market. Canadian law was, as we have demonstrated, second in regulating its own territory. Imperial protection obtained in accordance with international arrangements or publications of works in London trumped its application. This body of early cases '... deals with, as the court will put it in *Joubert v. Geracimo*, protection of foreign authors' copyright.'[73] They are cases involving imports, reprints or performance of American, French or English works being literary, dramatic works or musical compositions.[74] They will serve as the backdrop to our comments on

---

François Melançon, 'The Book in New France' in Lockhart Fleming, Gallichan & Lamonde, *supra* note 11, vol.1 at 46. John Bushell set up the first printing press in Canada in 1752, issuing the first number of the *Halifax Gazette* in that year.

[72] George L. Parker, 'The Evolution of Publishing in Canada' in Lockhart Fleming, Gallichan & Lamonde, *ibid.* at 17.

[73] *Joubert v. Géracimo*, *supra* note 28, injunction granted, judgment in favour of the French rightholder of a play who sought protection in application of the Berne Convention, the *Imperial Act implementing the treaty*, 1886 (UK), 49–50 Vict., c. 12 and the *Imperial Dramatic Literary Act,* 1833 (UK), 3–4 Will. IV, c. 15. Evidence showed that the play was performed 14 times in Quebec without authorization. The plaintiff did not comply with the Canadian *Copyright Act* – which did not at the time provide for protection of dramatic work – and grounded its claim of British law successfully arguing that the effect of the Royal Proclamation of adhesion to the Berne Convention was to give application in Canada to the 1833 *Dramatic Literary Property Act*. Justice Pelletier, dissenting, laments the anomalous position of Canada (at 122): '...if it is true that Canada is a nation, at least to the extent that the Confederation Act indicates, we should, I believe, interpret our laws in light of a definite principle of autonomy they seemingly embody and avoid leading British Parliament to believe that it should legislate, even indirectly, for us....' (our translation). See also *Hubert v. Mary*, *supra* note 28, affirming *Smiles v. Belford* (1877), 1 O.A.R. 436 (Ont. C.A.) and *Routledge v. Low*, *supra* note 28. *Contra*: refusing to apply in Canada the imperial *Fine Arts Copyright Act, 1862* (UK), 25–26 Vict., c. 68 in a case involving copies made in Canada without authorization of Maud Earl's painting 'What we have we'll hold', deciding that the Act is limited to the UK.

[74] The *Anglo-Canadian Music Publisher's Association v. Dupuis* (1903), 27 C.S. 485 (Que. S.C.); *Hubert v. Mary*, *supra* note 28, granting an injunction against the person who published in Canada the French copyrighted work 'Tante Berceuse' without authorization. The Imperial legislation was actionable by the French author in Canada, by reason of obtaining copyright protection in his own country which was a member of the Berne Union. Justice Lavergne concluded that the Imperial Parliament legislates for all the colonies.

the situation Canada endured under the Imperial ordeal. The second group of cases, more limited in number, consists of traditional and topical infringement cases. They are of particular interest, since they submerge the reader in a young cultural and social Canadian society. They constitute as many windows on nineteenth century cultural and economical preoccupations. Our ambition is simply to present some early moments in Canadian copyright law as staged before our courts. *Langlois v. Vincent,*[75] decided in 1874, portrays a very traditional and religious Quebec. In this case, the plaintiff, representing the church, complained about the fact that Langlois produced and published its own edition of *Le Grand Catéchisme*. The text was composed around the year 1700 by the second Bishop of Quebec, Monseigneur Saint-Vallier – Jean Baptiste de La Croix de Chevrière de Saint Vallier was his full name – a pious ecclesiastic from a noble family.[76] At the time of the proceedings, the work had already gone through 12 editions, and the Court had no difficulty in dismissing the plaintiff's claim. It concluded that '... said Catechism has been for a century and three quarters in public use, and is no longer susceptible of being made private property.'[77] The story does not tell if the church was vindicated by having the defendant excommunicated. The latter was certainly acquainted with the mortal nature of his initiatives. *Bernard v. Bertoni*[78] and *Beullac Ltée. v. Simard*[79] unveil two other iconic figures of Canadian history. In *Bernard v. Bertoni*, the plaintiff successfully sued on the ground of common law copyright for the sale of infringing copies of the bust of Elzéar-Alexandre Taschereau, co-founder of Laval University in Quebec City, appointed Archbishop of Quebec in 1871 and first Canadian Cardinal. Several minorities championing the right to devotion in Quebec, personified by the French plaintiff in this particular case, blamed the Italians for illegally producing and selling infringing copies of the bust.

---

75 *Langlois v. Vincent* (1874), 18 Lower Canada Jurist 160 (Que. S.C.).

76 Saint-Vallier came to Canada in 1685 on the same ship as the newly-appointed Governor of New France, the Marquis de Denonville, who was succeeded by Frontenac. 'We have two accounts of Canada at this time, wrote Le Sueur, one from the pen of the bishop designate, the other from that of the new governor after a residence of a little than three months in the country. [...] Saint Vallier sees everything *couleur de rose,* and detects the odor of sanctity everywhere. Denonville, on the contrary, sees license, insubordination, idleness, luxury, debauchery, running riot throughout the land'. W. D. Lesueur, *Count Frontenac* (Toronto: Morang, 1906) at 192. F. Melançon noted that Saint Vallier entrusted French printers with the printing of a catechism and book of rites for his diocese that he would import. Hence, the lack of local presses did not completely hinder the completion of projects initially conceived in New France. See Melançon, *supra* note 71 at 46.

77 *Langlois v. Vincent*, *supra* note 75 at 163.

78 (1888), 14 Q.L.R. 219 (Que. S.C.).

79 (1910), 39 C.S. 97 (Que. S.C.); aff'd (1911), 39 C.S. 517 (Que. S.C.-Revision).

Beullac v. Simard, decided in 1910 by the Superior Court of Montreal, presents similar facts. In this case, the successful plaintiff sued for infringement of its copyright in a papier maché model of Samuel de Champlain on the occasion of the 300th anniversary of the founding of Quebec City.[80] *Beauchemin v. Cadieux*[81] is another of these historic encounters. Decided in 1900, the case involves the largest Quebec French publisher, La Maison Beauchemin. From early 1842 until the present day, Beauchemin has been a publisher of major literary works and popular fiction, as well as a noted publisher in the field of educational textbooks in the Province of Quebec.[82] In *Beauchemin v. Cadieux*, the plaintiff claimed that the defendant copied and sold infringing copies of a dictionary in which Beauchemin had secured copyright. Dictionaries or atlases were popular products since specialized books were not in high demand for the vast majority of Canadians. They were traditionally composed of texts of various origins, ranging from geography to history compositions, often old or taken from the public domain in order to limit the cost of production and make them accessible to a larger public. The work at issue was no exception, since the dissenting judge noticed that both works in dispute '... are nothing more than works of abridged compilation of fact, dates and statistics, previously belonging to the public, in the domain of history, geography and biography.'[83] Unfortunately, it is beyond the scope of this paper to further pursue this voyage into Canadian jurisprudence. We hope, however, that we have been able to render a glimpse of Canadian culture through the selective presentation of the foregoing cases.

II THE PROBLEM WITH CANADA

Prior to 1842, the colonies of British North America exercised their own legislative powers without much encumbrance or interference from the Home Government, as long as matters of legislative activities related to their internal affairs. Because it was linked to education and culture, two essential tutors of

---

80 Champlain, great navigator and founder of Quebec in 1608, is also the author of a monumental work: *Voyages et descouvertures faites en la Nouvelle France* (Paris: 1619).

81 *Beauchemin v. Cadieux* (1900), 10 Que. KB 255 at 264; aff'd (1901), 31 S.C.R. 370.

82 George L. Parker, 'The Evolution of Publishing in Canada', *supra* note 72 at 26, reported that '...Étienne Roby, manager of Beauchemin's retail operations, observed in 1905 that French-language authors suffered because of the sales of Quebec reprints and cheap American editions of French authors'.

83 Another work of compilation will find itself in the midst of legal turmoil in *Garland v. Gemmill* (1887), 14 S.C.R. 321.

sustainable progress, intellectual property was perceived, on the Canadian side, as falling under colonial jurisdiction. Based on this assumption, the Parliament of Lower Canada adopted its first intellectual property statute in 1824: an *Act to Promote the Progress of Useful Arts in this Province*.[84] The Imperial Government refrained from interfering. It neither objected nor meddled. However, in copyright matters, the Imperial Parliament's deference vanished when it passed the *Copyright Act* in 1842. The enactment of this statute put Canada in a rather anomalous position, since it literally harnessed the colonial markets to British commercial interests. A British author, or an author residing in a country having a reciprocity agreement with Great Britain,[85] benefited from Imperial copyright protection which extended throughout the British Empire. The British North American provinces immediately denounced this incursion. The House of Assembly of Nova Scotia made an address to the Queen in April 1845 to '...relieve your Majesty's faithful and loyal subjects in British North America from the serious evils inflicted by said statutes...'.[86] Beginning in 1846, the government of New Brunswick protested through Lieutenant-Governor Colebrooke,[87] and Canada sent official reprimands to the British authorities denouncing the effect of the law of 1842, which deprived the colonist '...of that intellectual food so necessary to prevent him from retrograding in civilization and refinement.'[88]

The *Copyright Act* of 1842 had the effect of giving British publishers control over the international distribution of books, since they could avail themselves of the importation remedies laid down by British law. This was a way of promoting the trade in book exports from Great Britain, while at the

---

84 (Can.) 4 Geo. IV, c. 25. See Margaret Coleman, 'The Canadian Patent Office from Its Beginnings to 1900' (1976) 8 *Bulletin of the Association for Preservation Technology* 56 at 56. Also, Gordon Asher, 'The Development of the Patent System in Canada since 1767' (1965) 45 C.P.R. 56.

85 When the enactment of the 1842 *Copyright Act* and the treaty with Great Britain became law 1852, French authors would benefit from Imperial law as applicable in the colonies. *Convention du 3 novembre 1851, conclue entre la France et la Grande-Bretagne, Au sujet de la propriété littéraire et artistique*, reproduced in Paul Laboulaye, *Études sur la propriété littéraire en France et en Angleterre* (Paris: Auguste Durand, 1858) at 183–190. *An Act to enable Her Majesty to carry into effect a Convention with France on the Subject of Copyright, 1852* (UK), 15 & 16 Vict., c.12.

86 Great Britain – Colonial Office, *Colonial Copyright: return to an address of the Honourable the House of Commons, dated 12 April, 1872, for 'Copies or Extracts of Correspondence between the Colonial Office, the Board of Trade, and the Government of Canada, which preceded the passing of the Act 10 & 11 Vict. c. 95'* (London: HMSO, 1872) Dispatch No. 1, online: <http://www.canadiana.org/ECO/mtq?doc=9_02154> [*Papers Relating to Colonial Copyright*].

87 *Ibid.*, Dispatch No. 6.

88 *Ibid.*, Dispatch No. 12 at 11.

same time maintaining the means of production at home. It also provided the British author or his assignee with complete control of the Canadian publishing market, since no printing of works first published in Great Britain could be made without permission. The right to publish and reprint was retained and used as a commercial veto inflicted on the colonial publishing industry.

The import and reproduction rights were hence the hammer and anvil that paralyzed Canadian publishing, a situation that unexpectedly benefited the American publishing industry. Canada, as Parker stated, became the battlefield for American and British publishers.[89]

Importation

For many years, Canadian bookstores were supplied with books printed and imported from the United States. British book pricing practices made English language literature far too expensive for the Canadian book buyer and reader.[90] In addition to high pricing, one had to add taxes and transportation fees. The latter charges did not include the costs and hazards of such transportation which, due to climate conditions, rendered sea road traffic impossible for a good part of the year.[91] Canada was cut off from England and the main maritime routes for up to five months of the year. During this period, the only mode of access to the New World was through the United States. This, of

[89] Parker, *The Beginnings of the Book Trade in Canada*, *supra* note 12 at 258.

[90] Prices of English books '...come far beyond the means of our population, and hence if our sources of literature were confined to them, the mass of the people would in fact be entirely deprived of the productions of the English press. That in addition to the first cost, there is to be added the expense, the difficulty, and delay of importation.' See '*The Committee appointed to inquire into the question of the copyright referred to as the Petition of Arthur W. Godfrey and others, Halifax 11 March 1845, Colonial Copyright, Copies or Extracts of Correspondence*' in *Papers Relating to Colonial Copyright*, *supra* note 86, Dispatch No 1 at 2.

[91] J.J. Barnes, *Authors, Publishers and Politicians – The Quest for an Anglo-American Copyright Agreement 1815-1854* (Columbus: Ohio State University Press, 1974) at 140: 'Even if Britain could have supplied Canada with special and cheaper colonial editions, there were considerable obstacles in the way. To send publications across the Atlantic was a slow and costly business. Although newspapers were allowed to go by post at the reduced rate of one penny per printed sheet, no such concessions applied to books and periodicals. They had to be sent at the full letter rate and were limited in weight to sixteen ounces. An English magazine which might sell for 5s. in Canada required 2s–4s. postage, so the only practical method was to send magazines and books by freight, which inevitably involved delays of up to six months, insurance charges, Customs clearance, and additional handling. From November to May Canadian waterways were frozen, making it necessary to go overland, and though the postal service managed this trek twice a week, freight companies only made deliveries sporadically. Meanwhile American reprints continued filtering into Canada'.

course, made for difficult conditions and 'weaned' those in the book import trade from the home country. The Royal Commission of 1878 realized this:

> [...] In this country the disadvantage arising from the custom of publishing books in the first instance at a high price, is greatly lessened by the facilities afforded by means of clubs, book societies and circulating libraries. These means are not available, and indeed are impracticable, owing to the great distances and scattered populations, in many of the colonies, and until the cheaper English editions have been published, the colonial reader can only obtain English copyright books by purchasing them at high publishing prices, increased as those prices are by the expense of carriage and other charges incidental to the importation of the books from the United Kingdom.[92]

The United States became a particularly attractive partner, not only because of the possible land routes, but also because of their pricing practices. Reprints were often made on paper of a lesser quality and generally without having to pay royalties, although some printers and publishers offered payment to British authors on a discretionary and voluntary basis. Until 1891, a foreign author would be eligible for copyright protection provided he was an American resident or citizen. This point was, for a long time, a source of friction with European publishers, since the commerce of printing their books prospered across the United States.[93] Similarly – and this point is hardly to be found in English literature – American authors were often refused copyright protection in the British Empire on the grounds of non-compliance with formalities. Of course, the flow of works was largely to the United States' advantage; but literary America had its share of rising new authors, whose promise ensured great success abroad. To benefit from English copyright laws, the American author had to be a resident of Great Britain and had to have proceeded there with the first publication of his work.[94] In comparison, the

---

92 'Report of the Commission of 1878' in Putnam, *supra* note 7 at 258, paras. 183–6.

93 Absent any protection in the United States, a group of American publishers agreed to rely on a courtesy copyright, a form of auto regulation which ultimately failed. The participation in such a pool being voluntary, some publishers neither respected nor felt bound by it: 'To claim this privilege a publisher had only to secure the first copy of the foreign work to reach American shores. This induced leading publishers like Carey & Lea to arrange the prompt dispatch of new books by an agent in London. Once such book reached America, publishers hastily decided which ones to reprint and announced their intentions in the press, expecting that by so doing their brethren of the trade would acknowledge this priority, and would not reprint copies themselves. It was understood that they would then place orders with those publishers who had been first in the market.' See, Barnes, *supra* note 91 at 84–5.

94 See *Jefferys v. Boosey* (1854), 24 L. J. Ex. 81 (H.L.). Lord Cranworth for the House of Lords relying on a strict interpretation of the law: 'Prima facie the legislature

mere momentary presence of the author in Great Britain or its territory at the moment of publication would apparently suffice to meet the requirement of residence under English law. American authors would then be advised by their publishers to spend time in Canada at the moment of the publication of their works in Great Britain. They would cross the Saint Lawrence River for a day, thus obtaining copyright protection throughout the British Empire. British law was not only more advantageous than Canadian law, the latter being of limited application, but it was even more accessible. Canadian law, echoing American law, required more than just an occasional visit to be eligible. This refinement had important legal implications. Mark Twain, for example, was refused registration of one of his works by Ottawa, but was admitted for registration in London.[95]

As of the 1840s, colonial book trade became a highly desirable commercial pursuit which coincided with the rise of Great Britain as the first industrial nation and venue for international trade.[96] At this time, the Home Government was lured by the benefits of commercial expansion. The Central Government facilitated the export and import trade and the colonial implantation of British enterprises. In the case of Canada, this facilitation was especially strong in the area of pulp and paper. In the meantime, Canadian demand for books of all sorts increased considerably. The Act of 1842 was then felt as an outrageous intervention, since it placed the Canadian market in the hands of British publishers with all the inconveniences we have discussed. As of 1846, representations were made to the Imperial Government to exempt from authorization the importation of reprints made in the United States, the main source of affordable books. The British Government acceded to the repeated Canadian

---

of this country must be taken to make laws for its own subjects exclusively. […]. I do not doubt that a foreigner resident here, and composing and publishing a book here, is an author within the meaning of the statute. […]. But if at the time when copyright commences by publication the foreign author is not in this country, he is not, in my opinion, a person whose interests the statute meant to protect.' Barnes wrote that the effect of *Jefferys v. Boosey* '...was to throw open the floodgates to the republication of American works. Reprinters no longer feared court injunctions, and publishers like Sampson Low could only appeal to a sense of honour within the trade not to reprint a new work assigned to him by Harriet Beecher Stowe.' Barnes, *supra* note 91 at 172.

95 Dawson, 'Copyright in Books', *supra* note 52 at 22. See also, *New York Times* (17 December 1881), online: <http://www.twainquotes.com/18811225.html>: 'The application of Samuel L. Clemens (Mark Twain) for a Canadian copyright of his new book has been refused by the Department of Agriculture and Arts. The claim was based on Clemens's visit and domicile for two weeks in Montreal. The authorities decided that such residence is not a domicile'.

96 Ross Cranston, 'Law Through Practice: London and Liverpool Commodity Markets c. 1820–1975' (2007) 14 LSE Law, Society and Economy Working Papers, online: <http://www.lse.ac.uk/collections/law/wps/WPS14-2007Cranston.pdf>.

demands. In practice, the establishment of an effective customs control system appears to be illusory, since the Canadian border with the United States could not be rendered impermeable.[97] Thus, in 1847, the Imperial Parliament quietly enacted the *Foreign Reprints Act*.[98] Although this measure did not appear to be of great importance for the British administration, discontent and complaints were voiced by the English publishers. Not only were their expectations of lucre thwarted as far as the North American market was concerned, but reprints imported under the 1847 system could find their way into Great Britain and compete with home editions of the same works.[99]

Although general in its terms, the statute of 1847 was indeed a specific response to the North American problem. It removed the ban on the import of books which were printed abroad without authorization, on the condition that a minimal protection be given to British authors. 'The principle of this Act, commonly known as the Foreign Reprints Act, is to enable the colonies to take advantage of reprints of English copyright books made in foreign states, and at the same time to protect the interests of British authors.'[100] The law of 1847 does not specify in its text what was meant by the expression 'reasonable

[97] The Royal Copyright Commission concludes that: '[...] it is highly desirable that the literature of this country should be placed within easy reach of the colonies, and that with this view the Imperial Act should be modified, so as to meet the requirements of colonial readers. In this country the disadvantage arising from the custom of publishing books in the first instance at a high price, is greatly lessened by the facilities afforded by means of clubs, book societies and circulating libraries. These means are not available, and indeed are impracticable, owing to the great distances and scattered populations, in many of the colonies, and until the cheaper English editions have been published, the colonial reader can only obtain English copyright books by purchasing them at high publishing prices, increased as those prices are by the expense of carriage and other charges incidental to the importation of the books from the United Kingdom'. 'Report of the Commission of 1878' in Putnam, *supra* note 7 at paras. 183–186.

[98] *An Act to amend the Law relating to the Protection in the colonies of Works entitled to Copyright in the United Kingdom, 1847* (UK), 10 & 11 Vict., c. 95 [*Foreign Reprint Act*]. See 'Letter from John Murray and Thomas Longman to Gladstone, dated March 1870 complaining about the effect of the 1847 Foreign Reprints Act and ask for its prompt repeal' in *Papers Relating to Colonial Copyright*, *supra* note 86, Dispatch No 47 at 46.

[99] Briggs notes that: 'There is a present danger to English authors that cheap reprints authorised in any particular colony by special arrangement may be imported thence to others in which the book sells at full price. In spite of customs officers thousands of Tauchitz and other English Books published abroad at low price find their way into England.' W. Briggs, *The Law of International Copyright* (London: Stevens & Haynes, 1906) at 41.

[100] 'Report of the Commission of 1878' in Putnam, *supra* note 7 at para. 188.

protection', and leaves the Imperial Government the discretion to reject or validate any bill that would be presented to it by the colonies.[101] With alacrity, Canada availed itself of the *Foreign Reprints Act*,[102] and six days later, on 28 July 1847, it voted *An Act to Extend the Provincial Copyright Act to Persons Resident in the United Kingdom*.[103] This was a 'marvel of subterfuge' according to Barnes.[104] Interpreting the *Copyright Act* 1842 requirement of 'reasonable protection', the Canadian legislation provided that British subjects were protected in the same way as a person or persons residing in that province; provided that the work in question be *printed and published in the Province*. In effect, it created an exclusive colonial market, but so little consideration was given to Canadian affairs that the Board of Trade blindly approved the Act. The Canadian solution clearly conflicted with the Imperial legislation, whose central feature was the first publication in Great Britain. In other words, the Canadian government attempted to subtly eclipse Imperial competence in matters of copyright. The British government was late in reacting. If the Canadian Act was given assent, it was because '...[n]othing in it directly alluded to the Foreign Reprints Act but instead granted copyright protection to British authors who ...printed and published their works in the Province. Since British authors were under the impression that they already enjoyed such privilege under the Imperial Act of 1842, they took little notice.'[105]

Nonetheless, an irregularity remained. The issuance of an Order in Council was necessary to suspend the application of the importation provisions contained in the 1842 *Copyright Act* and to give full effect to the colonial

---

101 '[...] in the case Her Majesty shall be of the opinion that such act or ordinance is sufficient for the purpose, and shall be of the opinion that such act or ordinance is sufficient for the purpose of securing to British authors reasonable protection within such possession, it shall be lawful for Her Majesty [...] to issue an order in council declaring that so long as the provisions of such act or ordinance continue in force within such colony the prohibition [...] against the importing, selling, letting out to hire, exposing for Sale or Hire, or possessing Foreign Reprints of Books first composed, written, printed, or published in the United Kingdom, and entitled to Copyrights therein, shall be suspended so far as regards such Colony: [...].' *Foreign Reprint Act*, *supra* note 98, s. 1.

102 *Supra* note 98.

103 *An Act to extend the Provincial Copyright Act to persons resident in the United Kingdom, 1847* (Can.), 10 Vict., c. 28. Other colonies, including Nova Scotia (1848) and New Brunswick (1848), passed a regulation pursuant to the *Foreign Reprints Act*. See E. J. MacGillivray, *A Treatise Upon The Law of Copyright* (London: John Murray, 1902) at 187, n. 2; J. Shortt, *Law of Copyright*, 2nd ed. (London: Reeves and Turner, 1884) at 136; and W. A. Copinger, *The Law of Copyright*, 2nd ed. (London: Steven and Haynes, 1881) at 499.

104 Barnes, *supra* note 91 at 149.

105 *Ibid*.

provisions. The Governor-General at the time, Lord Elgin, requested that such formality be completed. By doing this and in the face of much resistance, the British authorities proceeded with a new examination of the Canadian statute and ultimately refused to endorse the issuing of the Order. The colonial statute of 1847 attempted a 'divorce' which Imperial law would not tolerate. Canada thus found itself in a stalemate, and returned to the drawing board in order to remedy the situation and find a way to accommodate the Imperial requirement.[106] Since the Canadian law of 28 July 1847 was stillborn, the sitting Parliament of the Province of Canada adopted a new Act in 1850.[107] This second attempt satisfied the British government. Following other colonies' initiatives,[108] the Act established a compensation system by which British authors would receive an *ad valorem* royalty '...not to exceed more than twenty percent on imported books in this province, upon which a literary property right exists, and which are originally composed or written in the United Kingdom.' The royalty was set at 12.5 per cent.[109]

Canada capitulated on its very legitimate attempts to be master on its territory. Importing was still permitted and the reader could read, but at what cost? The reader barely remained the sole owner of his culture, the fruits of which belonged to others. He was deprived of the right to reprint English works, as we will see; and forced to import books from abroad at a prohibitive cost (British publications). Canadian printers and publishers emerged from the stalemate as big losers. By contrast, American printers greatly benefited from colonial and Imperial measures. They continued with impunity to manufacture and supply Canada with new editions of English books, an exportation that was sanctioned by the *Foreign Reprints Act*. Excluded from this *de facto*

---

106 'Canadians took the better part of two years to secure the passage of a new Act which conformed to the provisions of the Foreign Reprints Act, and in the meantime conditions became increasingly chaotic. [...] According to the prevailing Copyright and Customs Acts of 1842 British authors and publishers had to notify the Customs of their latest copyright works which were then incorporated into lists forwarded to the colonies every three months. Clever booksellers and publishers in Canada recognized the time-lag between the date of publication and the receipt of quarterly lists and simply imported all the American reprints they wished during the interval.' Barnes, *supra* note 91 at 150.

107 *An Act to impose duty on Foreign re-prints of British Copyright Works, 1850* (Can.), 13 & 14 Vict., c. 6.

108 Bermuda, for instance, adopts in 1848, an *ad valorem* duty of 15 per cent on importation, *Papers Relating to Copyright (colonies), Colonial Copyright Acts* (Ottawa: 1875) at 25. There is also indication that acts to the same effect were passed in Jamaica, British Guiana, Bahamas, St. Vincent, Cape, Natal, Mauritius, Barbados, St. Lucia, Antigua and St. Kitts. We learn in addition that the rates of duty imposed by these Acts vary from 15 to 25 per cent *ad valorem*.

109 Copinger, *supra* note 103 at 500.

reprinting privilege,[110] some Canadian publishers decided to take the law into their own hands. In order to benefit from the same Imperial regime, they installed their printing presses in the United States, and then supplied their own bookshops in Canada.[111] According to Parker,

> Few people foresaw in the 1840s that the Americans would gain control of the Canadian market because a British act was passed in order to provide Canadians with cheap reading material; after all, one of the great liberal platforms of the nineteenth century was cheap reading for everyone. This situation led to the Canadian market becoming a battleground for American and British publishers, and skirmishes continued into the twentieth century because the British presence remained significant until the 1920s.[112]

For the British Government, the licensing scheme did not have the anticipated success. Although Canadian customs authorities regularly received the list from London of protected works for which a right of entry had to be collected, collecting remained difficult and proved to be a burden for Canadian authorities. During a period of 10 years, ending in 1876, the total amount collected by the 19 British colonies in application of the statute of 1847 amounted to £1,155.13, with Canada having contributed the amount of £1084.13 during this same period.[113] At the end of the 1850s, both the Canadian and the British governments began a new round of negotiations in order to find better arrangements. This was most needed from the Canadian side, since the importation exemption had already done great damage to the Canadian industry. Its presses remained silent while its bookshops were inundated with books printed in the United States. For its part, the British Government pressured the Canadian Government for better protection of its authors.

The *British North America Act* of 1867 – which united Nova Scotia, New Brunswick and Canada – subjected intellectual property matters to Federal

---

110 'They contended that although they might import and sell American reprints on paying the duty, they were not allowed to republish British works, and to have the advantage of the trade, the sole benefit of which was, in effect, secured for Americans', 'Report of the Commission of 1878', in Putnam, *supra* note 7 at 260, para. 195.

111 Seville, *supra* note 10 at 98.

112 Parker, *supra* note 12 at 258.

113 Briggs, *supra* note 99 at 608. Numbers are reproduced in *Report of the Royal Commission of 1878*, in Putnam, *supra* note 7 at 260, para. 193. Other figures are presented in the report sent by the Board of Trade to the Colonial Office: 'It appears from the last return (which is for 1866), that in that year 145*l*. 0*s*. 9*d*. was received from the whole of the 19 Colonies which have taken the advantage of the Act, of which 117*l*. 1*s*. 6*d*., was remitted by the colonists now forming the Canadian Dominion': *Papers Relating to Colonial Copyright*, *supra* note 86, Dispatch No 33 at 27.

Parliamentary competence and provided the occasion for both parties to reopen the copyright question. In 1868, two important legislative initiatives unfolded. First, Canadian Parliament passed *An Act Respecting Copyrights, 1868*[114] which set out the requirements for printing and publication in Canada. Second, *An Act to Impose a Duty on Foreign Reprints of British Copyright Works*[115] reintroduced the *ad valorem* duty on imported works. This legislation received Royal Assent that same year, but it did not seem to satisfy British authorities, since it still required publication and printing in the colony. Doubts also existed as to the expediency of the duty system in light of the British demand of a reasonable protection. Canada, after three attempts, passed the 1875 Act which granted full protection to British authors provided that they *reprint* or *republish*. In the meantime, the *Foreign Reprints Act* (1847) regime had not been explicitly repealed. Confusion as to its effect was complete. In 1877, the Court of Appeal in *Smiles v. Belford* was of the view that its regime was still valid and noticed, in passing, that the only solution for a British author to protect himself from undesirable foreign imports was to subject his work to the Canadian statute of 1875. Upon examination of the effect of the Canadian legislation, the Court stated that: '...it was intended to preserve intact so much of the Imperial Act as prohibits the printing of a British copyright work in Canada, but giving to the author a further right on certain conditions of securing a Canadian copyright, and thus preventing the importation into Canada of foreign reprints.'[116] This reading of the Canadian law appears to have been followed by a number of specialists. In 1894, a Canadian law on custom tariffs[117] eliminated the 12.5 per cent royalty collected on foreign editions of English works. Was the importation under the exception set out in 1847 still possible? With duty abolished, some felt that the full effect of the Imperial *Copyright Act* of 1842[118] should be restored and, therefore, be used as a ban on imports of foreign editions of the British author. This was also the opinion of MacGillivray:

> Although Canada came under the Foreign Reprints Act, 1847, and in accordance therewith imposed duties on foreign reprints for the benefit of the owner of the copyright, the collection of those duties has now been abandoned by the Tariff Customs Act (Canada), 1894, the result of which is that as regards Canada the

---

114 *An Act respecting Copyrights, 1868* (Can.), 31 Vict., c. 54.

115 *An Act to impose a duty on Foreign Reprints of British Copyright Works, 1868* (Can.), 31 Vict., c. 56.

116 *Smiles v. Belford, supra* note 73 at 445.

117 *An Act to consolidate and amend the Acts Respecting Customs, 1894* (Can.), 57–58 Vict., c. 33.

118 See also *Morang and Co. v. Publishers' Syndicate* (1900), 32 O.R. 393.

provisions of the Imperial Act, 1842, section 17, are revived and the importation of foreign copies of works having an Imperial copyright is again prohibited.[119]

Ironically, Canadian publishers who had started to negotiate private arrangements with English counterparts to reprint or republish British works in Canada (an encouraging result of the 1875 Canadian *Copyright Act*) shared similar concerns over the question of importation. It appears that the Canadian publisher desirous of publishing a British work in Canada remained without recourse against importation. The Imperial law reserved this right to the British author or publisher, should the *Copyright Act* 1842 be given full effect. The law did not yet provide him with any of the guarantees that he needed in order to pursue his activities in Canada. Following continued representations in London, Canada took the lead and managed to eliminate a 'double lock' of, first, the reproduction right and, then, the importation right. Both rights had originally been reserved for the British rightholder. In 1889, the Canadian Parliament adopted an act authorizing Canadian publishers, under certain conditions, to print and publish works for which a copyright would have been obtained in Canada, but which were not published in sufficient quantities to respond to the demand. It also implemented the obligation incumbent on British publishers to publish in Canada. Then, in 1900, the Canadian legislature amended the law of copyright allowing Canadian publishers to forbid all imports or competing distribution of works protected by imperial laws.[120] The statute granted the Minister of Agriculture the power to decree a ban on the import of a book printed outside of Canada.

Embargo on the Reproduction Right

The operation of the legal provisions regarding the importation remedies and that of the reproduction right are interconnected. British publishers relied on the reproduction right as a means to achieve British exportation. Faithful

[119] MacGillivray, *supra* note 103 at 188. See also, Kevin Garnett, Jonathan Rayner James & Gillian Davies, *Copinger and Skone James on Copyright*, 14th ed. (London: Sweet & Maxwell, 1999) at 1546.

[120] *An Act to amend the Copyright Act, 1900* (Can.), 63-64 Vict., c. 25, s. 1: 'If a book as to which there is subsisting copyright under The Copyright Act has been first lawfully published in any part of Her Majesty's dominions other than Canada, and if it is proved to the satisfaction of the Minister of Agriculture that the owner of the copyright so subsisting and of the copyright acquired by such publication has lawfully granted a license to reproduce in Canada, [...] the Minister may, notwithstanding anything in The Copyright Act, by order under his hand, prohibit the importation, except with the written consent of the licensee, into Canada of any copies of such book printed elsewhere [...].'

companion and complement of importation remedies, the reproduction right granted to British authors (by virtue of the Imperial *Copyright Act* of 1842) served to furnish its rightholders with a definite production and distribution monopoly. It is worth noting however, that – even if the idea has been suggested in legal literature for some time – copyright was generally perceived as an assignable, but not a divisible right. Publishers rarely resorted to territorial assignment of copyright. This would explain, in part, their hesitation to entrust Canadian publishers with the reprinting of their books. Evidence of this limitation is to be found in the 1884 edition of Shortt's work entitled *Law of Copyright*: 'The point has not been expressly decided in any case, but the opinions of several eminent judges are in favour of the view that copyright is not divisible as to locality.'[121] True, s. 13 of the 1842 British *Copyright Act* already provided that copyright may be granted in whole or in part. However, the concession contemplated by the legislature consisted more of a division in time or on a part of the work, as opposed to a territorial allocation. In addition, British publishers did not truly believe in a market in which exploitation depended directly on the fate reserved to the protection of British authors in the United States, a larger and far more threatening market. American publishers and printers constituted competition which would be difficult to thwart unless a reciprocity agreement was concluded. For these reasons, British diplomatic and commercial efforts would essentially be directed towards the conclusion of an arrangement with the United States, with Canada remaining in the shadow of the negotiations. While the Board of Trade recognized the anomalous position of Canadian publishers with respect to their counterparts in the United States, the British authorities were of the opinion that the Canadian question should be considered in connection with any negotiations conducted with the United States.[122]

The *Foreign Reprints Act* of 1847 contributed to the draining of the Canadian publishing industry, since it diverted the means of production and fabrication of books to the United States and England.[123] Canada strove to repatriate the reproduction right within its jurisdiction; first with the enactment

---

[121] Shortt, *supra* note 103 at 166.

[122] 'Board of Trade to Colonial Office, 22 July 1868' in *Papers Relating to Colonial Copyright*, *supra* note 86, Dispatch N. 27 at 22.

[123] In a letter dated 11 June 1868 and addressed to John Rose, Minister of Finance, John Lovell wrote: 'It is undeniable that Canadian printers would be enabled to comply with the requisite conditions and produce books, thanks to local advantages, at much cheaper rate than they can be produced in the States, and so bring about a large export business. This would have the happy effect of bringing back a large number of our skilled workmen who have been forced to leave the Dominion to find a remunerative field of labour': *Papers Relating to Colonial Copyright*, *supra* note 86, Dispatch No 20 at 18.

of the 1847 Canadian Act implementing the 1847 *Foreign Reprints Act*, and then in 1868 imposing upon any person residing in Great Britain or Ireland the requirement to print and publish in Canada in order to benefit from the Act's protection. The colonial ambition was challenged in the courts, and their decisions caused great disillusionment: they affirmed the pre-emption of Imperial Government over copyright matters in the colonies as far as British authors' interests were concerned.[124] Until the passing of the Canadian *Copyright Act* 1921, the British *Copyright Act* of 1842 would therefore be given authority. Commenting on British law ruling, Dawson wrote: 'And yet so selfish were the framers of that measure, so reckless of the interests of all but English manufacturers, that they made it extend over the whole Empire. They were determined to centre the printing trade in the British Isles.'[125] The *Home and Colonial Library* Project serves to illustrate the views of London publishers on Canada. In an effort to discourage smuggling of American reprints, and aware of the shortage of books felt in the colonies, John Murray, an influential English publisher – and a man of good intentions some would argue – proposed a catalogue of works offered in an economical format which was destined for colonial readers. Judging from the titles listed in the *Colonial Library*, one could question his motives. Amongst old classics, the reader could opt for *The Missionary Life in Canada*, *The Southey's Life of Nelson*, and *The French in Algiers*.[126] Enduring the seemingly fraternal, yet patriarchal, yoke of the laws of Westminster, and then having a list of old and chosen works imposed on them was simply inappropriate to colonial readers.

Conflict with the Imperial Government on this point reached its climax in 1872. The text adopted by the Canadian Parliament provided for a legal licensing scheme for the reproduction right – an *ad valorem* duty of 12.5 per cent – adopted from the model put into force by the 1847 *Foreign Reprints Act* on importation. It was, as Seville states, '...an extraordinary challenge to the imperial Parliament',[127] which ultimately was, as we know, defeated when Royal Assent was withheld. The commercial situation substantially improved with the Canadian *Copyright Act* of 1875, which invited British publishers to republish and reprint their works to obtain protection, including, as we have seen, the additional right to prevent importation of foreign reprints in Canada.

---

[124] *Smiles v. Belford*, *supra* note 73 at 443, Burton, J, following the decision in *Routledge v. Low*, *supra* note 28. See also, *Hubert v. Mary*, *supra* note 28; and *Black v. The Imperial Book Company*, *supra* note 28. *Contra*: *Hodge v. The Queen* (1883), 9 App. Cas. Rep. 17; *Harris v. Davies* (1885), 10 App. Cas. Rep. 282; and *Riel v. The Queen* (1885), 10 App. Cas. Rep. 675.

[125] Dawson, 'Copyright in Books', *supra* note 52 at 18.

[126] Barnes, *supra* note 91 at 144.

[127] Seville, *supra* note 10 at 103. See *An Act to remove Doubts as to the Validity of Colonial Laws, 1865* (UK), 28 & 29 Vict., c. 63.

These measures definitely contributed to the encouragement of trade and arrangements between British and Canadian publishers. Nonetheless, this evolution in trade practices was slow, and the participation of British publishers in Canadian interests was inconsistent. Canadian publishing would therefore depend largely on the future of the colonial situation of Canada as a whole.

CONCLUSION

The coexistence of two distinct laws in Canada has led to much confusion and disappointment. Canadians' struggles with the last gasp of Imperial interventionism did not pass unnoticed. It prompted diplomatic initiatives from the French government towards an arrangement with Great Britain in order, among other things, to secure protection of its authors in the lost colony of Canada. In January 1896, a memorandum prepared by French literary and artistic associations was forwarded to the interested governments protesting against British approval of any Canadian act which would make manufacture in Canada a prerequisite to copyright.[128] European exporters and publishers thus supported the long-armed Imperial statute. The Canadian experience, we believe, precipitated the conclusion of bilateral instruments, as well as the signature of the Berne Convention. From one side of the Atlantic, the circulation of pirated – or rather, should we say, copies legally reprinted without authorization of the foreign author – reprints manufactured in reckless countries was the evil to be eradicated. The protection in Canada and in the United States of English and French authors depended largely on their acquiescence to the national treatment principle, a newly devised rule that would facilitate control over dependent markets of the New World. On the other hand, readers' voices were raised to claim cheaper books. In addition, the right of making print in its territory was vital for the Canadian cultural and commercial future.

In an act of great defiance (or perhaps of exasperation), Canada declined to be bound by the actions of the Imperial government and withdrew from the Berne Convention. It became a signatory to the 1886 Convention in 1928, more than 30 years after Great Britain. What is remarkable in this unique history is Canada's resistance to the Imperial *diktat*. Even more remarkable, when Canada was given the means to its aspirations in 1911, it adopted the exact same language as that contained in the *British Copyright Act* of 1911. It

[128] Putnam, *supra* note 7 at 473. A special 'Manufacturing Clause' was also inserted in the American *Chace Act* of 1891 in order to secure the interests of the American printing industry. See *Chace Act*, *supra* note 5, s. 4956. See also Briggs, *supra* note 99 at 642.

was as if the accession to political and economical independence suddenly sufficed to wash away decades of frustration. The position of Canada with respect to the copyright question in those colonial years was certainly an anomaly; having achieved great progress in material prosperity, the conditions for its cultural development were yet to be asserted. The colonial copyright episode was a quest for legislative and commercial independence, and for its accession to the international scene.

7. Canadian originality: remarks on a judgment in search of an author[1]

Abraham Drassinower

The standard of originality in Canadian copyright law has recently undergone significant transformation. Traditionally a jurisdiction that, in the eyes of many, had adopted a 'sweat of the brow' standard, Canada is now a 'skill and judgment' jurisdiction.[2]

This chapter (1) describes and contextualizes the shift; (2) analyzes its presuppositions in respect of the Canadian conception of the purpose of copyright law; and (3) identifies difficulties and ambiguities that may preclude its full development. I will argue that the doctrinal shift is in tension with certain

---

[1] I would like to thank Ysolde Gendreau for the opportunity to contribute to this discussion of Canadian copyright and its implications. I would also like to thank Bruce Chapman, Andrea Slane, and Arnold Weinrib for helpful conversations during the preparation of this paper; Arnold Weinrib and an anonymous reviewer for comments on an earlier draft; Sooin Kim for her excellence as a librarian; and the Social Sciences and Humanities Research Council of Canada and the Centre for Innovation Law and Policy at the University of Toronto Faculty of Law for ongoing support.

[2] See *CCH Canadian Ltd. v. Law Society of Upper Canada*, [2004] 1 S.C.R. 339 at para. 16 [*CCH*]. For commentary, see Teresa Scassa, 'Original Facts: Skill, Judgment, and the Public Domain' (2006) 51 McGill Law Journal 253; Ramón Casas Vallés, 'Bibliotecas jurídicas y propiedad intelectual: El caso de la Gran Biblioteca del Colegio de Abogados de Ontario' (2005) 4 Revista Jurídica de Catalunya 26; Carys Craig, 'The Evolution of Originality in Canadian Copyright Law: Authorship, Reward and the Public Interest' (2005) 2 University of Ottawa Law & Technology Journal 425; Abraham Drassinower, 'Taking User Rights Seriously' in Michael Geist, ed., *In the Public Interest: The Future of Canadian Copyright Law* (Toronto: Irwin, 2005), 462 [Drassinower, 'User Rights']; Michael Geist 'Low-Tech Case Has High-Tech Impact' *Toronto Star* (22 March 2004); Daniel J. Gervais, 'Canadian Copyright Law Post-CCH' (2004) 18 Intellectual Property Journal 131 [Gervais, 'Post-CCH']; Matthew Rimmer, 'Canadian Rhapsody: Copyright Law and Research Libraries' (2004) 35 Australian Academic & Research Libraries 193; Teresa Scassa, 'Recalibrating Copyright Law? A Comment on the Supreme Court of Canada's Decision in CCH Canadian Ltd. v. Law Society of Upper Canada' (2004) 3 Canadian Journal of Law and Technology 89 [Scassa, 'Recalibrating']; Barry B. Sookman, 'CCH: A Seminal Canadian Case on Originality and the Fair Dealing Defence' (2004) 18 BNA World Intellectual Property Report 08.

aspects of the vision of the purpose of copyright law in the name of which it took place. I will also speculate as to the conditions for the possibility of a resolution of that tension. In short, my point is that the historical struggle between originality schools has not been overcome. It has transmuted into a struggle between a value paradigm and an authorship paradigm of copyright law.

I *CCH v. LAW SOCIETY* AND THE COPYRIGHT TRADITION

In *CCH*, the Supreme Court of Canada set out to settle the meaning of originality in Canadian copyright law.[3] Faced with a battle between two opposing originality schools, the 'sweat of the brow' and the 'creativity' schools, the Court refused to take sides in the debate.[4] It posited, rather, a third standpoint, for which the requirement of originality is a requirement of 'skill and judgment'. The Court formulated its refusal to side with either school by invoking a vision of the purpose of copyright law as a 'balance' between 'promoting the public interest' and 'obtaining a just reward for the creator'.[5] On this basis, the Court found that while the sweat of the brow school supports too author-centred a standard, the creativity school supports too public-centred a stan-

3 The case opposed plaintiff publishers CCH Canadian, Thomson Canada, and Canada Law Book, and defendant library Great Library at Osgoode Hall in Toronto, operated by the Law Society of Upper Canada. Members of the Law Society, the judiciary and other authorized researchers could request photocopies of materials from the library. The materials were copied by the library staff and delivered in person, by mail or by fax to the requesters. The publishers commenced an action against the library in respect of alleged infringements of copyright resulting from the library's photocopying service, and also from usage by the patrons of self-service photocopiers provided by the library. The Court held, *inter alia*, (1) that the publishers' materials were original works subject to copyright protection; (2) that the self-service photocopiers did not implicitly authorize reproduction of the materials; and (3) that the library successfully made out the defence of fair dealing for research purposes in respect of the photocopying service. In the course of its reasoning the Court defined originality as 'skill and judgment' and fair dealing as a 'user's right' not to be interpreted restrictively.

4 On the struggle between the sweat of the brow and creativity schools, see Abraham Drassinower, 'Sweat of the Brow, Creativity, and Authorship: On Originality in Canadian Copyright Law' (2004) 1 University of Ottawa law & Technology Journal 105 [Drassinower, 'Sweat of the Brow']. See also Yo'av Mazeh, 'Canadian Originality and the Tension Between the Commonwealth and The American Standards for Copyright Protection' (2003) 16 Intellectual Property Journal 561.

5 *CCH*, *supra* note 2 at para. 10.

dard.[6] In this vein, the Court presented its own skill and judgment standard as 'workable, yet fair'.[7] Thus the Court viewed the skill and judgment standard as an in-between truly attuned to the dual purpose animating copyright law as a whole.

The Court defined 'skill and judgment' as follows:

> I conclude that the correct position falls between these extremes. For a work to be 'original' within the meaning of the *Copyright Act*, it must be more than a mere copy of another work. At the same time, it need not be creative, in the sense of being novel or unique. What is required to attract copyright protection in the expression of an idea is an exercise of skill and judgment. By skill, I mean the use of one's knowledge, developed aptitude or practised ability in producing the work. By judgment, I mean the use of one's capacity for discernment or ability to form an opinion or evaluation by comparing different possible options in producing the work. This exercise of skill and judgment will necessarily involve intellectual effort. The exercise of skill and judgment required to produce the work must not be so trivial that it could be characterized as a purely mechanical exercise. For example, any skill and judgment that might be involved in simply changing the font of a work to produce 'another' work would be too trivial to merit copyright protection as an 'original' work.[8]

The difference between sweat of the brow and skill and judgment is sufficiently clear. The sweat of the brow standard provides that labour and industry, even in the absence of skill and judgment, may be sufficient to make out a finding of originality.[9] Under the sweat of the brow standard, the labour invested in the collection of the information that makes up an ordinary phone directory, for example, gives rise to copyright protection. The phone directory is original in the sense that it was not copied from another work. The fact that

---

6 *Ibid.* at para. 24: 'The "sweat of the brow" approach to originality is too low a standard. It shifts the balance of copyright protection too far in favour of the owner's rights, and fails to allow copyright to protect the public's interest in maximizing the production and dissemination of intellectual works. On the other hand, the creativity standard of originality is too high. A creativity standard implies that something must be novel or non-obvious – concepts more properly associated with patent law than copyright law. By way of contrast, a standard requiring the exercise of skill and judgment in the production of a work avoids these difficulties and provides a workable and appropriate standard for copyright protection that is consistent with the policy objectives of the *Copyright Act*.'

7 *Ibid.*

8 *Ibid.* at para. 16.

9 See, for example, *U & R Tax v. H & R Block* (1995), 62 C.P.R. (3d) 257 at 264 (F.C.T.D.): 'A work must be "original" in order to be afforded copyright. Industriousness ("sweat of the brow") as opposed to creativity is enough to give a work sufficient originality to make it copyrightable.' See also *Kelly v. Morris* (1866), L.R. 1 Eq. 69.

the production of an alphabetically arranged phone directory could be characterized as a merely mechanical and automatic task does not affect the directory's copyrightability.

The difference between creativity and skill and judgment, however, is more elusive. This impression is reinforced by the peculiar and surprising fact that in *CCH* the Canadian Supreme Court misrepresented the creativity standard. In the context of a discussion of the landmark US Supreme Court case, *Feist Publications v. Rural Telephone Service*,[10] the Court stated that the creativity standard entails a patent-like requirement of novelty or non-obviousness.[11] The Court then added that its own Canadian skill and judgment standard is therefore preferable for copyright purposes. In *Feist*, however, the US Supreme Court explicitly stated that 'originality does not signify novelty' and, moreover, that the creativity standard is 'extremely low'.[12] Thus, it is hard to avoid the impression that, given its misunderstanding of the creativity standard, the Supreme Court of Canada happens to occupy with the phrase 'skill and judgment' the very same space generally thought to be occupied by the word 'creativity'.[13] Otherwise, one would have to credit the Supreme Court of Canada with the mysterious achievement of having found a significant midpoint between zero and 'extremely low'.

While important ambiguities regarding the difference between the Court's skill and judgment standard and the creativity standard have been noted, few have doubted that *CCH* represents an unambiguous rejection of the sweat of the brow standard, a standard many regard as the traditional Anglo-Canadian standard.[14] This rejection of the traditional sweat of the brow approach to orig-

---

10 499 U.S. 340 (1991) [*Feist*]. The US Supreme Court denied copyright protection to an ordinary white pages phone directory, establishing explicitly and definitively that 'creativity', not 'sweat of the brow', is the applicable originality standard in the US.

11 *CCH*, *supra* note 2 at para. 24: 'A creativity standard implies that something must be novel or non-obvious – concepts more properly associated with patent law than copyright law.'

12 *Feist*, *supra* note 10 at para. 10. See also paras. 41 and 49.

13 See, for example, Daniel J. Gervais and Elizabeth Judge, *Intellectual Property: The Law in Canada* (Toronto: Carswell, 2005) at 23: 'But it seems that the Supreme Court [of Canada] chose a "middle-path" only in appearance. Canada instead has taken on a standard essentially identical to those of our American neighbours and to the Continental systems.' See also Drassinower, 'Sweat of the Brow', *supra* note 4 at 123; Gervais, 'Post-CCH', *supra* note 2 at 7; Scassa, 'Recalibrating', *supra* note 2 at 91.

14 See, for example, Norman Siebrasse, 'Copyright in Facts and Information: Feist Publications is Not and Should Not be, the Law in Canada' (1994) 11 Canadian Intellectual Property Review 191 [Siebrasse, 'Facts and Information'].

inality is one manifestation of the judgment's status as a landmark transformation of the originality standard in Canadian copyright jurisprudence.

Of course, while it is not incorrect to emphasize the innovative dimension of the judgment, and hence its discontinuity with antecedent case law, it would be incorrect to forget that the judgment settled an ongoing struggle between originality schools, and that therefore elements of the side that emerged victorious in *CCH* were themselves present in the copyright tradition from which *CCH* apparently seeks to differentiate itself. The continuity between *CCH* and the copyright tradition should not be underestimated.[15] Moreover, just as it is to be expected that elements of the victorious side were already present in the copyright tradition, it is equally to be suspected – contrary to first impressions – that elements of the defeated side, albeit in altered or disguised form, remain operative in *CCH*. This is all the more likely where – at least in the Court's own self-understanding – *CCH* did not so much pick a side in the struggle it settled, as much as framed a mid-point between the contending schools.

In what follows I analyze two classic authorities on originality, *University of London Press v. University Tutorial Press* and *Walter v. Lane*. My purpose in doing so is twofold. First, I want to find in these two classic authorities traces of the struggle between sweat of the brow and creativity schools, and hence to appraise the presence in each of these authorities of an alternative to the sweat of the brow standard. Second, I expect to learn from that exercise what some of the fundamental implications of the shift from sweat of the brow to skill and judgment must be. It is only in this way that we can hope to understand the relationship between *CCH* and the copyright tradition, and therefore the significance of *CCH* for the development of that tradition.

II *UNIVERSITY OF LONDON PRESS v. UNIVERSITY TUTORIAL PRESS*

Briefly stated, the facts in *University of London Press* pertinent to the originality question were as follows. Professor Lodge and Mr Jackson were hired

15 Consider, for example, *Caron v. Association des Pompiers* (1992), 42 C.P.R. (3d) 292 at 294–295 (F.C.T.D.) [*Caron*]: 'In this regard, I consider that they [the defendants] were not able to show on a balance of probabilities that the compilations produced by the plaintiff required no creativity.' See also *Tele-Direct (Publications) Inc. v. American Business Information, Inc.* (1997), 76 C.P.R. (3d) 296 at 303, 307–8 (F.C.A.) [*Tele-Direct*]; *Kilvington v. Goldberg* (1957), 8 D.L.R. (2d) 768 at 770 (Ont. H.C.) [*Kilvington*]; *Cramp v. Smythson*, [1944] A.C. 329 at 335–6 [*Cramp*]; and *MacMillan v. Cooper* (1923), 93 L.J.P.C. 113 at 186–7, 40 T.L.R. 186 (J.C.P.C. – India) [*Macmillan*].

by the University of London to set entrance examinations in mathematics. It was a condition of their being hired that copyright in the examination papers vested in the University. Together they set three examination papers, one in arithmetic and algebra, a second in geometry, and a third in more advanced mathematics. (Accordingly, the Court referred to the first two papers as 'elementary', in contrast to the third paper in more 'advanced' mathematics.)[16] The University then assigned the copyright in the examinations to the plaintiff, University of London Press. The Press published the examination papers. But, having obtained copies of the examination papers from students who had taken the examinations, the defendant, University Tutorial Press, also published the examination papers. University of London Press sued for copyright infringement.

In a famous passage, the Court defined 'originality' as follows:

> The word 'original' does not in this connection mean that the work must be the expression of original or inventive thought. Copyright Acts are not concerned with the originality of ideas, but with the expression of thought, and, in the case of 'literary work', with the expression of thought in print or writing. The originality which is required relates to the expression of the thought. But the Act does not require that the expression must be in an original or novel form, but that the work must not be copied from another work – that it should originate from the author.[17]

This passage involves three closely related propositions worth parsing. Two of these propositions tell us what originality is not, and one tells us what it is.

The first proposition is that originality is not novelty of thought. It is trite copyright law that to express an old or familiar idea anew in one's own words is to be original for copyright purposes.[18] Originality is not about *what* the work says – whether novel or otherwise – but about *how* the work says it. It pertains not to content but to form, not to idea but to expression.

The second proposition is that originality is not about novelty in expres-

---

[16] *University of London Press v. University Tutorial Press*, [1916] 2 Ch. 601 at 609 [*University of London Press*].

[17] *Ibid.* at 608–9.

[18] On the idea/expression dichotomy, see, for example, *Moreau v. St. Vincent*, [1950] Ex. C.R. 198 at 203 (Can. Ex. Ct.): 'It is .... an elementary principle of copyright law that an author has no copyright in ideas but only in his expression of them. The law of copyright does not give him any monopoly in the use of the ideas with which he deals or any property in them, even if they are original. His copyright is confined to the literary work in which he has expressed them. The ideas are public property, the literary work is his own. Every one may freely adopt and use the ideas but no one may copy his literary work without his consent.' For commentary on the idea/expression dichotomy, see Abraham Drassinower, 'A Rights-Based View of the Idea/Expression Dichotomy in Copyright Law' (2003) 16 Canadian Journal of Law and Jurisprudence 3.

sion. While it is true that originality pertains exclusively to expression, this does not mean that the expression must itself be novel. This is aptly captured in the defence of independent creation. As Justice Learned Hand put it, 'if by some magic a man who had never known it were to compose anew Keats's Ode on a Grecian Urn, he would be an "author", and, if he copyrighted it, others might not copy that poem, though they might of course copy Keats's.'[19]

The third proposition is already contained in the second. What is required for originality is not that the expression be novel in the sense that it has never been composed by anyone else before, but that it be not-copied from another work – that is, that it be original in the sense of being the author's own product. One does not cease to have said something in one's own words just because, coincidentally, another person happens to have used those very same words. The co-incidence, however unexpected or unlikely, does not make one's expression any less one's own. It is this sense of 'one's own' – that of the origins or pedigree of the expression – that originality recognizes. Original means independently created.

Having described the originality standard, the Court in *University of London Press* proceeded to apply it to the facts of the case. Peterson J. pointed out that Professor Lodge and Mr Jackson had proved that they had themselves thought of the questions which they set. They had notes or memoranda proving that they had themselves come up with the questions – that is, that they had not copied them. The examination papers were therefore original within the meaning of the Copyright Act.[20]

The Court then moved on to consider four objections to its holding. Three of them are directly relevant to our present purposes. In essence, the Court's response to these objections was that they are all rooted in a misunderstanding of the meaning of originality. In particular, the objections misunderstand the crucial proposition that originality does not mean novelty. Examining these objections is instructive because, in the course of its response to them, the Court's reasons appear to give rise to a struggle between two distinct views of originality. One of these views is consistent with the Court's manifest formulation that 'original' means 'not-copied from another work'. The other view announces, as it were in latent form, the proposition that 'original' means – to use the Court's own words – involving 'selection, judgment and experience'.[21]

The first objection dealt with by the Court was that, in composing the examinations, the authors '*drew upon* the stock of knowledge common to

---

19 *Sheldon v. Metro-Goldwyn Pictures Corp.*, 81 F.2d 49 at 54 (2d Cir. 1936).
20 *University of London Press*, *supra* note 16 at 609.
21 *Ibid.*

mathematicians'.[22] The Court replied that drawing from the common stock of knowledge does not preclude originality. Originality is not novelty, otherwise 'only those historians who discovered fresh historical facts could acquire copyright for their works'.[23] The objection is untenable in that it suggests that originality turns on the novelty of the information conveyed in a work. The work of Professor Lodge and Mr Jackson met the originality standard because they did not copy from the common stock; they only drew upon it. While *copying* from the common stock is indeed inconsistent with originality, *drawing* from the common stock does not preclude originality.

The second objection was that the examination questions set by Professor Lodge and Mr Jackson were questions in 'book work' – that is, 'questions set for the purpose of seeing whether the student has read and understood the books prescribed by the syllabus'.[24] This objection is but a version of the first; namely, that a work is not original if it draws from another. The Court therefore responds by affirming once again the proposition that originality is not novelty and that drawing from another work does not preclude originality. To be sure, the objection here is not that the examiners drew from the common stock but rather that they drew from the specific books prescribed by the syllabus. Still, the answer is basically the same in that it restates that original means not-copied: 'the questions set are not copied from the book'.[25]

Yet the passage in which the Court responds to the 'book work' objection gives us reason to pause:

> Some of the questions, it was urged, are questions in book work, that is to say, questions set for the purpose of seeing whether the student has read and understood the books prescribed by the syllabus. But the questions set are not copied from the book; they are questions prepared by the examiner for the purpose of testing the student's acquaintance with the book, *and in any case it was admitted that the papers involved selection, judgment, and experience*. This objection has not, in my opinion, any substance; if it had, it would only apply to some of the questions in the elementary papers, and would have little, if any, bearing on the paper on advanced mathematics.[26]

The Court's additional remark that the papers involved 'selection, judgment and experience' is puzzling. The remark is at best unnecessary and at worst counter-productive. It is unnecessary in that, on the view that original means not-copied from another work, the papers would be original even if they had

22 *Ibid.* [emphasis added].
23 *Ibid.*
24 *Ibid.*
25 *Ibid.*
26 *Ibid.* [emphasis added].

involved no selection, judgment and experience. The Court does not need to assert that the papers involved 'selection, judgment, and experience' in order to find them original.

The remark is counter-productive in that the criteria of 'selection, judgment and experience' are not necessarily consistent with the 'not-copied from another work' criterion. Garden variety phone directories, to use once again the classic example, can be both 'not copied from another work' *and* involve no 'selection, judgment and experience' in their production. Peterson J. himself raises the possibility of works of such a kind when he comments that the 'book work' objection 'would only apply to some of the questions in the elementary papers, and would have little, if any, bearing on the paper on advanced mathematics'. It is as if Peterson J. were saying that if originality were about 'selection, judgment, and experience', the 'elementary papers' could be denied protection. Thus the comment seems to be some kind of concession on Peterson J.'s part that the originality determination is easier in respect of the paper on advanced mathematics because it is easier to characterize that paper as involving 'selection, judgment and experience'. Paradoxically, then, Peterson J. invoked the admission that the papers involved 'selection, judgment, and experience' as a response to the objection that the papers were mere 'book work', yet in so doing he in fact wound up raising the spectre of a standard of originality that at least some of the papers in issue could have some difficulty meeting.

The Court's treatment of the third objection, however, consolidated the proposition that 'selection, judgment, and experience' are not necessary for originality. The third objection was that 'the questions in the elementary papers were of common type'.[27] That is, even if the advanced examination were to be regarded as original on the grounds that its production involved 'selection, judgment, and experience', the elementary examinations could not be so regarded because they were of 'common type'. Note that the objection here was not that the elementary examinations *drew* from the common, but rather that they *were* common, too common – so the objection goes – for the Court to hold that their production involved anything other than copying from the common. Whereas *drawing* from the common in the absence of copying likely involves 'selection, judgment, and experience', *being* common or ordinary is not clearly the result of anything other than purely mechanical or automatic repetition.

Nonetheless, the Court dismissed this objection. The Court once again affirmed the proposition that original does not mean novel – that to be original is simply to be not-copied from another work. Thus, the Court insists that

---

27 *Ibid.*

the elementary examinations, even if common, were not copied from other papers, and therefore, they were original within the meaning of the Copyright Act. What is original as a matter of copyright law may well be common, even ordinary, like the questions in the elementary examinations: 'I suppose that most elementary books on mathematics may be said to be of a common type, but that fact would not give impunity to a predatory infringer. The book and the papers alike originate from the author and are not copied by him from another book or other papers.'[28]

In the wake of the suggestion that 'selection, judgment, and experience' may have a role to play in the determination of originality, the Court's insistence that original means not-copied may seem slightly less persuasive. Yet it is precisely this insistence that renders the judgment a classic 'sweat of the brow' authority. The word 'original' did not find its way into the English Copyright Act until 1911. At the very least, this represented an opening, not seized by the *University of London Press* 1916 Court, to introduce criteria such as 'selection, judgment, and experience' into the copyrightability determination. Had the Court done so, it could have of course reached the same result it actually did. It could have held that the elementary papers, too, involved 'selection, judgment, and experience', even if to a lesser degree than the paper in more advanced mathematics. Such interpretive path would have inevitably brought with it a distinction between mere products and works, as well as between producers and authors. Products lacking 'selection, judgment, and experience' could not be regarded as works of authorship subject to copyright protection, and the requirement of originality would have arisen – however slightly – as a more robust way of guarding entry into the world of copyright. If not the elementary examinations in issue in the case, some products – such as ordinary phone directories – would be refused entry, and by implication, some producers would be denied the honours of authorship. The Court's refusal in 1916 to take up this opportunity is all the more telling in light of the introduction of the word 'original' into the Act in 1911. The refusal is nothing less than a self-conscious decision to affirm a view decisively foreign to any rendering of originality premised on a distinction between production and authorship, between the labour of mere production and the specific work of authorship.

The Court's decision to steer away from narrowing the meaning of originality in response to the 1911 legislative amendment had at least two related determinants. On the one hand, the Court relied on precedents evidencing a wide conception of copyrightability. Before discussing the originality issue, the Court discussed the question whether the examination papers could be

---

28 *Ibid.*

regarded as 'literary work' within the meaning of the Act. 'Under the Act of 1812, which protected "books" ', Peterson J. wrote, 'many things which had no pretensions to literary style acquired copyright; for example, a list of registered bills of sale, a list of foxhounds and hunting days, and trade catalogues; and I see no ground for coming to the conclusion that the present Act was intended to curtail the rights of authors'.[29] If a list of foxhounds and hunting days is worthy of copyright protection, and its producer is therefore an author within the meaning of the Act, then it is understandable that elementary examination papers, and Professor Lodge and Mr Jackson, must also be worthy of the same status. Peterson J. found no reason to hold that 'originality' should be given a more restrictive meaning.

On the other hand, the Court derived inspiration from a particular conception of the purpose of copyright law. Famously, Peterson J. concluded his examination of originality as follows:

> The objections with which I have dealt do not appear to me to have any substance, and, after all, there remains the rough practical test that *what is worth copying is **prima facie** worth protecting*. In my judgment, then, the papers set by Professor Lodge and Mr. Jackson are 'original literary work' and proper subject for copyright under the Act of 1911.[30]

David Vaver makes an important point when he remarks that 'As a legal invitation, this is too crude to be overtly accepted. Taken literally, it begs all questions of copyrightability, infringement, and substantiality.'[31] In *University of London Press*, to give but the nearest of examples, the question was whether copying by the defendants amounted to a wrong to the plaintiff. Naturally, the answer to this question required a determination whether the material copied was subject to copyright. After all, no wrong can be found in the absence of a right. It was precisely in order to determine whether a right had been obtained that Peterson J. examined the issue of originality. Thus, even if only under the guise of a 'rough practical test', inferring the existence of the copyright from the fact of copying is at best puzzling. The procedure raises a presumption that copying is wrongful, yet before any determination as to whether an exclusive right to copy obtains to begin with. The presumption is as odd as would be one establishing that, in negligence cases, damage suffered by a plaintiff is worthy of compensation, yet before reaching a determination as to whether the damage caused was reasonably foreseeable (that is, negligently caused). Just as, in the law of negligence, not all damage caused by the defendant is actionable, so in

---

29 *Ibid.* at 608.
30 *Ibid.* at 609–10 [emphasis added].
31 David Vaver, *Copyright Law* (Toronto: Irwin Law, 2000) at 148.

the law of copyright not all copying amounts to copyright infringement. The maxim that 'what is worth copying is prima facie worth protecting' threatens to collapse any viable distinction between harm and wrong, between mere loss and actionable injury.

A more sympathetic rendering of the maxim would point out that the Court seems concerned with the unauthorized transfer of value from plaintiff to defendant as a result of the defendant's act of reproduction. The defendant could not have denied that what he copied was worth copying – his very act is an affirmation of that proposition. It does not lie in his mouth, so to speak, to deny the appropriation of value involved in his act.[32] The fact of copying thus permits us to deploy against the defendant the inference that the material produced by the plaintiff is worth copying – that is, that in the defendant's own view there is value to be taken. The defendant has after all copied the plaintiff's examination papers in order to publish them in a book of his own, in the expectation of selling that book to students interested in studying previous examinations.

The first 'worth' in the maxim 'what is worth copying is prima facie worth protecting', then, is about *value* – it is literally about the worth of the material copied. But the second 'worth' in the maxim is about *entitlement*. It is less about the value of the plaintiff's product *per se* than about the plaintiff's legally recognized right to exclude others from that value. It is not about the worth of the material, but about whether that material is, so to speak, worthy of legal protection as a matter of copyright law.

As a whole, then, the maxim conveys an affinity between value and entitlement, between the production of value and the entitlement to exclude others from benefits to be derived therefrom; in a word, between origination and copyright protection. From the point of view of this affinity, the purpose of copyright law is to prevent defendants from reaping where they have not sown. Copyright guarantees plaintiffs the value generated through the sweat of their brow.

Peterson J.'s classic judgment is a decision to opt for a standpoint for which originality as a matter of copyright law is a proxy for value-origination, and for which the purpose of copyright law is to remedy the misappropriation of that value. The decision is also a refusal to distinguish the labour of value-production from the specific work of authorship. From this viewpoint, the

---

[32] Consider in this regard *International News Service v. Associated Press*, 248 U.S. 215 (1918) at 239: '[D]efendant, by its very act, admits that it is taking material that has been acquired by complainant as the result of organization and the expenditure of labor, skill, and money, and which is salable by complainant for money, and that defendant in appropriating it and selling it as its own is endeavoring to reap where it has not sown.'

question whether any given value is properly the subject matter of copyright law is to be decided not through an investigation of the specificity of authorship but rather through an interpretation of particular categories of subject matter listed in the statute. Thus, for example, copyright protects not works of authorship, but – to use the language of the Act of 1812 – the value of 'books': whether these are the writings of Robert Louis Stevenson, registered bills of sale, a list of foxhounds and hunting days, trade catalogues, examinations in elementary mathematics, ordinary phone directories, or the poems of Lord Byron.

III *WALTER v. LANE*[33]

The opening lines of Lord Halsbury's classic judgment in *Walter v. Lane* eloquently capture the sweat of the brow approach to originality:

> I should very much regret it if I were compelled to come to the conclusion that the state of the law permitted one man to make profit and to appropriate to himself the labour, skill, and capital of another. And it is not denied that in this case the defendant seeks to appropriate to himself what has been produced by the skill, labour, and capital of others. In the view I take of this case I think the law is strong enough to restrain what to my mind would be a grievous injustice. The law which I think restrains it is to be found in the Copyright Act, and that Act confers what it calls copyright – which means the right to multiply copies – which it confers on the author of books first published in this country.[34]

The affirmation of the normative significance of the sweat of the author's brow generates a vision of copyright law as a remedy for the grievous injustice of misappropriation. Copyright is there in order to preclude reaping by those who have not sown.

---

33 [1900] A.C. 539. The following discussion of *Walter v. Lane* follows closely, though with some alterations, parts of the text of Drassinower, 'Sweat of the Brow', supra note 4.

34 *Walter v. Lane*, *ibid.* at 545. Strictly speaking, use of the phrase 'sweat of the brow' to denote Lord Halsbury's judgment is anachronistic. The phrase describes a school of thought with respect to the originality requirement, but the word 'original' did not find its way into the English Copyright Act until 1911, eleven years after *Walter v. Lane*. Still, in the pre-1911 jurisprudence, including *Walter v. Lane*, the debate about copyrightability took place through inquiry into the meaning of the word 'author'. See Robert Howell & Ysolde Gendreau, 'Qualitative Standards for Protection of Literary and Artistic Property' (Canadian report to the 1994 International Congress of Comparative Law, Athens, 1994) in *Contemporary Law 1994* (Cowansville, Que.: Yvon Blais, 1994) 518 at 521–2, 542–5.

Walter v. Lane involved several public speeches delivered by the Earl of Rosebery. Journalists attended the speeches and reported them *verbatim* in *The Times* newspaper. Sometime after publication of the reports of the Earl of Rosebery's speeches, the defendant published a book that consisted of reports of the very same speeches, preceded by short notes. It was admitted that these reports were taken from the reports in *The Times*. *The Times* sued for copyright infringement, asserting copyright in the verbatim reports of the speeches.

Five judgments were delivered. Four (Earl of Halsbury L.C., Lord Davey, Lord James of Hereford, and Lord Brampton) found in favour of the plaintiff. Lord Robertson dissented.

In *Walter v. Lane*, the Court of Appeal had found in favour of the defendant on the grounds that the reporters were not 'authors' for copyright purposes. To *produce* a verbatim report of a speech is not to *author* a work subject to copyright protection. In Lord Halsbury's view, however, the Court of Appeal's judgment was based on too narrow and misleading a use of the word 'author'. Whatever the word 'author' means in some ordinary or general sense, the word 'author' within the meaning of the Act cannot exclude the producers of a verbatim report such as the one in the case at hand. Lord Halsbury relied on the directory cases, which hold that garden variety phone directories are subject to copyright protection.[35] 'If the producer of such a book [i.e. a phone directory] can be an author within the meaning of the Act,' he writes, 'I am unable to understand why the labour of reproducing spoken words into writing or print and first publishing it as a book does not make the person who has so acted as much an author as the person who writes down the names and addresses of the persons who live in a particular street.'[36] Lord Halsbury's reliance on the directory cases displays an insistence, echoed by Peterson J. in *University of London Press*, that no meaningful distinction can be drawn for copyright purposes between producers and authors, and, by that same token, between products and works. Once again, what is at stake is not 'authorship' in any special sense, but rather the 'grievous injustice' involved in the misappropriation of another's effort – in reaping where another has sown.

Before moving on to Lord Robertson's dissent, I want to pause briefly on Lord James's judgment. Lord James's view is of interest at this point because, while Lord James agrees with Lord Halsbury as regards the result, he nonetheless reaches that result from the standpoint of a distinction between production and authorship. Lord James frames the issue by stating that the report of the speech is 'something different' from and beyond the speech itself.[37] The question is whether this difference represents a 'something' of which any one can

---

35 See, for example, *Kelly v. Morris*, *supra* note 9.

36 *Walter v. Lane*, *supra* note 33 at 546.

37 *Ibid.* at 553.

be regarded as 'the author' within the meaning of the Copyright Act.[38] Lord James finds this mysterious 'something' in what he calls the 'reporter's art'.[39] Taking down the words of a speaker, and certainly of a rapid speaker, Lord James points out, is 'an art requiring considerable training'.[40] In fact, reporters less skilled are 'deficient in this quality of accuracy'.[41] It is on the basis of this quality that Lord James concludes that 'a reporter of a speech under the conditions existing in this case is the *meritorious producer of the something necessary to constitute him an "author"* within the meaning of the Copyright Act.'[42] Thus, although Lord James applies an authorship standard, he nonetheless concurs with Lord Halsbury at the level of the result. Lord James finds the features of authorship in the verbatim reports.

In his dissent, Lord Robertson restricts the meaning of 'authorship' even further than does Lord James. Nothing but literal accuracy, Lord Robertson notes, is required to produce the verbatim reports in question.[43] The reporter of a speech is a good reporter by virtue of a contribution of a purely negative kind. The good reporter 'does not interfere, but faithfully acts as a conduit'.[44] The merit of the verbatim reports, says Lord Robertson, is that 'they present the speaker's thoughts untinctured by the slightest trace of colour of the reporter's mind'.[45] Thus, Lord Robertson's view is that the very merit of the reports is what indicates that the reports are not copyrightable. The rival of a good stenographer is the phonograph, and it is hard to see, says Lord Robertson, 'how, in the widest sense of the term "author", we are in *the region of authorship*'.[46] Lord Robertson's judgment is thus premised on an affirmation of the specificity of the work of authorship, and, therefore, on a distinction between mental products *per se* and the specific works of authorship.

As regards the directory cases on which Lord Halsbury relies, Lord Robertson insists that they are not inconsistent with his affirmation of the specificity of authorship. Thus Lord Robertson admits that there are cases that apply the words of the Act to 'very pedestrian efforts of the mind', such as furniture catalogues and timetables.[47] Still, he insists that even such pedestrian efforts of the mind nonetheless exhibit 'structure and arrangement on the part

38 *Ibid.*
39 *Ibid.* at 554.
40 *Ibid.*
41 *Ibid.* at 555.
42 *Ibid.* [emphasis added].
43 *Ibid.* at 560.
44 *Ibid.*
45 *Ibid.* at 561.
46 *Ibid.* [emphasis added].
47 *Ibid.*

of the maker'.[48] In the end, Lord Robertson's view is that 'the recording by stenography the words of another is in a *different region* from the making-up a timetable'. 'I do not say it is [a] lower or higher [region],' he is careful to add, 'but in a different plane, *because there is no construction*'.[49]

Thus, if Lord Halsbury does not require anything more than the undifferentiated and unspecified labour of production, and Lord James requires, in addition, the application of a 'skill' of some kind, Lord Robertson requires not the application of just *any* skill, but the application of *a particular skill or faculty he identifies with 'authorship'*: 'The word "author" ', he writes, 'seems to me to present a criterion consistent with the widest application of the Act to all who can claim as embodying their own thought, whether humble or lofty, the letterpress of which they assert their authorship'.[50] Whatever else he might be, a stenographer is not an author, and copyright is about authorship.

Whereas Lord Halsbury affirms a view of copyright concerned with the origination and protection of value, Lord Robertson affirms a view of copyright concerned with the specificity of authorship. This tension *between* the two judgments appears internalized as a tension *within* Peterson J.'s judgment in *University of London Press*. It is as if the intervening insertion of the word 'original' into the Act had compelled Peterson J. to gesture, albeit unnecessarily and counter-productively, toward 'selection, judgment, and experience' in his discussion of the distinction between elementary and advanced examinations. Lord Halsbury was far less ambiguous: '[I]f I have not insisted upon the skill and accuracy of those who produce in writing or print spoken words', he wrote, 'it is not because I think the less of those qualities, but because, as I have endeavoured to point out, neither the one nor the other are conditions precedent to the right created by the statute'.[51]

IV *CCH* REVISITED

It will be recalled that in *CCH* the Supreme Court of Canada affirmed the skill and judgment originality standard by invoking a vision of the purpose of copyright law as a balance between two objectives, promoting the public interest, on the one hand, and obtaining a just reward for the creator, on the other. As noted above, it was in terms of this balance that the Court dismissed both the sweat of the brow and the creativity standards as extremes of which the skill

48 *Ibid.*
49 *Ibid.* [emphasis added].
50 *Ibid.* at 562.
51 *Ibid.* at 549.

and judgment standard is the appropriate mean – in between inappropriately 'low' and inappropriately 'high' alternatives.

Neither the metaphor of a balance, nor that of a continuum from 'low' to 'high', however, provide sufficient basis either to explain or to justify the shift from sweat of the brow to skill and judgment. The result of this justificatory vacuum is truly striking. In *CCH* the skill and judgment rhetoric of a copyright model centred on the specificity of authorship co-exists with the generation and distribution of benefits rhetoric of a copyright model centred on the origination of value. If *University of London Press* exhibited traces, however slight, of an internalized struggle, so to speak, between Lord Halsbury and Lord Roberston, *CCH* manages to reconstitute the tension in altered form: a vision of copyright fundamentally preoccupied with the balancing of value presides over a doctrinal shift in the direction of authorship.

Nothing about the concept of copyright as a balance between dual objectives necessarily entails the proposition that the sweat of the brow standard is too low. On the contrary, many regard the sweat of the brow standard as appropriate from the standpoint of copyright law as a balance between authors and users, ownership and access.[52] After all, the vision of copyright law as a balance is by no means novel. In 1785, in *Sayre v. Moore*, for example, Lord Mansfield famously formulated the task of copyright law as one in which:

> [w]e must take care to guard against two extremes equally prejudicial; the one, that men of ability, who have employed their time for the service of the community, may not be deprived of their just merits, and the reward of their ingenuity and labour; the other, that the world may not be deprived of improvements, nor the progress of the arts be retarded.[53]

The sweat of the brow standard is part and parcel of a centuries old tradition that, at least nominally, devoted itself to finding an in-between 'two extremes equally prejudicial'. To be sure, there can be no doubt that in *CCH* the Supreme Court of Canada presents its dismissal of the sweat of the brow standard in the name of the copyright balance. But a bare assertion that the traditional originality standard is too low is surely insufficient in a context that has always aspired to that balance precisely through that standard. The same is true of the Court's dismissal of the creativity standard as too high. Once again, a bare assertion is simply insufficient in light of the adherence to that standard in the name of a balanced copyright in US copyright jurisprudence.

---

[52] See Siebrasse, 'Facts and Information', supra note 14. Consider also *CCH Canadian Ltd. v. Law Society of Upper Canada* (2002), 18 C.P.R. (4th) 161 at para. 59 (F.C.A.) [*CCH FCA*].

[53] *Sayre v. Moore*, 1 East 361, 102 Eng. Rep. 139 (K.B. 1785) at 139.

Moreover, even if we were to accept that varying originality standards can somehow be understood and classified as more or less conducive to the achievement of a balance between authors and public, it seems clear that the degree to which any given standard would either promote or be consistent with the balance in question would depend crucially on one's construal of other copyright doctrines, such as, for example, fair dealing. The Court of Appeal in *CCH*, for example, addressed in its reasons the relation between originality and fair dealing in this light. It suggested that the interaction between originality and fair dealing as central copyright doctrines, not either one in isolation, is to be considered as instrumental in achieving the requisite balance.[54]

In other words, conclusions about the role of the originality standard in the achievement of the copyright balance cannot possibly be persuasive in the absence of more integrated assessments of its combined and concurrent action in light of other copyright doctrines. Because the Supreme Court's dismissal of the sweat of the brow standard takes place in the absence of any such integrated assessment, it cannot help but remain at best unpersuasive, and at worst short-lived and precarious. (Once again, the same can be said of the Court's dismissal of the creativity standard.) While *CCH* did deal extensively with fair dealing, it did not deal explicitly with the balanced and integrated interaction between originality and fair dealing. It seems prima facie clear that a decision, such as *CCH*, that both narrows originality and widens fair dealing in the same breath must do more than merely invoke the copyright balance and assert without more ado that the sweat of the brow standard is too low, or that the creativity standard is too high.

Finally, even if we were to assume that originality standards can (whether in isolation or along the lines of more integrated assessments) be correlated with certain outcomes at the level of the copyright balance, there is no self-evident reason to believe that these correlations would be industry neutral. That is, it is entirely plausible, perhaps even probable, that one originality standard may be more conducive to 'balance' in one industry or field of activity (such as phone-directory production), and another in another industry or

---

[54] *CCH FCA*, *supra* note 52 at para. 59: 'Admittedly, the public interest in the dissemination of works may be a policy reason to impose a high standard of "creativity" as a prerequisite to copyright protection. There is also the concern that overprotection of certain works will thwart social and scientific progress by precluding persons from building upon earlier works. However, I would suggest that copyright monopolies are better controlled through the avenues that Parliament has established than through the imposition of an arbitrary and subjective standard of "creative spark" or "imagination". As will be discussed below, a fair interpretation of user rights can counteract the apparent imbalance potentially generated by a low threshold (see Vaver, *Copyright Law, supra* at 169–70). For example, the fair dealing provisions of the *Act* provide a mechanisms [sic!] whereby user rights are better considered.'

field of activity (such as sculpture or painting).[55] In short, the Supreme Court's holding that the sweat of the brow and creativity standards are inadequate may well be correct, but unfortunately the Court has hardly provided any reasons for its holding.

A similar situation obtains as regards the metaphor of a continuum from 'low' to 'high' in terms of which originality standards can somehow be meaningfully classified. The image of the continuum presupposes that the sweat of the brow standard requires less of authors than the skill and judgment standard, and that, in turn, the skill and judgment standard requires less than does the creativity standard. It is by no means clear, however, what it is that these standards share, so as to make it meaningful to place them in a continuum moving from less to more, or – for that matter – in any kind of continuum. It may be that what the Court has in mind is that the sweat of the brow standard is 'lower' in that the requirements it imposes for admission to the world of copyright protection are such that any work qualifying under the other two standards would also qualify under the sweat of the brow standard, whereas the reverse is simply not true. Similarly, it may be that what the Court also has in mind is that any work qualifying under the creativity standard would also qualify under the skill and judgment standard, whereas the reverse, again, is simply not true. Nonetheless, these observations are radically insufficient. They do nothing by way of providing reasons for the view that there is a shared something at all, or by way of providing a description of what this shared something is.

Consider the Court's conclusions regarding the nature of 'originality'. The text of the judgment suggests that the Court does indeed have in mind a kind of creativity continuum moving from 'none' (sweat of the brow), through 'enough' (skill and judgment), to 'more than enough' (creativity):

> For these reasons, I conclude that an 'original' work under the *Copyright Act* is one that originates from an author and is not copied from another work [i.e. sweat of the brow]. That alone, however, is not sufficient to find that something is original. In addition, an original work must be the product of an author's exercise of skill and judgment. The exercise of skill and judgment required to produce the work must not be so trivial that it could be characterized as a purely mechanical exercise. While *creative works will by definition be 'original' and covered by copyright*, creativity is not required to make a work 'original'.[56]

---

55 See, for example, Alfred Chueh-Chin Yen, 'The Legacy of Feist: Consequences of the Weak Connection Between Copyright and the Economics of Public Goods' (1991) 52 Ohio State Law Journal 1343.

56 *CCH*, *supra* note 2 at para. 25 [emphasis added].

Thus, whereas the sweat of the brow standard is too low in that it would admit a 'purely mechanical' yet 'not copied' product into the world of copyright, the creativity standard is too high in that, as the Court puts it in this context, it 'implies that something must be novel or non-obvious – concepts more properly associated with patent law than copyright law'.[57] The Court, then, appears to affirm the following three propositions:

(1) sweat of the brow, skill and judgment and creativity are part of a continuum of which creativity is the highest form;
(2) this highest form must be ruled out as an originality standard because it requires novelty or non-obviousness, which are associated with patent law, not copyright law;
(3) creative works will by definition be original and covered by copyright.

The problem with these propositions is that if proposition (2) is true, then proposition (3) is false. Proposition (2) defines creative works as novel or non-obvious. Proposition (3) asserts that such works will by definition be covered by copyright. But that is simply not true. Patentable subject matter is indeed novel and non-obvious. But it is trivially true that such subject matter is *not* – and certainly not 'by definition' – subject to copyright protection.[58]

The point is not that patentable inventions are in some sense not sufficiently creative. Nor is the point that inventions do not involve skill and judgment in their production. The point, rather, is that the human faculty exercised in the production of a patentable invention, even where such exercise is significant and cannot possibly be characterized as purely mechanical, is qualitatively distinct from that exercised in the production of works of authorship. The invention of a mouse-trap, for example, no doubt requires creativity and/or skill and judgment. But a mouse-trap is not a literary work, and an inventor is not an author. It is as absurd to place these human faculties in a continuum as it is to suggest that an author is less creative than an inventor, or that Lord Byron is somehow better at compiling phone directories than your local telephone company. It seems far more fruitful to regard these activities as distinct, to refrain from regarding them as belonging in a continuum moving from low to high, and to attempt the elaboration of the specificity of each.

Of course, there is no denying that the *CCH* Court specifies that the skill and judgment it has in mind is not *any* skill and judgment but rather the skill

---

57 *Ibid.* at para. 24.

58 For discussion of the distinction between copyright and patent, see Abraham Drassinower, 'A Note on the Distinction Between Copyright and Patent' in *Intellectual Property at the Edge: New Approaches to IP in a Transsystemic World* (Montreal: Centre for Intellectual Property Policy, 2006) 285.

and judgment *of an author*: 'an original work must be the product of *an author's* exercise of skill and judgment'.[59] Similarly, the Court also specifies that the skill and judgment in issue is specifically the skill and judgment involved in the expression of an idea: 'What is required to attract copyright protection *in the expression of an idea* is an exercise of skill and judgment'.[60] Moreover, the Court's definition of judgment arguably excludes certain modes of judgment, such that not all exercise of judgment would qualify for copyright protection. Finally, even where the Court asserts that 'creative *works* will by definition be ... covered by copyright', the letter of its text is careful to refer to 'works', not to just any product of intellectual effort.

These aspects of the *CCH* decision fruitfully engage issues pertinent to the specificity of authorship vis-à-vis inventorship, or to the specific work of authorship vis-à-vis productive labour more generally. It is these aspects that would indicate that the continuum from 'low' to 'high' should not be understood quantitatively but rather as a series, so to speak, of copyright models differing from each other at the level of their conception of the conditions defining a copyrightable work. Thus, it is not so much, for example, that Lord Halsbury's standard was 'lower' than Lord Robertson's. It is rather that Lord Halsbury and Lord Robertson operated with different definitions of the nature of a 'work'.

Still, even with these aspects in mind, it seems difficult to avoid the impression that the *CCH* decision remains undeveloped in this respect. The problem is not that the judgment does not elaborate the content of skill and judgment, and therefore of originality, beyond the indication that a 'purely mechanical exercise' will not do, or beyond the example that 'simply changing the font of a work to produce "another" work would be too trivial to merit copyright protection as an "original" work'. One may after all take some comfort in the well-settled view that 'originality' is ultimately a finding of fact.

The problem is rather that the pervasive images of a continuum and a balance generate a conceptual environment not ideally conducive to an independent inquiry into the nature or specificity of skill and judgment, and therefore into the findings of fact that are to determine the outcome of any given case. This is because, once it has been understood as falling between two extremes, one 'low' and the other 'high', the inquiry into skill and judgment appears less as an inquiry into the defining conditions of a copyrightable work, than as an inquiry into the amount of protection to be regarded as consistent with the copyright balance. Thus originality is less about the nature of skill and judgment or authorship than about the amount of value-protection and distribution that would be

---

59 *CCH*, *supra* note 2 at para. 25 [emphasis added].

60 *Ibid.* at para. 16 [emphasis added].

attuned to the purpose of copyright. The crucial question of *what* it is that is being protected and distributed, as distinct from the question of *how much* of it to protect and *how much* of it to distribute, remains undeveloped, as it were hidden behind the veil of the balance-cum-continuum metaphor. Not a way to think through the nature of authorship, originality is but a way to talk about value-distributions magically formulated elsewhere.

Preoccupying about this standpoint is that it puts obstacles in the way of a fully articulated elaboration of a viable alternative to the sweat of the brow position. To be sure, there can be no doubt that, by jettisoning the sweat of the brow standard, the Court jettisons the view that authors should appropriate the value they originate. To put it otherwise, the Court jettisons the presumption, characteristic of the sweat of the brow school, that the author is *prima facie* entitled to the value she originates, and that, therefore, instances in which copyright law does not guarantee her that value ought to be regarded as exceptions. It is in this vein that the Court insists that such so-called 'exceptions' are rather 'user rights', integral to the innermost structure of copyright law.[61] But what the Court alters in this way is the nature of the default distribution of value between authors and users, ownership and access. It does not, however, challenge the deeper and more fundamental assumption, also characteristic of the sweat of the brow standpoint, that authorship is fundamentally about value-origination.

In his dissent in *Walter v. Lane*, Lord Roberston was careful to avoid 'disparaging the gifts of the shorthand writer'. He in fact discussed in some detail, and not without eloquence, the value and merit of the 'art of stenography'. As noted above, he concluded his discussion as follows:

> These observations apply to the stage of taking down in shorthand what the speaker says. The next stage, copying out the notes, is purely clerical work. Now I recognise the skill of the stenographer, I find that, for the reasons which I have mentioned, an educated man is the better qualified to be a faithful reporter. *But I fail entirely to see how, in the widest sense of the term 'author', we are in the region of authorship.*[62]

This metaphor of a specific region of authorship, as distinct from other regions wherein skill and/or judgment may also be found, is fruitful. It is certainly more fruitful than the metaphor of a continuum through which variegated aspects of human agency are homogenized and commodified by being reduced to mere quantities to be measured or balanced. Lord Robertson was surely correct when he insisted that the region of authorship is not 'lower or higher,

---

61 *Ibid*. at para. 48.

62 *Walter v. Lane*, *supra* note 33 at 561 [emphasis added].

but in a different plane'. In so doing, he identified not value-origination as such but the specificity of authorship as the pivotal concern.

V CONCLUDING REMARKS

In my view, *CCH* situates Canadian copyright culture at a juncture analogous to that faced by Peterson J. in *University of London Press* in 1916. In 1916, in the wake of the introduction of the word 'original' into the English Copyright Act in 1911, Peterson J. opted to affirm an affinity between value-origination and entitlement as the organizing principle of copyright law. Thus he rejected 'selection, judgment, and experience' as relevant criteria in the originality determination, and concluded his examination of originality with the maxim that 'what is worth copying is prima facie worth protecting'. Almost a century later, the Supreme Court of Canada in *CCH* unambiguously affirmed a skill and judgment originality standard. This is by any account a decisive movement away from the sweat of the brow standard. Yet this movement at the level of doctrine has not yet crystallized at the level of principle. By way of the skill and judgment standard, *CCH* alters the prima facie default distribution of value, but it does not question the very concept of the author as a value-originator. It is only that the author is now, in the name of balance, entitled to less of that value.

Faced with this juncture, we can retain the vision of copyright law as a mode of governing the origination and distribution of value. Should we follow this option, the immediate task will be to distinguish the specific kind of value or values to which copyright applies. Available for this task is not only the Court's concept of skill and judgment, but also the arsenal of copyright doctrines that separates out different kinds of values and reserves protection for only some of them. Thus, for example, the idea/expression dichotomy refuses protection to ideas, regardless of their value, and regardless also of the kind of skill and judgment, if any, that their production may have involved. This is a decision to curtail the value to which the author is entitled. The same could be said of fair dealing as a refusal to grant protection for the use of copyright subject matter in respect of certain purposes. Again, this is a decision to distribute value towards users rather than authors.

Alternatively, we can seize the unambiguous affirmation of skill and judgment at the doctrinal level as an invitation to elaborate the specificity of authorship. Should we choose this option, the immediate task will be the elaboration of an interpretation of *CCH* bringing into relief those aspects of the decision that emphasize that the skill and judgment at issue are specifically the skill and judgment of authorship. Lord Robertson's judgment in *Walter v. Lane* is by no means the only helpful referent in this respect. The tradition of originality jurisprudence is not monolithic, and a vigorous constellation of judgments inconsistent with the sweat of the brow school does exist.[63] *CCH* is not as innovative as we at times appear to assume.

Most recently, it was the Federal Court of Appeal in *Tele-Direct (Publications) Inc. v. American Business Information, Inc.* that invoked that constellation most forcefully:

> The use of the word 'copyright' in the English version of the Act has obscured the fact that what the Act fundamentally seeks to protect is 'le droit d'auteur'. While not defined in the Act, the word 'author' conveys a sense of creativity and ingenuity. I do not read these cases which have adopted the 'sweat of the brow' approach in matters of compilations of data as having asserted that the amount of labour would in itself be a determinative source of originality. If they did, I suggest that their approach was wrong and is irreconcilable with the standards of intellect and creativity that were expressly set out in NAFTA and endorsed in the 1993 amendments to the Copyright Act and that *were already recognized in Anglo-Canadian law*.[64]

Deploying this constellation would set the stage for an elaboration of the content of skill and judgment as well as for an effort to link that elaboration with an affirmation of the inherent dignity of authorship as the organizing principle of copyright law. Essaying this task in the current juncture in the development of Canadian copyright would also require an interpretation of copyright law integrating the recognition of the inherent dignity of authorship characteristic of Continental copyright with the openness to fair dealing in particular and to the public domain in general more palpably present, albeit in different modes and degrees, in common law copyright. This is a difficult and perhaps impossible task.[65] As a bi-jural jurisdiction, however, Canada is well placed to attempt it.

We would in any case do well to keep in mind that the altered yet still ongoing struggle between the sweat of the brow and skill and judgment schools in Canadian copyright is not a struggle between pro-author and pro-user construals of originality. From the standpoint of the region of authorship, the pro-author/pro-user squabble is but a disagreement about domestic relations in a foreign country – a country for which copyright is less about authorship than about the generation and distribution of value. It is to be hoped that the future growth of Canadian copyright jurisprudence will manage, as it were retrospectively, to seize the promise of authorship that *CCH* evokes but does not quite capture.

---

63 See, for example, *Tele-Direct*, *supra* note 15; *Caron*, *supra* note 15; *Kilvington*, *supra* note 15; *Cramp*, *supra* note 15; *Macmillan*, *supra* note 15.

64 *Tele-Direct*, *ibid.* at 308 [emphasis added].

65 For an interpretation of *CCH* from an authorship standpoint, see Drassinower, 'User Rights', *supra* note 2.

8. Moral rights in Canada: an historical and comparative view

Elizabeth Adeney*

INTRODUCTION

To a person tracing the development of moral rights in the copyright[1] countries, Canada stands as a forerunner and an example. In 1928, when moral rights were introduced for the first time into the Berne Convention, it was only the Canadian legislators who, unlike their counterparts in the UK and Australia, were prepared to accept that the law then current in Canada, whether common law or statute, did not render Canada compliant with Article 6 *bis* of the new Convention text. While spokespersons in Australia and the UK took the view that their common law and statute provided sufficient protection for authorial moral interests[2] the Canadian parliament immediately set about upgrading its legislation. By 1931 the task was accomplished. Canada became the first of the copyright countries to enact a clear moral rights provision.[3]

* Some of the matters discussed in the present chapter are pursued in more detail in Elizabeth Adeney, *The Moral Rights of Authors and Performers: an International and Comparative Analysis* (*Moral Rights*) (Oxford: Oxford University Press, 2006). English translations in this chapter are the author's unless otherwise stated. French versions of treaties and legislation are official versions.

[1] Namely the countries which have formulated their copyright legislation according to British models, these models centering on the concept of copyright ownership. Such countries can be contrasted with countries which have taken the concept of authors' rights as the basis for their legislation.

[2] The British delegates to Rome reported in 1928 that 'no extensive changes were made in the Convention' that year: United Kingdom, *Rome Copyright Conference, 1928, Report of the British Delegates*, Public Record Office FO 371/13444, 3. In 1936, an eminent British commentator wrote that the Rome Convention had 'not necessitated any changes in English municipal law': F. E. Skone James, ed., *Copinger on the Law of Copyright*, 7th ed. (London: Sweet & Maxwell, 1936) at v. For the Australian attitude, see Australia – Delegate to the International Copyright Conference, Rome, May and June 1928, *Report of the Australian Delegate (Sir W. Harrison Moore)* (Canberra: Green, 1928) at n° 255.

[3] Through the operation of S.C. 1931, c. 8, s. 5.

Why was it that Canadian legislators did not follow the example of the UK and Australia and shy away from amendment of their still relatively recent legislation?[4] Why did they accept the need for change so readily? Has this early acceptance had implications for moral rights in Canada? How does the Canadian model of moral rights, the *droits moraux*, differ from that of Canada's common law peer group? This chapter will attempt to answer the first two of these questions by tracing the early development of moral rights in that country. The current Canadian moral rights provisions will then be examined and compared with certain of their counterparts in other countries.

DEVELOPMENT PRIOR TO 1928

The Nineteenth Century

Moral rights thinking had been present in Canada as far back as the 1880s, at a time when the concept of the rights was still in a developmental stage even in Europe.[5] At this stage the rights had not yet received legislative recognition anywhere in the world. Yet in Canada the barrister Mignault had the following to say about publishers to whom the production of a literary work had been entrusted:

> The publisher cannot cut anything at all from the book, by changing its title or removing the name of the author without this person's consent...
>
> The writer has the right to make changes to his book, as long as they are not of such a nature as to cause additional expenses for the publisher…
>
> The publisher cannot destroy the work. He is obliged to publish it, because the author has not intended to alienate his hope of reputation.[6]

---

4 *An Act to amend and consolidate the Law relating to Copyright*, S. C. 1921, c. 24 [*Copyright Act of 1921*].

5 The term appears to have been coined in the 1870s, when it was first used by Morillot in France: see André Morillot, 'De la personnalité du droit de publication qui appartient à un auteur vivant' (1872) 2 Revue critique de législation et de jurisprudence 29 and André Morillot, 'De la nature du droit d'auteur considéré à un point de vue général' (1878) 7 Revue critique de législation et de jurisprudence 111.

6 '[L]'éditeur ne peut rien retrancher du livre, en changer le titre ou supprimer le nom de l'auteur sans le consentement de ce dernier...l'écrivain a le droit de faire tout changement à son livre, pourvu, toutefois, que ce ne soit pas de nature à entraîner des dépenses additionnelles à l'éditeur...l'éditeur ne peut pas détruire l'ouvrage, il est obligé de le publier, car l'auteur n'a pas entendu aliéner l'espoir de la réputation': Pierre-Basile Mignault, 'La Propriété Littéraire' (2nd article) (1880) 2 *La Thémis* 367 at 372.

Mignault was, in these last three words, echoing the wording of French judicial decisions,[7] indicating very early familiarity, at least in French speaking circles in Canada, with concepts that were attracting significant interest on the other side of the globe.[8] No subsequent discussion of moral rights in Canada could thereafter occur in a vacuum. Mignault's early pronouncement was to be built on in the new century.

The Twentieth Century and Judicial Developments

As in Europe, the first practical steps towards the protection of moral rights in Canada were taken in the courts.[9] In 1911, in *Morang v. LeSueur*, a common law contract case heard before the Supreme Court of Canada, Sir Charles Fitzpatrick C.J.C. recognised the existence of personal authorial rights that could be exercised against the publisher, namely rights to carry out improvements to the work and against incorrect attribution of authorship:

> Nor could the author be denied by the publisher the right to make corrections …; nor could the manuscript be published in the name of another. After the author has parted with his pecuniary interest in the manuscript, he retains a species of personal or moral right in the product of his brain. Lyon Caen, note to Sirey, 1881.1.25. … [W]hat is called literary property has a character and attributes of its own and… such a contract as we are now called upon to consider must be interpreted and the rights of the parties determined with regard to the special nature of the thing which is the subject of the contract.[10]

Relying on the French source to which he referred, Fitzpatrick C.J.C. considered that the protection of non-economic interests was a consequence of

---

7 For example the decision in *Delpit et Lacour c. Gué et consorts* where it was stated that the assigning author could not be '*présumé avoir aliéné l'espoir inévaluable de la réputation que peut…donner la publicité*' ('presumed to have alienated the inestimable hope of reputation which…publicity can give': Bordeaux, 24 August 1863, S. 1864.II.194. See also Trib. civ. Seine, 16 December 1899, D. 1900.II.152 (*Agnès dit A. Sorel c. Fayard frères*).

8 The rights were the subject of commentary by the major authors' rights scholars, among them Josef Kohler, *Das Autorrecht* (Jena: G. Fischer, 1880); André Morillot, *De la protection accordée aux œuvres d'art, aux photographies, aux dessins et modèles industriels et aux brevets l'invention dans l'empire d'Allemagne* (Paris: Cotillon; Berlin: Puttkammer & Mühlbrecht, 1878); and Eugène Pouillet, *Traité théorique et pratique de la propriété littéraire et artistique et du droit de représentation* (Paris: Marchal, Billard & Co., 1879).

9 For this early period see also Elizabeth Adeney, 'Moral Rights: a brief excursion into Canadian history' (2001) 15 Intellectual Property Journal 205.

10 *Morang and Co. v. LeSueur* (1911), 45 S.C.R. 95 at 98. The case was on appeal from the Court of Appeal for Ontario: (1910), 20 Ont. L. R. 594.

the author having property in a work.[11] Although his remarks were not echoed by the other members of the court, they show the early influence in Canadian courts, at the highest level, of the rights that Mignault had referred to 30 years earlier.

Six years later, in 1917, we see the Court of King's Bench recognising an apparently natural right of authors to respect and fair play in relation, this time, to the work's correct designation. The case was *Joubert v. Geracimo*.[12] Joubert, a French music publisher, had come before the Canadian courts seeking national treatment under the Berne Convention. Relying on the UK *Dramatic Literary Property Act* of 1833,[13] which was still in force in Canada, he had complained of three types of offence (*délit*) for which he sought statutory damages. The first was the unauthorized representation of a number of works, the second was the suppression of the author's name in association with the works and the third was the suppression of the works' titles. The Act did not provide for the second and third types of offence and ultimately the three were treated together as the offence of unauthorized representation. Although the action was necessarily based on the provisions of the 1833 legislation and hence on proven interference with property interests, the court discussed the significance of the suppression of the work's title and of the author's name. These acts were treated by the majority as being relevant to the quantum of damages.[14] Most interestingly, the judgment of the majority (per Carroll J.) contained a statement of what were considered to be the rights of the author:

> An author has a right to credit for his work, to respect for his texts, and also to the material advantage that can accrue to him from the prestige of his name and the popularity of his works.[15]

The comment suggests a natural right, based on the labour of production, derived by the author from the act of authorship. By virtue of this right, the author could require both the work and the author's connection with it to be respected, the benefits flowing from this respect being at least partially economic.

---

[11] Indeed much early moral rights thinking in France had been based on the property concept, present in the Law of 19–24 July 1793.

[12] (1916), 26 B.R. 97, 35 D.L.R. 683 (Que. K. B.). This was an appeal decision, the initial decision having been handed down in 1914.

[13] 3–4 Will. IV, c. 15.

[14] *Ibid.* at 110.

[15] *Ibid.* at 111: 'Un auteur a droit au crédit de son travail, au respect de ses textes, et aussi au bénéfice matériel qui peut lui résulter du prestige de son nom ou de la vogue de ses œuvres.'

Statutory Amendments in the Twentieth Century

From early in the twentieth century commentators in Canada asserted a need for the improved legislative protection of authors.[16] As demonstrated by the facts that gave rise to the *Joubert* case, copyright material was being introduced to the country from abroad, from France and Belgium, and misused in Canada. The imported works were stripped of their authorial designation and exploited under a different title, to the prejudice of the economic interests of the rightsholders.[17] Canada's first legislative move was typical of the times. Instead of creating a regime of civil liability, the legislators chose to co-opt the criminal law to assist the authors. They incorporated a new s. 508b into the Canadian criminal code, establishing penalties for those who, among other things, altered the authorial designation or removed it from the work with a view to having the work performed.[18] This move does not appear to have been a resounding success.

The section was utilized with disappointing results in a 1915 legal action – the case of *Helbronner v. Daoust*.[19] This was a private prosecution brought in Quebec in reliance on the Berne Convention coupled with these new provisions in the Criminal Code. A representative of a French author was seeking to enforce the criminal provisions against a Canadian offender who had, among other things, suppressed the author's name. The case was initially decided against the accused but the fine was minimal ($5) and, upon appeal, the accused was acquitted.[20]

The provisions of the Criminal Code were subsequently incorporated in the *Copyright Act 1921*, as a regime of summary offences.[21] The offences are embodied now in s. 43(2). Quebec too passed a more limited protection of authorial identification in its *Theatrical Performance Act* of 1919,[22] a provision that has subsequently been repealed.[23]

---

16 *House of Commons Debates* (15 February 1915) at 196–203.

17 House of Commons, Special Committee on Bill 2, *Proceedings of the Special Committee appointed to consider and report upon Bill no. 2, an Act to amend and make operative certain provisions of the Copyright Act* (Ottawa: F.A. Acland, 1925) at 154.

18 *An act to amend the Criminal Code*, S.C. 1915, c. 12, s. 508b assented to 15 April 1915. See also [1916] Droit d'Auteur 14.

19 (1915), 49 C.S. 65, [1917] Droit d'Auteur 58 (Que. S.C.).

20 For an account of the ultimate acquittal of the accused see 'Le Canada et la protection des auteurs unionistes' [1916] Droit d'Auteur 40 at 43.

21 *Copyright Act, 1921*, S.C. 1921, c. 24, s. 25(2), later to become s. 26(2).

22 S.Q. 1919, c. 47, s. 3712a. See [1926] Droit d'Auteur 95 for a brief discussion of the section, comments on it by M. Louvigny de Montigny indicating that it was indeed seen as pertaining to moral rights protection, and an account of an action taken under it.

23 By *An Act to repeal certain statutory provisions*, S.Q. 1988, c. 27 (repealing the then *Theatrical Performances Act*, R.S.Q. c. R-25).

The above provisions cannot be seen as having instituted moral rights protection, since they do not grant rights. Keyes and Brunet have since commented that:

> a right has not been enforced, in the strict sense, when the infringer has been punished. Apart from being 'avenged', the offended copyright owner derives no benefit from a criminal sanction…The onus of pursuing legal remedies should lie with the owner of the copyright and not with society as a whole. Individual rights should be asserted by individuals.[24]

The provisions did, however, cover some of the authorial interests that are likewise addressed by moral rights, among them the author's interest in correct attribution. These various judicial and legislative developments gave moral rights or notions analogous to moral rights a very early presence in Canadian law. They formed a basis from which further attempts at moral rights protection in Canada could be launched.

Developments in the 1920s

The main push for explicit moral rights protection occurred in the 1920s, in a decade that saw growing acceptance of the moral rights idea worldwide.[25] Year after year, from 1925 to 1930, private members' bills were introduced to the Canadian parliament, seeking the protection of authorial moral rights.[26] It

---

[24] Andrew A. Keyes & Claude Brunet, *Copyright in Canada. Proposals for a revision of the law* (Ottawa: Consumer and Corporate Affairs Canada, 1977) at 185–7.

[25] In 1933 one commentator wrote that the idea of the *droit moral* could be found in most legislation aimed at reform of 'copyright' law in the post World War 1 period. He listed the legislation of Greece (1920), Hungary (1921), Bulgaria (1921), Romania (1923), Czechoslovakia (1926), Poland (1926), Portugal (1927), Finland (1927), China (1928), Russia (1928), Yugoslavia (1929) and Norway (1930): D. M. Kauschansky (1933), 'Evolution des Autorrechts, die moderne Auffassung über die soziale Funktion der Erzeugnisse geistiger Tätigkeit und die Förderung des faktischen Schutzes des Autors' UFITA 24, 43. Syria and Lebanon too achieved moral rights protection in 1921: Elizabeth Adeney, *The Moral Rights of Authors and Performers: an International and Comparative Analysis* (Oxford: Oxford University Press, 2006) at para. 1.71 [Adeney, *Moral Rights*].

[26] The series of Bills began in 1924 with Bill 28 of that year (*An Act to amend and make operative certain provisions of the Copyright Act, 1921*), a private member's bill, which, however, contained no reference to moral rights. From 1925 onwards moral rights protection was sought in the following bills: Bill 2, *An Act to amend and make operative certain provisions of The Copyright Act, 1921*, 4th Session, 14th Parliament, 1925; Bill 3, *An Act to amend and make operative certain provisions of The Copyright Act, 1921*, 1st Session, 15th Parliament, 1926; Bill 45, *An Act to amend and make operative certain provisions of The Copyright Act, 1921*, 1st Session, 16th Parliament,

was during this very active period in Canadian moral rights history that the rights finally received more than passing recognition in the Berne Convention, through the incorporation of Article 6 *bis*.[27] Years before this amendment to Berne, however, it was proposed in Canada that the *Copyright Act* should contain the following wording:

> Any person, corporation or association charged under this Act with having reproduced, performed or executed a work contrary to the provisions of this Act, shall not be allowed to set up as a means of defence that the work was so reproduced, performed or executed from copies of such work bearing an altered title or from copies failing to disclose the name of the author of the original work; and any assignment of a work shall not entitle the assignee to suppress or change the name of the author of the said work nor in any way whatsoever change the nature of the work, *nor in any other way affect the moral right of the author therein*.[28]

The provision would have been groundbreaking if passed since it makes express mention of moral rights, something that even Article 6 *bis* of the Berne Convention was not to do in 1928. It implies that moral rights were not to be conceived of as rights brought into existence by legislation, but rather as natural rights recognised and protected, but not created, by statute. The words that followed the above extract are even more extraordinary in that they give a definition of moral rights, something that no other national legislation appears ever to have done.

> For the purpose of this section 'moral right' means the author's personal privilege of enjoying the prestige or influence which he may derive or which may accrue to him from his production, notwithstanding any assignment of his property rights.

1927; Bill 16, *An Act to amend and make operative certain provisions of the Copyright Act, 1921*, 4th Session, 16th Parliament, 1930; and Bill 37, *An Act to Amend the Copyright Act*, 4th Session, 16th Parliament, 1930.

[27] '(1) Independently of the author's copyright, and even after the transfer of the said copyright, the author shall have the right to claim authorship of the work, as well as the right to object to any distortion, mutilation or other modification of the said work which would be prejudicial to his honour or reputation. (2) The determination of the conditions under which these rights shall be exercised is reserved for the national legislation of the countries of the union. The means of redress for safeguarding these rights shall be regulated by the legislation of the country where protection is claimed': *Berne Convention for the Protection of Literary and Artistic Works*, revised at Rome on 2 June 1928, 123 L.N.T.S. 233.

[28] Clause 18 of: Bill 2 of 1925, Bill 3 of 1926 and Bill 45 of 1927, all proposing new s. 25D [emphasis added]. The wording was also contained in clause 19 of Bill 16 of 1930, proposing new s. 26D. The reference to the moral right reappeared in clause 1 of Bill 37 of 1930.

In clarifying that assignment of the work (presumably the economic rights in the work) would not of itself permit a free use of the work to the detriment of the author's personal interests, the provision both reflected current European thinking and foreshadowed the opening words of Article 6 *bis*. But it went much further than Article 6 *bis* was to go in 1928 in that it specified the type of benefit that the moral right bestowed on the author, namely the personal privilege of enjoying the fruits of one's labour. This was a great deal more than the type of protection offered by the Criminal Code. The history of moral rights in Canada could have been very different had any of the bills containing these words been passed.

1931 – Legislative Protection at Last

The bills of the 1920s came to nothing, but they meant that legislators in 1931 were receptive to the idea that moral rights needed greater protection under Canadian law. The legislators were no strangers to the moral rights concept and they knew that their existing statute contained nothing like what had been proposed in the earlier bills. Nor did it contain anything that would satisfy Article 6 *bis* of Berne,[29] which required specific author-centred protection for the benefit of foreign authors seeking redress in Canada. There also appears to have been no argument in Canada at the time that common law and equity were capable of filling the gap.[30] Therefore, when a provision in almost identical terms to Article 6 *bis* was proposed, it must have seemed an easy way of bringing Canada into compliance with its international obligations as well as satisfying those who had for so long been pressing for change. The provision passed through Parliament without significant resistance. Only one member of the House of Commons refused to vote for it, and that was on the grounds that it did not go far enough.[31] The provision read:

Independently of the author's copyright, and even after assignment, either wholly or partially, of the said copyright, the author has the right to claim authorship of the work, as well as the right to restrain any distortion, mutilation, or other modification of

Indépendamment de ses droits d'auteur, et même après la cession partielle ou totale desdits droits, l'auteur conserve la faculté de revendiquer la paternité de l'œuvre, ainsi que le privilège de réprimer toute déformation, mutilation ou autre modification de ladite œuvre,

[29] See *supra*, note 27.
[30] In any event parliamentary discussion does not reveal it.
[31] *House of Commons Debates* (8 June 1931) at 2402 (Mr Chevrier).

the work that would be prejudicial to his honour or reputation.

qui serait préjudiciable à son honneur ou à sa réputation.[32]

These words embodied moral rights regulation in Canada until 1988. They existed alongside the summary offence provisions discussed above.

Criticism and Use of the 1931 Clause

The 1931 provision, commonly known as s. 12(7),[33] subsequently aroused quite spirited criticism within Canada, though it was well received in Berne Convention circles.[34] Its attribution right was described by one eminent commentator as 'conceived in vagueness, poorly drafted, sententious in utterance, and useless in practical application'.[35] The fault lay, however, not so much with Canadian drafting techniques as with the fact that the provision was lifted practically word for word from the Berne Convention. The wording of a multilateral international treaty such as the Berne Convention is unlikely, on its own, to furnish the optimal wording for a domestic provision on the same subject since the treaty exists above all to set broad benchmarks acceptable to all member nations. The domestic statute, by contrast, exists to regulate behaviour within the state in a way that is responsive to prevailing conditions there. Particularly in countries of the English legal tradition, it is generally expected that the legislature will provide a regulation more detailed than a bare statement of rights.

Section 12(7)'s shortcomings were various. It did not, for example, address the issue of remedies in enough detail or with enough clarity to have significant effect domestically. It was seen, probably rightly, as leading almost exclusively to injunctive relief.[36] The option of damages had been neglected, no doubt partly because an award of damages had long been considered worthless in

---

32 The provision was introduced through s. 5 of *Copyright Amendment Act, 1931*, S.C. 1931, c. 8, providing for the creation of a new s. 12(5) in the *Copyright Act*.

33 The provision was initially s. 12(5) of the amended legislation, then s. 12(7) and, later, s. 14(4) but referred to in this chapter as s. 12(7).

34 [1932] Droit d'Auteur 5 and 113. European writers saw this as the introduction of real moral rights into Canada though they considered the formula adopted 'un peu étroite'. The approbation of the Berne Union may have been based on an overestimation of the provision's capacity for enforcement.

35 Harold G. Fox, 'Some points of interest in the law of copyright' (1945) 6 U.T.L.J. 100 at 126. See also Ysolde Gendreau, 'Moral Rights' in Gordon F. Henderson, ed., *Copyright and Confidential Information Law of Canada* (Scarborough, Ont.: Carswell, 1994) 161 at 168.

36 The word 'restrain' had been substituted for the Berne word 'object', allowing injunctive relief to be sought for breach of the right of integrity.

most circumstances.[37] The section also did not indicate the duration of the rights and was unclear about the opportunity for their waiver. And it did not answer fundamental questions about the exercise of the rights after the death of the author, assuming that the rights continued to exist post mortem.

For decades there was talk of amending or replacing s. 12(7). Various suggestions were considered, various reports commissioned by government, various viewpoints represented – all of them casting further light on what a moral rights provision could or should look like in a copyright country.[38] In these suggestions the viewpoints of both the commercially oriented common law tradition and the less economically oriented civil law tradition – the two components of Canada's bijural legal system – could be heard. The push towards amendment finally came to fruition in 1988 with the passage of the *Copyright Amendment Act* of that year.

In the meantime, however, inadequate as it may have been, the provision still offered to the rest of the world an example of a working moral rights provision in a jurisdiction mostly based on the English legal tradition.[39] It is worth considering what kind of guidance the Canadian provision gave, especially since the principles developed under s. 12(7) remain persuasive today.

CASES UNDER SECTION 12(7)

Although s. 12(7) prompted little litigation, the case law that it did generate was not all negative from the author's point of view. In particular, the judg-

---

[37] This was the gist of the discussions in the early years of the century, leading at that stage to the creation of criminal sanctions which were considered more protective than any damages awarded to the author. For a detailed discussion of the problems facing the foreign author see the speech of M. Rodolphe Lemieux, *House of Commons Debates* (15 February 1915) at 196–203. See also 'Le Canada et la protection des auteurs unionistes' [1916] Droit d'Auteur 40.

[38] Royal Commission on Patents, Copyright, Trade Marks and Industrial Designs (1957), *Report on Copyright*, Ottawa: Queens Printer; Economic Council of Canada (1971), *Report on Intellectual and Industrial Property*, Ottawa: Information Canada, accompanied by Bruce McDonald (1971), *Copyright in Context: the Challenge of Change. Background Study to the Report on Intellectual and Industrial Property,* Economic Council of Canada; Keyes & Brunet, *supra* note 24; Judy Erola & Francis Fox, *From Gutenberg to Telidon: A White Paper on Copyright* (Ottawa: Consumer and Corporate Affairs, 1984); Canada. Parliament, House of Commons, Sub-Committee on the Revision of Copyright, Standing Committee on Communications and Culture, *A Charter of Rights for Creators* (Ottawa: Standing Committee on Communications and Culture, 1985).

[39] Only Quebec has a civil law system.

ment in *Snow v. The Eaton Centre Ltd.*[40] has long exemplified a notably pro-author interpretation of the 'integrity' component of moral rights.

This case concerned a sculptor whose work, consisting of 60 sculpted geese, was sold and displayed in a major shopping mall in Toronto. One Christmas, the owner of the geese hung decorative ribbons around the birds' necks, prompting the author to sue. The author claimed a breach of his integrity right, alleging that the addition of the ribbons had altered his work in a way that prejudiced his honour or reputation. The court found in his favour. In giving judgment, O'Brien J. of the Ontario High Court of Justice rejected the argument that s. 12(7) should be read as giving no greater rights than the law of libel or slander. He stated that the words 'prejudicial to his honour or reputation' involve 'a certain subjective element or judgment on the part of the author so long as it is reasonably arrived at'.[41] In considering this subjective element, the judge noted the plaintiff's belief that he had been made to look ridiculous, a belief that was 'reasonable under the circumstances' given that certain other 'well respected artists and people knowledgeable in his field' agreed with the sculptor.[42]

Thus, the case stands for a number of principles: that the moral right of integrity can be infringed even when the physical embodiment of an artistic work is not damaged, destroyed or even altered; that the right can be infringed through an altering of the image that the work presents to those who see it, in other words through superficial and removable embellishments of the work; and that the honour or reputation test contains a subjective element, albeit modified by the application of a reasonableness test. The judgment also reminds us of a fundamental fact in moral rights jurisprudence – that the content of the 'honour or reputation' test should not be read solely in the light of defamation law, that moral rights are independent rights and are not to be confined by pre-existing common law notions.

This judgment is still looked to as a leading authority in Canada. Referring to *Snow*, Ducharme J. in the Supreme Court of Justice of Ontario noted in 2003 the need for corroborative opinions from others knowledgeable in the field in cases where an author had claimed prejudice to his or her honour or reputation.[43] Such opinions had served in the *Snow* case to establish the reasonableness of the plaintiff's claims.

Snow was not the only case that discussed s. 12(7). In 1973, in the case of

---

40 (1982), 70 C.P.R. (2d) 105 (Ont. H.C.J.).

41 *Ibid.* at 106.

42 *Ibid.*

43 *Ritchie v. Sawmill Creek Golf & Country Club Ltd* (2003), 27 C.P.R. (4th) 220 at 236–7 (O.S.C.J.).

Gnass v. Cité d'Alma,[44] a Quebec court had considered damage, through negligent treatment, of works of sculpture assigned to a public authority. Here the judicial statement was made that:

> This moral right consists in the right of the author to make sure that the artistic integrity of the work is maintained in so far as it is accessible to the public. The artist who transfers his work to another, whether for payment or otherwise, divests himself of his property but does not relinquish *the hope of reputation that publicity can give him*.[45]

The Court here was taking its words directly from nineteenth century French cases, showing a line of influence that owed nothing to the Berne Convention.[46] The phrase 'hope of reputation' reinforced the fact that the reputation at issue here is not of a type that need be capable of current objective proof and that harm to existing reputation is not the only type of harm against which the right of integrity guards. The 'prejudice' of which the section speaks is that which would prevent or stunt the accrual of the desired reputation or distort the nature of that reputation.

In 1982, the first court[47] to discuss the right of attribution under s. 12(7) quoted a French author of the 1930s, Michaélidès-Nouaros, to the effect that an architect had the right to demand attribution on the façade of his building. Should alterations to the building either disfigure it or distort the architect's artistic vision, however, the architect would be entitled to demand removal of the attribution.[48] The case demonstrates the extension of moral rights into the industrial field but also foreshadows the legislative device now utilized in the UK of allowing removal of attribution to ameliorate the harm caused by infringement of the integrity right.[49] The pragmatism of the solution offered

---

44 (23 November 1973), Roberval A-158 (Que. C.S.); (30 June 1977), Quebec 09-000032-745 (Que. C.A.).

45 'Ce droit moral consiste dans le droit pour l'auteur de veiller à la conservation de l'integrité artistique de l'œuvre en tant qu'elle est accessible au public. L'artiste qui fait cession de son œuvre, à titre gratuit ou à titre onéreux, se dépouille de sa propriété, mais n'aliène pas *l'espérance de réputation que peut lui assurer la publicité*' (emphasis in French original). The statement was made by Judge Mignault in the Superior Court ((23 November 1973), Roberval A-158 (C.S.Q.) at 30) and quoted with approval by Judge Crete in the Court of Appeal ((30 June 1977), Quebec, 09-000032-745 (C.A.Q.) at 7).

46 See *supra*, note 7.

47 *John Maryon International Ltd v. New Brunswick Telephone Co. Ltd* (1982), 141 D.L.R. (3d) 193 at 249 (N.B.C.A.).

48 Georges Michaélidès-Nouaros, *Le droit moral de l'auteur* (Paris: Arthur Rousseau, 1935) at 258.

49 *Copyright, Designs and Patents Act 1988* (UK), c. 48, s. 80(5) [*CDPA 1988*]

by Michaélidès-Nouaros was no doubt a response to the industrial context of the infringement. There is nothing in the current Canadian Act that entrenches such a solution, though the removal of attribution could be effected under the common law of contract and this would then make damage to reputation under the *Copyright Act* a great deal harder to prove.

CANADIAN MORAL RIGHTS TODAY – WHAT IS ESPECIALLY CANADIAN ABOUT THEM?

When the Swedish scholar Strömholm wrote, in the 1960s, about the possible incorporation of moral rights into the law of common law countries, he saw '*la technique législative britannique*' as presenting difficulties. The tendency towards detail, precision and exhaustive regulation that he associated with the common law systems seemed to him inimical to the reception of moral rights there.[50] His implication seemed to be that moral rights, as they had developed to the 1960s, depended largely on a shared understanding of their underlying premises. While the spirit of moral rights was readily understood in the civil law systems, and much could therefore remain unstated by legislation, every last detail would have to be spelled out if the rights were to be transplanted into other legal systems.

Of course, at the time Strömholm wrote this, moral rights had already existed in the Canadian statute for upwards of 30 years, though they were constricted in their operation. In that sense his comments were somewhat over-inclusive. But the comments do serve to cast light on the current differences between Canada's moral rights provisions and those of other copyright countries which adhere more closely than Canada does to the '*technique britannique*' – most notably Australia, the UK and to some extent the US.

In these countries, and particularly the UK and Australia, the moral rights provisions are, as in Canada, based loosely on Article 6 *bis* of the Berne Convention. Nevertheless they differ significantly from Canada's, both in their detail and in the way the rights link with the copyright system. The US system departs even more radically from the Canadian system than the other two do. The following account attempts to give some impression of the distinctive

[where the author of a derogatorily treated building is identified on it s/he has the right to require removal of the identification]; s. 81(6) [where the author has been identified infringement will not occur where disclaimer is made]; s. 82(2) [the right of integrity is not infringed where there is sufficient disclaimer].

50 Stig Strömholm, *Le droit moral de l'auteur en droit allemand, français et scandinave avec un aperçu de l'évolution internationale*, vol. 1 (Stockholm: Norstedt & Söners Förlag, 1967) at 428.

features of current Canadian moral rights law as viewed from outside the Canadian legal system and by comparison with the laws of other copyright countries.

Theoretical Relationship with Copyright

One of the central features of a country's 'copyright' system will always be the relationship between the moral rights and copyright, or between the non-economic rights of the author and the economic rights of the author/copyright owner. Typically in the common law countries, the moral rights are seen as separate from copyright, as statutory rights not having the nature of property. The two sets of rights are not linked in the way that they often are in the civil law countries, where both are seen as sub-groups of 'authors' rights', the '*Urheberrecht*', the '*droit d'auteur*'. Canada's rights are slightly different from those in the purely common law countries in this regard.

In Canada the rights subsist in relation to all copyright works and are in some contexts seen as part of the 'copyright' concept. In other contexts they are not. To put it differently, the term 'copyright' is inherently ambiguous in Canada, sometimes embracing and sometimes excluding the moral rights. The complication is compounded by the fact that the word 'copyright' is rendered in the French text of the Act by '*droit d'auteur*', a term capable in other countries – for example France – of comprehending both the economic and the moral rights. In the Canadian statute, however, the term '*droit d'auteur*', like 'copyright', only expressly comprehends the economic rights.[51] By contrast, judicial opinion at the highest level treats the moral rights as part of an overarching copyright/*droit d'auteur* theory. They are, however, subject to the economic imperatives of copyright.[52]

This judicial position contrasts with the position in the UK and Australia, where moral rights, as statutory rights separate from copyright, are not theoretically subservient to the aims of copyright. This lack of theoretical subservience is, however, belied in those countries by the rights being expressly limited in ways that serve the copyright interests.[53] In the US these limits are so extreme as to preclude moral rights protection for all but a very small range of works.[54]

---

[51] *Copyright Act*, R.S.C. 1985, c. C-42, s. 3.

[52] *Desputeaux v. Éditions Chouette (1987) inc.*, [2003] 1 S.C.R. 178.

[53] See for example the reasonableness defence in Australia: *Copyright Act 1968* (Cth), ss. 195AR and 195AS [*Copyright Act 1968*]. In the UK see the limitations put on the works that sustain protection: *CDPA 1988*, *supra* note 49, ss. 79, 80(5), 81 and 82(1).

[54] The limits take the form of the exclusion of most copyright works from the

What is the Role of Moral Rights in Canada?

Moral rights provisions in any jurisdiction cannot be sensibly interpreted unless their role in the legislative scheme is understood. Canada's legislation does not state any purpose for the rights in the way that a number of US jurisdictions do for their counterpart rights.[55] This might be taken as leaving questions of the rights' purpose open in Canada, or it might be taken as indicating that to ask the 'purpose' of the rights is to ask the wrong question. The rights, it might be thought, do not exist for instrumentalist reasons; they are not tools in social policy but rather expressions of the way the Canadian nation regards its authors. One might properly argue that the rights exist as a form of human rights protection, consistently with the statements of principle in the *Universal Declaration of Human Rights*[56] and the requirements – binding on Canada – of the *International Covenant on Economic, Social and Cultural Rights*.[57] This is a concept of the rights that is particularly strong in France and Germany.[58]

In the promotion of a more instrumentalist rationale, it is sometimes argued that moral rights in Canada serve the purpose of protecting culturally important material, that the public interest in cultural protection is at least one of the rights' *raisons d'être*.[59] Analogies with similar or counterpart rights in the US certainly encourage this view.[60] There are a number of reasons, however, why this argument is not convincing.

---

ambit of protection, leaving only the narrow category of 'works of visual art'. Most notably, the US federal rights do not protect the author against anything done to a reproduction of a work, even a work of visual art. For further commentary on the US rights see Adeney, *Moral Rights*, supra note 25 at c. 16.

55 Cal. Civ. Code § 987(a); Mass. Gen. Laws Ann., ch. 231, § 85S(a); N. J. Stat. Ann. title 2A, § 24A-2; Pennsylvania Fine Arts Preservation Act, PA. Stat. Ann., title 73, Preamble. See also HR Rep. No. 101–514 (1990), reprinted in 1990 USCCAN 6915.

56 'Everyone has the right to the protection of the moral and material interests resulting from any scientific, literary or artistic production of which he is the author'.

57 *International Covenant on Economic, Social and Cultural Rights*, 16 December 1966, 993 U.N.T.S. 3, Article 15(1): 'The States Parties to the present covenant recognize the right of everyone … to benefit from the protection of the moral and material interests resulting from any scientific, literary or artistic production of which he is the author'. Canada acceded to the Covenant in 1976.

58 Paris, 1ère Ch., 1 February 1989, (1989) 142 R.I.D.A. 301 (Annot. Sirinelli) (*Bragance c. Olivier Orban et Michel de Grèce*); in Germany, the moral right is based partly on articles 1 and 2 of the *Basic Law*, the German constitutional safeguard of human dignity.

59 See in particular R. D. Gibbens, 'The Moral Rights of Artists and the Copyright Act Amendments' (1989) 15 *Canadian Business Law Journal* 441 at 449 and 456; David Vaver, 'Authors' Moral Rights in Canada' (1983) I.I.C. 329 at 351.

60 It is clear in the US that the cultural protection rationale underpins the federal statute and also the California Art Preservation Act, among others. See HR Rep No 101–514, 14 and 17–18 (1990); and Cal Civ Code § 987(a).

When moral rights were first discussed in *Morang v. LeSueur*, they were treated as part of 'literary property'.[61] This established the rights as upholding proprietary, individualist and not community values. Later, in 1931, the legislators chose to draft the rights in the same form as Article 6 *bis* of the Berne Convention. It is therefore reasonable to interpret the 1931 provision according to the interests that Article 6 *bis* was designed to protect, namely the author's interest in maintaining his or her personal bond with the work.[62] Subsequent discussion has reinforced these conclusions. The Keyes and Brunet study in particular endorsed moral rights as protective of authorial personality.[63] One must also take into account the continuing influence of civil law, personalist, concepts on the judicial interpretation of the rights. The writings of learned commentators are cited by the courts when considering the rights' application, many of these commentators being francophone writers from the civil law tradition.[64] By this means focus is maintained on the rights' personalist aspect.[65]

These conclusions are also supported by various practical features of the current Canadian moral rights regime, and these will be noted below.

The Effects of a Bilingual and Bijural System

The interpretation of the moral rights provisions in Canada is both complicated and enriched by the bilingual nature of the statute and the bijural nature of the legal system. Each language version of the *Copyright Act* is as authoritative as, but not necessarily a perfect image of, the other. In cases where a provision in one language is ambiguous, the other language version is to be consulted before any further means of resolving the ambiguity are used. As the Canadian Supreme Court has said:

---

61 *Morang & Co. v. LeSueur*, supra note 10 at 98.

62 See further Adeney, *Moral Rights*, supra note 25, c. 6 on the drafting of Article 6 *bis*.

63 Keyes & Brunet, *supra* note 24 at 55.

64 For example, Carrière, Gendreau and Tamaro in *Lapierre-Desmarais v. Éditions Fides*, J.E. 99-1424 (C.Q.); Bertrand (France), Gendreau and Tamaro in *Les Ateliers Tango Argentin Inc v. Festival d'Espagne et d'Amérique Latine Inc.* (1997), 84 C.P.R. (3d) 56 (Que. S.C.); Tamaro in *Armand Vaillancourt v. Carbone 14*, [1999] R.J.Q. 490 (Que. S.C.); Colombet (France), Goudreau and Toupin in *Desputeaux v. Éditions Chouette (1987) inc.* (2001), 16 C.P.R. (4th) 77 (Que. C.A.); Goudreau in *Desputeaux v. Éditions Chouette (1987) inc.*, *supra* note 52 (S.C.C.).

65 In 2003 the Supreme Court, responding to a judgment of the Court of Appeal in Quebec, admitted that the work is a 'manifestation of the personality of the author' and made reference (loosely, one imagines) to 'copyright as a moral right': *Desputeaux v. Editions Chouette (1987) inc.*, *supra* note 52 at paras. 49 and 55 respectively. This is hardly an instrumentalist rhetoric.

statutory interpretation of bilingual enactments begins with a search for the shared meaning between the two versions. Where the words of one version may raise an ambiguity, courts should first look to the other official language version to determine whether its meaning is plain and unequivocal. …[66]

If the words in the second language version are unequivocal, the matter is settled.[67] If the words of the second language version are equivocal, the court will look for a reading that is clear, that is sufficiently limited to be common to both language versions and that is also consistent with the intention of parliament in drafting the statute.[68] If both versions are clear, the narrower of the versions is the correct one,[69] always provided that it is consistent with parliamentary intention. These principles have relevance to moral rights in Canada, since there appear to be several differences in meaning or scope between the one language version of the provisions and the other.[70] It is important for an accurate reading of the statute, therefore, that the French and English texts be read side by side.

Laconic Drafting

A further hallmark of the Canadian provisions is what has been called their laconic quality.[71] In common with continental European legislation, the central moral rights provisions are brief, with relatively little attempt made to regulate all possible situations that may arise in the exploitation of the work. In this the provisions differ from their counterparts in the UK, Australia and the US. For example, in Canada the right of attribution is stated in a fraction of a sentence.[72] In Australia 11 sections (and 20 subsections) cover the same area, stating the nature of the right/s (a right against false attribution is included), the way attribution should be made, the degree of attribution

---

66 *R. v. Mac*, [2002] 1 S.C.R. 856 at para. 5. The court was citing Pierre-André Côté, *Interpretation of Legislation in Canada*, 3d ed. (Scarborough, Ont.: Carswell, 2000) at 327.

67 *R. v. Mac*, *ibid.* at para 6.

68 *Medovarski v. Canada (Minister of Citizenship and Immigration)*; *Esteban v. Canada (Minister of Citizenship and Immigration)*, [2005] 2 S.C.R. 539 at paras. 23–6 and referring also to *R. v. Daoust*, [2004] 1 S.C.R. 217 and *Schreiber v. Canada (Attorney General)*, [2002] 3 S.C.R. 269.

69 If neither version is ambiguous, or if they both are, the common meaning is normally the narrower version: *R. v. Daoust*, *ibid.* at para. 29.

70 For example, see below note 90 and associated text and note 126 and associated text.

71 The word has been applied particularly to the attribution right: *Desputeaux v. Les Editions Chouette (1987) inc.*, *supra* note 64 at para. 38 (C.A.Q.).

72 *Copyright Act*, *supra* note 51, s. 14.1.

required, the circumstances under which attribution should be made, and the circumstances under which a work will be considered falsely attributed.[73] Infringement and defences to infringement of the attribution right are covered separately and also at length.[74] In the UK three sections (and 21 subsections[75]) regulate the attribution right, with particular attention given to circumstances where the right does not arise or will not be infringed.[76] This creation of detailed exceptions is largely foreign to the Canadian regime.

What is the result of Canada's laconic drafting? It would probably be true to say that the courts have less to interpret, though they have to deal with the complexity of a bilingual statute. (This in turn will mean that provisions will tend to be read narrowly, so that both language versions can be accommodated.)[77] The courts are, on some issues, left to infer principles or standards that in other countries are made express.[78] The lack of explicit exceptions to the rights means that the Canadian courts can be more generous to authors than other courts are free to be.[79] The courts are not told what considerations must be taken into account in making their decisions, as is sometimes the case under the Australian statute.[80] There is, in short, more space left in Canada for judicial discretion and lawmaking.

CANADIAN MORAL RIGHTS AND HOW THEY ARE INFRINGED – THEIR KEY ELEMENTS

Under the current law in Canada the author has a right of integrity, a right to be associated with a work as its author, and a right to remain anonymous.[81] The first two are effectively the rights outlined in Article 6 *bis* of the Berne

---

[73] *Copyright Act 1968*, *supra* note 53, ss. 193, 194, 195, 195AA, 195AB–AH.

[74] *Ibid.*, ss. 195AO, 195AP, 195AR.

[75] *CDPA 1988*, *supra* note 49, ss. 77–9.

[76] *Ibid.*, s. 79.

[77] See above note 69 and associated text.

[78] For example, the degree and type of attribution that should be made to an author are mandated in Australia: *Copyright Act 1968*, *supra* note 53, ss. 195, 195AA and 195AB.

[79] For example, they are not constrained to deny protection because of the nature of the work, because it has come into existence in certain circumstances, or because formalities (such as a formal assertion of the right) have not taken place, as is the case in the UK: *CDPA 1988*, *supra* note 49, s. 77(1).

[80] *Copyright Act 1968*, *supra* note 53, ss. 195AR, 195AS, 195AVA, 195AZA.

[81] *Copyright Act*, *supra* note 51, s. 14.1(1): 'L'auteur d'une œuvre a le droit, sous réserve de l'article 28.2, à l'intégrité de l'œuvre et, à l'égard de tout acte mentionné à l'article 3, le droit, compte tenu des usages raisonnables, d'en revendiquer, même sous pseudonyme, la création, ainsi que le droit à l'anonymat.'

Convention. The last is within the spirit but not the wording of Article 6 *bis*.[82] Since 1988 strict adherence to the words of the Berne Convention has no longer been an aspect of Canadian moral rights, though the key elements of the Berne wording are retained.

The Right of Integrity

The content of Canada's right of integrity is expressed not in the provision stating the right[83] but through a statement of the acts that will infringe it.[84] It is infringed only if the work is distorted, mutilated or otherwise modified or if it is used in association with a product, service, cause or institution.[85] Such an act must be 'to the prejudice of the honour or reputation of the author'.[86] Destruction of the work, no matter how prejudicial to the accrual of a future reputation, is not stated to be capable of infringing.[87] Most destructions would, however, probably be interpreted as extreme forms of mutilation and brought under the operation of the provisions in this way.[88]

No derogatory treatment concept

The right of integrity differs from the counterpart right in Australian and UK law in that no mediating concept is used, such as the notion of 'derogatory treatment'.[89] This means that the Canadian statute is less cluttered by terms needing interpretation than its counterparts in the other countries. On the other

---

82 Elizabeth Adeney, 'The Mask of the Author – Anonymity and Pseudonymity in Two Common Law Countries' (2000) 31 I.I.C. 913.

83 *Copyright Act*, *supra* note 51, s. 14.1 (1).

84 *Ibid.*, s. 28.2.

85 *Ibid.*, s. 28.2(1) 'Il n'y a violation du droit à l'intégrité que si l'œuvre est, d'une manière préjudiciable à l'honneur ou à la réputation de l'auteur, déformée, mutilée ou autrement modifiée, ou utilisée en liaison avec un produit, une cause, un service ou une institution.'

86 *Ibid.*: 'd'une manière préjudiciable à l'honneur ou à la réputation de l'auteur.'

87 While the inclusion of a destruction clause was mooted in the Committee hearings, the balance of opinion appeared to be that it was inconsistent with the conventional view of moral rights: '…to include destruction might in a perverse way offend the principle of preserving a moral right': Mr Edwards (Member of the Committee), agreeing with the Minister and another speaker: *Committee Proceedings, Bill C-60* 9:49 (10 December 1987). However it should be remembered that Mignault, in 1880, had regarded the author as entitled to prohibit a destruction of the work. See *supra* note 6 and associated text.

88 This happened in *Armand Vaillancourt v. Carbone 14*, *supra* note 64.

89 See *Copyright Act 1968*, *supra* note 53, s. 195AI(2); *CDPA 1988*, *supra* note 49, s. 80(1). The wording derives from the current English text of Article 6 *bis* and its reference to 'other derogatory action'.

hand the lack of any such broad concept throws the focus onto specific authorial prerogatives and infringing acts rather than a general concept of those types of treatment of the work that authors cannot be expected to tolerate. This tends to have a limiting effect on the provision's ambit.

The harm to the author

The French and English versions of the Canadian right of integrity differ slightly. The French version speaks of the distortion, mutilation or modification being carried out 'd'une manière préjudiciable à l'honneur ou à la réputation de l'auteur'. The English version speaks of the act being carried out 'to the prejudice' of the author. The English version is hence drafted to focus on the result of the treatment, the prejudice to the author.[90] The French version, on the other hand, is drafted to focus on the moment of distortion and the prejudicial manner in which the distortion takes place. The difference is highlighted in at least one judgment.

In the Federal Court judgment in *Prise de parole Inc v. Guérin, éditeur Ltée*, Denault J., working with the French statutory text, emphasized that the plaintiff did not need to prove actual damage (*un préjudice*) to honour or reputation, but rather that the work had been treated in a manner that could harm these interests:

> I note that paragraph 28.2(1) does not oblige the plaintiff to prove harm to his honour or to his reputation [*un préjudice à son honneur ou à sa réputation*], but to prove that the work has been distorted, mutilated or otherwise modified 'in a manner prejudicial to the honour or to the reputation of the author'.[91]

Judge Denault saw this wording ('in a manner prejudicial') as particularly significant and as 'justifying the use of a subjective criterion – the author's opinion – in assessing whether the infringement is prejudicial'.[92] Referring to the *Snow* case, however, Denault J. also considered an objective evaluation of the prejudice (presumably whether the author's opinion had been reasonably

---

90 The word 'prejudicial', like the word 'harmful', seems to contemplate the relevant harm in two stages. While an act may be presently prejudicial to reputation, the actual loss of standing or esteem may occur later, for example when a distorted work is published.

91 English translation as reported in *Prise de parole Inc. et al v. Guérin, éditeur Ltée* (1995), 66 C.P.R. (3d) 257 at 266 (F.C.T.D.). The French text read: 'Je note que le paragraphe 28.2(1) n'oblige pas le demandeur à prouver un préjudice à son honneur ou à sa réputation, mais à prouver que l'œuvre a été déformée, mutilée ou autrement modifiée "d'une manière préjudiciable à l'honneur ou à la réputation de l'auteur"': as quoted by Judge Locas in *Lapierre-Desmarais v. Editions Fides*, *supra* note 64.

92 *Prise de parole Inc. v. Guérin, éditeur Ltée*, *ibid.* at 265.

arrived at) to be necessary.[93] A judge working solely from the English version of the statute might not have been prompted to emphasise the manner of treatment as Denault J. did, though the rather uncertain meaning of 'to the prejudice' in the English text might have prompted consideration of the French text with a view to clarification.

Although it has been argued in Canada that the occurrence of actual harm is necessary for infringement to be made out,[94] the *Prise de parole* reading of the provision seems most likely to reflect the intention of the Canadian legislators and is close to international formulations of the right. The formulations used in Australia and the UK – 'prejudicial to the author's honour or reputation' in both countries – seem to allow for the case to be made out through the establishment of propensity alone. In the US the legislators (both at state and federal level) have chosen the wording 'which would be prejudicial' in their equivalents of the integrity right,[95] drawing on the current English version of the Berne Convention to do so.[96] The conditional construction used in the US allows for infringement to be established where actual or quantifiable harm is still in the future. This is, furthermore, similar to the way the German counterpart provision is drafted, providing for infringement where only *endangerment* of authorial interests is established.[97] This notion of unrealised future harm seems to have found a Canadian analogue in the French text of the provision. Its location of the infringement in the *manner* in which the distortion takes place, so that the author's view of the likely outcome becomes relevant, places the time of infringement well before that of the ultimate harm.

As for the question of what constitutes 'honour' and 'reputation', there has been only modest comment in Canada on these concepts. Honour, according to the Canadian commentator Carrière, is moral dignity which is enjoyed when

---

93 Ultimately Denault J. found that: '... although the author has shown that his novel was substantially modified without his knowledge and that he was shocked and distressed by this, the evidence has not shown that, objectively, as required by s. 28.2(1) of the Act, his work was modified to the prejudice of [in a manner prejudicial to] his honour or reputation': *ibid.* at 266 [official translation].

94 Gibbens, *supra* note 59 at 452.

95 *Copyright Act*, 17 U.S.C. § 106A(a). In the Nevada Revised Statutes publication of a defaced or mutilated work is prohibited 'if damage to the reputation of an artist is reasonably foreseeable': Nev. Rev. Stat. 597.740(1). In the New York and Louisiana statutes the impugned act must be 'reasonably likely to result' in damage to reputation: NY Arts and Cult. Aff. Law § 14.03; La Rev. Stat. Ann. § 51:2154(C).

96 *Berne Convention for the Protection of Literary and Artistic Works*, revised at Paris on 24 July 1971, 1161 U.N.T.S. 3, Article 6 *bis*(1).

97 'The author has the right to prohibit a distortion or any other impairment of his work that is *apt to endanger* his legitimate intellectual or personal interests in the work': *Urheberrechtsgesetz* (Germany), § 14.

one has the feeling of meriting respect and of maintaining self esteem. Reputation, on the other hand, is a matter of being honourably regarded from a moral point of view.[98]

As noted in relation to the *Snow* case, the concept of reputation used here should not necessarily be interpreted as co-extensive with reputation in defamation law.[99] Avoiding such interpretation, Carrière suggests that the phrase should be read as 'prejudicial to the honour and to the reputation, artistic or literary, of the author, with regard to this work or to the aggregate of his works'.[100] Despite this rather narrow approach to honour or reputation sometimes being followed in Europe,[101] the UK[102] and the US,[103] the limitation to artistic or literary reputation may not represent the intention of the negotiating parties in Brussels when they discussed this aspect of Article 6 *bis*. Here it was stated, on behalf of the Berne Union, that the reputation of the author as author and also as personality on the literary stage was protected. Acts which injured the 'man' (*l'homme*) through a distortion of his work were the target of the protection.[104]

The droit d'aval – contextual infringement

The Canadian statute does not contain any broad concept of contextual abuse – the infringement of the integrity right through the use of the work in a prejudicial environment or context. This is a significant limitation on the integrity right and a surprising one, since the latest version of Article 6 *bis*, covering '*other derogatory action* in relation to [the work], which would be prejudicial to [the author's] honor or reputation'[105] was drafted to address concerns about contextual abuse.[106] Australia, by contrast, has relatively robust provision for

[98] Laurent Carrière, 'Droit d'auteur et droit moral: quelques réflexions préliminaires' in *Développements récents en droit de la propriété intellectuelle (1991)* (Cowanville: Yvon Blais, 1991) 243 at 270.

[99] See above note 40 and associated text.

[100] Carrière, *supra* note 98 at 270.

[101] This is particularly the case in Scandinavia. See Norway, *Act No 2 of May 12, 1961, Relating to Copyright in Literary, Scientific and Artistic Works*, s. 3. See also Denmark, *Act on Copyright 1995,* s. 3(1).

[102] *Pasterfield v. Denham*, [1999] F.S.R. 168 at 182 (Plymouth County Ct., U.K.).

[103] *Carter v. Helmsley-Spear*, 861 F.Supp 303 at 323 (S.D.N.Y. 1994).

[104] *Documents de la conférence de Bruxelles 5–26 juin 1948* (Berne: Bureau de l'Union Internationale pour la Protection des Œuvres Littéraires et Artistiques, 1951) at 97–8.

[105] *Berne Convention for the Protection of Literary and Artistic Works*, revised at Paris on 24 July 1971, 1161 U.N.T.S. 3, Article 6 *bis*(1) [emphasis added].

[106] See, on the problems the amendment was intended to remedy, Adeney, *Moral Rights*, supra note 25 at para. 7.19.

contextual infringement.[107] It is, however, the only one of its peer group of countries that allows for such infringement.

Although contextual abuse is not generally subject to sanction in Canada, the Act does contain what is called in French the *droit d'aval*. The author may oppose the use of the work in association with a product, service, cause or institution, by this means being able to control certain uses of the work that alter neither one of its embodiments nor its intellectual content. Although only a very narrow range of uses is contemplated, the right has sometimes been seen in Canada as too broad. The current wording was objected to in committee hearings, for example, on the basis that the words 'in association with' would catch too many acts. It was proposed that the word 'promoting' be substituted for them,[108] with a view to limiting this right to the advertising or similar contexts. Although this attempt at limitation was unsuccessful, it would seem that, for example, the reproduction of a religious work in a pornographic magazine would not infringe the right, whereas this might well constitute an infringement in Australia.

The deeming of prejudice

Canada is the only copyright country where it is possible for a distortion, mutilation or modification of a work, without more, to result in an infringement. The relevant provision[109] is drafted in the interests of artistic authors who might otherwise find the task of establishing prejudice to honour or reputation insurmountable.[110] But they are only assisted under very limited circumstances. The deeming relates solely to a small and traditional group of artistic works, namely paintings, sculptures and engravings. The legislative intention, as far as one can judge from the preliminary discussions, was to protect the authors of works that exist only in a single embodiment.[111] Nevertheless, as Vaver points out, the statutory wording is broad enough to apply to works as

---

[107] *Copyright Act 1968*, *supra* note 53, s. 195AK: 'doing anything else in relation to the work'. This latter part of the definition is intended to address those instances where a work is used in an inappropriate context and prejudices the author's honour or reputation: Revised Explanatory Memorandum, Copyright Amendment (Moral Rights) Bill 1999 (Cth) at 44.

[108] *Committee Proceedings, Bill C-60* 4:8 (27 October 1987) (M. Jacques Alleyne).

[109] *Copyright Act*, *supra* note 51, s. 28.2(2): 'Toute déformation, mutilation ou autre modification d'une peinture, d'une sculpture ou d'une gravure est réputée préjudiciable au sens du paragraphe (1)'.

[110] *From Gutenberg to Telidon: A White Paper on Copyright*, *supra* note 38 at 26–7.

[111] *Committee Proceedings, Bill C-60* 9:50 (10 December 1987) (Ms. Wanda Noël).

they exist not only in original embodiments, but in reproductions.[112] Should the courts read the provision as broadly as its words allow, Canada would be the most liberal country in the copyright world in its protection of certain visual artists' moral rights. This liberalism would approach that of Germany, where the prejudice to authorial interests tends to be assumed by the courts if sufficient interference with the work has been proven.[113] Neither Australia, the UK nor the US allows for the deeming of prejudice under any circumstances.[114]

At least in its application to original embodiments, the deeming provision seems a reasonable response to the difficulty that artists are likely to have in proving prejudice to honour or reputation. It also helps to address longstanding international criticism of the 'honour or reputation' limb of the integrity right.[115] This criticism is particularly justified where indigenous art is concerned and where the distortion of a work may be deeply offensive to the cultural group, including the author, without the individual author's honour or reputation necessarily being affected.[116]

Exceptions to distortion, mutilation and modification

Having somewhat broadened the application of the integrity right, s. 28.2 then proceeds to circumscribe it, enumerating circumstances in which a work will not be considered distorted, mutilated or modified. Neither a change in the location of a work, nor the physical means by which a work is exposed, nor the physical structure containing a work, nor steps taken in good faith to restore or preserve the work will, 'by that act alone', constitute distortion, mutilation or modification of the work.[117]

---

[112] David Vaver, *Copyright Law* (Toronto: Irwin Law, 2000) at 163.

[113] Haimo Schack, *Urheber und Urhebervertragsrecht*, 2nd ed. (Tübingen: Mohr Siebeck, 2001) at 165, citing OLG Munich, [1992] ZUM 307 at 310.

[114] Though this was once mooted in the US. See *Visual Artists Rights Act*, H.R. 2690, 101st Congress § 3 (1989) as introduced by Representative Kastenmeier on 20 June 1989.

[115] The criticism of such wording has been made both by international commentators on the Berne Convention (see Adeney, *Moral Rights*, supra note 25 at para. 7.24) and more recently in France. In relation to the right of integrity in computer programs, Lucas considers that the test renders the right merely symbolic: André Lucas & Henri-Jacques Lucas, *Traité de la propriété littéraire et artistique* (Paris: Litec, 1994) at para. 419.

[116] See further Elizabeth Adeney, 'The Moral Right of Integrity: the Past and Future of "Honour"' (2005) 11 Intellectual Property Quarterly 111 at 131–3.

[117] '(3) Pour l'application du présent article, ne constitue pas nécessairement une déformation, mutilation ou autre modification de l'oeuvre un changement de lieu, du cadre de son exposition ou de la structure qui la contient ou toute mesure de restauration ou de conservation prise de bonne foi.'

The words 'by that act alone' limit the scope of the exception. They suggest that any of the abovementioned acts could still produce a distortion, mutilation, or modification if they caused accompanying changes to the work. Furthermore, in the absence of good faith, that is, in the absence of genuinely restorative work, alterations under the guise of restoration still have the potential to infringe.

The Right of Attribution (Right of Paternity or Right of Association)

The main provision governing the right of attribution describes a right to be associated with the work as its author by name or under a pseudonym and the right to remain anonymous.[118] The right to be associated with the work arises when the work is utilized in certain prescribed ways,[119] and 'where reasonable in the circumstances' ('compte tenu des usages raisonnables'). It is notable that the Canadian legislators have not required the author to 'assert' the right as a condition precedent to its exercise, as the UK legislators have done.[120] In this Canadian law is consistent with both Australian and US law, where no formal assertion is required.

The interests that the right protects, the values that it safeguards, are not stated in the legislation. One court, however, has commented that:

> The right to have the work properly attributed to oneself, just like the right to respect for one's name, has a purely moral connotation that is tied up with the dignity and honour of the work's creator.[121]

This statement is one of the few internationally that indicate the attribution right's general purpose of safeguarding the honour and dignity of the creator. Such a statement ignores notions of consumer protection (a justification often given for the attribution right),[122] focusing instead

---

118 For the purposes of this discussion the anonymity right will be treated as a limb of the attribution right.

119 Listed in *Copyright Act*, *supra* note 51, s. 3.

120 See *CDPA 1988*, *supra* note 49, s. 77(1).

121 'Le droit de se voir justement attribuer la paternité d'une œuvre tout comme le droit au respect du nom revêtent une connotation purement morale tenant à la dignité et à l'honneur du créateur de l'œuvre': *Desputeaux v. Les Editions Chouette (1987) inc.*, *supra* note 64 at para. 40. Français writes to similar effect: Jean-Arpad Français, 'Le droit moral comparé: entre problématique classique et moderne' (2000) 12:2 Cahiers de propriété intellectuelle 315 at 336.

122 See David Vaver, 'Authors' moral rights and the copyright law review committee's report: w(h)ither such rights now?' (1988) 14 Monash University Law Review 284 at 286; Jane C. Ginsburg, 'Moral Rights in a Common Law System' in Peter Anderson & David Saunders, eds, *Moral Rights Protection in a Copyright System*

on the personal harm occasioned by misrepresentation of the author-work bond.

The right to be associated with the work as its author

'The right to be associated with the work as its author', 'le droit...d'en revendiquer...la création', is a broad formulation, not mandating the form that attribution must take and apparently satisfied by either tangible or intangible forms of attribution. The very broadly expressed French language version of the right – the right to 'claim the work's creation' – reinforces the view that the manner of association with the work is unconstrained. There is no indication here that the name must appear on the work or in proximity to a particular embodiment of the work. The sole stated limitation, apart from the reasonableness requirement, is that the right arises only when the work is used or exploited in the ways listed in s. 3 (which is also a list of the exclusive rights of the copyright owner).

It may be asked whether the right of attribution applies where the work is mentioned in media or other discussion. It is true that discussion of the work is not an exclusive right of the copyright owner listed in s. 3. However, if the work were performed (or published or exhibited – acts embraced by s. 3) and the performance, publication or exhibition discussed, one might infer a right to be associated with the work as its author in 'connection with' the performance, publication or exhibition. Such an interpretation would mean that the Canadian right is broader than its UK and Australian counterparts, where only physical proximity of the name to the work appears to have been envisaged by the legislators.[123]

The notion of being 'associated with the work as its author' has received welcome attention in Canada. One judge has stated that a purported attribution nominating a person as having 'prepared' the work is insufficient to denote authorship.[124] If a person has written (or painted or composed etc) a work, then this authorship must be acknowledged for what it is and not labelled as some lesser contribution to the final work. Since this point has subsequently been reinforced in a UK decision,[125] it is to be hoped that courts and users of

---

(Brisbane: Institute for Cultural Policy Studies, 1992) at 15–16 (also published in (1990) 1 Ent. L. R. 121 (U.K.)) and Sam Ricketson, 'The Case for Moral Rights' (1995) 25 Intellectual Property Forum 37 at 40–41.

[123] *CDPA 1988*, *supra* note 49, s. 77; *Copyright Act 1968*, *supra* note 53, ss. 193 and 194.

[124] *Dolmage v. Erskine* (2003), 23 C.P.R. (4th) 495 (O.S.C.J., Small Claims).

[125] The words 'With thanks to Dr Lionel Sawkins for his preparation of performance materials for this recording' were not considered adequate to identify Dr Sawkins as the author of the material in question: *Hyperion Records Ltd v. Sawkins*, [2005] 1 W.L.R. 3281 at 3297 (England and Wales C.A. (Civil Division)) approving a judgment of Mr Justice Patten in *Sawkins v. Hyperion Records Ltd.*, [2004] 4 All E.R. 418.

copyright material in other jurisdictions will make this distinction, attaching proper importance to the difference between authorship and mere preparation.

The reasonableness criterion

The association of the name with the work must be 'reasonable in the circumstances'; this is a condition precedent to the existence of the right. In the words of the French version of the Act, attribution must be made 'compte tenu des usages raisonnables'. This was a concession to the realities of, for example, the television industry, which saw great difficulty in making attribution in all cases.[126] However, the import of this criterion appears to have been interpreted differently by various Canadian courts.

The English-language formulation of the right, stating a right to attribution 'where reasonable in the circumstances', suggests that the plaintiff must make the case that the attribution would have been reasonable. This is consistent with the fact that this provision's dominant purpose is to describe the subsistence of a right rather than dealing with infringement and defences. Consistently with this view, some authors have expressed concern that the need to prove reasonableness may significantly impinge on the author's basic right to receive attribution: 'Article 14.1(1) could even be interpreted as placing on the author the burden of proving that reasonable usage gives him the right to affix his name.'[127] In a 2003 decision Ducharme J. of the Superior Court of Justice of Ontario noted, in line with this interpretation of the term, that it was not reasonable for a plaintiff to believe that he would continue to be associated with some of his photographs which appeared on a website.[128] He had no right to complain of such utilization.

There is other authority, however, suggesting that it is the defendant who may wish to establish reasonableness. In *Tat-ha v. Centre hospitalier de l'Université Laval* an employed author lost her action for attribution to her of a report written in the course of her employment. The institutional practice in

---

[126] *Committee Proceedings, Bill C-60* 4:8 (27 October 1987) (M. Jacques Alleyne) spoke in support of the limitation: 'On the matter of paternity, it is essential to say "where reasonable in the circumstances", because otherwise…I could recite to you the coverage of various events – parades…We have no idea in television how many works appear in television, of all kinds, of all natures. Even covering a parade, you would have artistic craftsmanship; you would have anything you can think of. Even covering a football game, you could have some visual elements you would have to identify. So I think "when reasonable" will at least take away what is unreasonable in the common intendment of people, and that would be an improvement.'

[127] Mistrale Goudreau, 'Le droit moral de l'auteur au Canada' (1994) 25 Revue générale de droit 403 at 413 citing Victor Nabhan, 'Coup d'œil sur les modifications à la Loi sur le droit d'auteur au Canada' (1989) R.I.D.A. 142 at 175 and 195.

[128] *Ritchie v. Sawmill Creek Golf & Country Club Ltd*, *supra* note 43 at 237.

her workplace was for the team leader to sign work to which institution members had contributed. This was considered by the court a 'reasonable practice'.[129] Similarly, in a case where a photograph had initially been used without attribution, the prompt and *bona fide* action of the defendant in attaching the name as soon as she became aware of it negated the infringement. The defendant had, in the judge's view, respected 'les usages raisonnables de l'article 14.1 de la Loi' ('the reasonable usages of section 14.1 of the Act').[130] In a third case, where the plaintiff won, it was pointed out that the defendant had failed to show a good reason for the inadequate attribution made to the plaintiff. The failure of attribution was therefore unreasonable.[131]

It may be that, if what the defendant has done conforms to concepts of reasonable usage, the plaintiff's action against the defendant will not be considered reasonable. But a certain inconsistency remains between the two alternative readings of the provision, encouraged by the two different language versions of the Act.

A right against false attribution of authorship?

In Australia, a special right against false attribution of authorship is given, protecting the author against attribution of his or her work to another.[132] Canadian law does not expressly give the author such a right. Despite this, it seems that false attribution, as the term is understood in Australia, is covered by the Canadian right of attribution as interpreted by the courts. For example, where a photographer's work – subject, layout, design, lighting and so on – was copied by another photographer (who had not, however, copied the actual negatives or prints made by the first photographer) and the second photographer's name appeared on the copy, a court found that the second photographer had infringed the attribution right.[133]

This Canadian protection of the author's interest in not having his or her work attributed to another contrasts with the apparent lack of this right in the UK, despite the UK having what its legislation calls a 'right against false attribution'.[134] In that country, however, the right is primarily a right against misuse of a person's name on the work of another, or against misuse of the

---

129 *Tat-ha v. Centre hospitalier de l'Université Laval* (1999), BE 99-259 at para. 22, [1999] AQ 181 (Que. S.C.).

130 *Lapierre-Demarais v. Éditions Fides*, *supra* note 64.

131 *Dolmage v. Erskine*, *supra* note 124 at 526–7 (O.S.C.J., Small Claims).

132 *Copyright Act 1968*, *supra* note 53, ss. 195AC-195AH. The right also protects the author against the misattribution to the author of an altered work.

133 *Les Ateliers Tango Argentin Inc. v. Festival d'Espagne et d'Amérique Latine Inc.*, *supra* note 64. This decision was made under s. 12(7), but nothing in the new legislation indicates that the case would be decided differently today.

134 *CDPA 1988*, *supra* note 49, s. 84(1).

artist's name on an artistic work that has been altered after it has left his or her hands.[135] The right against misuse of a person's name is not covered by the moral rights provisions in Canada,[136] and rightly so. In as far as it relates to *any* person's name and is unrelated to a work by that person, it is not an authorial right on accepted principles at all.[137]

The right of anonymity

Probably the most striking aspect of the Canadian moral rights regime is the express right of anonymity, whose presence in the statute is not required by the Berne Convention. In protecting authorial anonymity so unambiguously, Canada has aligned itself with civil law thinking,[138] and has given the author a useful means of (1) preventing the association of the author's name with works that may no longer reflect his or her convictions and (2) protecting him/herself against violent reactions to the work's contents.

This express provision for anonymity indicates Canada's commitment to protection of the author above protection of the public since, by and large, the public interest lies in the full identification of the author. The express allowance made for pseudonymity in Canada,[139] as elsewhere, also indicates a particular concern for the authorial interest above the public interest since pseudonymity constitutes, in some senses, a deliberate misleading of the public.[140] Canada, in other words, has been sturdily pro-author in its approach to attribution.

The Absence of Express Defences

The Canadian statute does not cut back the authorial rights through the granting of express defences. The defendant in Canada can argue neither fair dealing[141] nor fair use.[142] Likewise, despite the concept of reasonableness being

---

135 See further Adeney, *Moral Rights*, *supra* note 25 at 14.46–14.59.

136 *682330 Ont. Inc. v. Cineplex Odeon Corp.* (1990), 33 C.P.R. (3d) 408 at 411 (F.C.T.D.), aff'd (1990), 33 C.P.R. (3d) 413 (F.C.T.D.).

137 See, for the comments of a number of authors on this issue, Adeney, *Moral Rights*, *supra* note 25 at 8.58.

138 See particularly Germany where the author has the right to determine how *and whether* to receive attribution: *Urheberrechtsgesetz* (Germany), § 13.

139 *Copyright Act*, *supra* note 51, s. 14.1(1).

140 It must be admitted, however, that the consistent use by an author of a pseudonym does at least allow the public to allocate a sequence of works to a particular, albeit unknown, source.

141 The Australian defence covered by *Copyright Act 1968*, *supra* note 53, ss. 40–42 (in relation to works); the UK defence covered by *CDPA 1988*, *supra* note 49, s. 30 and associated with the right of attribution by s. 79(4).

142 See 17 U.S.C. § 107(1). In Australia, in the moral rights context, the concept

built into the right of attribution,[143] the reasonableness of an act is no *general* defence to infringement of moral rights in Canada. The lack of a fair use/fair dealing defence in particular means that courts are not perplexed by the need to apply concepts which take their meaning from the economic context in which they were developed to an entirely different type of right.[144] There is a cost, however. These defences of fairness or reasonableness represent areas of flexibility in the statutory scheme, where the court's discretion may be invoked. Without them the scheme becomes more rigid.

The Absence of Indirect Infringement

While the absence of express defences works in favour of the plaintiff, the absence in Canada of any notion of indirect infringement of moral rights (infringement through sale or importation of, or dealing with, infringing material) reduces the number of parties who may be joined as defendants. Carrière writes of the right of attribution that it can be claimed only with regard to s. 3 acts. It is not possible to assert the right in relation to indirect violations.[145] His comments appear to be equally true of the right of integrity. In this respect Australia, unlike the UK or the US, provides more complete protection to the plaintiff author, since this country provides expressly for infringement through importation and sale.[146]

A LIBERAL APPROACH TO WAIVER AND CONSENT

As in any other country, moral rights in Canada are incapable of assignment.[147] Moreover the assignment of the economic rights does not of itself effect a waiver of the moral rights.[148] The Canadian legislators have, however,

---

of reasonableness has been substituted: *Copyright Act 1968*, *supra* note 53, ss. 195AR(2) and (3), 195AS(2)(h) and 195AS(3)(i).

143 *Copyright Act*, *supra* note 51, s. 14.1(1): 'The author of a work has, subject to section 28.2, … in connection with an act mentioned in section 3, the right, *where reasonable in the circumstances*, to be associated with the work as its author by name or under a pseudonym and the right to remain anonymous' [emphasis added].

144 Peter H. Karlen, 'What's Wrong with VARA: a Critique of Federal Moral Rights' (1993) 15 Hastings Communications and Entertainment Law Journal 905 at 912–913.

145 Carrière, *supra* note 98 at 254.

146 *Copyright Act 1968*, *supra* note 53, ss. 195AU, 195AV.

147 *Copyright Act*, *supra* note 51, s. 14.1(2): 'Moral rights may not be assigned but may be waived in whole or in part.'

148 *Ibid.*, s. 14.1(3).

made very liberal provision for the moral rights to be waived.[149] It seems that this was done to preserve authorial autonomy:

> [R]espect for works of the mind and their creators should not take the form of paternalism. ...Freedom is vital to the creative environment. Concerns expressed that hard-pressed and non-established creators may be tempted to give away too much control over their works are well meant, but lead to undesirable constraints. All copyright rights – economic as well as moral – should be assignable and waivable. It is through negotiations about rights that creators derive benefit from their works.[150]

Perhaps it is for the reasons mentioned in this extract that statutory allowance for waiver, whether written or oral, express or implied,[151] has never aroused much dissention in Canada. This is surprising from an extra-Canadian perspective. Waiver is an abandonment of rights,[152] and the notion of abandonment does not sit well with the 'human rights' aspect of authorial moral rights and their entrenchment in both the *Universal Declaration of Human Rights* and the *International Covenant on Economic, Social and Cultural Rights*.[153] This is not to say that Canada is alone in its tolerance of waiver. Both the UK and the US legislation allow waiver of the moral rights, though in the latter country there has been concern that a waiver provision is a potential threat to the rights.[154] The UK statute also allows for common law waiver-like abandonment of the rights.[155] Australia's legislation does not mention waiver, but allows authorial consent to otherwise infringing acts so freely that such consent may well amount to implied waiver of the rights.

Consent vitiating infringement is also envisaged in Canada, though it is not formulated as an authorial prerogative in the way that waiver is. An infringement

---

149 *Ibid.*, s. 14.1(2).

150 *A Charter of Rights for Creators*, *supra* note 38 at 7–8. The objection to paternalism somewhat misses the point that moral rights are conceived of as natural rights in the nature of human rights.

151 The legislation does not limit the concept of waiver in any way.

152 This, in any event, is the way it is treated in the UK and the way Lord Beaverbrook described it in the House of Lords: *Hansard*, 5th ser., vol. 491, col. 395 (10 December 1987).

153 See above, notes 56 and 57.

154 In case the waiver provision allowed the unequal bargaining power of the artist to be taken advantage of, the legislature provided for a study to be conducted by the Copyright Office on the use and effect of waiver during the 18 months after the passing of the legislation: *Waiver of Moral Rights in Visual Artworks: Final Report of the Register of Copyrights, March 1, 1996* (Washington, D.C.: United States Copyright Office, 1996). The Report was, however, inconclusive on the effects of waiver on visual artists.

155 *CDPA 1988*, *supra* note 49, s. 87(4).

of the rights occurs when authorial consent to the prima facie infringing act is absent.[156] Nothing indicates that a consent must be in writing, so it seems that it may be spoken or even implied. The treatment of consent in the Canadian scheme is quite unlike the detailed and complex arrangements made for consent in Australia.[157] It may be criticized for taking no account of the unequal bargaining positions of authors and users of the copyright material and the ease with which consents can be extracted from the impecunious author.[158]

CANADA'S 'SHORT' PROTECTION PERIOD

The duration of the moral rights in Canada is the same as for copyright – 50 years after the author's death as a rule of thumb.[159] Canada has therefore not followed France's concept of indefinite moral rights protection.[160] Nor is the 50-year period consistent with the US approach of generally not allowing the counterpart (visual artists') rights to persist beyond the author's death.[161] Neither has Canada succumbed to pressure from the United States to extend its copyright (and hence, in Canada, moral rights) term to 70 years post mortem. The basic term of protection is now 20 years shorter than the basic term in Australia,[162] and in those countries of continental Europe where the moral rights are coextensive with the economic rights.[163] Unlike Australia, Canada has created no exceptions to its duration rule for particular types of work.[164]

---

156 *Copyright Act*, *supra* note 51, s. 28.1.

157 *Copyright Act 1968*, *supra* note 53, ss. 195AW–195AWB.

158 In Australia special provision is made to protect authors from the consequences of consents made under duress, though such protection may in any event form part of the common law: *Copyright Act 1968*, *supra* note 53, s. 195AWB.

159 *Copyright Act*, *supra* note 51, s. 14.2(1).

160 *Code de la Propriété Intellectuelle*, art. L. 121-1.

161 17 U.S.C. § 106A(d).

162 *Copyright Act 1968*, *supra* note 53, s. 195AM(2) and (3) together with s. 33.

163 For example Germany, Austria, Belgium and the Netherlands. For a table of moral rights durations around the world see Adeney, *Moral Rights*, *supra* note 25 at 712 'Comparative Table of National Moral Rights'.

164 Australia makes one exception in relation to the integrity right in films. The right in this case subsists only for the author's lifetime: *Copyright Act 1968*, *supra* note 53, s. 195AM.

THE FULL HERITABILITY OF THE RIGHTS

Provision for inheritance of the moral rights in Canada is unusually detailed, allowing the moral rights to pass, on the death of the author, first to a person by way of specific bequest, second to the testamentary inheritor of the copyright, and otherwise to 'the person entitled to any other property in respect of which the author dies intestate'.[165] Whether the last of these persons would be interested in defending the rights is another matter. When the above persons die, the same rules apply to the moral rights that have been entrusted to them.[166] The Canadian provision for inheritance contrasts starkly with the position in Australia, where the rights, though generally lasting for the full copyright period, cannot be inherited and can be exercised *post mortem auctoris* only by the author's legal personal representative.[167] This Australian limitation significantly curtails the likelihood of the rights' exercise post mortem.

CONCLUSION

In the decades since 1980, authorial interests have achieved a new importance in the copyright legislation of Canada, the UK, Australia and, to a lesser extent, the US. Through the development or redevelopment of moral rights regimes in all these countries, the authorial interests have been repositioned and strengthened in relation to the competing interests of the copyright owner, the commercial bodies exploiting the work, the derivative creator, and the broader society seeking access to intellectual material. The new moral rights provisions exist not only to protect the domestic authors of the countries concerned but also to allow authors from any Berne Union state to seek recovery for harm that accrues to them outside their own country. The moral rights provisions of all Union countries are therefore of general international interest, and their effectiveness is a measure of how seriously that country takes its treaty obligations.

At the time of writing, in 2007, Canada has the most developed moral rights jurisprudence among its common law peer group. In the UK, moral rights case law is scanty[168] and in Australia its development has only just

---

165 *Copyright Act*, *supra* note 51, s. 14.1(2).

166 *Ibid.*

167 If they are to be exercised post mortem in Australia they must be exercised by the author's legal representative: *Copyright Act 1968*, *supra* note 53, s. 195AN(1).

168 The six main cases to date are: *Morrison Leahy Music Ltd. v. Lightbond Ltd.*, [1993] E.M.L.R. 144 at 151 (Ch.D.); *Confetti Records (a firm) and others v. Warner Music UK Ltd (trading as East West Records)*, [2003] E.W.H.C. 1274 at para. 147 (Ch.D.); *Tidy v. Trustees of the Natural History Museum* (1995), 39 I.P.R. 501, [1996]

begun.[169] The United States, although it has developed a substantial body of case law around the provisions of its federal *Visual Artists' Rights Act*,[170] does not have sufficiently extensive moral rights coverage for its decisions to provide guidance in any area beyond the visual arts. For the UK and Australia, bound to each other and to Canada by their common juridical heritage, Canadian developments in moral rights are of particular interest. In the past the *Snow* case has been regarded as furnishing relevant indications of how moral rights provisions might be interpreted.[171] What is not sufficiently appreciated outside Canada is that its moral rights jurisprudence is more extensive than this and is continuing to expand under the 1988 amendments.

As moral rights litigation grows in the countries of the copyright tradition, we can expect to see the case law of one country increasingly influencing that of the others. Counsel and courts, conscious of the limited moral rights jurisprudence in their own countries, are likely to seek guidance from related jurisdictions abroad. Such influence is desirable in the interests of harmonising at least the judge-made aspects of moral rights law around the globe. It is also important that the copyright countries remain as far as possible in step with the countries of the civil law, authors' rights, tradition, so that the universal protection striven for by the framers of the Berne Convention achieves a degree of reality. It is undoubtedly in Canada that civil law influence on concepts of authorial rights is strongest. Standing as it does at the intersection of the civil and common law traditions, Canada's approach to moral rights is deserving of close attention, both now and into the future.

E.I.P.R. D-81 (H.C.); *Pasterfield v. Denham, supra* note 102 and *Sawkins v. Hyperion Records Ltd., supra* note 125 (both at first instance and on appeal).

169 The first decided case is *Meskenas v. ACP Publishing Pty Ltd*, [2006] FMCA 1136, concerning attribution and false attribution of authorship.

170 See *Carter v. Helmsley-Spear*, 852 F.Supp 228 (S.D.N.Y. 1994); 861 F.Supp 303 (S.D.N.Y. 1994); 71 F.3d 77 (2nd Cir. 1995); *Pollara v. Seymour and Casey*, 150 F.Supp 2d 393 (S.D.N.Y. 2001; 206 F.Supp 2d 333 (N.D.N.Y. 2002); *Flack v. Friends of Queen Catherine Inc et al.*, 139 F.Supp 2d 526, 531 (S.D.N.Y. 2001); *Phillips v Pembroke Real Estate, Inc.*, 288 F.Supp 2d 89, 99 (D. Mass. 2003); *Martin v. City of Indianapolis*, 982 F.Supp 625 (S.D. Ind. 1997), 4 F.Supp 2d 808 (S.D. Ind. 1998), 28 F.Supp 2d 1098 (S.D. Ind. 1998); 192 F.3d 608 (7th Cir. 1999) among others.

171 See *Tidy v. Trustees of the Natural History Museum, supra* note 168 at 504.

9. A uniquely Canadian institution: the Copyright Board of Canada

Daniel J. Gervais[1]

What is uniquely Canadian? I first should apologize for putting the question so directly. I do not ask this question to fill the reader's mind with images of the Rockies, canoes, Niagara Falls, Pier 21 in Halifax, igloos, old Quebec City or Prairie skies.[2] Nor does this chapter argue that the Copyright Board of Canada should have made the list. Still, according to experts,[3] Canadian uniqueness is a secret blend of efficiency, inexpensive clothes, and friendliness. Canadians are also law-abiding, and have a noted penchant for compromise and self-criticism.[4] Arguably, there is no better environment to develop the best possible copyright regulatory scheme, especially with subfreezing temperatures helping cooler heads prevail.[5] Perhaps it's not a wonder, but this chapter will suggest that the Copyright Board is uniquely Canadian.

[1] The author wishes to acknowledge the assistance and contribution of Mario Bouchard, Esq., General Counsel, Copyright Board of Canada, for his many helpful suggestions. However, the views expressed are the author's own, as are any mistakes or omissions. The author wishes to acknowledge the financial contribution of Bell University Labs and the Social Sciences and Humanities Research Council of Canada (SSHRC).

[2] Unofficially, the seven wonders of Canada. See <http://www.cbc.ca/sevenwonders/>.

[3] Will Ferguson & Ian Ferguson, *How to be Canadian* (Vancouver: Douglas & McIntyre, 2001).

[4] As illustrated by a recent report by the Conference Board according to which Canada is fast becoming a mediocre country. Heather Scoffield 'Canada a land of mediocrity, Conference Board says' *Globe and Mail* (13 June 2007) A1. A note of reassurance to the reader of this book who is suddenly thinking of asking for a refund: if we were truly a mediocre nation, that report would not have been written, let alone published.

[5] Interestingly, another great step forward in copyright history was made in another cool climate: the Nordic countries invented the extended repertoire system discussed in section II below. See Tarja Koskinen-Olsson, 'Collective Management in the Nordic Countries' in Daniel J. Gervais, ed., *Collective Management of Copyright and Related Rights* (The Hague: Kluwer, 2006).

With the maple leaf thus set as backdrop, let us now consider the context. Several countries have fostered the growth of Collective Management Organizations (CMOs) through legislative initiatives in the belief that CMOs offer a viable solution to the problems associated with individual licensing, collecting royalties and enforcing copyright against large numbers of users. In theory, collective licensing enables creators to exercise rights in a fair, efficient and accessible manner. It ensures copyright protection when individual management of it becomes difficult or impracticable.[6] However, collective management is not a panacea, and questions have been raised about the efficiency and the transparency of CMOs and their continued relevancy in the digital age.[7] A first set of criticisms targets structural issues such as governance, the absence of competition among CMOs and tariff-setting processes. A second set of issues, of a conjonctural or cyclical nature, includes fast-changing market conditions and online business models that have added to the pressure to adapt put on CMOs by their members,[8] users of copyright material and regulators.[9]

Can collective management work in the digital environment, and what if any is the role of regulators in optimizing its efficiency? It is with those questions in mind that this chapter attempts to demonstrate that Canada has developed one of the most efficient (though far from perfect) systems of collective management of rights and that a key vector of this relatively successful endeavour has been the Copyright Board.

In Part I of the chapter, we first take a snapshot of the current state of collective management in Canada and then at the establishment and functioning of the Copyright Board. In Part II, we consider the pros and cons of the

---

[6] For example, tens of thousands of radio stations worldwide cannot possibly clear individually the rights of authors, composers, performers and producers of each song they play. That said, the concentration of media ownership in certain countries may progressively render centralized (direct) licensing less difficult to envisage.

[7] For example, rights are often managed by multiple collective management societies within a particular territory. Coordination is required not only between national collective management societies, but then on an international basis between collective management societies. There is also a significant lack of standards among many collective management societies. Identification alone of an underlying right (and rightsholder(s)) can be a convoluted process.

[8] This term is used generically in this chapter, even though some CMOs are not membership organizations proper.

[9] Licensing, collecting and enforcing copyright may now be done on an individual basis through the aid of technologies such as digital rights management systems. While most authors do not adopt the view that collectives will no longer have a role to play in the digital environment, the point is that new technologies alleviate some concerns relating to the inefficiency of individual licensing, collecting and enforcement of copyright.

Canadian system and lessons that may be drawn to improve collective management in Canada generally and the functioning of the Board in particular.

I COLLECTIVE MANAGEMENT OF RIGHTS IN CANADA

The Four Legal Regimes in the Canadian Act

In 1997, bill C-32[10] amended the *Copyright Act* by adding a definition of the expression 'collective society', as follows:

> A 'collective society' means a society, association or corporation that carries on the business of collective administration of copyright or of the remuneration right conferred by section 19 or 81 for the benefit of those who, by assignment, grant of licence, appointment of it as their agent or otherwise, authorize it to act on their behalf in relation to that collective administration, and (*a*) *operates a licensing scheme*, applicable in relation to a *repertoire* of works, performer's performances, sound recordings or communication signals of *more than one* author, performer, sound recording maker or broadcaster, pursuant to which the society, association or corporation *sets out classes of uses* that it *agrees to authorize* under this Act, and the *royalties and terms and conditions* on which it agrees to authorize those classes of uses, *or* (*b*) *carries on the business of collecting and distributing royalties or levies* payable pursuant to this Act.' (Emphasis added)

This definition is important to create uniformity in the Canadian collective management regime, a uniformity greatly reinforced by the fact that all those regimes are subject to the supervisory authority of the Board. However, in spite of this conceptually-unifying definition and the breadth of the Board's authority, the *Act* contains four legal regimes concerning the collective administration of copyright and neighbouring rights. These regimes (since 1997) are as follows:

- A regime for music performing rights (and certain neighbouring rights)
- A general (or 'residual') regime
- A 'particular cases' regime for retransmissions and certain uses by educational institutions; and
- A regime for private copying levies.

The formation of the four regimes stem in part from historical evolution –

---

10 S.C. 1997, c. 24 (assented to 25 April 1997).

notably the separate regime for music performing rights, which, as noted above, was the original realm of collectives. Yet those four regimes also reflect policy choices. The Canadian regulatory context is unique in that it differentiates the original/classical regime of music performing rights, from regimes based on compulsory licenses (that is, the particular cases regime), regimes based on voluntary assignments,[11] and a regime for private copying of music under which collectives do not license. They are established to collect a compensatory remuneration for copying only on certain types of media.[12]) The copying is deemed uncontrollable, as a practical or normative matter, or both.

Music performing rights and certain neighbouring rights

The first regime concerns the *performance or telecommunication of musical works and sound recordings of musical works.*[13] This type of collective management is regulated by s. 67 of the *Copyright Act*. CMOs active in this field grant licences for the public performance and communication to the public by telecommunication of music (the underlying musical work, the performer's performance and the producer's sound recording). In the case of authors, the Society of Composers, Authors and Music Publishers of Canada (SOCAN), the only collective representing copyright holders in this field,[14] represents approximately 70,000 holders of an exclusive copyright under s. 3 of the *Act*. Authors voluntarily assign their rights to SOCAN. In theory, authors and publishers who own rights in musical works can avoid the application of the regime by managing their rights on their own.[15] However, in practice, SOCAN's repertoire includes virtually every musical work communicated or performed in Canada.

---

11 Which, as is discussed below, may include an extended repertoire or limited liability option.

12 *Copyright Act*, R.S.C. 1985, c. C-42, ss. 79–80 [*Copyright Act* or *Act*]. The royalty applies to blank 'recording medium, regardless of its material form, onto which a sound recording may be reproduced and that is of a kind ordinarily used by individual consumers for that purpose.' This was interpreted as not including 'devices' (such as iPods) on which music may be stored. See *Canadian Private Copying Collective v. Canadian Storage Media Alliance* (2004), 36 C.P.R. (4th) 289, [2005] 2 F.C. 654 (F.C.A.).

13 *Copyright Act*, ss. 67 to 69.

14 SOCAN was formed in 1990 by the merger of its two predecessors: The Composers, Authors and Publishers Association of Canada (CAPAC) and the Performing Rights Organization of Canada (PROCAN).

15 That option is not open to performers and record producers, since only a collective can collect royalties for the performance or telecommunication of sound recordings of musical works: *Copyright Act*, s. 19(2)(a). The remuneration right for the performance or telecommunication of other sound recordings can be paid to either the performer or the record producer: *Copyright Act*, s. 19(2)(b).

The *Act* imposes collective management of the rights to remuneration of performers and makers of sound recordings.[16] The Neighbouring Rights Collective of Canada (NRCC), a non-profit umbrella collective, was established in 1997 to administer such rights. NRCC does not directly deal with individual rights holders, however. It has five member collectives.[17]

Collective management of rights for dramatic and literary works contained in sound recordings (notably through ArtistI[18]) is voluntary.

In fixing tariffs in this area, the *Act* imposes specific criteria to be applied by the Copyright Board, including a single payment for the equitable remuneration of producers and performers.[19] All tariffs must be certified by the Copyright Board before they can be enforced. CMOs who do not file proposed tariffs for a given use or market are no longer allowed to seek legal redress for that use or market[20] and a user who offers to pay the appropriate tariff cannot be prosecuted for violation of copyright, even if the CMO refuses to issue a licence.[21] Given the nature of the powers of the Board under this regime, it has been argued that agreements between a collective and a user are null and void as a matter of public policy.[22]

The general regime

The regime that governs CMOs in s. 70.1 and following is known as the general (or residual) regime because it applies to all voluntary licensing

---

16 *Copyright Act*, s. 19(1) and (2).

17 Namely, the American Federation of Musicians and the ACTRA Performers' Rights Society, which receive royalties for the benefit of most performers; ArtistI, which manages the rights of some 600 performers (mostly singers) from the province of Québec; and SOPROQ and AVLA, which receive the producers' share are described below. In 2004, NRCC collected some CAN $12M and distributed CAN $10.2M.

18 ArtistI is the collective society of the *Union des artistes* (UDA) for the remuneration of performers' rights. <http://www.uniondesartistes.com>.

19 *Copyright Act*, s. 68(2).

20 Absent a tariff, an action may be commenced with the permission of the relevant Minister: *Act*, ibid., s. 67.1(4). In practice, however, that permission has never been sought, and, barring exceptional circumstances, would not be granted.

21 *Copyright Act*, s. 68.2(2). SOCAN still can enjoin a person who does not conform to the tariff from using its repertoire: see *e.g., Society of Composers, Authors and Music Publishers of Canada v. Kicks Roadhouse Inc. (c.o.b. How-Dee's)* (2005), 39 C.P.R. (4th) 238 at para. 27 (F.C.T.D.).

22 Stéphane Gilker, 'Statut des ententes négociées hors du processus de la Commission' in Ysolde Gendreau, ed., *Copyright Administrative Institutions* (Montreal: Yvon Blais, 2002) at 140–1. In practice, SOCAN does have agreements with a variety of users. They clarify which tariffs apply to certain uses, offer discounts on the rates set out in the tariffs or even set prices for uses that are outside any of the tariffs certified by the Board.

schemes other than those of s. 67 just described[23] and unless another regime applies.[24] It is important to note, however, that in terms of financial flows, s. 67 CMOs (under the first regime above) collect and distribute more money than all s. 70.1 collectives combined.

In theory, this regime applies to all voluntary collective management of the rights of reproduction, adaptation, rental, publication and public performance in the area of copyright (s. 3) and to the rights of performers concerning the first fixation of their performances, reproduction and communication to the public of live performances (s. 15) and to certain rights of sound recording producers (s. 18) and broadcasters (s. 21). In practice, however, it applies to:

- Reprography, where the two main societies are the Access Copyright (previously CANCOPY)[25] and the *Société québécoise de gestion collective des droits de reproduction* (COPIBEC).[26]
- Mechanical rights. CMOs such as (a) the Society for Reproduction Rights of Authors, Composers and Publishers in Canada (SODRAC), which 'administers royalties stemming from the reproduction of musical works';[27] and (b) the Canadian Musical Reproduction Rights Agency (CMRRA), 'a Canadian centralized licensing and collecting agency for the reproduction rights of musical works in Canada.'[28] The two CMOS are collaborating in certain areas, including online use of music through a joint agency known as CMRRA/SODRAC Inc. (CSI).[29]

---

23 Or more precisely any CMO which operates 'a licensing scheme, applicable in relation to a repertoire of works of more than one author, pursuant to which the society sets out the classes of uses for which and the royalties and terms and conditions on which it agrees to authorize the doing of' a protected act: *Act*, s. 70.1.

24 According to one author, some forms of collective management may escape that definition: '[a] company that licenses the use of the works of multiple authors to users can avoid the application [of the general regime]...if that company does not deal with users on a general tariff basis but negotiates each use individually.' See Peter Grant, 'Competition and the Collectives in Canada: New Developments in the Relationship between Copyright and Antitrust Law' (1990–91) 1 Media and Communications Law Review 191 at 199.

25 <http://www.accesscopyright.ca>.

26 <http://www.copibec.qc.ca>.

27 <http://www.sodrac.ca>.

28 <http://www.cmrra.org>.

29 'CSI (CMRRA/SODRAC Inc.) is an administrative entity established by CMRRA and SODRAC, enabling these two organizations, through CSI, to negotiate agreements with users for various reproduction rights and issue licences to them, as well as to submit tariff proposals to the Copyright Board. CSI also facilitates the payment process for users, enabling the user to issue only one payment instead of two': Canadian Heritage, *CSI*, online: <http://music.gc.ca/enreg_fichi_Creat_csi_e. asp>.

- Visual arts. The Canadian Artists' Representation Copyright Collective (CARCC) was 'established in 1990 to create opportunities for increased income for visual and media artists. The services it provides to artists include negotiating the terms for copyright use and issuing an appropriate license to the use.'[30] This area also includes previously-mentioned SODRAC and the *Société de droits d'auteur en arts visuels* (SODART) 'created by the *Regroupement des artistes en arts visuels du Québec* (RAAV) and responsible for collecting rights on behalf of visual artists. It negotiates agreements with organizations that use visual arts, such as museums, exhibition centres, magazines, publishers, audio-visual producers, etc. SODART issues licences to these organizations and collects royalties due to the artists it represents.'[31]
- Sound recordings and music videos. Here, the *Société de gestion collective des droits des producteurs de phonogrammes et vidéogrammes du Québec* (SOPROQ) represents mostly Francophone record producers from Québec while the major record companies, many independent labels, performers and producers are [Audio-Video Licensing Agency] AVLA members. AVLA members represent 95% of all sound recordings and music videos produced and/or distributed in Canada.[32] Both collectives administer the copyright in master audio and music video recordings. Both license the exhibition and reproduction of music videos and the reproduction of audio recordings for commercial use. Both receive a part of the makers' share of neighbouring rights royalties and private copying levies.
- Audiovisual and multimedia rights where the Directors Rights Collective of Canada (DRCC) acts for film and television directors; and the Producers Audiovisual Collective of Canada collects royalties on behalf of producers for the sale of blank audiovisual media for the rental and lending of video recordings. In both cases, royalties are mostly from foreign sources. The *Société civile des auteurs multimédia* (SCAM), a French collective, administers reproduction rights of literary works intended for audio-visual media such as cinema, television and radio.
- Off-Air Program Taping. Two collectives license off-air taping of television and radio programs. The Educational Rights Collective of Canada (ERCC), established in 1998, collects royalties pursuant to a tariff that is set by the Copyright Board, for the off-air taping and public performance of television and radio programs by educational institutions. It collected

30 <http://www.carfac.ca>.
31 <http://www.raav.org/sodart>.
32 <http://www.avla2007.ca>.

less than CAN $20,000 in 2004.[33] The Canadian Broadcasters Rights Agency (CBRA) licenses the use of programs owned by Canadian private television and radio broadcasters by media monitoring firms and by government entities that operate in-house monitoring services, pursuant to a combination of individual licences and a tariff set by the Copyright Board. CBRA's media monitoring royalties are in the order of CAN $800,000 per year.

- Other Areas. A variety of other CMOs play a role in distributing royalties collected in Canada or elsewhere. The Canadian Screenwriters Collection Society (CSCS) deals in royalties payable to film and television writers under Canadian and foreign copyright legislation, including retransmission royalties.[34] The Playwrights Union of Canada, a service organization for professional playwrights, also acts as agent for the distribution of rights and collection of royalties. SACD, a French collective, represents authors, composers and choreographers of dramatic and audiovisual works. SOQAD redistributes royalties (around CAN $90,000) agreed to with the Ministry of Education of the Province of Québec to playwrights whose works are performed in pre-school, primary and secondary schools.

CMOs operating under the general regime can file tariffs for approval by the Board[35] or conclude agreements with users[36] that will take precedence over tariffs.[37] A CMO may, under this regime, file a copy of an agreement concluded with a user with the Board, which prevents the application of s. 45 of the *Competition Act*[38] (dealing with conspiracies to limit competition). The Board then sets the royalties payable under the agreement, as well as the related terms and conditions. However, the Commissioner of Competition may

---

[33] Educational institutions apparently prefer to deal with specialized distributors, who supply pre-recorded videocassettes along with the right to perform the underlying work in the classroom, rather than to make use of the tariff set by the Board.

[34] CSCS receives retransmission royalties through another collective society, CRC.

[35] *Copyright Act*, s. 70.3 and following. To date, the Board has certified tariffs pursuant to this aspect of the general regime for the reproduction of radio and television programs for the purpose of media monitoring as well as the reproduction of musical works by radio stations by distributors of video-copies of feature films (and the music they contain). Tariffs currently under examination target the reproduction of musical works in a variety of contexts (podcasting, Internet use) and the reprographic reproduction of literary works by educational institutions.

[36] *Copyright Act*, s. 70.12(b).

[37] *Copyright Act*, s. 70.191.

[38] R.S.C. 1985, c. C-34.

ask the Copyright Board to examine the agreement if he considers it is contrary to the public interest.[39] The Board may also be asked to determine the royalty applicable in individual cases (arbitration).[40] To date, the Board has issued only one decision pursuant to this aspect of the regime.[41]

Retransmissions and certain uses by educational institutions (section 71)
The third regime applies to non-voluntary licences for the retransmission of distant radio and television signals as well as for the reproduction and public performance by educational institutions, of radio or television programs, for educational or training purposes.[42] No royalties can be collected except pursuant to a tariff certified by the Copyright Board and all royalties must transit through one or more CMOs, each of which collects a share set by the Board in the tariff.

There are eight retransmission CMOs who operate in whole or in part under this regime. Each gets a share of the royalties set in a single tariff, certified by the Copyright Board.[43] They are:

- Border Broadcasters' Inc. (BBI);[44]
- Canadian Broadcasters Rights Agency (CBRA);[45]
- Canadian Retransmission Collective (CRC);[46]
- Canadian Retransmission Right Association (CRRA);[47]
- Copyright Collective of Canada (CCC);[48]
- FWS Joint Sports Claimants (FWS);[49]

---

39 *Copyright Act*, s. 70.5(2) to (5). As of this writing, this has never been done.

40 *Copyright Act*, s. 70.2. If an agreement is reached between the parties, the Board 'shall not proceed': s. 70.3.

41 See *Society for Reproduction Rights of Authors, Composers and Publishers in Canada v. MusiquePlus Inc.* (2000), 10 C.P.R. (4th) 242 (Cop. Bd.).

42 *Copyright Act*, ss. 71 to 76.

43 *Television Retransmission Tariff 2001–2003* (22 March 2003), Copyright Board, s. 15, online: <http://www.cb-cda.gc.ca/tariffs/certified/r22032003-b.pdf>.

44 Border Broadcasters Inc. (BBI) represents US border broadcasters.

45 <http://www.cbra.ca>.

46 <http://www.crc-scrc.ca>.

47 An association representing the Canadian Broadcasting Corporation (CBC), the American Broadcasting Company (ABC), the National Broadcasting Company (NBC), the Columbia Broadcasting System (CBS) and *Télé-Québec*.

48 It represents copyright owners (producers and distributors) of the US independent motion picture and television production industry. Should not be confused with the United States Copyright Clearance Center, Inc. (CCC – <http://www.copyright.com>), the US Reproduction Rights (reprography) Organization (RRO).

49 It represents a number of major sports leagues.

- Major League Baseball Collective of Canada (MLB);[50] and the
- Society of Composers, Authors and Music Publishers of Canada (SOCAN).

Another collective, the Educational Rights Collective of Canada (ERCC) licenses copy and use of radio or television programs for educational use in classrooms[51] except for news and news commentary programs copied and played at school within the period of one year from the time that the program was copied.[52] This regime is another illustration of the Board's jurisdiction beyond tariffs and the uniqueness of the Canadian regime. Here, it is given clear regulatory powers by the *Act*. Section 29.9(2) reads as follows:

> The Board may, with the approval of the Governor in Council, *make regulations*
> (a) prescribing the information in relation to the making, destruction, performance and marking of copies that must be kept under subsection (1),
> (b) prescribing the manner and form in which records referred to in that subsection must be kept and copies destroyed or marked, and
> (c) respecting the sending of information to collective societies referred to in section 71.[53]

Non-member rightsholders may claim royalties collected on the basis of an approved tariff, subject to conditions applicable to member rightsholders.[54]

Private copying

A specific regime was put in place in 1998 concerning the private copying of sound recordings.[55] As noted in the introductory part of this section, the regime only applies to music and to limited types of media. It does not involve licensing as such, but rather remuneration designed to compensate rightsholders for a use of musical works, performances and sound recordings that is made non-infringing by a parallel exception allowing users to make copies of

---

50 It collects for the retransmission of major league baseball games in Canada.

51 *Copyright Act*, s. 29.6(2), which was added by S.C. 1997, c. 24, s. 18(1). It came into force on 1 January 1999.

52 See <http://www.ercc.ca> and *Statement of Royalties to be Collected by ERCC from Educational Institutions in Canada, for the Reproduction and Performance of Works or Other Subject-Matters Communicated to the Public by Telecommunication for the Years 2003 to 2006* (14 January 2005), Copyright Board, online: <http://www.cda-cb.gc.ca/decisions/e14012005-b.pdf>.

53 Added by S.C. 1997, c. 24, s. 18(1). In force 1 January 1999.

54 *Copyright Act*, s. 76. See also *Re SARDEC* (1998), 86 C.P.R. (3d) 481 (Cop. Bd.).

55 *Copyright Act*, s. 79–88, added by S.C. 1997, c. 24, s. 50 and came into force 19 March 1998.

music for private use.[56] The scheme replicates the retransmission (third) regime in all relevant respects but two. First, the levy must be collected through a single collecting body designated by the Board.[57] Second, rather than apportioning royalties among collectives, the Board sets the share of the levies to which all eligible authors, eligible performers and eligible makers (or record producers) are respectively entitled;[58] how these shares are then divided within each college of rights holders is up to the relevant collectives.

The CMOs entitled to receive a share of this remuneration created the Canadian Private Copying Collective (CPCC), which is responsible for distributing the funds generated by the levy to the collective societies representing eligible authors, performers and makers of sound recordings. The member collectives of the CPCC are the previously-mentioned CMRRA, SODRAC, SOCAN and NRCC (itself an umbrella organization).

The Establishment of the Board

Though the origins of copyright tribunals in Commonwealth jurisdictions can be traced back to the findings of a Parliamentary Select Committee set up in the UK in 1929,[59] the creation of a copyright tribunal[60] in that country was deferred until the 1956 Copyright Act.[61]

Hence, the Canadian oversight authority was established first. This means there was no obvious model to follow at the time. Consequently, the Canadian model, and the transition from a traditional regulatory tribunal (the model in place in the UK and several Commonwealth jurisdictions whose 'primary task

---

56 *Copyright Act*, s. 80(1).

57 *Copyright Act*, s. 83(8)(d).

58 *Copyright Act*, s. 84.

59 M. J. Freegard, 'Quis Custodiet? The Role of Copyright Tribunals' (1994) 16:7 Eur. Int. Prop. Rev. 286.

60 Originally known as the 'Performing Right Tribunal', its function was 'to determine disputes arising between licensing bodies and persons requiring licences or organisations claiming to be representative of such persons'. [...], the Tribunal's jurisdiction was limited, to public performance, broadcasting and cable diffusion licences. *Ibid.* at 289.

61 Freegard traces the impact of the UK model on several jurisdictions, Australia, Ireland, South Africa, but also to a lesser degree Bangladesh, Hong Kong, India, Jamaica, Pakistan, Singapore and Zimbabwe, and a number of others with distinct 'competent authority' (though not referred to as a Board or tribunal). *Ibid.* at 290–1. For a much more detailed review of the functioning of copyright tribunals and oversight authorities in a number of jurisdictions, see Gendreau, *supra* note 22. The book also contains several interesting papers on the operations and history of the Canadian Board (some of which are mentioned in other notes) and is recommended reading for anyone wishing to learn more about the topic discussed in this chapter.

...is to determine the amount of the licence fee payable for the exploitation of certain rights in copyright works'[62]) to a professional body consisting of full-time members and research staff, may properly be considered unique. It is also unique among Commonwealth member States because, as we shall see below, its jurisdiction far exceeds what Continental European commentators view as *de minimis* control by copyright tribunals essentially limited to tariffs and terms of the licence.[63]

In 1931, the *Copyright Act*[64] was amended to require that the CPRS (the Canadian 'subsidiary' of the British Performing Rights Society (PRS)) file its statements of royalties. Cabinet could modify the statements following an investigation and report by a commission of inquiry.[65] In 1936, following a recommendation of a Commission,[66] the *Act* was further amended so that performing rights tariffs would have to be certified by a new administrative agency, the Copyright Appeal Tribunal, before coming into force, and a CMO could not commence infringement proceedings it if refused or neglected to file a statement of royalties.[67] Following the establishment of the tribunal, the oversight of collective management organizations in Canada proceeded fairly smoothly, with the Tribunal concentrating its time and efforts on tariffs.

The year 1989 represented something of a watershed for Canadian CMOs. The *Act* was amended in two important respects. First, the Copyright Appeal Tribunal was replaced by the Copyright Board. The government recognized at the time that the growth of collective management, both in the importance of

62 Edward Bragiel, 'Is the Copyright Tribunal Showing Irrational Tendencies' (2001) 23:8 E.I.P.R. 371.

63 Pavel Tuma, 'Pitfalls and Challenges of the EC Directive on the Collective Management of Copyright and Related Rights' (2006) 28:4 E.I.P.R. 220 at 220–2; Uma Suthersanen, 'Collectivism of Copyright: The Future of Rights Management in the European Union' in Eric M. Barendt & Alison Firth, eds., *The Yearbook of Copyright and Media Law* (Oxford: Oxford University Press, 2000) at 20–4. Tuma writes: 'On one side of the scale is the UK model. Collecting societies are entirely formed as private corporations and the collective management is exercised mostly according to contractual provisions. Neither any public law regulation nor any specific authority supervision is applied.'

Changes to the regulatory situation in the European Union will induce changes in the UK system. See Lucie Guibault & Stef van Gompel, 'Collective Management in the European Union' in Gervais, *supra* note 5.

64 At the time R.S.C. 1927, c. 32.

65 *Copyright Amendment Act, 1931*, S.C. 1931, c. 8, ss. 5, 10.

66 *Report of the Royal Commission appointed to investigate the activities of the Canadian Performing Rights Society, Limited, and similar societies* (Ottawa: King's Printer, 1935) (Chair: James Parker).

67 *An Act to Amend the Copyright Act, 1931*, S.C. 1936, c. 28, s. 2. The Canadian Tribunal thus predates the British Performing Rights Tribunal by some 21 years.

the monies collected and the increasing breadth of its reach (even more so in 1997 with the formation of collectives in the field of reprography, and the formation of new collectives to administer the rights introduced in respect of neighbouring rights and private copying[68]), required a supervisory authority empowered to look beyond mere tariff setting and beyond a legalistic approach based strictly on evidence adduced by parties to a tariff case. The new Board was empowered to supervise dealings between collectives and individual users or groups of users in areas other than music performing rights. Collective management was thus recognized as an integral part of the system and its relationship with competition law was somewhat clarified.

In 1997, collective management received further recognition. CMOs were no longer limited to dealing with users on a case-by-case basis; they could secure tariffs that would apply to all current and future users. Even more significantly, Parliament used collective management as the tool of choice in dealing with a number of areas where access had to be guaranteed in exchange for a form of compensation, including music neighbouring rights,[69] educational uses of television programs,[70] private copying[71] and some forms of ephemeral recordings and transfer of format.[72] These developments led to a further increase in the number of collectives, and to a significant expansion of the role the Copyright Board was asked to play in regulating the relationship between collectives and users.

---

[68] In the 1989 amendments, the use of protected works in retransmitted distant radio and television signals was subjected to a compulsory licensing scheme according to which rights holders could seek remuneration only through a CMO; in that area, collective management became the only possible course of action.

[69] Those neighbouring rights in this context were rights of performers and producers (makers) of sound recordings to a remuneration for the broadcasting of their performances and recordings, respectively and to prohibit the reproduction of fixations of performances and recordings (*Copyright Act*, ss. 15, 18 and 19(2)(a)).

[70] *Copyright Act*, ss. 71–76.

[71] *Copyright Act*, ss. 79–88. The private copying regime introduced an exception for private copies made on certain audio media but remuneration on blank media was introduced to compensate rightsholders. The right to collect this remuneration is necessarily managed by a collective, namely the Canadian Private Copying Collective (see <http://www.cpcc.ca>).

[72] *Copyright Act*, ss. 30.8(8) and 30.9(6); pursuant to these provisions, exceptions that allow broadcasters to make ephemeral and transfer of format copies do not apply if a CMO offers a licence for the use of the relevant work, performance or sound recording.

The Copyright Board Today

Administration

The Copyright Board of Canada[73] is an independent administrative tribunal. It consists of not more than five members, appointed by the government for a set term of up to five years. Members can serve either full-time or part-time; in practice, all members except the Chairman serve full-time. The Board has a small permanent staff which includes a Secretary General, a General Counsel and a Director of Research and Analysis. Copyright tribunals often do not and must thus rely on the parties' evidence and analysis, which may limit their ability to factor in broader public policy considerations, especially those requiring empirical data not provided by the parties. In addition, not being a traditional tribunal, over the past 15 years, more hearings of the Canadian Board have been chaired by one of two Vice-Chairmen, including a non-lawyer, than by one of three judicial Chairmen.

With respect to the participation of experts and other persons not representing one of the parties, the Canadian Board's policy has been extremely liberal. It has made full use of its ability to control its own proceedings to allow interventions from persons or groups who are not directly interested but who are likely to provide a useful point of view.

The Board presents two unique characteristics among Canadian regulatory agencies. First, for historical rather than practical reasons,[74] the Chairman is a sitting or retired judge of a superior court. Second, because the Chairman thus usually serves part-time, the Board's direction is two-headed: the Chairman directs the work of the Board, but the Vice-Chairman is its Chief Executive Officer.

Procedures before the Copyright Board

The procedure leading to the certification of a tariff is similar in all four regimes.[75] A proposed tariff is filed on or before 31 March of the year preceding the year in which the tariff is to come into effect. The Board publishes the proposal in the *Canada Gazette* and users or their representatives[76] may object to the proposal within 60 days of the publication. The Board then issues a

---

[73] *Copyright Act*, ss. 66–66.5.

[74] When the Copyright Appeal Tribunal was set up in 1936, it was a common practice in Canada to ask a judge to preside over the deliberations of administrative tribunals. This is no longer the case.

[75] *Copyright Act*, ss. 67.1, 68 (performing rights regime); 70.13–70.15 (general regime, tariffs); 71–73 (statutory licences); 83(1)–83(10) (private copying).

[76] In the private copying regime, anyone is entitled to object.

directive on procedure and sets a timetable for the proceedings.[77] The CMO and objectors are given the opportunity to argue their case in a hearing before a panel usually constituted of three members.[78]

The nature of the evidence offered varies considerably and the Board is not bound by specific rules of evidence.[79] After deliberations, the Board certifies the tariff, publishes it in the *Canada Gazette* and provides written reasons for its decision.[80] A tariff comes into effect on 1 January following the date by which the proposed tariff was filed and is effective for one or more calendar years.[81]

The powers of the Board

Further to an important decision by the Federal Court of Appeal which recognized the broad discretion of the Board,[82] the Board redefined its role from simply protecting users against the potential misuse of monopoly power by CMOs (a view which still seems to inform the work of several national copyright tribunals) to regulating the balance of market power between copyright holders and users. This was perhaps the defining moment of what made the Canadian Board so unique. The Board has asserted not only that a market price is only one of several possible rational bases for a tariff, but that in certain circumstances, public policy would lead it to ignore market considerations altogether.[83]

---

77 The Board has the power to adopt rules of procedure, but has not exercised it.

78 In exceptional cases, no hearing will be held if proceeding in writing accommodates a small user or if the issues at hand do not warrant a hearing. The hearing is also dispensed with on most preliminary or interim issues.

79 According to the Supreme Court of Canada, a Canadian administrative tribunal that blindly follows the rules of evidence applicable to ordinary courts of law may unduly fetter its discretion: *Université du Québec à Trois-Rivières v. Larocque*, [1993] 1 S.C.R. 471.

80 Board decisions are available online: <http://www.cb-cda.gc.ca/decisions/index-e.html>.

81 *Copyright Act*, ss. 67.1(3), 70.14, 71(4) and 83(5).

82 *Re Statement of Royalties to be Collected for Performance in Canada of Dramatico-musical or Musical Works in 1990, 1991, 1992 and 1993* (1993), 52 C.P.R. (3d) 23 at 34 (Cop. Bd.) [*SOCAN Tariff 2.A, 1993*], aff'd *Canadian Association of Broadcasters v. SOCAN* (1994), 58 C.P.R. (3d) 190 at 196 (F.C.A.). The Federal Court of Appeal stated in part:

> The Board properly understood its function when it stated that it had to regulate the balance of market power between copyright owners and users...the Board is in a better position than this Court to strike a proper balance between the interests of copyright owners and users and this Court will not interfere unless the result reached is patently unreasonable.

83 *SOCAN Tariff 2.A, 1993*, *ibid.* at 34 b–c, 39 c–d.

There are no conditions in the *Act* respecting the corporate structure of a CMO (as a for-profit entity, a membership organization, etc), the manner in which it secures the repertoire it administers or the nature of its relationship with rights holders or users or the way in which it surveys and distributes the income collected on behalf of rights holders. Not surprisingly, then, practices vary considerably, and interactions between CMOs are sometimes complex. Somewhat surprisingly given the centrality of its role, the Board has no direct powers over any of those aspects. Hence, subject to the intervention of Canadian competition authorities, rights holders are free to organize their affairs as they wish; even when a compulsory licensing scheme applies, nothing forces them to join a given collective or to organize CMOs along predetermined rules; as a result eight retransmission CMOs, some of which administer similar rights, receive a share of the royalties directly from copyright users. While no authorization from the Board or any other governmental entity is required to establish a new collective, the Board does have two obligations that influence the ability of a CMO to enter a market; as noted earlier, the Board must ensure that the payment of royalties for the performance or communication of sound recordings of musical works is made in a single payment and that the levy on blank media to compensate for private copying is collected by a single collecting body. In addition, as is shown below,[84] by using its discretion on setting conditions associated with monetary and other aspects of tariffs, the Board indirectly regulates a number of aspects that affect the governance of Canadian CMOs.

Indeed, as with any administrative tribunal, the Copyright Board has powers of a substantive and procedural nature. Some are expressly granted; others are implicit. Thus the Act grants the Board the power to issue interim decisions, to vary earlier decisions, to make regulations governing its procedure and to cause the publication and distribution of notices.[85] The Board also enjoys some of the powers of a superior court of record:[86] for example, it can compel the production of evidence or the appearance of witnesses. The Board even can formulate its own objections to proposed tariffs.[87] However, contrary to most Commonwealth copyright tribunals, the Board does not have the power to award costs. The Board has some implicit powers, such as to regulate its proceedings, to decide questions of law that are necessarily incidental to the exercise of its core function[88] and even to set royalties at a higher rate than requested by the CMO.[89]

---

84 See *infra* note 93 and accompanying text.

85 *Copyright Act*, ss. 66.51, 66.52, 66.6 and 66.71 respectively.

86 *Ibid.*, s. 66.7(1).

87 *Ibid.*, ss. 68(1), 70.14, 72(2) and 83(7).

88 *Canadian Cable Television Association v. Canada (Copyright Board)*, [1993] 2 F.C. 138 (F.C.A.).

89 *Canadian Private Copying Collective v. Canadian Storage Media Alliance*, *supra* note 12 at para. 167ff (F.C.A.).

The Board's powers are obviously constrained not only by the Act,[90] but also by regulations, general principles of administrative law and court decisions. The government can, by regulation, issue policy directions to the Board and establish general criteria that the Board must apply or have regard to.[91] In certain cases, as noted above, it is expressly empowered to issue regulations.[92]

The Board has made ample use of its power to certify royalties and their related terms and conditions 'with such alterations...as the Board considers necessary'[93] to influence the structure of CMO markets. It has carved new tariffs out of existing ones to suit the purposes of certain groups of users, imposed reporting requirement, authorized audits and imposed interest on late payment.[94] The Board is allowed to develop a tariff structure that is completely different from the one proposed by the collective or the users:[95] in the first retransmission proceedings, the Board set aside 11 separate proposals to adopt a single tariff based on a tariff formula that it developed.[96] The Board has imposed identical tariff structures on separate collectives; in the case of the performing rights tariff for commercial radio, for example, until SOCAN became the sole collective,[97] an overall rate was set and then apportioned, instead of dealing with each collective's tariff separately. The Board has even certified single tariffs for the combined use of the repertoires of SOCAN and

---

90 For example, the *Act* provides that performing rights tariffs must not place broadcasters at a financial disadvantage because of linguistic or content requirements imposed pursuant to the *Broadcasting Act*, S.C. 1991, c. 11, that the neighbouring rights royalties must be made in a single payment, that the private copying levy must be collected by a single body and that small cable systems are entitled to preferential rates (*Copyright Act*, ss. 68(2)(a)(iii) (single payment), 83(8)(d) (single collecting body) and 68.1(4), 74(1) (preferential rate)).

91 That power has been exercised with respect to retransmission royalties: see *Retransmission Royalties Criteria Regulations*, SOR/91-690, 28 November 1991.

92 See *supra* note 53 and accompanying text.

93 E.g., *Copyright Act*, ss. 68(3) and 70.15(1).

94 See, e.g., *Statement of Royalties to be Collected for Performance or Communication in Canada of Dramatico-musical Works in 1992, 1993 and 1994* (1994), 58 C.P.R. (3d) 79 at 83–87 (Cop. Bd.) (new tariff); *Maple Leaf Broadcasting Company Limited v. CAPAC*, [1954] S.C.R. 624; *FWS Joint Sports Claimants v. Canada (Copyright Board)*, [1992] 1 F.C. 487 (F.C.A.).

95 *Canadian Broadcasting Corp. v. Copyright Appeal Board* (1986), 17 C.P.R. (3d) 460 (F.C.A.).

96 *Re Royalties for Retransmission Rights Of Distant Radio and Television Signals* (1990), 32 C.P.R. (3d) 97 (Cop. Bd.).

97 SOCAN was formed in 1990 as a result of the merger of two former Canadian performing rights societies: The Composers, Authors and Publishers Association of Canada (CAPAC) and the Performing Rights Organization of Canada (PROCAN).

NRCC.[98] Perhaps the Board could even impose a single payment rule in retransmission or even merge tariffs filed pursuant to separate regimes.[99]

The Board and interaction among CMOs

Canadian CMOs often form strategic alliances. Sometimes, these are dictated by the structure of the regulatory regimes: this explains in part the creation of CPCC and NRCC as umbrella collectives.[100] Others respond to the structure of the market. It is considerably easier for CMRRA and SODRAC to jointly seek a tariff for commercial radio stations, since the use of their respective repertoires varies considerably between French- and English-speaking stations. It is also easier for Access Copyright and COPIBEC to act for each other in their respective 'home territories'. Other alliances probably are perceived by the relevant CMOs as arranged marriages (imposed by the Board): such is arguably the case with SOCAN and NRCC in those markets where the Board has certified a single tariff for both collectives.[101]

Alliances between CMOs can be used to prevent the Copyright Board from dealing with an issue. When two performing rights societies merged to form SOCAN, the need to allocate royalties between them disappeared. By filing a single tariff that applies to commercial radio stations irrespective of their relative use of the repertoires of CMRRA and SODRAC, the two collectives are free to apportion between them as they see fit the royalties collected pursuant to the tariff certified by the Board. Having joined CPCC, CMRRA, SODRAC and SOCAN removed from the Board the determination of their individual share of music creators' remuneration for private copying.

Rights holders also can bring to the table divergent points of view, either through the relevant CMOs or the associated industry associations. Makers of

---

98 *Re Statement of Royalties to be Collected by SOCAN and by NRCC for Pay Audio Services (Tariff 17.B)* (2002), 19 C.P.R. (4th) 67 (Cop. Bd.); *Neighbouring Rights Collective of Canada v. Society of Composers, Authors and Music Publishers of Canada* (2003), 26 C.P.R. (4th) 257 (F.C.A.).

99 Daniel J. Gervais, 'Essai sur le fractionnement du droit d'auteur' (2002) 15 Cahiers de propriété intellectuelle 501 at 532-33.

100 The neighbouring rights regime, under which NRCC operates, requires a single payment for the use of a given sound recording: *Copyright Act*, s. 68(2)(a)(iii). The private copying regime, under which CPCC operates, requires that a single body be designated to collect the levy (*ibid.*, s. 83(8)(d)).

101 *Statement of Royalties to be Collected by SOCAN and NRCC in Respect of Commercial Radio (Tariff 1.A – 2003–2007)* (15 October 2005), Copyright Board, online: <http://www.cb-cda.gc.ca/tariffs/certified/m15102005-b.pdf>; *Statement of Royalties to be Collected by SOCAN and NRCC in Respect of Pay Audio Services (2003–2006)* (26 February 2005), Copyright Board, online: <http://www.cb-cda.gc.ca/tariffs/certified/m26022005-b.pdf>.

sound recordings[102] recently opposed a request by CMRRA and SODRAC for the tariff that applies to the licensing of online music services. The variety of Canadian retransmission collectives is explained in part by the fact that some rights holders wished to convince the Board to attribute a higher value for the viewing of certain programs than to others.[103] One CMO, representing scriptwriters, even filed a proposed tariff with the intention of having the Board determine the share of a television program's royalties that should be paid to the program's scriptwriter.[104]

II ANALYSIS

The Copyright Board of Canada has had a significant degree of success is ensuring that 'copyright works'. Any analysis of the causes of its successes, and of its shortcomings, is partly speculative of course, but may nonetheless offer lessons on how collective management should be overseen by governments, and which measures could be adopted to further improve the Canadian system.

Advantages of the Canadian System

When compared to its Australian and UK counterparts,[105] the Canadian regulatory framework for collective management may work better for at least three sets of reasons. First, its *structure* as an administrative agency not tied by the strict rules of evidence and procedure (beyond the few rules contained in the Act and fundamental principles of natural justice) allows the Board to consider data that would not necessarily be seen (either because no party is its possessor or is willing to bring it forward) or admitted (for example, as hearsay). We suggest that this is actually more in keeping with the role that the Board should

---

102 Represented by the Canadian Recording Industry Association (CRIA), online: <http://www.cria.ca>.

103 These attempts were unsuccessful: *FWS Joint Sports Claimants Inc. v. Border Broadcasters Inc.* (2001), 16 C.P.R. (4th) 61 (F.C.A.).

104 See *Statement of Proposed Royalties to be Collected by CSCS for the Retransmission of Distant Television Signals, in Canada, in 2002 and 2003* (14 April 2001), Copyright Board, online: <http://www.cb-cda.gc.ca/tariffs/proposed/r14042000-b.pdf>. The issue was eventually settled between the association representing script writers and the CMO of which they previously had been members.

105 Paul L. C. Torremans, 'Collective Management in the United Kingdom (and Ireland)' in Gervais, *supra* note 5 at 227; and Mario Bouchard, 'Collective Management in Commonwealth Jurisdictions: Comparing Canada with Australia' in *ibid.* at 283.

play in taking account not just of the immediate interests of those involved in a proceeding, but also more broadly the interests of the general public and the operation of the market for copyright material. Information and ideational goods are public goods, or at least they behave as such in the marketplace. As such, any restriction on their use (as an ex ante incentive or ex post reward for their creation) is likely to generate negative welfare outcomes, which may be necessary but should form part of the policy equation examined by the Board in setting tariffs. On a more mundane level perhaps, a tariff imposed on a corporate user (for example, a broadcaster, hotel or online music delivery service) may ultimately be reflected in the price paid by the consumer. Because consumers and other groups may not always be able to participate in Board proceedings, it is certainly valuable and arguably essential to provide the Board with the necessary leeway and discretion to ensure that all interests, including those of the public (which is not formally represented at Board hearings), are adequately protected. The regulation of the balance of market power between copyright holders and users requires no less.[106]

A second set of reasons revolve around the organization of the Board, with its full-time commissioners and a (albeit small) research staff. The permanent nature of the commissioners' appointment allows them to gain appreciable expertise in the various complex issues at play.[107] The Board's role, as explained above, greatly exceeds the function of a competition law safety valve, and its decisions exceed finding the right 'number' for a given tariff in the absence of an agreement between CMOs and users. An administrative body of this type with its own internal research and ability to contract out for additional expertise seems better suited to tackle questions of this nature than a traditional tribunal limited to an adversarial process. This may in turn have generated the restraint shown by the Federal Court of Appeal[108] in revising the Board's decision, especially in matters concerning the specialized nature of the Board's work, such as tariffs.[109] The Board has also striven to give detailed

---

[106] See *supra* note 82 and accompanying text.

[107] The complexity follows at least in part from the Board's own decision to move beyond the role of a competition law safety valve into a much broader market regulation body.

[108] According to s. 28(1)(j) of the *Federal Courts Act*, R.S.C. 1985, c. F-7, that Court has exclusive jurisdiction for any revision of a decision rendered by the Board.

[109] See *supra*, note 82 and *Neighbouring Rights Collective of Canada v. Society of Composers, Authors & Music Publishers of Canada*, supra note 98 at para. 62:

> Parliament established the Copyright Board to administer the scheme by approving royalties and invested it with the powers necessary for it to discharge its regulatory responsibilities in a complex area. Rapid and profound technological developments

reasons on the legal aspects of its decisions and has not hesitated to produce original decisions, such as its 1999 decision on the application of copyright to online transmissions of music,[110] the first decision of its kind on the merits anywhere in the world, most findings of which were later upheld by the Supreme Court of Canada.[111]

The third set of reasons is the extent of the powers given to the Board under the Act. As indicated above, there is a significant degree of public interest in copyright tariff-setting processes and outcomes, and in the operation of the copyright system. Whether and on which terms users can access copyright works they need, for business, academic or personal use, ultimately affects everyone. To limit the powers of the oversight authority to a strict 'numbers game' may obfuscate the real questions or at least the complete picture. The 'conditions' that attach to the tariff itself (defined as payment for access to a repertory for a limited period of time) are probably as important as the price to be paid, perhaps more. The amount and purpose of authorized use is directly relevant of course, but also the reporting requirements (which are necessary to survey usage in order to pay rights holders accordingly but impose an additional burden on users), the collection mechanism (for example, a single payment for one economic use independently of the number of rights holders involved), and the efficiency and transparency of the CMO concerned, which reassures rights holders that they will get the appropriate payment in due course but also the users, many of whom probably prefer not to pay into a 'black hole'. The Board's powers to merge tariffs and tariff hearings, the publication of decisions, reports, proposed tariffs and so on, its ability to obtain information about and from CMOs and users and more broadly to engage the various stakeholders has resulted in greater transparency.

With the transition from a tribunal to a board, the Copyright Board moved copyright regulation into the sphere of public law in the sense that (a) its functions are best viewed as regulatory rather than adjudicatory; and (b) its

---

are reshaping the market and require sophisticated regulatory responses in order to ensure that all who contribute value to the recording of a musical work are fairly compensated and that consumers are not prejudiced. In *Dr. Q.* [*v. College of Physicians and Surgeons of British Columbia*, [2003] 1 S.C.R. 226] at paragraph 31, the Supreme Court recently re-emphasized that deference is indicated by a statutory scheme in which a specialized tribunal is granted broad discretion to balance in the public interest competing rights and economic interests.

[110] *SOCAN – Tariff 22 (Transmission of Musical Works to Subscribers via a Telecommunications Service not covered under Tariff Nos. 16 or 17)* (1999), 1 C.P.R. (4th) 417 (Cop. Bd.).

[111] *Society of Composers, Authors and Music Publishers of Canada v. Canadian Assn. of Internet Providers*, [2004] 2 S.C.R. 427.

normative profile moved beyond the interests or even the requests of the litigants to those of the public interest in a fair and well-functioning copyright system.[112] Given the broad impact of copyright tariffs on culture, media and society at large, this may, in this author's opinion, be seen as a positive development.

Disadvantages and Shortcomings of the Canadian System

The Canadian system, including the Copyright Board, is not perfect, far from it, even though it seems better equipped legally, structurally and organisationally to perform its duties in the interests of all those concerned, including the public when compared to more traditional tribunals.

The Board has been criticized by a number of stakeholders. The costs and duration of proceedings, including the delay to get a hearing date are most often mentioned.

The criticism levelled at the Board is surprisingly not as much about the tariffs as about its operations – in particular the long delays in setting up hearings and the costs associated with long hearings. While part of the criticism is well-founded – it may take close to two years to obtain hearing dates (from the date of filing of a proposed tariff), which means that any certification would necessarily be retroactive (when counted from the decision date) – the Board is of course not responsible for delays in the appeal process.[113] Part of the delays may be due to inadequate and insufficient staffing. Other delays are caused by the sheer number of parties who wish to be heard, though this problem has been lessened somewhat by combining hearings on certain tariffs. Other issues are structural. For example, some CMOs have no choice but to apply for a tariff, thus increasing the workload. Additionally, the inability of the Board to award costs has sometimes resulted in it having to deal with matters that could have been addressed more expeditiously. Conversely, the fact that some Canadian CMOs must obtain a tariff from the Board before collecting any royalties seems to have had positive effects. This sometimes has accelerated the process leading to the effective implementation of a collective in a market. In Canada, a retransmission tariff was in place less than ten

---

[112] The Board may take account of 'any factor that it considers appropriate' (s. 68(2)(b) – but see also 66.71, 68(1), 70.14, 70.16 *in fine*, 72(2), 83(7), 68(3), 70.15(1), 73(1)(ii), and 83(8)(ii)) and may decide beyond the proposed tariff, in spite of the traditional rule of *ultra petita*. See *Canadian Private Copying Collective v. Canadian Storage Media Alliance*, *supra* note 12 at para 7.

[113] In that connection, Parliament has already eliminated one step (the Trial Division of the Federal Court).

months after royalties became payable.[114] The Board can also ensure a certain level of uniformity in the terms and conditions of the various tariffs without having to wait for a dispute to arise between a collective and its users.

As to the delays in setting up hearings, there is no published data on the delays caused by one party (for example, not being available or asking for a postponement) as opposed to those created by the Board's inability to work faster. If the problem is the latter, one would need an administrative audit process to determine whether there are administrative deficiencies or simply a lack of resources. If this author may venture a personal opinion based on observations of the Board's operations, the second factor is certainly part of the explanation.

The length of hearings (from a few days to several weeks) likely stems from good intentions: letting everyone speak, in order to increase transparency and engender respect for the decisions. Perhaps some parties abuse the process and the Board's rules could most probably be improved to streamline the process. That said, while those are important organizational matters for stakeholders, especially those who must pay the bills associated with submissions to the Board and hearings, the bigger picture of a well-functioning copyright system seems paramount. There may, however, be a few ways in which processes could be improved, including awarding costs to parties who at great expense have presented a valid case to the Board or against any party who is considered to have abused the process.

Finally, the flip side of the move from a rather limited adjudicatory function to a regulatory one mentioned as an advantage earlier, and the Board's embracing of the broader 'public interest' and other criteria 'as it sees fit' (as opposed to a strict limit to what is argued before it) and its ability to go beyond what is requested by the parties (that is, the traditional rule of *ultra petita* does not apply) is necessarily accompanied by a certain normative fuzziness, which theoretically may lead to unpredictability of outcomes. This, however, has not generally been observed.

Future Growth

Given the growing importance of copyright in the Canadian economy (and more generally in the global knowledge economy) as a key determining factor

---

[114] Collectives subject to the general regime have even started to use the filing of a proposed tariff as a tool to enter a market and force recalcitrant users to the bargaining table: see *Statement of Royalties to be Collected by CBRA for the Fixation and Reproduction of Works and Communication Signals, in Canada, by Commercial Media Monitors for the Years 2000–2005 and Non-commercial Media Monitors for the Years 2001–2005* (2005), 39 C.P.R. (4th) 152 (Cop. Bd.).

in the extent and depth of knowledge, art, entertainment and information production, dissemination and use in Canada, the Board should be given both additional resources and additional powers. Its supervisory function of CMOs could be enhanced by helping CMOs (other than well-established CMOs in the music field) secure the necessary authority to license, that is, the right to authorize the use of a complete (or appropriate) repertoire (of works, performances or recordings). The inability to license works, performances or recordings is frustrating for users (who may then claim that the copyright system is broken), but leads to losses for rightsholders when that inability is not a (*a priori* legitimate) use of their right to prohibit the use but the fact that the CMO was unable to find them to obtain the authority to represent them.[115]

One specific suggestion contained in a study published in 2003 by Heritage Canada[116] (which shares responsibility for copyright policy with Industry Canada) has been to allow Canadian CMOs to apply for world-wide extension of their repertoire. Under such a system, the CMO's repertoire (of rights administered) becomes 'opt out' rather than 'opt in', once a CMO can show that (a) it has obtained the voluntary support of a substantial number of Canadian rights holders of the category concerned by its proposed licensing scheme; and (b) that it is in the public interest to do so. This system, known as extended repertoire (or extended licensing) has been in use for almost 40 years in Northern Europe where apparently it has worked rather well because those countries use a significant amount of foreign material – in respect of which obtaining licensing authority is often far more complicated. If such a system were introduced, CMOs would have to apply to the Board to show that they should get the extension.

There are other ways in which the role of the Board may be expanded even further over the coming years. To mention but one, for the first time since the establishment of CMOs to administer reprographic rights, no agreement was reached between one such CMO (Access Copyright) and educational institutions in Western provinces, thus leading to a hearing and a first tariff to be set by the Board, probably towards the end of 2007. Educational uses are increasingly contentious, and interventions by the Board (and perhaps also by Parliament) are on the policy radar screen.

Independently of those possible changes, it seems that 'blanket' or repertory-based solutions to license massive online uses are likely to grow expo-

---

115 Daniel J. Gervais, 'The Changing Role of Copyright Collectives' in Gervais, *supra* note 5 at xx–xxi.

116 Daniel Gervais, *Application of an Extended Collective Licensing Regime in Canada: Principles and Issues Related to Implementation* (June 2003), online: <http://www.canadianheritage.gc.ca/progs/ac-ca/progs/pda-cpb/pubs/regime/regime_e.pdf>.

nentially. Collectives may be able to offer the rights associated with online content, as some have already begun to do. Collective licensing is a fair alternative between prohibition and free use, at least for uses for which imposing an exception would be unfair to creators and publishers (for example, an educational exception to allow free use of textbooks and other forms of academic material) and a violation of the international norm known as the three-step test.[117] On the other hand, prohibition of use on the Internet (a) is very difficult to achieve technologically; and (b) does not generate revenue for authors and other rights holders, at least not directly.[118]

In 2001, the US Supreme Court upheld the rights of freelance journalists to control the electronic reuse of texts submitted to newspaper and periodical publishers, including the *New York Times*, for publication in their paper edition.[119] The decision is interesting because, while the Court fully recognized that copyright vests in the author (absent an express transfer), it refused to enjoin the publishers from using the material. Instead, it 'forced' the parties to negotiate:

> ...it hardly follows from today's decision that an injunction against the inclusion of these [freelance] Articles in the [publisher] Databases (much less all freelance articles in any databases) must issue. [...] The Parties (Authors and Publishers) may enter into an agreement allowing continued electronic reproduction of the Authors' works; they, and if necessary the courts and Congress, may draw on numerous *models* for distributing copyrighted works and remunerating authors for their distribution.[120]

The only 'model' the US Supreme Court referred to in that decision was the licensing of musical works for broadcast use, that is, collective management. The decision implicitly recognized that properly functioning collective licensing models can reduce the transaction costs associated with obtaining an authorization to use copyright material, while allowing authors and other rightsholders to benefit economically, thus ensuring that the historical reward and incentive function of copyright is fulfilled.[121]

---

117 Sam Ricketson & Jane C. Ginsburg, *International Copyright and Neighbouring Rights: The Berne Convention and Beyond*, vol. 1 (Oxford: Oxford University Press, 2006) at 756–76; Daniel J. Gervais, *TRIPS Agreement : Drafting History and Analysis*, 2nd ed. (London: Sweet & Maxwell, 2003) at 143–52.

118 Daniel J. Gervais, 'The Purpose of Copyright Law in Canada' (2005) 2:2 Univ. Ottawa L & Tech. J. 315 at 331–32, online: <http://www.uoltj.ca/articles/vol2.2/2005.2.2.uoltj.Gervais.315-356.pdf>.

119 *Tasini et al. v. New York Times et al.*, 121 S. Ct. 2381 (2001).

120 *Ibid.* at 2393 [Emphasis added].

121 Unfortunately, though perhaps not surprisingly in that jurisdiction, the matter led to further litigation and a tendency on the part of publishers to ask for full assign-

CONCLUSION

In Canada, the growth of collective management has been significant, as is the number of areas in which CMOs operate, especially for a common law jurisdiction. This seems to be the result of deliberate policy choices on the part of successive Canadian governments, combined with the ability of the Copyright Board to develop some of the tools that allow it to best implement those choices. In effect, it would seem that the rapid evolution of collective management in Canada has been intimately linked to the emergence, in the *Act*, of mechanisms to oversee the relationship between collectives and copyright users.

The main oversight mechanism is the Copyright Board of Canada. By functioning as an administrative body with permanent staff, somewhat more liberal rules than law courts, and its own research resources, the Board has been able to consider facts and opinions not limited to evidence presented by parties to a hearing, and to render decisions that take account of the broader public interest at play in most recent copyright-related debates. The Board's ability to examine the functioning of Collective Management Organizations beyond the strict financial aspects of tariffs has allowed the rationalization of both tariff-setting processes and tariffs, including the determination of some of the conditions of operation of CMOs, for example, to ensure transparency and thus build trust in the system by users and the general public. Comparatively speaking, the Board seems to have performed significantly better as a copyright regulator than entities functioning as pure, generally part-time tribunals.

More needs to be done. The Board needs additional resources and perhaps internal process reviews to streamline hearings. This could include the possibility of awarding costs. But overall the Board has achieved many of its goals and ensured that Canadians can have access on reasonable terms to the music, films, books and other copyright material they want and love. This is largely due to a structure that gives it broad powers and its own resource – and, some might add, a policy role, or at least one that clearly goes well beyond that of a tariff tribunal and competition law safety valve. As copyright law is called upon to regulate more and more individ-

ment of rights, thereby excluding many authors from a share in any ongoing revenues generated by their work. Admittedly, the matter is complex because a significant portion of online revenue made by news providers consist of advertising, placement fees, etc, not individual article downloads, but a collective management approach can work well, at least for those paid downloads, as the RightsLink project, managed by the US reprography collective, Copyright Clearance Center Inc., shows. See <http://rightslink.copyright.com>.

ual uses and reuses of copyright material, especially in the online environment, the management of copyright by individual rightsholders becomes more difficult, at least for mass uses. This may lead to an increased reliance on collective management and an increasingly more visible role for the Board.

PART 3

Overlapping issues

10. Battleground between new and old orders: control conflicts between copyright and personal data protection

Margaret Ann Wilkinson[1]

INTRODUCTION

In 2005, the Federal Court of Appeal had the opportunity to consider the relationship between notions of privacy and conceptions of intellectual property in *BMG Canada Inc. v. John Doe*.[2] Justice Sexton, for the court, wrote:

> Modern technology…must not be allowed to obliterate those personal property rights which society has deemed important. Although privacy concerns must also be considered, it seems to me that they must yield to public concerns for the protection of intellectual property rights in situations where infringement threatens to erode those rights.[3]

In the context of exploring the issues that were before the Court of Appeal in that case, this chapter will explore three themes emanating from this paragraph. First, Justice Sexton equates intellectual property with property rights – an increasingly prevalent rhetoric in an age when property rights holders who have come into the ascendancy during the industrial age are challenged by the recent migration of wealth from manufacturing to the internet, from the industrial age to the information age. Second, Justice Sexton juxtaposes

1 The author has been supported in this work through funding received from the Social Sciences and Humanities Research Council of Canada. Law student Vanessa Bacher provided timely research assistance. The author would also like to thank the reviewer of an earlier draft of this paper for most thoughtful suggestions.

2 *BMG Canada Inc. v. John Doe*, [2005] 4 F.C.R. 81, (2005), 39 C.P.R. (4th) 97, Sexton J.A. [*BMG FCA* cited to F.C.R.], aff'g *BMG Canada Inc. v. John Doe*, [2004] 3 F.C.R. 241, (2004), 32 C.P.R. (4th) 64, von Finckenstein J. [*BMG FC* cited to F.C.R.].

3 *Ibid.* at para. 41.

privacy and intellectual property – and gives priority to intellectual property. Third, Justice Sexton cites 'public concerns for the protection of intellectual property rights' and this begs an examination of notions of the public interest.

It is perhaps not unexpected that a dispute such as this would arise from the present highly charged environment of music. Music is an area where industrial players have, in the past, particularly benefited from past extensions of copyright law. In the immediate past, the music industry is also one that has enjoyed considerable success, particularly in the US, in influencing legislators to further amend copyright legislation to perpetuate and shore up the industrial model.[4] In Canada, the music industry has a long history of collective representation,[5] recently strengthened by further legislative recognition of collectives for all rights holders.[6] In this litigation, the music companies themselves were the plaintiffs: BMG is just the first named plaintiff – the other plaintiffs are fellow members of the Canadian Recording Industry Association (CRIA).[7]

---

[4] See Pamela Samuelson, 'Digital Rights Management {and, or, vs.} the Law' (April 2003) 46:4 Communications of the ACM 41. Samuelson writes that the Hollywood industry has long influenced copyright policy in the United States, using such measures as the *Audio Home Recording Act* (AHRA) of 1992, which required the installation of copy management chips in digital audiotape technologies and videocassettes, and today through their ownership of key patents for DVD players, thus controlling the anti-copying technology built into them. They also have a mandate to increase the prevalence of Digital Rights Management technology in their products. For further illustration of the recording industry's influence, see Amy Harmon 'Music Industry in Global Fight on Web Copies' *The New York Times* (7 October 2002), online: New York Times <http://www.nytimes.com/2002/10/07/technology/07SWAP.html> (on legal action taken over file-sharing programs in the US). See also *Metro-Goldwyn-Mayer Studios Inc. et al. v. Grokster, Ltd. et al.*, 545 U.S. 913 (2005) at para 1, where the Supreme Court ruled against file-sharing software providers, concluding: 'one who distributes a device with the object of promoting its use to infringe copyright, as shown by clear expression or other affirmative steps taken to foster infringement, is liable for the resulting acts of infringement by third parties.'

[5] Dating back to 1925 when the Canadian Performing Rights Society, an offshoot of the British Performing Rights Society, was established. In 1940, BMI Canada emerged.

[6] In 1988 the Canadian *Copyright Act*, R.S.C. 1985, c. C-42 [*Copyright Act*] was amended to except rightholders' collectives from the rigours of the *Competition Act*, R.S.C. 1985, c. C-34. This encouraged the formation of many rightsholders' collectives. See Mario Bouchard, 'Collective Management in Commonwealth Jurisdictions: Comparing Canada and Australia' in Daniel Gervais, ed., *Collective Management of Copyright and Related Rights* (The Netherlands: Kluwer Law International, 2006) 283 at 285.

[7] EMI Music Canada, a Division of EMI Group Canada Inc., Sony Music Entertainment (Canada) Inc., Universal Music Canada Inc., Warner Music Canada Ltd., BMG Music, Arista Records Inc., Zomba Recording Corporation, EMI Music Sweden AB, Capitol Records, Inc., Chrysalis Records Limited, Virgin Records

CRIA is not a copyright collective:[8] rather it is 'a non-profit trade organization that was founded in 1964 to represent the interests of Canadian companies that create, manufacture and market sound recordings',[9] although it maintains 'a Division to enforce the various rights in copyright of its members and to investigate and initiate legal action in response to piracy'.[10] Further, '[i]n association with its international affiliates, CRIA's Anti-Piracy Division monitors internet sites in Canada for unauthorized use of sound recordings'.[11] Unlike the practice of many copyright collective associations,[12] CRIA does not take

---

Limited, Sony Music Entertainment Inc., Sony Music Entertainment (UK) Inc., UMG Recordings, Inc., Mercury Records Limited, and WEA International Inc.

[8] In the 1988 reforms, copyright holder collectives were exempted from the rigours of the *Competition Act*. See *Copyright Act*, *supra* note 6, s. 70.5. For an interesting discussing of the situation of users' collectives, as opposed to copyright holders' collectives, see Catherine A. Maskell, 'Consortia: Anti-competitive or in the public good?' (2008) 26:2 Library Hi-Tech 164. The definition of 'collective society' was added to the Canadian *Copyright Act* in 1997 by S.C. 1997, c.24, s. 1(5):

> a society, association or corporation that carries on the business of collective administration of copyright or of the remuneration right conferred by section 19 [re: rights in sound recordings] or 81 [re: private copying of sound recordings] for the benefit of those who, by assignment, grant of license, appointment of it as their agent or otherwise, authorize it to act on their behalf in relation to that collective administration, and
> (a) operates a licensing scheme, applicable in relation to a repertoire of works...or more than one author ... pursuant to which the society, association or corporation sets out classes of users that it agrees to authorize under this Act, and the royalties and terms and conditions on which it agrees to authorize those classes of users, or
> (b) carries on the business of collecting and distributing royalties, or levies payable pursuant to this Act.

CRIA is not included in the compendium of Canadian collective societies available on the website of the Copyright Board of Canada, Copyright Board of Canada, 'Copyright Collective Societies', online: <http://www.cb-cda.gc.ca/societies/index-e.html>.

[9] Canadian Recording Industry Association, 'About CRIA', online: <http://www.cria.ca/about.php>.

[10] See #1 in CRIA's list of anti-piracy efforts: CRIA, 'What we do?', online: <http://www.cria.ca/whatwedo.php>. Also see Jonathan Fowlie 'Music police trumpet piracy bust' *The Globe & Mail* (9 July 2004) A1, A10. On Thursday 8 July 2004, the RCMP announced that, tipped off by the CRIA, they had confiscated an enormous cache of over 1,100 DVDs and 1,500 VHS tapes, 'the most ever taken at one time,' bootlegged from music concerts and shows. An individual from Hamilton was charged with five counts of copyright infringement. On the following Monday, 12 July 2004, the members of CRIA filed their appeal from the decision of Justice von Finckenstein.

[11] See #6 in CRIA's list of anti-piracy efforts, *ibid.*.

[12] The Society of Composers, Authors and Music Publishers of Canada

an assignment from its members of the copyright interest it represents and thus is not directly a litigant in proceedings such as this case.

CRIA's members, then, launched this lawsuit against 'John Doe, Jane Doe and all those persons who are infringing copyright in the plaintiffs' sound recordings'. In particular,[13] the plaintiffs alleged that the defendants were infringing their rights:

- To reproduce sound recordings in a material form[14]
- To authorize the reproduction of sound recordings in a material form[15]

The infringements alleged were both primary infringement[16] and, by distributing (to such an extent as to affect prejudicially the owner of copyright) unauthorized reproductions and possessing the unauthorized reproductions in order to effect the distribution, secondary infringement.[17]

The challenge facing the plaintiffs as they commenced this litigation in the Federal Court was inherent in the technology of the internet: although they knew that works in which they held copyright interests were circulating widely on the internet without their permission, they did not know the identities of those whom they alleged were infringing their rights to reproduce or authorize reproduction. They alleged that activity at 29 internet service provider addresses was evidence of infringement.[18] However, all 29 addresses could be identified by the plaintiffs only in terms of the online pseudonyms that the internet users at those addresses used. Thus the plaintiffs brought the interlocutory motion, which created the context for the judgments on which this article focuses. The motion was brought before Justice von Finckenstein under Federal Court Rules 233[19] and 238,[20] against five Canadian internet

(SOCAN), for example, takes an assignment from its members of performing rights in music, including rights to communicate music by telecommunication, and therefore, in litigation proceedings, SOCAN is itself a party.

13 *BMG FC*, *supra* note 2 at para. 22.

14 *Copyright Act*, supra note 6, s. 18(1)(b).

15 *Ibid.* at s. 18(1).

16 *Ibid.* at s. 27(1).

17 *Ibid.* at s. 27 (2)(b), (d). This is a relatively new section of the Act, added in 1997.

18 *BMG FC*, *supra* note 2 at para. 3. The plaintiffs submitted that over 1000 songs had been downloaded by users at each of these 29 internet addresses.

19 *Federal Court Rules,* S.O.R./98-106, r. 233 (1). On motion, the Court may order the production of any document that is in the possession of a person who is not a party to the action, if the document is relevant and its production could be compelled at trial.

20 *Ibid.* at r. 238 (1). A party to an action may bring a motion for leave to examine for discovery any person not a party to the action, other than an expert witness for a party, who might have information on an issue in the action.

service providers[21] to compel these ISPs to disclose the names of their customers who used the ISP addresses alleged to be relevant to the infringement lawsuit.[22] It is important to note that all parties to this motion agreed on two points:

> [1.] ISP account holders have an expectation that their identity will be kept private and confidential. This expectation of privacy is based on both the terms of their account agreements with the ISPs and sections 3 and 5 of the *Personal Information Protection and Electronic Documents Act* (PIPEDA).
> [2.] The exceptions contained in PIPEDA apply in this case and an ISP by virtue of s. 7(3)(c) of PIPEDA may disclose personal information without consent pursuant to a court order.[23]

In the first instance, Justice von Finckenstein decided that the test that he ought to apply, in deciding whether to grant the applicants' motion,[24] had the following five parts:[25]

(a) the applicant must establish a *prima facie* case against the unknown alleged wrongdoer;
(b) the person from whom discovery is sought must be in some way involved in the matter under dispute, he must be more than an innocent bystander;

---

21 Shaw Communications Inc., Roger Cable Communications Inc., Bell Canada, Telus Inc., and Vidéotron Ltée.

22 *BMG FC*, *supra* note 2 at para. 6. Electronic Frontier Canada and the newly established Canadian Internet Policy and Public Interest Clinic of the Faculty of Law at the University of Ottawa (CIPPIC) were granted intervener status for the purpose of making arguments.

23 *Ibid.* at para. 9.

24 *Ibid.* at para. 15.

25 *Ibid.* at para. 13. See also *Federal Court Rules*, *supra* note 19, r. 238(3) set out in Annex A to the judgment:

> The Court may, on a motion under subsection (1) [set out above], grant leave to examine a person and determine the time and manner of conducting the examination, if it is satisfied that
> (a) the person may have information on an issue in the action;
> (b) the party has been unable to obtain the information informally from the person or from another source by any other reasonable means;
> (c) it would be unfair not to allow the party an opportunity to question the person before trial; and
> (d) the questioning will not cause undue delay, inconvenience or expense to the person or to the other parties.

(c) the person from whom discovery is sought must be the only practical source of information available to the applicants;
(d) the person from whom discovery is sought must be reasonably compensated for his expenses arising out of compliance with the discovery order in addition to his legal costs;
(e) the public interests in favour of disclosure must outweigh the legitimate privacy concerns.

Of these criteria, Justice von Finckenstein found that the applicant plaintiffs had satisfied (b),[26] (d),[27] but not (a),[28] (c),[29] or (e).[30] Therefore, he denied the motion.[31]

The plaintiff applicants appealed the denial of their motion to the Federal Court of Appeal. Justice Sexton, as mentioned above, delivered the judgment for himself, Justice Noël and Chief Justice Richard.[32] The Court of Appeal itself characterized the outcome of the appeal as one of 'divided success'[33] – however, the appeal was dismissed.[34] The characterization of 'divided success' was made because this dismissal was 'without prejudice to the plaintiffs' right to commence a further application for disclosure of the identity of the "users" taking into account these reasons'.[35]

The Court of Appeal upheld Justice von Finckenstein's view that Rule 233 of the Federal Court was not available to the plaintiffs on these facts.[36] The Court of Appeal agreed that Justice von Finckenstein had used the appropriate five criteria to determine the outcome of the motion with respect to Rule 238.[37] The Court of Appeal also agreed in the result with Justice von Finckenstein's finding that the plaintiffs had failed to establish a *prima facie* case against the unknown alleged wrongdoer.[38] However, the Court of Appeal,

---

26 *Ibid.* at para. 30.
27 *Ibid.* at para. 35.
28 *Ibid.* at para. 43.
29 *Ibid.* at paras. 31, 43.
30 *Ibid.* at paras. 42–3.
31 *Ibid.* at para. 47. In *obiter* in paras. 44–6, Justice von Finckenstein described the scope and terms of the order he would have given had the motion succeeded.
32 Only CIPPIC intervened in the case at this level.
33 *BMG FCA*, *supra* note 2 at para. 56.
34 *Ibid.* at para. 55.
35 *Ibid.* at paras. 55, 56. All parties had to bear their own costs of the appeal.
36 *Ibid.* at paras. 17–19.
37 *Ibid.* at para. 30, Sexton J. 'In my view, the plaintiffs could invoke either Rule 238 or equitable bills of discovery and, in either case, the legal principles relating to equitable bills of discovery would be applicable', this agreement was subject to a caveat concerning the first branch of the test, which will be set out just below.
38 *Ibid.* at para. 21.

in agreeing that this motion should be denied, focussed on the deficiencies in the evidence presented in this proceeding, which was primarily hearsay:[39] the Court of Appeal, on the other hand, confirmed that it *is* possible to bring a motion to compel identification of persons committing infringements of copyright under Rule 238.[40] Moreover, the Court of Appeal disagreed with Justice von Finckenstein's statement of the first branch of the test, that, to succeed on such a motion, the plaintiffs had to provide evidence of a *prima facie* case,[41] and stated that the correct test was whether the plaintiffs had a *bona fide* claim.[42] It would have been sufficient, therefore, in the eyes of the Court of Appeal, if the plaintiffs had been able to establish, on this branch of the five part test, that 'they really do intend to bring an action for infringement of copyright based upon the information they obtain, and that there is no other improper purpose for seeking the identity of these persons'.[43]

The Court of Appeal specifically agreed with Justice von Finckenstein's 'characterization of the 5th criteria – that is – the public interest in favour of disclosure must outweigh the legitimate privacy concerns of the person sought to be identified if a disclosure order is made'.[44] Justice von Finckenstein had written that:

> This motion is not a novel proceeding. In the past, third parties have been compelled to disclose documents identifying the name and address of a defendant previously identified solely by an Internet Protocol address. In no case have privacy or other concerns weighing against disclosure outweighed the interest in obtaining documents and information necessary to identify the defendants [authorities omitted].
>
> In this case, the plaintiffs have a legitimate copyright in their works and are entitled to protect it against infringement...[45]

In the same vein, Justice Sexton, for the Court of Appeal, held 'in my view, in cases where plaintiffs show that they have a bona fide claim that unknown persons are infringing their copyright, they have a right to have the identity revealed for the purpose of bringing action'.[46] Justice von Finckenstein in the first instance found, that despite the plaintiffs' legitimate interests in protecting

---

39 *Ibid.*.

40 *Ibid.* at para. 25.

41 *BMG FC, supra* note 2 at paras. 13, 43. See the language of Von Finckenstein J. referring to 'a *prima facie* case.'

42 *BMG FCA, supra* note 2 at para. 32.

43 *Ibid.* at paras. 34, 54. FCA judgment specifically did not accept Justice von Finckenstein's statements of copyright law and findings relating to the merits of the claim for infringement.

44 *Ibid.* at para. 36.

45 *BMG FC, supra* note 2 at paras. 41–2.

46 *BMG FCA, supra* note 2 at para. 42.

themselves against infringers, they had left too long a period of time between the alleged infringements and their quest for the infringers' identities and that this gap raised 'the serious possibility of an innocent account holder being identified'.[47] Justice Sexton, for the Court of Appeal, was also concerned about delay – and for the same reasons:

> it is possible that the privacy rights of innocent persons would be infringed and legal proceedings against such persons would be without justification. Thus the greatest care should be taken to avoid delay between the investigation and the request for information. Failure to take such care might well justify a court in refusing to make a disclosure order.[48]

Justice Sexton went on to say:

> In any event, if a disclosure order is granted, specific directions should be given as to the type of information disclosed and the manner in which it can be used. In addition, it must be said that where there exists evidence of copyright infringement, privacy concerns may be met if the court orders that the user only be identified by initials, or makes a confidentiality order.[49]

Thus, at the end of the day, much of what the Court of Appeal in *BMG Canada Inc. v. John Doe* says about privacy and personal data protection is obiter – just as the decision of the original motions judge, Justice von Finckenstein, did not depend upon his findings about the relationship between the plaintiffs' intellectual property rights and the privacy or personal data protection interests of the owners of the targeted internet accounts. Nonetheless, and notwithstanding the fact that there are other decisions which have involved disclosure of identities in litigation involving the internet, both Justice von Finckenstein and the Federal Court of Appeal express in this case attitudes toward the relationship between privacy and personal data protection interests and intellectual property interests that bear close scrutiny.

This scrutiny is particularly warranted in light of the comments made by Justice LeBel, dissenting in part, in *Society of Composers, Authors and Music Publishers of Canada v. Canadian Association of Internet Providers*.[50] This decision, also involving music in the internet environment, was released on 30 June 2004,[51] between the time that Justice von Finckenstein gave his judgment

---

47 *BMG FC*, *supra* note 2 at para. 42.

48 *BMG FCA*, *supra* note 2 at para. 43.

49 *Ibid.* at para. 45.

50 *Society of Composers, Authors and Music Publishers of Canada v. Canadian Assn. of Internet Providers*, [2004] 2 S.C.R. 427, Binnie J. [*Tariff 22*].

51 The majority decision was written by Justice Binnie, for himself and Justices Iacobucci, Major, Bastarache, Arbour, Deschamps, Fish and Chief Justice McLachlin.

in *BMG Canada Inc. v. John Doe*, on 31 March 2004, and the judgment of the Court of Appeal on 19 May 2005, and was not referred to by the Court of Appeal. In the *Tariff 22* decision, Justice LeBel writes

> ...In general, once the content provider has posted content on a host server, it is available to the public. Owners of copyright works and their collective societies can easily monitor such public content by trawling the publicly accessible servers with specially designed software. Privacy concerns are diminished because it is the content provider who has made the information public by posting it on the server. Although privacy concerns are attenuated, they are not eliminated [by the approach he was proposing in the *Tariff 22* case]. It is now common for Internet site operators to collect personal data from end users when users visit their Web site...But that is a question for another day.[52]

That 'other day', forecast by Justice LeBel, was indeed before the courts in *BMG v. John Doe*, but Justice LeBel gave an indication of his perspective in such a case when, as the only member of the Supreme Court to raise privacy issues in *Tariff 22*, he warned:

> By contrast, the real and substantial connection test [the test adopted by the majority in the *Tariff 22* decision], insofar as it looks at the retrieval practices of end users, encourages the monitoring of an individual's surfing and downloading activities. Such habits tend to reveal core biographical information about a person. Privacy interests of individuals will be directly implicated where owners of copyrighted works or their collective societies attempt to retrieve data from Internet Service Providers about an end user's downloading of copyrighted works. We should therefore be wary of adopting a test that may encourage such monitoring.[53]

The industry and environment concerned are identical in the two cases. The Supreme Court, in *Tariff 22*, noted '[t]he issue of the proper balance in matters of copyright plays out against the much larger conundrum of trying to apply national laws to a fast-evolving technology that in essence respects no national boundaries'.[54] The *Tariff 22* litigation concerned 'the difficult issue of who should compensate musical composers and artists for their Canadian copyright in music downloaded in Canada from a foreign country via the Internet'.[55] In *BMG v. John Doe*, participants in the music industry were also trying to enforce their rights in the internet environment, seeking compensation for music. As in the interim motion proceedings involved in *BMG v. John Doe*, the

52 *Tariff 22*, *supra* note 50 at para. 154, LeBel J., dissenting.
53 *Ibid.* at paras. 153–155, LeBel J., dissenting.
54 *Ibid.* at para. 41.
55 *Ibid.* at para. 1.

targets in the *Tariff 22* litigation were the internet service providers (ISPs).[56] In the *Tariff 22* situation, the root of the litigation lay in the factual reality that '[a]t this point the prospect of seeking to collect royalties from foreign infringers is not an attractive prospect for SOCAN'[57] – and therefore SOCAN sought (unsuccessfully, in the end) to obtain revenue by imposing tariff obligations on Canadian ISPs. The root of the *BMG v. John Doe* litigation lies in the fact that 'Canada's music producers and recording industry are very concerned about infringement of copyright in their musical works through the use of Internet file sharing' and they did not have access to the identities of the alleged infringers; but the ISPs did.[58]

In finding that Canadian ISPs could not be made subject to the tariff at issue before them in the *Tariff 22* case, the Supreme Court observed:

> The knowledge that someone might be using neutral technology to violate copyright...is not necessarily sufficient to constitute authorization...An overly quick inference of 'authorization' would put the Internet Service Provider in the difficult position of judging whether the copyright objection is well founded, and to choose between contesting a copyright action or potentially breaching its contract with the content provider.[59]

The Court went on to observe:[60]

> Parliament made a policy distinction between those who abuse the Internet to obtain 'cheap music' and those who are part of the infrastructure of the Internet itself. It is clear that Parliament did not want copyright disputes between creators and users to be visited on the heads of Internet intermediaries, whose continued expansion and development is considered vital to national economic growth.[61]

Moreoever, Justice LeBel, concurring with the majority on this part of the judgment, but alone in specifically raising privacy concerns, stated:

---

[56] In the *Tariff 22* context, the ISPs were the targets of the action itself: the litigation before the Supreme Court of Canada was an interim proceeding taken to determine whether the Copyright Board of Canada had jurisdiction to impose a tariff for the benefit of SOCAN on Canadian ISPs.

[57] *Tariff 22*, *supra* note 50 at para. 81.

[58] *BMG FCA*, *supra* note 2 at para 2.

[59] *Tariff 22*, *supra* note 50 at para. 127 (Binnie, J. for the majority of the Court, LeBel, J., concurring in these areas).

[60] In the context of s. 2.4(1)(b) of the *Copyright Act* which was at issue in the case.

[61] *Tariff 22*, *supra* note 50 at para. 131 (Binnie, J. for the majority of the Court, LeBel, J., concurring in these areas).

> Insofar as is possible, this Court should adopt an interpretation of [the section at issue] that respects end users' privacy interests, and should eschew an interpretation that would encourage the monitoring or collection of personal data gleaned from Internet-related activity within the home…

The attitudes of both the majority[62] and minority in *Tariff 22* may be contrasted with the attitudes of both Justice von Finckenstein and the Federal Court of Appeal in *BMG v. John Doe*, expressed most forcefully in the judgment of Justice Sexton: 'in my view, in cases where plaintiffs show that they have a bona fide claim that unknown persons are infringing their copyright, they have a *right* to have the identity revealed [by ISPs] for the purpose of bringing action [emphasis here added]'.[63] Indeed, by lowering the requirement on the first branch of the test from establishing a bona fide case (Justice von Finckenstein's threshold) to establishing a bone fide claim, the Court of Appeal gave even greater priority to intellectual property rights (and other civil claims) over privacy interests – with the result that ISPs, whatever their contractual obligations to their clients, would be more frequently required to reveal their clients' identities in civil proceedings brought by third parties.

INTELLECTUAL PROPERTY AND PROPERTY

What is the nature of the interests that are declared by Justice Sexton to be competing for priority in society? He discusses intellectual property and property and he also describes both 'privacy concerns'[64] and 'public concerns for the protection of intellectual property rights'.[65]

It may be useful to begin first by setting aside the equation of intellectual property and property articulated by Justice Sexton. Copyright is intellectual property, not property.[66] Mis-characterizing its essential nature will not assist

---

62 The majority was particularly leery of imposing obligations on ISPs (*ibid.*). The precedent created by the Federal Court of Appeal in *BMG v. John Doe*, if correct, can impose obligations on ISPs and does directly affect the ability of ISPs to guarantee confidentiality to their clients.

63 *BMG FCA*, *supra* note 2 at para. 42.

64 *Ibid.* (See also the opening quotation in this chapter.)

65 *Ibid.*

66 See, for example, W.A. Adams, 'Personal Property Law and Information Assets: Rehabilitation and Relevance,' (2002) 36 Canadian Business Law Journal 267. This perspective may be perceived to run counter to the argument made by Norman Siebrasse that, rather than attempting to balance dissemination and the incentive to create works through copyright law, copyright law should focus on ensuring that property rights are clearly defined: Norman Siebrasse, 'A Property Rights Theory of the Limits of Copyright' (2001) 51 University of Toronto Law Journal 1. On the other

with the resolving of the important questions facing lawmakers.[67] Daniel Gervais has recently pointed out that there are both economic and instrumentalist justifications for copyright and rights-based justifications for copyright made – but '[t]rying to squeeze copyright on one side of that philosophical fence is incorrect in historical perspective, both in common law and civil law jurisdictions'.[68]

It has been widely acknowledged that copyright, in its current form in Canada, is a purely statutory system.[69] Further, in s. 3 of the Canadian *Copyright Act*, it is made absolutely clear that rights exist for rights holders only in the whole or a substantial portion of works. Authors, therefore, do not have an exclusive or exclusionary right over their works – only rights over substantial portions or whole dealings with their works. Where insubstantial portions of their works are involved, authors and copyright holders have no interest.[70] Moreover, the holders of economic rights in copyright under Canadian law are only compensated if they have a right that would, without their consent, be infringed:

---

hand, his need to make the argument itself demonstrates that copyright, as a branch of intellectual property, cannot be considered pure property. See R.J. Roberts, 'Canadian Copyright: Natural Property or Mere Monopoly' (1979) 40 C.P.R. (2d) 33; *Compo Co. v. Blue Crest Music Inc.*, [1980] 1 S.C.R. 357 at 373, Estey J.; *Bishop v. Stevens*, [1990] 2 S.C.R. 467 at 477.

[67] It should be noted that there have been calls to create a property right in personal data. For example, James Rule and Lawrence Hunter, 'Towards Property Rights in Personal Data' in Colin J. Bennett & Rebecca Grant, eds., *Visions of Privacy: Policy Choices for the Digital Age* (Toronto: University of Toronto Press, 1999) 168. It should also be noted that the authors do not discuss the relationship between this proposed property interest and existing interests in intellectual property.

[68] Daniel Gervais, 'The Changing Role of Copyright Collectives' in Daniel Gervais, ed., *Collective Management of Copyright and Related Rights* (The Netherlands: Kluwer Law International, 2006) 3 at 6.

[69] As Plowman J. writes in *Universities of Oxford and Cambridge v. Eyre & Spottiswoode Ltd.*, [1964] 1 Ch 736 at 750, [1963] 3 All E.R. 289 at 293, 'until 1709 [the Statute of Anne] private copyright did not exist.' And, explicitly, in 1911, the *Imperial Copyright Act* abolished any common law copyright: s. 31. This provision is carried forward in s. 89 of the current Canadian *Copyright Act*.

[70] A point recognized by the Copyright Board in *Application by Pointe-à-Callière, Montreal Museum of Archeology and History for the Reproduction of Quotations* (29 March 2004), Copyright Board Decision, online: <http://www.cb-cda.gc.ca/unlocatable/other/1-b.pdf>, when the Board declined to give applicants licenses for unlocatable copyright holders that they were seeking because the Board found the use being contemplated was not one over which the copyright holders had rights. *CCH Canadian Ltd. v. Law Society of Upper Canada*, [2004] 1 S.C.R. 339 at para. 56 [*CCH*], 'if the amount taken from a work is trivial, the fair dealing analysis need not be undertaken at all because the court will have concluded that there was no copyright infringement' because, under s. 3, 'copyright subsists in every work or every substantial portion…'.

> It is an infringement of copyright for any person to do, without the consent of the owner of the copyright, anything that by this Act only the owner of the [economic] copyright has the right to do.[71]

This is far from vesting a property right in works. Indeed the Canadian *Copyright Act* embraces three independent sets of rights. Two of these systems of rights take the form of limited term monopolies[72] emanating from the creation of works: the economic rights in copyright and the moral rights in copyright. The moral rights are inalienable interests held by the creators of works.[73] The third set of rights is based on particular uses of information: this third set is the users' rights. The fair dealing exceptions under the Canadian *Copyright Act* are the cornerstone of this set of rights.[74] As the Chief Justice expressed it, for a unanimous Supreme Court,

> User rights are not just loopholes. Both owner rights and user rights should therefore be given the fair and balanced reading that befits remedial legislation.[75]

It is true that the Supreme Court has recently considered the role of licenses in the context of the *Copyright Act* and specifically approved the following explanation of the relationship between rights and permissions under the Act:

> The 'grant of an interest' referred to in s. 13(4) [of the *Copyright Act*] is the transfer of a property right as opposed to a permission to do a certain thing. The former gives the licensee the capacity to sue in his own name for infringement, the latter provides only a defence to claims of infringement.[76]

---

[71] *Copyright Act*, *supra* note 6, s. 27(1).

[72] *Ibid.* at s. 6. (Both sets of rights run for the life of the author plus approximately fifty years).

[73] *Ibid.* at ss. 2, 14.1, 14.2, 28.1 and 28.2. (These rights in Canada include the rights to paternity and integrity as well as rights to determine with what the creator's work will be associated. While they can be waived, they cannot be assigned.)

[74] Margaret Ann Wilkinson 'Filtering the flow from the fountains of knowledge: access and copyright in education and libraries' in Michael Geist, ed., *In the public interest: the future of Canadian copyright law* (Toronto: Irwin Law, 2005) 331. (The users' rights language of the Supreme Court of Canada is strong, rights-based language and offers a powerful alternative to the potential tyranny of rights holders' interests signalled by the mandatory language in the *Berne Convention*, *NAFTA* and *TRIPS* agreements. The Government may wish to bear in mind that a strong connection may be drawn between the rights-based language of the Supreme Court of Canada in this area and the right to freedom of expression, including rights to access information, under s. 2(b) of the *Charter of Rights and Freedoms*.)

[75] *CCH*, *supra* note 70 at para. 48, quoting with approval from David Vaver, *Copyright Law* (Toronto: Irwin Law, 2000) 171.

[76] *Robertson v. Thomson Corp.*, [2006] 2 S.C.R. 363 at para. 56, LeBel and Fish JJ., for the majority (quoting *Ritchie v. Sawmill Creek Golf & Country Club Ltd.*

However, this statement is specifically made with reference to certain economic rights granted under the *Copyright Act*. Failure to distinguish between various uses of expressions of facts and ideas (information), which are reserved to the holders of the economic rights in copyright under the Canadian *Copyright Act*, and the works associated with these economic copyright interests, or the facts and ideas lying behind the expressions, will distort the role and contribution of economic rights in copyright to society[77] and eclipse the contribution of both moral rights under the Canadian *Copyright Act* and users' rights under the Canadian *Copyright Act*, such as fair dealing.

A key feature of intellectual property is that these devices carry with them aspects of public interest. In the *Copyright Act*, all three bundles of rights (the economic, the moral and the users') serve the public interest. Justice Binnie, writing for the majority in *Théberge v. Galerie d'Art du Petit Champlain*, emphasized that the *Copyright Act* provides 'a balance between promoting the public interest in the encouragement and dissemination of works of the arts and intellect and obtaining a just reward for the creator (*or, more accurately, to prevent someone other than the creator from appropriating whatever benefits may be generated*).'[78] He went on to recognize the special – and limited – nature of the economic copyright holders' rights under copyright:

> The proper balance…lies not only in recognizing the creator's rights but in giving due weight to their limited nature. In crassly economic terms, it would be as ineffi-

(2004), 35 C.P.R. (4th) 163 (Ont. S.C.J.)). See also paras. 57–8 (the majority of the Court further held that 'the content of these licenses is a live issue that should go to trial... Parties are, have been, and will continue to be, free to alter by contract the rights established by the *Copyright Act*').

77 To consider meeting the *information* needs in a society one must factor in many who are not, and may never become, 'authors' within the meaning of the *Copyright Act* – but who are nonetheless communicators of ideas and facts. Abraham Drassinower has promulgated an interesting analysis, in various publications, that essentially reduces copyright players to authors and non-authors: see Abraham Drassinower, 'A Rights-Based View of the Idea/Expression Dichotomy in Copyright Law' (2003) 16 Canadian Journal of Law and Jurisprudence 3. He has been unable to extend his analysis to the patent arena (see Margaret Ann Wilkinson, 'National Treatment, National Interest and the Public Domain' (2003–2004) 1:1-2 University of Ottawa Journal of Technology Law 23) because not all non-patent holders can realistically be considered potential patent holders. That Drassinower cannot articulate his theory for patents may in fact be because the patent situation more clearly points out an essential weakness in the whole theory, even for the copyright context: not all non-authors *are* potential authors – there is a class of non-authors who, nevertheless, are important *information* users *and* disseminators.

78 *Théberge v. Galerie d'Art du Petit Champlain inc.*, [2002] 2 S.C.R. 336 at para. 30 [*Théberge*] [italics added], *Tariff 22*, *supra* note 50 at para. 40. All but the italicized section is also restated and approved in *CCH*, *supra* note 70 at para. 10.

cient to overcompensate artists...as it would be self-defeating to under-compensate them...

Excessive control by holders of copyrights and other forms of intellectual property may unduly limit the ability of the public domain to incorporate and embellish creative innovation in the long-term interests of society as a whole, or create practical obstacles to proper utilization.[79]

The Chief Justice further expressed this concept in *CCH v. Law Society of Upper Canada*: 'the purpose of the copyright law was to balance the public interest in promoting the encouragement and dissemination of works of the arts and intellect and obtaining a just reward for the creator.'[80]

Thus equating intellectual property rights such as copyright with property is not accurate, but perhaps more importantly, it does nothing to assist in the resolution of problems involving competing legal interests and, indeed, leads to mischaracterization of interests by obscuring such values as the encouragement and dissemination of innovations and works of the art and intellect.

PRIVACY AND INTELLECTUAL PROPERTY

Justice Sexton characterized the challenge before the court in *BMG v. John Doe* as one requiring consideration of privacy rights in light of intellectual property concerns – and gave intellectual property priority. However, in terms of 'privacy concerns', two different ideas occur in *BMG v. John Doe*. First, acknowledged in the agreement of the parties, are the statutory obligations imposed upon the ISPs under the *PIPEDA*. Second are notions of privacy that pre-date the coming into force of *PIPEDA*: 'the legitimate privacy concerns' referred to in the fifth branch of the test for granting equitable bills of discovery and now declared by Justice Finckenstein, approved by the Court of Appeal, applicable to applications under Rule 238 of the Federal Court.

Turning first to the statutory obligations, Justice von Finckenstein wrote his judgment, released on 31 March 2004, just months after the *Personal Information Protection and Electronic Documents Act* (*PIPEDA*) came into force in respect of businesses such as ISPs, on 1 January 2004.[81] Indeed, up until 2000, no such legislation existed at all in the private sector in Canada (except in Quebec where the *Act Respecting the Protection of Personal*

---

79 *Théberge, ibid.* at paras. 31–2.

80 *CCH, supra* note 70 at para. 23, McLachlin, C.J. (citing *Théberge, supra* note 78 at 335, Binnie J.).

81 *Personal Information Protection and Electronic Documents Act,* S.C. 2000, c. 5 [*PIPEDA*], discussed in *BMG FC, supra* note 2 at paras. 38–40.

Information in the Private Sector[82] dates from 1993). The personal data protection aspects of *PIPEDA* came into force for federally regulated businesses (for example, shipping companies) and any inter-provincial transfers of information by Canadian businesses on 1 January 2001,[83] except where the information involved was personal health information,[84] but, as mentioned, by 1 January 2004, all private sector organizations engaged in 'commercial activities' in Canada were included in the regime[85] (including those dealing with personal health information).[86]

Personal data protection is a statutory regime that has swept across Canada since 1977, when it was first introduced into the public sector in Part IV of the *Canada Human Rights Act*.[87] It was later combined with the access to government information initiative,[88] becoming, in 1982, the federal *Privacy Act*[89]– passed together with the federal *Access to Information Act*.[90] Similar legislation was passed in Quebec in the same year.[91] Combined access and personal data protection legislation now governs the vast majority of public sector orga-

---

82 *Act Respecting the Protection of Personal Information in the Private Sector*, R.S.Q. c. P-39.1.

83 *PIPEDA*, *supra* note 81 at s. 30(1).

84 *Ibid.* at s. 30(1.1).

85 *Ibid.* at ss. 30(2), (2.1).

86 The federal government, for constitutional reasons, left room for, and indeed encouraged, provincial regulation of private sector activities – and some provinces have taken up this invitation. The federal legislation anticipates the passage of 'equivalent' provincial legislation, by providing that, once recognized as equivalent by the federal Cabinet, such provincial legislation will replace *PIPEDA* for provincial matters within that province (*PIPEDA*, *supra* note 81 at s. 26(2)(b)). Quebec's pre-existing *Act respecting the protection of personal information in the private sector*, *supra* note 82 has already been recognized by the federal government as equivalent to *PIPEDA*. Several other provinces have passed legislation for the private sector – but have not succeeded in persuading the federal government that the legislation is equivalent to *PIPEDA* (Alberta, *Personal Information Protection Act*, S.A. 2003, c. P-6.5 and British Columbia, *Personal Information Protection Act,* S.B.C. 2003, c. 63.) – thus organizations in those provinces must satisfy both regimes. Several other provinces have passed specific personal data protection legislation for the health sector. In Ontario's case, this legislation has been deemed equivalent to *PIPEDA* by the federal government. See, in this connection: Wil Peekhaus, 'Personal Medical Information: Privacy or Personal Data Protection?' (July 2006) 5:2 Canadian Journal of Law and Technology 87.

87 *Canadian Human Rights Act,* R.S.C. 1985, c. H-6.

88 In a unique move, the two separate statutes, now separately located and identified, were passed in one bill: *Access to Information Act and Privacy Act*, S.C. 1982, c. 111.

89 *Privacy Act*, R.S.C. 1985, c. P-21.

90 *Access to Information Act*, R.S.C. 1985, c. A-1.

91 *An act respecting access to documents held by public bodies and the Protection of personal information*, R.S.Q. c. A-2.1.

nizations.[92] It must be noted, however, that personal data protection legislation in the private sector is not combined with access legislation.

This difference between public and private sector personal data protection legislation – that the former is invariably combined with access legislation but the latter never is – becomes important in examining one precedent discussed by both Justice Finckenstein and the Court of Appeal in *BMG v. John Doe*: *Glaxo Wellcome PLC v. Minister of National Revenue*.[93] At the time of the *Glaxo Wellcome* case, Revenue Canada would indeed have been subject to public sector personal data protection legislation.[94] However, as noted, all public sector institutions governed by personal data protection legislation are also subject to access legislation[95] and, indeed, the *Glaxo Wellcome* decision stands for the proposition that a litigant seeking production of documents in

---

92 There are arguably 14 jurisdictions in Canada: the federal government, nine provinces and three territories (although technically territorial governments are subordinate to the federal government). Municipalities are subordinate to the legislatures of the provinces. In some provinces they are included in the personal data protection legislation that governs provincial organizations (Alberta, British Columbia, Quebec and Newfoundland) and in some cases provinces have passed separate legislation for them (Ontario and Saskatchewan). In other jurisdictions municipalities *per se* are not covered (New Brunswick, Nova Scotia, and Prince Edward Island). Thus the public sector legislation in force is as follows: *Privacy Act,* R.S.C. 1985, c. P-21 (Canada), *Freedom of Information and Protection of Privacy Act,* R.S.A. 2000, c. F-25 (Alberta), *Freedom_of Information and Protection of Privacy Act,* R.S.B.C. 1996, c. 165 (British Columbia), the *Freedom of Information and Protection of Privacy Act,* S.M. 1997, c.50 (Manitoba), *Access to Information and Protection of Privacy Act*, S.N.L. 2002, c. A-1.1 (Newfoundland and Labrador), *Right to Information Act,* S.N.B. 1978, c. R-10.3 (New Brunswick), *Freedom of Information and Protection of Privacy Act,* S.N.S. 1993, c.5 (Nova Scotia), *Freedom of Information and Protection of Privacy Act,* R.S.O. 1990, c. F.31 (Ontario), *Freedom of Information and Protection of Privacy Act,* S.P.E.I. 2001, c. 37 (Prince Edward Island), *An Act Respecting Access to Documents Held By Public Bodies and the Protection of Personal Information, supra* note 91 (Quebec), *Freedom of Information and Protection of Privacy Act,* S.S. 1990–91, c. F-22.01 (Saskatchewan), *Access to Information and Protection of Privacy Act*, S.N.W.T. 1994, c. 20 (Nunavut & Northwest Territories), *Access to Information and Protection of Privacy Act*, R.S.Y. 2002, c. 1 (Yukon), *Municipal Freedom of Information and Protection of Privacy Act*, R.S.O. 1990, c. M56 (Ontario), *Local Authority Freedom of Information and Protection of Privacy Act*, S.S. 1990–91, c. L-27.1 (Saskatchewan). It also must be noted that in four provinces public health information has been moved to separate legislation: *Health Information Act,* R.S.A. 2000, c. H-5 (Alberta), *Personal Health Information Act*, C.C.S.M. c. P33.5 (Manitoba), *Personal Health Information Protection Act,* 2004, S.O. 2004, c. 3, Sch. A (Ontario) and *Health Information Protection Act,* S.S. 1999, c. H-0.021 (Saskatchewan).

93 *Glaxo Wellcome PLC v. M.N.R.* (1998), 81 C.P.R. (3d) 372 (F.C.A.) [*Glaxo*] (Considered in *BMG FCA*, *supra* note 2 at para. 32).

94 *Privacy Act*, *supra* note 89.

95 *Access to Information Act*, *supra* note 90.

the possession of a public sector institution governed by *access* legislation need not apply under the access legislation but can, instead, seek a court order for production. Justice Sexton cited the decision because the plaintiff obtained a disclosure order requiring Revenue Canada to identify certain importers who were alleged to have infringed its patents. However, personal data protection focuses exclusively on individuals, not corporate bodies, and is only relevant in the case of information about identifiable individuals – it has no application in the case of the identities of corporate persons. The identities of corporate persons were at issue in the *Glaxo Wellcome* case, not the identities of individuals, and the Federal Court of Appeal in that case, accordingly, was only considering the *Access to Information Act*, not the *Privacy Act*.[96] The thrust of the *Access to Information Act* is in favour of public access to information held by public sector organizations – the opposite thrust of *PIPEDA*, which was the legislation applicable in the *BMG v. John Doe* case. Thus, the reliance placed upon the *Glaxo Wellcome* case by both courts, but particularly the Court of Appeal, in *BMG v. John Doe* is entirely misplaced.

Although related to the concept of privacy, personal data protection is not privacy legislation. It neither confers upon an organization subject to it the ability or duty to gather information from individuals nor prohibits an organization from gathering information from individuals. Rather than dealing with *whether* information can be gathered about individuals or from individuals, personal data protection statutes begin by regulating *how* information is to be gathered about individuals if the organization either needs or is mandated elsewhere to gather that type of information. That personal data protection legislation is not strictly privacy legislation is evidenced by the fact that the Organisation for Economic Co-operation and Development Guidelines, with which Canada's regimes deliberately concur,[97] articulate a dual purpose: not only to protect personal information but also to ensure the free flow of data between countries.[98]

---

[96] *Glaxo*, *supra* note 93 (note that the *Privacy Act* is not judicially considered).

[97] Organisation for Economic Co-operation and Development, *Guidelines on the Protection of Privacy and Transborder Flows of Personal Data* (Paris, 1981) [*OECD Guidelines*]. Canada became a signatory in 1984. Canada's regimes are also designed to make Canadian organizations compatible with the EC, *Directive 95/46/EC of the European Parliament and of the Council of 24 October 1995 on the protection of individuals with regard to the processing of personal data and on the free movement of such data*, [1995] O.J. L.281/31. The EU has given this domestic directive an international application in that it prohibits those subject to its Directive from sharing information with organizations elsewhere who are not obliged to treat personal information in comparable ways.

[98] Colin Bennet, *Regulating Privacy: Data Protection and Public Policy in Europe and the United States* (Ithaca: Cornell University Press, 1992) 136–140. See also *OECD Guidelines*, *ibid*.

But privacy, as distinct from statutory personal data protection, clearly has a role to play in *BMG v. John Doe*: the fifth branch of the test for disclosure, which certainly predates personal data protection in Canada, concerns 'legitimate privacy concerns'. What are these concerns?

Privacy, since the late nineteenth century, has popularly come to be understood as 'the right to be let alone'[99] and there has been increasing debate about whether, and to what extent, it should be protected by law – even though it has become enshrined in international instruments (to which Canada is signatory). First, the *Universal Declaration of Human Rights (*1948)[100] provides in Article 12 that:

> No one shall be subjected to arbitrary interference with his privacy... Everyone has the right to the protection of the law against such interference or attacks.[101]

Second, Article 17 of the *International Covenant on Civil and Political Rights*[102] provides:

> (1) No one shall be subject to arbitrary or unlawful interference with his privacy, family, home or correspondence, nor to unlawful attacks on his honour or reputation.
> (2) Everyone has the right to the protection of the law against such interference or attacks.

These instruments do not provide definitions of the concept of privacy and the classic 'right to be let alone', involving the description of privacy as a right, goes beyond articulating the concept of privacy and makes a claim to legal, or at least normative, status. This, in turn, may obscure, rather than assist, the quest to understand the concept of privacy. A better conception might be 'the *state* of being let alone'.[103]

---

99 Samuel Warren & Louis Brandeis, 'The Right to Privacy' (1893) 4 Harv.L.Rev. 193 at 213.

100 *Universal Declaration of Human Rights*, GA Res. 217(III), UN GAOR. 3d Sess., Supp. No. 13, UN Doc. A/810 (1948) 71.

101 *Ibid.* at Art. 27 contains provisions related to intellectual property: (1) Everyone has the right freely to participate in the cultural life of the community, to enjoy the arts and to share in scientific advancement and its benefits. (2) Everyone has the right to the protection of the moral and material interests resulting from any scientific, literary or artistic production of which he is the author.

102 *International Covenant on Civil and Political Rights*, 999 U.N.T.S. 171 (entered into force 1976), online: <http://www.unhchr.ch/html/menu3/b/a_ccpr.htm>.

103 Which concurs with the early usage of privacy recorded in the *Oxford English Dictionary* as dating from 1450: 'The state or condition of being withdrawn from the society of others, or from the public interest.'

While personal data protection is confined by statute to information *about* an identifiable individual,[104] privacy can embrace rights to refuse to divulge any information held by an individual that she or he desires to keep secret, including information about her or himself.[105] Moreover, while personal data protection, as its name implies, encompasses only data issues,[106] privacy encompasses concerns about a much wider range of interferences with the individual.[107]

Nonetheless, while in other societies, at other times, the value of privacy as it relates to personal information may not have been highly regarded,[108] an individual's interest in personal information privacy has been enshrined in Canada as a value to be protected against government incursion. In the criminal context, the majority of the Supreme Court held:

> In fostering the underlying values of dignity, integrity and autonomy, it is fitting that s. 8 of the Charter should seek to protect a biographical core of personal information which individuals in a free and democratic society would wish to maintain and control from dissemination to the state. This would include information which tends to reveal intimate details of the lifestyle and personal choices of the individual.[109]

Again in the criminal context, the Supreme Court held in 1990 that '[p]rivacy may be defined as the right of the individual to determine when, how, and to what extent he or she will release personal information'.[110] In this context, the Court identified its notion of privacy with the context of personal information, thus limiting its conception of information privacy. Alan Westin, in the 1960s,

---

[104] *Privacy Act*, *supra* note 89 at s. 3.

[105] Margaret Steig, 'The Nineteenth-Century Information Revolution' (1980) 15 Journal of Library History 22 (Illustrates the attitude of early industrial British employers who considered information about their employees to be the private affair of the employer and therefore not to be made available to the government or anyone else).

[106] That is, information contained in records.

[107] The *Canadian Charter of Rights and Freedoms*, for example, does not contain a direct reference to privacy, but both s. 7 ('Everyone has the right to life, liberty and security of the person and the right not to be deprived thereof except in accordance with the principles of fundamental justice') and s. 8 ('Everyone has the right to be secure against unreasonable search or seizure') have been interpreted to protect Canadians against government incursion of privacy interests beyond informational privacy.

[108] David Flaherty, *Privacy in Colonial New England* (Charlottesville, VA: University Press of Virginia, 1972) at 243–5. (Described the situation in the original New England colonies of America where the social consensus was that the individuals harbouring interest in being let alone were suspect.)

[109] *R. v. Plant*, [1993] 3 S.C.R. 281 at para. 20, Justice Sopinka, speaking for Justices LaForest, Gonthier, Cory, Iacobucci, and then Chief Justice Lamer. Justice McLachlin (as she then was) dissented on other grounds.

[110] *R. v. Duarte*, [1990] 1 S.C.R. 30 at para. 25.

interpreted privacy in similar language, as including an 'informational right': a right of people and organizations 'to determine when, how, and to what extent information about them is *communicated* to others'.[111] However, as then Chief Justice Lamer pointed out, in his dissent in *Aubry v. Editions Vice-Versa*, there are additional limitations on the notion of constitutionally protected informational privacy in Canada:

> the decisions of this Court relating to s.8 [of the Charter] recognize that there is a fundamental difference between a person's reasonable expectation of privacy in his or her dealings with the state and the same person's reasonable expectation of privacy in his or her dealings with ordinary citizens... It would therefore be wrong to define the scope of the right to privacy between citizens solely on the basis of the decisions relating to s. 8... the right to privacy can have a different scope in private law.[112]

---

111 Alan F. Westin, *Privacy and Freedom* (New York: Atheneum, 1967) at 7.

112 *Aubry v. Editions Vice-Versa*, [1998] 1 S.C.R. 591 at paras. 8–9 [*Aubry*]. A recent decision in the Ontario Superior Court of Justice has comprehensively considered the place of privacy under the *Canadian Charter of Rights and Freedoms*. In *Cheskes et al v. A.G.(Ont.)*, [2007] O.J. no. 3515, 2007 CanLII 38387 (Ont. S.C.), released 19 September 2007, Justice Belobaba held that the disclosure provisions of Ontario's *Adoption Information Disclosure Act*, S.O. 2005, c.25, proclaimed in force 17 September 2007, as part of the *Vital Statistics Act*, R.S.O. 1990, c. V.4, as amended, violated s. 7 of the Charter and are invalid and are of no force or effect. In terms of this analysis, several aspects of Justice Belobaba's reasons are worth noting. First, while setting out ten background points on which the judgment is based, Justice Belobaba equates personal data protection legislation with privacy [at para.62] and cites the existence of personal data protection and personal data protection commissioners ['privacy commissioners'] as evidence that the protection of privacy is a fundamental value in modern democracies. Second, the breach of the Charter which Judge Belobaba finds occurred in this case is characterized [at para.91] as a breach of the right to liberty under s.7 of the Charter: 'I have found a breach of the right to liberty by focussing on the informational privacy interest and applying the reasoning in *R. v. O'Connor* [[1995] 4 S.C.R. 411 at para.120].' Justice Belobaba agrees with the analysis herein that 'there is no freestanding right to privacy in the Charter. If a right to privacy exists under the Charter, it has to be found in the provisions that touch on matters of individual autonomy.' [para. 79, footnote omitted]. It should be noted that the Ontario government has subsequently passed *An Act to Amend the Vital Statistics Act in relation to adoption and to make consequential amendments to the Child and Family Services Act, 2008,* S.O. 2008, c.15), which received Royal Assent 14 May 2008, by which, since adoptions prior to 2008 were under different premises with respect to privacy than the new 2008 provisions, adult adoptees and birth parents whose adoptions were registered in Ontario prior to 1 September 2008 can place a disclosure veto on their file, but, if they do so, they will be asked to provide medical history so that the birth relatives can obtain personal health information. In addition, adult adoptees and birth parents may continue to place a no-contact notice on their files

Even in the context of the protection of personal information from government intrusion, the value of informational privacy has been recognized in many instances to be secondary to other interests. Indeed, the majority of the Supreme Court in *R. v. Plant* itself held that the accused's reasonable expectation of privacy was outweighed by the public interest in criminal enforcement in the situation at bar. Other examples of legislated incursions on informational privacy are the census legislation and income tax legislation, both of which have become very controversial, on privacy grounds.[113]

By contrast, although there is a recognition in Canada of at least *some* limitations on the ability of government to intrude into the lives of Canadians and disrupt their 'state of being alone', including situations involving information privacy, in the private sector, there is not a strong body of consistent jurisprudence establishing the existence of a tort of invasion of privacy. The Manitoba Court of Appeal, in 1986, stated:

> It would appear that at common law the tort of violation of privacy in regard to disclosure of personal information has not been recognized in Canada. Neither counsel has supplied us with a case indicating that this tort has been recognized. Counsel for defendants states simply that the tort has not been recognized although recognized in the United States of America. This is certainly not a proper or adequate factual situation to develop new law on the tort of invasion of privacy rights at common law.[114]

In Ontario, in 1996, a case arose which the court of first instance decided on privacy grounds, *Gould Estate v. Stoddart Publishing*.[115] But the decision of

---

113 There was a recent controversy in Canada about the full release of post-1911 census records: see *Beatty v. Canada (A.G.)* (2004), [2005] 1 F.C.R. 327, [2004] F.C.J. No. 1162. Beginning in 1911 the enumerators were required by Order-in-Council (31 March 1911 at 11) as follows 'The facts and statistics of the Census may not be used except for statistical compilations, and positive assurances should be given on this point if a fear is entertained by any person that they may be used for taxation or any other object.' There was no time limit placed upon this undertaking and so it clashed with the legislated time limits for personal data protection in the public sector (the *Privacy Act* and the *Access to Information Act*, infra) legislated by Parliament much later in the twentieth century. The result was *An Act to Amend the Statistics Act*, S.C. 2005, c. 31 (introduced first through Senate) – whereby the censuses taken between 1910 and 2005 become public 92 years after the census – but beginning with the 2006 census, the individuals to whom the information relates in the census must consent to the release of their information after 92 years. In 2006, only 56% consented, which raises concerns, especially amongst genealogists and historians (see Gregory Bonnell 'Canadians lose "crucial" pieces of historical information in 2006 census: expert' *Canadian Press NewsWire* (15 March 2007)).

114 *Bingo Enterprises Ltd. v. Plaxton* (1986), 26 D.L.R. (4th) 604 (Man. C.A.).

115 *Gould Estate v. Stoddard Publishing Co.* (1996), 31 C.C.L.T. (2d) 224 (Ont.

that court was overturned in 1998 on appeal to the Ontario Court of Appeal. The Court of Appeal held that the case should be decided purely on copyright grounds. In a more recent Ontario decision, the court held that it was possible that a claim to privacy could be the subject of a successful lawsuit but the litigation never continued to trial.[116]

There is, however, legislation[117] in four common law jurisdictions of Canada that gives individuals a right to sue for certain violations of privacy: Saskatchewan (1978),[118] Manitoba (1987),[119] Newfoundland (1990)[120] and British Columbia (1996).[121]

Gen. Div.), rev'd (1998), 39 O.R. (3d) 545 (Ont. C.A.). (The facts in the case were challenging in terms of the claim to invasion of privacy: the person whose privacy was alleged to have been violated was the famous pianist Glenn Gould, who was dead before the litigation arose; the author of the published piece which was alleged to have violated the privacy interest, Jock Carroll, was also dead before the legislation arose; the litigation was being maintained by the estate of the musician and the publishers.)

116 *Somwar v. McDonald's Restaurant of Canada Ltd.* (2006), 79 O.R. (3d) 172 (Ont. S.C.J.).

117 Canada is a federated state and, under its constitution, legislative power was divided in 1867 between the provinces and the federal government according to enumerated headings (*Constitution Act, 1867* (UK), 30 & 31 Vict., c. 3, reprinted in R.S.C. 1985, App. II, No. 5). Naturally, given its nineteenth century origins, very few information topics are reflected in this list of powers – really only copyrights and patents (see *Constitution Act, 1867, ibid.*, ss. 91(22) (23)). However, the provinces retained exclusive power to legislate in areas of 'purely local and private interest' (see *Constitution Act, 1867,* and also *Re: Anti-Inflation Act*, [1976] 2 S.C.R. 373 and *R. v. Crown Zellerbach Canada Ltd.*, [1988] 1 S.C.R. 401). Matters that do not fall within provincial heads are legislated federally under the residual power stated in s. 91 (see *Constitution Act*, s. 91, where the opening words empower the federal Parliament 'to make laws for the peace, order, and good government of Canada, in relation to all matters not coming within the classes of subjects by this Act assigned exclusively to the Legislatures of the provinces…'). Constitutionally, there is little argument for federal legislative control over privacy since property and civil rights and matters of local concern were specifically allocated to the provinces and have typically been interpreted very broadly: Peter W. Hogg, *Constitutional Law of Canada* (Scarborough, Ont.: Carswell, 2006) 453. Privacy is generally considered as related to human rights as well as being a matter of local concern. On the other hand, personal data protection has been legislated by both the federal and provincial governments of Canada, as described elsewhere, as an adjunct to the named subject areas of power each level of government already has under the *Constitution Act*.

118 *Privacy Act*, R.S.S. 1978, c. P-24, s. 2.

119 *Privacy Act*, R.S.M. 1987, c. P125, s. 2(1).

120 *Privacy Act*, R.S.N.L. 1990, c. P-22, s. 3.

121 *Privacy Act,* R.S.B.C. 1996, c. 373, s. 1. The original *Privacy Act* in British Columbia was the first in Canada, enacted in 1968 (S.B.C. 1968, c. 39). In *J.M.F. v. Chappell*, [1998] B.C.J. No.276, it was determined that in criminal proceedings (governed under the federal *Criminal Code*, R.S.C. 1985, c. C-46), civil rules such as those represented by the *Privacy Act* could not be in conflict and did not apply.

Particularly in the first three of these provinces, the statutes are articulated in terms of a focus on particular situations: surveillance, eavesdropping, and certain itemized commercial situations. For example, in Saskatchewan:

> s. 2 It is a tort, actionable without proof of damages, for a person wilfully and without claim of right, to violate the privacy of another person.
>
> s. 3 Without limiting the generality of s.2, proof that there has been:
>
> (a) auditory or visual surveillance of a person by any means including eavesdropping, watching, spying, besetting or following and whether or not accomplished by trespass;
>
> (b) listening to or recording of a conversation in which a person participates, or listening to or recording of messages to or from that person passing by means of telecommunications, otherwise than as a lawful party thereto;
>
> (c) use of the name or likeness or voice of a person for the purposes of advertising or promoting the sale of, or any other trading in, any property or services, or for any other purposes of gain to the user if, in the course of the use, the person is identified or identifiable and the user intended to exploit the name or likeness or voice of that person; or
>
> (d) use of letters, diaries or other personal documents of a person; without the consent, express or implied, of the person or some other person who has the lawful authority to give consent is prima facie evidence of a violation of the privacy of the person first mentioned.

There appear to have been very, very few successful actions brought under any of these statutes.[122]

---

[122] There have been a number of cases argued in British Columbia but most have been unsuccessful, at least on the *Privacy Act* claims. *David v. McArthur* (1969), 10 D.L.R. (3d) 250, rev'd (1970) 17 D.L.R. (3d) (B.C.C.A.) involved the activities of a private investigator hired by a husband to conduct surveillance of a wife. *Belzberg v. British Columbia Television Broadcasting Ltd* (1981) (unreported but described in the *Silber* case below) was a case in which a privacy claim was made in addition to a claim in trespass, over photographs of a front door taken and broadcast without permission. In *Wooding v. Little* (1982), 24 C.C.L.T. 37, [1982] B.C.J. No. 1422 (B.C.S.C.) (QL) invasion of privacy and libel were both claimed and qualified privilege was held to be a defence to both causes of action. *Silber v. British Columbia Television Broadcasting System* (1985), 25 D.L.R. (4th) 345 involved the filming and broadcasting of an individual in a parking lot, as Justice Lysyk said:

> in the middle of the day, on a site open to unobstructed view from an adjoining heavily travelled thoroughfare, in a busy commercial neighbourhood. The property was private in the sense that the plaintiffs had the right to exclude trespassers from it, but Mr. Silber could hardly expect to enjoy a right of privacy with respect to what happened there because that was open for anyone happening by to see (para. 17).

In *Insurance Corporation of British Columbia v. Somosh* (1983), 51 B.C.L.R. 344, a counterclaim for invasion of privacy by defendants to an action by the insurer of an

Quebec, Canada's civil law jurisdiction, by contrast, has enacted a provincial statute which it has entitled the *Quebec Charter of Rights and Freedoms*.[123] In it, the province gives privacy its strongest and clearest legal expression in Canada:[124]

s. 4 Every person has a right to the safeguard of his dignity, honour and reputation

---

automobile against an owner and driver was successful. The main action was dismissed, but on the counterclaim, a private investigator's inquiries about the financial positions of the defendants were found to be invasions of privacy. On the other hand, in *Rusche v. Insurance Corp. of British Columbia*, [1992] B.C.J. No.87, 4 C.P.C. (3d) 12 (B.C. S.C.), a jury finding that there was no breach of the *Privacy Act* in the actions of private investigators was left undisturbed. In *Milton v. Savinkoff*, [1993] B.C.J. No. 2396 (B.C. S.C.), a woman did not succeed in her claim of violation of privacy having carelessly left photos of herself partially clothed in the defendant's jacket but objecting to their being distributed to another acquaintance. In *Hollingsworth v. BCTV, a division of Westcom TV Group Ltd.*, [1998] B.C.J. No.2451, [1999] 6 W.W.R. 54, 59 B.C.L.R. (3d) 121, in an action founded also in libel, the British Columbia Court of Appeal held that the *Privacy Act* did not apply in a claim against BCTV. In *St. Pierre v. Pacific Newspaper Group Inc.*, [2006] B.C.J. No. 259 (B.C. S.C.), the *Vancouver Sun* was exonerated from a claim under the *Privacy Act*, concerning publication of a photograph, on the grounds of consent (s. 2(2)(a)) although found liable for defamation. One successful case, *Poirier v. Wal-Mart Canada Corp.*, 2006 BCSC 1138 involved photographs:

> It is a tort, actionable without proof of damage, for a person to use the name or portrait of another for the purpose of advertising or promoting the sale of, or other trading in, property or services, unless that other ... consents to the use for that purpose (British Columbia *Privacy Act*, s. 3(2) cited in para. 74).

In that case, Wal-Mart was found to have violated its long-term employee's rights by posting the employee's name and photograph beside a message welcoming shoppers to a new Wal-Mart location. In an earlier case involving a photograph, a British Columbian court held that reproductions of a photograph of an unidentified torso did not violate the privacy rights of the model who posed for the photograph: *Joseph v. Daniels (Brent Daniels Photography)* (1986), 4 B.C.L.R. (2d) 239, 11 C.P.R. (3d) 544. In Manitoba, in 1988, an interlocutory injunction was granted on the grounds of either private nuisance or under the *Privacy Act* where the defendant was harassed by mail and telephone in *Pateman v. Ross*, [1988] 68 Man.R. (2d) 181, and in *Ferguson v. McBee Technographics Inc.* (1989), 24 C.P.R. (3d) 240 (Man. Q.B.), portions of an affidavit filed in a proceeding in slander and injurious falsehood were struck as inadmissible because they were based on conversations to which the affiant was not party and they therefore *prima facie* violated s. 3(b) of the *Privacy Act* and were not saved under s. 5(c) of the Act as 'reasonable, necessary for, and incidental to, the protection of the person, property or other interests'.

123 The Quebec *Charter of human rights and freedoms*, R.S.Q. c. C-12.

124 There is no exception in it for newspapers.

s. 5 Every person has a right to respect for his private life
s. 9 Every person has a right to non-disclosure of confidential information

In 1998, a majority of the Supreme Court of Canada, on appeal from the Quebec Court of Appeal,[125] reinforced that strong privacy protection in *Aubry v. Editions Vice-Versa*.[126]

Looking only at the chequered patchwork of privacy protection in Canada, especially in common law Canada, it may not be surprising that Justice Sexton felt that 'privacy concerns...must yield to...intellectual property rights...'[127] – but is there another approach to consider in the *BMG v. John Doe* scenario in evaluating 'privacy concerns'?

THE ROLE OF CONFIDENTIALITY IN PRIVACY AND PERSONAL DATA PROTECTION

It is interesting that the information privacy right in Quebec is framed in terms of non-disclosure of confidential information: in terms of confidentiality and not in terms of personal information. Justice La Forest, in the criminal context in 1988, quoted with approval from a 1972 federal government report: 'This notion of privacy derives from the assumption that all information about a person is in a fundamental way his own, for him to communicate or retain for himself as he sees fit.'[128] But Justice La Forest then went on to say:

> In modern society, especially, retention of information about oneself is extremely important. We may, for one reason or another, wish or be compelled to reveal such information, but situations abound where the reasonable expectations of the individual that the information shall remain confidential to the persons to whom, and restricted to the purposes for which it is divulged, must be protected.[129]

---

125 *Aubry, supra* note 112.

126 *Ibid.*, L'Heureux-Dubé J., Bastarache J. for the majority opinion, Gonthier J., Cory J., and Iacobucci J., concurring, Major J., and Lamer C.J.C., dissenting. Both Justices Lamer and Major dissented because there was no evidence of damages – but Chief Justice Lamer went on to dissent saying the right to privacy must be given a different scope in dealings between private parties than it is in dealings between individuals and government. Thus in the civil context of Ms Aubry's complaint, he would have required that the defendants in the case had committed a fault before giving the plaintiff Ms Aubry redress.

127 *Ibid.* at para. 41, quoted above.

128 *R. v. Dyment*, [1988] 2 S.C.R. 417 at para. 22 (citing Canada, *Report of the Task Force established by the Department of Communications/Department of Justice, Privacy, and Computers* (Ottawa: Information Canada, 1972) at 13).

129 *Ibid.*

Canadian criminal law has, for some time, created legal protections of confidences for Canadians who choose to disseminate information, in such offences as s. 183 prohibiting the interception of private communications 'made under circumstances where it is reasonable for the originator to expect that [the communication] will not be intercepted by any person other than the person intended by the originator thereof to receive it...'[130]

In the civil context, there have long been particular legally recognized duties of confidence and the courts have imposed penalties upon confiders for breach of their duties in cases where the individual whose confidence had been broken sued. The courts in these cases have focussed on the relationship between the parties rather than the subject matter of the confidence. The legal protection of these information exchanges has been about confidentiality, not privacy. Since the late 1980s Canadian courts have continually expanded their protection of confidences, particularly in the commercial context, to the point now where the action for breach of confidence embraces situations far wider than just those involving information exchanges between or about individuals.[131] Since the late 1980s in Canada, the courts have recompensed the confider for a breach:

(1) if the information is secret;
(2) if the information was imparted in confidence, and
(3) if the information is such that it would save the confidante time, energy and expense and is used in an unauthorized fashion to the detriment of the confider.[132]

It should be noted there is no apparent public participation in this area. In patent, the public is guaranteed the right to inspect the innovations patented;[133] in copyright there is the public's right to the free circulation of ideas and facts as well as users' rights.[134] And in both cases, the monopolies given the economic rights holders are temporally limited. As the intellectual property device of protection of confidential information is developing, the public has no right of access to the subject matter of the secret, in any form, ever (there is no time limit to the monopoly of the confider on the secret).[135]

---

[130] *Criminal Code*, *supra* note 121, s. 183.

[131] *Lac Minerals Ltd. v. International Corona Resources Ltd.*, [1989] 2 S.C.R. 574, [1989] S.C.J. No. 83; *Cadbury Schweppes Inc. v. FBI Foods Ltd.*, [1999] 1 S.C.R. 142.

[132] *Lac Minerals Ltd. v. International Corona Resources Ltd.*, *ibid.*

[133] *Patent Act*, R.S.C. 1985, c. P-4, s.10.

[134] Discussed more fully below.

[135] And because this is not an area of legislative law, there is no possibility of testing this legal development against the *Canadian Charter of Rights and Freedoms* (specifically, s. 2(b) the right to freedom of expression, which includes access).

Breach of confidence has gradually entered into the arena of international trade agreement. The fullest expression of obligations concerning confidential information is found in the *TRIPS Agreement*:[136]

> Natural and legal persons shall have the possibility of preventing information lawfully within their control from being disclosed to, acquired by, or used by others without their consent in a manner contrary to honest commercial practices so long as such information:
> (a) is secret in the sense that it is not, as a body or in the precise configuration and assembly of its components, generally known among or readily accessible to persons within the circles that normally deal with the kind of information in question;
> (b) has commercial value because it is secret; and has been subject to reasonable steps under the circumstances, by the person lawfully in control of the information, to keep it secret.[137]

Both Kim Scheppele and Elizabeth Neill have published doctoral dissertation work focussing on definitional issues germane to any attempt to draw distinctions between notions of privacy, personal data protection and confidential information. In *Legal Secrets*, Scheppele[138] has described an analytic framework which would identify the protection described in *R. v. Plant* as legal protection for direct transmission of 'secrets' from one individual (A) to another (B: the government). Scheppele treats as 'serial secrets' all secrets that have already moved from their original confider (A) *to* a confidante (B) where issues have arisen concerning further dissemination *from* that confidante (B) to another (C). She would place all such secrets under the rubric of 'confidentiality' rather than privacy. Neill,[139] in *Rites of Privacy and the Privacy Trade*, also wrestled with these issues and argued for a conception of privacy as an

---

[136] Member countries, including Canada, are limited in the exceptions they can create to those permitted under Article 13: 'Members shall confine limitations or exceptions to exclusive rights to certain special cases which do not conflict with a normal exploitation of the work and do not unreasonably prejudice the legitimate interests of the right holder.'

[137] *Trade-Related Aspects of Intellectual Property Rights Agreement* (1994), 33 I.L.M. 1197, section 7, art. 39 [*TRIPS*]. The *North American Free Trade Agreement Between the Government of Canada, the Government of Mexico and the Government of the United States*, 17 December 1992, Can. T.S. 1994 No. 2, 32 I.L.M. 289 (entered into force 1 January 1994) [*NAFTA*] also contains obligations for Canada, the United States and Mexico in this area, providing that trade secrets shall be protected if they are secret, are of actual or potential commercial value and the confider has taken reasonable steps to keep them secret – see Articles 1711 (1), (2) & (3).

[138] Kim Lane Scheppele, *Legal Secrets: Equality and Efficiency in the Common Law* (Chicago: University of Chicago Press, 1988).

[139] Elizabeth Neill, *Rites of Privacy and the Privacy Trade: On the Limits of Protection for the Self* (Montreal & Kingston: McGill-Queens University Press, 2001).

extension of our 'sacred selves'. Her argument is that, in imparting information under circumstances of confidentiality, an individual is extending the circle of the self to deliberately embrace other individuals – in the expectation of continued privacy. Neill specifically distinguishes her conception of the boundaries of privacy, which would generally include personal confidential relationships, from personal data protection, which she argues falls outside privacy.[140] While extending the legal remedy of breach of confidence to the corporate commercial environment might be argued to be an extension of privacy values to corporations (who are, after all, legally endowed with capacity as persons), such an extension would be an anathema to Neill's perspective on privacy. It seems far more persuasive that this extension of the law of breach of confidence is one that clearly illustrates the conceptual differences between confidentiality and privacy.

Organizations that fall under personal data protection regimes are required to adhere to the dictates of the legislation so long as the information they hold continues to be identified with an individual. This responsibility arises and continues whether or not the individual subject is even aware either of the information's existence within that organization or of the contents of that information. Moreover, in virtually all Canadian jurisdictions, this responsibility continues for a number of years after the death of the subject individual.[141] These characteristics of personal data protection differentiate it from

140 From the point of view of creating consistent information policy across Canada, Scheppele's conception, which distinguishes privacy and confidentiality, may be more useful – and, indeed, her approach may actually strengthen Neill's argument that personal data protection does not form a part of privacy policy. However, in the context of this discussion, since the ISPs had confidentiality agreements with their subscribers, Neill's conception would focus even greater attention on the implications of those arrangements.

141 The federal government, in the *Privacy Act*, *supra* note 89, protects personal information held by the governed public sector organizations for 20 years following death (s. 3 'personal information' (m)) whereas, under *PIPEDA*, *supra* note 81, it protects an individual's information held by private sector organizations either until 20 years after death or until 100 years after the document was created, whichever is the shorter (ss. 7(3)(h)(i), (ii)). British Columbia's legislation also operates with a 20 years after death time frame (*Freedom of Information and Protection of Privacy Act*, R.S.B.C. 1996, c. 165, s. 22(4) taken together with s. 36 (c)) and Nova Scotia's legislation is similar (*Freedom of Information and Protection of Privacy Act*, R.S.N.S. 1993, c. 5, s. 20(4) taken together with s. 30(c)). Newfoundland's legislation operates to protect information for 20 years after a person's death or for 50 years after the document was created, at least where the information is held in archives (*Access to Information and Protection of Privacy Act*, R.S.N.L. 2002 c. A-1.1, s. 42(c),(d)). Alberta and Saskatchewan protect personal information until 25 years after the individual's death (*Freedom of Information and Protection of Privacy Act*, R.S.A. 2000, c. F-25, s. 17(2)(i), the *Local Authority Freedom of Information and Protection of Privacy*

legislation and common law which have arisen in defence of privacy rights. Personal data protection statutes artificially limit the abilities of the organizations governed by them because they generally prohibit collection of information about individuals from sources other than those individuals. Though digitization and the internet increasingly make available information about various people, organizations subject to personal data protection legislation must often ignore available sources of information and limit their access to information about identifiable individuals to seeking information from those individuals personally. Organizations subject to these statutes, even having properly accessed and collected information about identifiable individuals, are also limited by the legislation in the uses to which the collected information can be put. Thus these statutes, since they do not deal with the right to require an individual to disseminate information to particular organizations, but do limit the scope of the organization's abilities to use the information collected from individuals about themselves and prohibit its further dissemination except in very strict circumstances, appear to be extensions of the law of confidentiality, rather than privacy statutes. These laws mandate a relationship of confidence between individuals providing information about themselves to organizations and the affected organizations.[142] The individual's entitlement

---

Act, R.S.S. 1990–91, c. L-27, 1 s. 29(1), the *Freedom of Information and Protection of Privacy Act*, R.S.S. 1990–1991, c. F-22.01, s. 30(1)). Prince Edward Island's legislation generally protects personal information for 25 years after death (*Freedom of Information and Protection of Privacy Act*, R.S.P.E.I., c. F-15.01, s. 15(2)(i)). Ontario protects personal information until 30 years after death (*Freedom of Information and Protection of Privacy Act*, R.S.O. 1990, c. F.31, s. 2(2); *Municipal Freedom of Information and Protection of Privacy Act*, R.S.O. 1990, c. M.56, s. 2(2)) and Quebec does the same, unless the record is over 100 years old (*An Act respecting the protection of personal information in the private sector*, *supra* note 82, s. 18.2.). Manitoba, on the other hand, protects information only until 10 years after an individual's death (the *Freedom of Information and Protection of Privacy Act*, C.C.S.M. 1997, c. F175 1997 s. 17(4)). New Brunswick's legislation contains no term of protection but appears to leave the matter open to regulation (*Protection of Personal Information Act*, S.N.B. c. P-19.1, s. 7).

[142] Viewing personal data protection as statutorily created relationships of confidence, rather than fundamental privacy protection, may help to explain certain decisions of governments to make public information which would otherwise fall under personal data protection. One might point to the Ontario government's recent decisions to protect participants in adoptions before September 2008 from disclosure of their identities while requiring that adoptions from now on are subject to disclosure, albeit limited (see *supra*, note 112).The Ontario legislature took this action over the objections of the Ontario Privacy Commissioner (Office of the Privacy Commissioner of Ontario, News Release, '*Controversial adoption disclosure bill faces final vote but much needed protection missing* (21 October 2005), online: <http://www.ipc.on.ca/ index.asp?layid=86&fid1=418>). Neither she nor any other can appeal to the Canadian *Charter of Rights and Freedoms* to insist upon privacy

to confidentiality in information supplied to organizations is limited under this legislation to information that is, and remain, identified with that individual personally. This is a much narrower scope of protection for confidences than is available in other areas of law providing legal protection for confidences. The narrow focus of this particular legal protection for confidentiality, limited as it is to confidences involving subject matter identified with the individual confider, is probably the source of much of the conceptual confusion between personal data protection legislation and privacy concepts.[143]

Moreover, it must be recalled that Canada's obligations under the *OECD Guidelines* are intended not only to protect personal information, but also to ensure the free flow of data between countries. One of the policy reasons that information about identifiable individuals held by affected organizations is to be gathered from those individuals directly is presumably to ensure integrity

---

protection for the parents (mothers) who put these children up for adoption years ago with assurances of privacy. Other examples of legal initiatives that counter the notions of privacy as a constitutional right are various provincial salary disclosure laws (in Ontario, see the *Public Sector Salary Disclosure Act, 1996*, S.O. 1996, c. 1, Sch. A, which requires that all employees making over $100,000 per year, and their exact salaries, be published by public sector institutions annually; in Nova Scotia, see *Ministerial Education Act Regulation* 80/97, as amended up to N.S. Reg. 120/2006, concerning annual reporting of school board salaries, made under s. 145 of the *Education Act*, S.N.S. 1995-96, c.1).

143 This confusion has only been exacerbated by the decision of the Supreme Court in *H.J. Heinz Co. of Canada Ltd. v. Canada (Attorney General)*, [2006] 1 S.C.R. 441, [*Heinz* cited to S.C.R], where the majority of the Court held that the 'privacy' right under personal data protection legislation can be exercised on behalf of individuals by corporations. Personal data protection legislation carefully distinguishes between the rights under these statutes given to 'individuals', rather than legal 'persons' (in order to exclude corporate 'persons' from the direct ambit of personal data protection), and those rights given to 'third parties' – corporations, companies, and businesses (which have their own exemptions and protections). The minority in *Heinz* believed that corporate parties should be limited to claiming the exemptions specifically targeted for them. The majority permitted Heinz to invoke personal data protection exemptions to the federal access legislation in order to block release of information to a requestor. The individuals identified in the disputed information were not party to the litigation. Not only does the decision greatly enhance the ability of corporations to censor the public discourse, it distorts the purpose of the personal data protection regimes by wresting some control of personal information away from individuals and putting it back into the hands of corporations. The Court used the vocabulary of privacy throughout the judgment. If the Court had conceptualized the problem in terms of a legislated confidence between an identified individual and the public sector organization holding the data, it is submitted that it is less likely that the majority would have acceded to the request of a third party corporation to represent the interests of the confider individual, without notice to the individual concerned, and step into the shoes of the confider to insist that the confidante government organization not divulge the information to a requestor.

in the data. This perspective is reinforced by the provision in these statutes requiring the affected organizations to either correct information held by identifiable individuals when an error is pointed out by the individual concerned or, at least, to keep a record of disagreement which reveals the related information provided by the subject which differs from the previously held information recorded by the organization. These provisions of personal data protection legislation cannot be interpreted as part of the concept of privacy. They provide a function in information terms that has long been provided by the law of defamation in situations where information about individuals is published. Libel law does not protect individual privacy – it does, however, protect individual reputations by limiting the publication of false information about individuals (where the individual is injured by the falsity) and, at the same time, provides protection for the integrity of published information about individuals. Personal data protection statutes provide the same functionality, ensuring data integrity, and thus contribute to the efficiency and effectiveness of flows of information between countries. This function of personal data protection is quite unrelated to notions of privacy.

Thus it would seem that Justice Sexton's characterization of the 'concerns' involved in the *BMG v. John Doe* case as 'privacy concerns' swept together a complex set of separate considerations involving personal data protection and confidential relationships. Juxtaposing such a set of complex concepts against the complex set of concepts which is intellectual property cannot lead to a clear resolution of any particular challenging situation – instead each situation must be fully analyzed in light of specific intellectual property interests and 'privacy concerns' actually at issue.

REVISITING *BMG v. JOHN DOE*

It will be recalled that the parties in *BMG v. John Doe* agreed 'an ISP by virtue of s. 7(3)(c) of PIPEDA may disclose personal information without consent pursuant to a court order'. The relevant section reads:

> (3) For the purpose of clause 4.3 of Schedule 1, and despite the note that accompanies that clause, an organization may disclose personal information without the knowledge or consent of the individual only if the disclosure is
>
> (c) required to comply with a subpoena or warrant issued or an order made by a court, person or body with jurisdiction to compel the production of information, or to comply with rules of court relating to the production of records.

Clause 4.3 of Schedule 1 deals with 'Principle 3 – Consent' and provides that '[t]he knowledge and consent of the individual are required for the collection, use, or disclosure of personal information, except where inappropriate'.

Records are defined under *PIPEDA*[144] and do not include records that an organization would have to create – so, it would appear, on the same logic as Justice Sexton applied in considering Rule 233,[145] that s. 7(3) of *PIPEDA* in this case would only apply in respect of the production of information (and not in terms of compliance with rules of court relating to the production of records) since there were no extant records at issue here. So the question would be whether the court had jurisdiction to compel the production of information.[146]

And this leads back to the realization that the only jurisdiction that the court had in this case to compel the production of information was a jurisdiction that includes consideration of whether the public interests in favour of the disclosure outweigh the legitimate privacy concerns.

So the key question becomes whether there is a public interest in favour of disclosure to the plaintiffs in this copyright infringement proceeding that outweighs the legitimate privacy concerns of the potential defendants. If legitimate privacy concerns prevail, then there is no jurisdiction in the court to compel production of this information and the provisions of s. 7(3) of *PIPEDA*, the data protection legislation dictating the terms of a confidential relationship between the ISPs and their customers, would require the ISPs to keep that information confidential.

This is a different approach from that taken by Justice Sexton in his analysis in *BMG v. John Doe*. Justice Sexton explicitly equates consideration of the privacy interests at stake in his consideration of the fifth criterion (for considering compelling disclosure of the identities at issue) with a consideration of *PIPEDA*: 'Privacy rights are significant and they must be protected. In order to achieve the appropriate balance between privacy rights and the public interest in favour of disclosure, PIPEDA provides protection...'[147] At this point Justice Sexton's analysis became completely circular: *PIPEDA* permits disclosure if

---

144 *PIPEDA*, *supra* note 81, s. 2 ('Record' includes any correspondence, memorandum, book, plan, map, drawing, diagram, pictorial or graphic work, photograph, film, microform, sound recording, videotape, machine-readable record and any other documentary material, regardless of physical form or characteristics, and any copy of any of those things).

145 *BMG FC*, *supra* note 2 at para. 15 (Justice von Finckenstein held that only Rule 238 could be relevant to the outcome of this motion because under Rule 233 there would have to be a relevant document in existence and, in this case, any such document would have to be created).

146 *An act respecting access to documents held by public bodies and the Protection of personal information*, *supra* note 91, ss. 18-26 (This provision does not appear to exist in the Quebec statute governing the private sector; sections governing communication to third persons).

147 *BMG FCA*, *supra* note 2 at para. 38.

there is a court order and the court used *PIPEDA* to determine whether there ought to be a court order – which inevitably led to a conclusion that there ought to be a court order – the conclusion Justice Sexton reached.[148]

It is not surprising, given his approach, that Justice Sexton then stated that 'privacy concerns may be met if the court orders that the user only be identified by initials, or makes a confidentiality order'[149] – but under personal data protection legislation, including *PIPEDA*, the only actions contemplated are either the release or the withholding of a record – there is no provision for qualified release of the type envisioned by Justice Sexton. And even from a privacy perspective, rather than that of personal data protection legislation, the use of initials or a confidentiality order would not save the alleged infringer from public notoriety, it would not protect the alleged infringer from the lawsuit or from the plaintiffs having knowledge of his identity or home computer habits.

THE PUBLIC INTEREST

Since *PIPEDA* governs the information being sought in this application, by virtue of its being held by ISPs, the overriding public interest, as expressed by Parliament for the public, in the situation before the courts in *BMG v. John Doe*, then, must be the purpose for *PIPEDA*:

> to establish rules [for organizations engaged in commercial activities]...in a manner that recognizes the right of privacy of individuals with respect to their personal information...and the need of [such] organizations [for] personal information for purposes that a reasonable person would consider appropriate[150]

Parliament has tempered this right to privacy and the needs of the organizations governed by *PIPEDA* through the inclusion of certain exceptions in the legislation. It is true that, as agreed by the parties in *BMG v. John Doe*, one of these exceptions to the right to privacy in *PIPEDA* is the requirement that a custodial organization disclose personal information where required by court order.[151] But when asking, in considering the question of disclosure under the five part test under the Federal Court Rule 238, whether the 'public interests in favour of disclosure' outweigh 'the legitimate privacy concerns', it must be borne in mind that there is, just since 2004, a clear articulation *against* disclo-

---

148 *Ibid.* at para. 42.
149 *Ibid.* at para. 45.
150 *PIPEDA*, *supra* note 81, s. 3.
151 *Ibid.* at s. 7(3)(c).

sure of personal data held by private sector organizations in Canada in legislation. Rather than outweighing legitimate privacy concerns, this legislation explicitly articulates those concerns as a part of its raison d'être.

Justice von Finckenstein[152] and Justice Sexton, for the Court of Appeal, cited a number of cases in support of the proposition that various public interests in favour of disclosure in civil proceedings had outweighed legitimate privacy concerns in the past. However, all of these cases arose prior to the full implementation of *PIPEDA* in the private sector.[153] Justice von Finckenstein noted Ontario *First Nations Limited Partnership v. John Doe,*[154] *Canadian Blood Services/Société du Sang v. John Doe,*[155] *Wa'el Chehab v. John Doe,*[156] *Kibale v. Canada,*[157] *Loblaw Companies Ltd v. Aliant Telecom Inc. and Yahoo.*[158] The Federal Court of Appeal in *BMG v. John Doe* particularly picked up on and noted the *Loblaw* case, where Rule 32.12 of the New Brunswick Rules of Court was used to compel production of the identity of someone who sent an e-mail spreading confidential information around the Loblaw operation.[159] *Irwin Toy v. Doe,*[160] also cited by both courts, was a 2000

---

152 *BMG FC, supra* note 2 at para. 41.

153 *Loblaw Companies Ltd. v. Aliant Telecom Inc.,* [2003] N.B.J. No. 208 (N.B.Q.B.) (QL) might have concerned *PIPEDA* even though it was heard prior to 1 January 2004 because Aliant Telecom operated in the federally regulated telecommunications environment (in close association with Bell Canada), and was governed by *PIPEDA* after 2001 – but no personal data protection legislation was considered in the order. The *Loblaw* decision refers to *Re Johnston and Frank Johnston's Restaurants Limited*, [1980] P.E.I.J. No.34 which also pre-dates any relevant personal data protection legislation. The Ontario Court of Appeal in *Straka v. Humber River Regional Hospital* (2000), 51 O.R. (3d) 1 specifically pointed out that the Ontario *Freedom of Information and Protection of Privacy Act* did not apply to hospitals and could not be relevant to that case (at para. 33). Therefore the court concluded that the applicant could not be granted access to a reference letter written about him. Now, hospitals in Ontario fall under the *Personal Health Information Protection Act*, 2004, S.O. 2004, c. 2, Sch. A. However, whereas under s. 2 of the federal *Privacy Act*, 'the views or opinions of another individual about the individual' are an element of an individual's own 'personal information' and therefore the letter of reference at issue in *Straka* would be considered information about the applicant to be disclosed (as under other public sector personal data protection in Canada and for federally regulated private sector enterprises governed by *PIPEDA*), Ontario's *Personal Health Information Protection Act* does not apply to employee information (see s. 4(a)).

154 (3 June 2002), (Ont. S.C.J.).

155 (17 June 2002), (Ont. S.C.J.).

156 (3 October 2003), (Ont. S.C.J.).

157 [1991] F.C.J. No. 634 (F.C.) (QL).

158 *Supra* note 153.

159 *BMG FCA, supra* note 2 at para. 27.

160 *Irwin Toy v. Doe* (2000), 12 C.P.C. (5th) 103 (Ont. S.C.J.) at para. 37. See also *BMG FC, supra* note 2 at para. 41.

case, decided at a time when personal data protection in common law Canada applied only to public sector organizations.[161] The Federal Court of Appeal picked up on and noted this case, decided under Rules 30.10 and 31.10 of Ontario's *Rules of Civil Procedure*, and holding that a third party could be compelled to produce the identity of senders of e-mail from ISPs in a defamation suit.[162] When these cases were decided, 'the public interests in favour of disclosure' might have been properly said to 'outweigh the legitimate privacy concerns' because there was no personal data protection regime in the private sector in common law Canada. However, in the circumstances of *BMG v. John Doe*, there is a personal data protection regime in place in Canada in the private sector – that clearly establishes a public interest in personal data protection – and thus renders these previous decisions inapplicable to the analysis that should have been undertaken by the courts in *BMG v. John Doe*. Were it otherwise, if the Court of Appeal in *BMG v. John Doe* is correct, then ISPs will be ordered to identify individuals in any case where a plaintiff can establish a civil claim, not even a prima facie case, against those individuals. There is surely no qualitative difference between the civil claims of a plaintiff for copyright infringement and those of a plaintiff in any other civil proceedings, for example in divorce proceedings or a debtor-creditor issue. One might expect those seeking personal information about others to launch suits that they might not otherwise pursue because of the information that could be made available in preliminary proceedings. And the 'protection' of *PIPEDA* would be rendered unstable, to say the least.[163] At any time an individual might discover that another had enough of a claim against her or him, in at least one area of law, to render the confidentiality of communications between that individual and her or his ISP defunct.[164]

---

[161] Except in Quebec, Canada's only civil law jurisdiction, where *An Act Respecting the Protection of Personal Information in the Private Sector*, *supra* note 82, came into force in 1994.

[162] *BMG FCA*, *supra* note 2 at para. 27.

[163] Jane Bailey's quite different analysis of the *BMG v. John Doe* case, in a comparative context comparing the United States and Canada ('The Substance of Procedure: Non-Party Disclosure in the Canadian and U.S. Online Music Sharing Litigation' (2006) 43 Alberta L.R. 615), leaves her with much the same concern about privacy. She finds that 'If anything, Canada should consider strengthening protections for online privacy in the civil non-party disclosure process' (at para. 5) and 'the Court risks its procedures being used as a tool to exacerbate existing inequalities in resources between the music industry and those against whom they seek to make claims' (at para. 69).

[164] It would seem that this might raise concerns in the context of Canada's international obligations under *TRIPS* and *NAFTA* because, in addition to the information concerning customers' personal data raising issues in the realm of personal data protection, it could lead to breaches of confidence 'contrary to honest commercial practices'.

What then are the 'public interests in favour of disclosure'? *PIPEDA* legislates those interests in disclosure that transcend personal data protection: they are laid out in s. 7(3) of the Act (which makes reference to the accompanying provisions from Schedule 1 to the Act). They are subsections relating to Canadians' overriding interest in law enforcement:

> ...an organization may disclose personal information without the knowledge or consent of the individual only if the disclosure is
>
> (c) made to a government institution or part of a government institution that has made a request for information, identified its lawful authority to obtain the information and indicated that
>
> (i) it suspects that the information relates to national security, the defence of Canada or the conduct of international affairs,
>
> (ii) the disclosure is requested for the purpose of enforcing any law of Canada, a province or a foreign jurisdiction, carrying out an investigation relating to the enforcement of any such law or gathering intelligence for the purpose of enforcing any such law, or
>
> (iii) the disclosure is requested for the purpose of administering any law of Canada or a province;[165]

Nowhere in *PIPEDA* are the interests of private litigants, or those of intellectual property rights holders, generally placed ahead of personal data protection interests. How then can it be said that 'public interests in favour of disclosure...outweigh the legitimate privacy concerns' in the *BMG v. John Doe* litigation?

In this context, then, properly weighing the public interest in privacy against the public interest in private litigation protecting copyright interests must be revisited: Justice Sexton's consideration of the social importance of intellectual property rights must also be revisited.

The answer to the question of whether there is a public interest in assisting private litigants to pursue their remedies under the *Copyright Act* must be yes – not because of the nature of these rights as property rights but because of their nature as legislated intellectual property rights. But where that interest in assisting private litigants to pursue their remedies involves disclosure of personal data protection held by private sector third parties engaged in commercial activities, does that interest necessarily outweigh other interests – specifically legitimate privacy concerns? The answer must be no.

On this analysis, the fifth element of the requirement for a disclosure order under Rule 238 or the equitable remedy for disclosure is not met. Therefore an order for disclosure should not be given in these circumstances. If such an order is not given, then there is no exemption from the rights of the internet

---

165 See also *PIPEDA*, *supra* note 81, ss. 7(3)(c.2), (d).

customers under *PIPEDA* and the ISPs must not disclose the identities of these customers to anyone other than the individual customers, upon request. What would the implications of such a finding be?

If the reasoning suggested herein is adopted and the identities of the ISP customers are not ordered disclosed in civil proceedings for copyright infringement, will the plaintiffs necessarily be completely without remedy? First of all, if the identities of the alleged infringers come to light other than through the channels of the ISPs, then the plaintiffs are free to continue their lawsuit. Secondly, the *Copyright Act* provides for criminal proceedings against those who infringe upon the rights of copyright holders.[166] In the case of criminal proceedings, the public interest is much clearer than in disputes between private parties in civil proceedings. If rights holders invoke the criminal process, it would seem that there would be a much greater argument that the privacy rights of those against whom a sufficient case for disclosure can be made should be suspended in favour of the Queen's justice.

Is this result inconsistent with the general regime of intellectual property? No. Even within the copyright regime itself, the economic interests in copyright must be balanced both with moral rights interests and with users' rights. The economic interests in copyright such as those held by the plaintiffs in *BMG v. John Doe* are not the only intellectual property rights related to the musical works and recordings involved in that case, and therefore it is too simplistic to conclude that the economic rights holders should necessarily be given priority[167] as opposed to other rights holders – whether other rights holders within the copyright regime (authors or users) or those whose interests lie under personal data protection legislation or the legal protection of privacy. Thus, given that there is a public interest in supporting the copyright holder's pursuit of economic interests under the *Copyright Act* that must be balanced even within the copyright regime against the legitimate interests of moral rights holders and users, is the economic interest of rights holders in pursuing infringers through civil remedy of the infringement lawsuit so compelling as to outweigh privacy interests affected by that pursuit?

Is this result consistent with what little explicit guidance there is in legislation about the relationships between intellectual property rights and personal data protection legislation? Yes – while the evidence is sparse and indirect.[168] It may be noted that s. 32.1(1) of the *Copyright Act* provides:

---

166 *Copyright Act*, *supra* note 6, s. 42–45(2).

167 As Sexton does in *BMG FCA*, *supra* note 2 at para. 42.

168 See Margaret Ann Wilkinson, 'The Copyright Regime and Data Protection Legislation' in Ysolde Gendreau, ed., *Copyright Administrative Institutions* (Cowansville, Que: Yvon Blais, 2002) 77.

> It is not an infringement of copyright for any person
> (a) to disclose, pursuant to the *Access to Information Act*, a record within the meaning of that Act, or to disclose, pursuant to any like Act of the legislature of a province, like material;
> (b) to disclose, pursuant to the *Privacy Act*, personal information within the meaning of that Act, or disclose, pursuant to any like Act of the legislature of a province, like information...

Nor is prioritizing personal data protection over disclosure for purposes of copyright litigation inconsistent with the positions of personal data protection and privacy under the *Charter of Rights and Freedoms* as compared to the position of intellectual property in terms of the *Charter*. As discussed earlier, informational privacy is not directly addressed in the *Charter*, although there are privacy-related provisions specifically set out in the *Charter* and jurisprudence around *Charter* protection for privacy has developed. The Supreme Court stated in *Lavigne v. Canada* that '...the *Privacy Act* has been characterized by this Court as "quasi-constitutional" because of the role privacy plays in the preservation of a free and democratic society'.[169] In the more recent *Heinz* case, Justice Deschamps, writing for herself and Justices Binnie, Fish, and Abella, in the majority, held that privacy trumps access to government-held information, and that privacy rights are quasi-constitutional.[170] On the other hand, in the intellectual property context, lower courts had suggested that intellectual property was not subject to *Charter* scrutiny.[171] However, in writing for the majority of the Supreme Court in *Harvard College v. Canada*,[172] Justice Bastarache considered the implications of the Canadian *Charter of Rights and Freedoms* on the issues before the court involving the patentability of the 'Harvard Mouse'.[173] Although he found the *Charter* was not helpful in deciding the issue before the Court, he was certainly prepared to apply the *Charter* in the context of intellectual property in an appropriate case.[174] And it may also be useful to

---

169 *Lavigne v. Canada (Office of the Commissioner of Official Languages)*, [2002] 2 S.C.R. 773 at 790. (It must be noted that the *Privacy Act* referred to is actually a federal personal data protection statute and not a privacy statute, as discussed above.)

170 *Heinz*, *supra* note 143 at para. 28.

171 *Compagnie Générale des Établissements Michelin-Michelin & Cie v. National Automobile, Aerospace, Transportation and General Workers Union of Canada (CAW-Canada)*, [1997] 2 F.C. 306 at para. 102, [1996] F.C.J. 1685 (F.C.T.D).

172 *Harvard College v. Canada (Commissioner of Patents)*, [2002] 4 S.C.R. 45, 2002 SCC 76 [*Harvard Mouse*].

173 *Ibid.* at paras. 177–182.

174 This scrutiny would be available for intellectual property devices legislated by Parliament – as is patent, the subject matter at hand in the *Harvard Mouse* case. This would also apply to copyright, trademark, or industrial design and so on. There would not be the possibility of *Charter* scrutiny over breach of confidential information at this time because this is a purely common law action and the *Charter* does not reach private parties.

recall that the Supreme Court pointed out in the *Heinz* case that intellectual property rights can be altered by contract.[175]

Therefore, on balance, it appears that the economic interest of rightsholders in pursuing infringers through the civil remedy of the infringement lawsuit is not so compelling as to outweigh privacy interests affected by that pursuit. The decision of the Court of Appeal in *BMG v. John Doe*, while correct in the result, has left open the door to future litigation. The principles enunciated by Justice Sexton to guide that future litigation are not appropriate in the current Canadian context. His concerns with the relationships between intellectual property and property rights and between privacy and intellectual property rights are misplaced. The critical factor determining such future cases is the extension of personal data protection into the private sector in Canada. Parliament, in creating this environment, has articulated a very narrow scope for disclosure in terms of personal information and enhanced the confidentiality of relationships between individuals and commercial organizations in Canada. Since privacy is one thrust of personal data protection legislation, and there is no element of public access connected to the enactment of this legislation in the private sector, legitimate privacy concerns about disclosure have been dramatically recognized by the enactment of personal data protection legislation in the private sector in Canada. Whatever the state of the law of privacy across the various jurisdictions in Canada, the evidence of the enactment of *PIPEDA* is that 'public concerns for the protection of intellectual property rights' – other than intellectual property rights that lie at the heart of criminal proceedings – have given way to the public interest in personal data protection. And, while distinct from privacy, personal data protection is intimately related to privacy and certainly limits disclosure of personal information to third parties, rather than encouraging it. Thus, as intimated in the *Tariff 22* decision, and consistent with Canada's international obligations, individuals confiding personal information to commercial organizations in Canada should be entitled to have those private confidences of personal information respected by the courts, whatever the civil litigation interests of third parties might be.

175 *Heinz*, *supra* note 143 at para. 20.

11. When intellectual property rights converge – tracing the contours and mapping the fault lines 'case by case' and 'law by law'

Myra J. Tawfik*

> Where then does this leave us as judges and lawyers? The challenge, as I see it, is to work out, case by case, law by law, a framework which recognizes the benefits to be obtained from regarding ideas as property, while delineating the limits on those property rights, which a society increasingly dependent on the free flow of ideas must permit, as a matter of practicality and morality.[1]

One of the more daunting challenges confronting intellectual property scholars, jurists and policy-makers alike is the task of identifying and circumscribing the nature and scope of the established categories of intellectual property rights. Born centuries ago, these venerable bodies of law – copyright, patent, trademarks and industrial designs – emerged at a particular time and place and have evolved in ways that may not have remained true to whatever underlying objectives had originally fashioned them. And while the law does not remain static and, indeed, should adapt to meet current economic, social and cultural needs, there is growing concern that intellectual property laws are now being extended and expanded beyond acceptable parameters.[2] With each measure to

* The author would like to thank Michelle Mulchan for her research assistance and the Law Foundation of Ontario for its financial support.

1 Beverley McLachlin 'Intellectual Property. What's it all About?' in Gordon F. Henderson, ed., *Trade-Marks Law of Canada* (Scarborough: Carswell, 1993) 391 at 397.

2 See for example, David Vaver, 'Need Intellectual Property Be Everywhere? Against Ubiquity and Uniformity' (2002) 25:1 Dalhousie Law Journal 1; James Boyle, 'A Manifesto on WIPO and the Future of Intellectual Property' [2004] Duke Law and Technology Review 9; Berndt Hugenholtz, 'Copyright, Contract and Code: What Will Remain of the Public Domain' (2000) 26 Brooklyn J. Int'l L. 77; Carys J. Craig, 'Locke, Labour and Limiting the Author's Right: A Warning against a Lockean Approach to Copyright Law (2002) 28 Queen's L.J. 1; Samuel E. Trosow, 'The Illusive Search for Justificatory Theories: Copyright, Commodification and Capital' (2003) 16

strengthen intellectual property rights, questions are raised and attempts made to find some logical coherence to each grounded in sound and principled policies. However, active engagement in this inquiry cannot start and end within the strict boundaries of each category of intellectual property right.

With intellectual property expansion, the potential for some or all forms of intellectual property to co-exist in the same subject matter has increased. The study of overlapping rights[3] – where the subject matter in question is susceptible to multiple protection – is a critical piece of the overall examination of contemporary intellectual property law. Determining the proper scope of each form of intellectual property right therefore necessitates an understanding both of their respective boundaries and of their inter-connectedness.

The origins of Canadian intellectual property laws follow patterns much like those of British and American laws.[4] Brad Sherman and Lionel Bently in their masterful exploration of British intellectual property history posit that intellectual property laws are historically and contextually specific.[5] They assert therefore that each category of right is not an inevitable construct but rather, accidental and arbitrary. To the extent that there was any attempt to understand their relationship, it was in terms of recognizing that each form addressed one aspect of human creativity – in other words, at a high level of abstraction. As the actual mechanics of each body of intellectual property law became crystallized in the latter half of the nineteenth century each category

---

Can. J. L. & Juris. 217. See too the Geneva Declaration on the Future of the World Intellectual Property Organization, online: <http://www.cptech.org/ip/wipo/ genevadeclaration.html>.

[3] In this chapter, I will use 'overlapping' 'co-existing' 'converging' intellectual property rights synonymously to signify the phenomenon of more than one form of intellectual property right attaching to the same subject matter. In addition, I make no general distinction between right holders asserting multiple rights concurrently or consecutively nor do I distinguish between cases in which a plaintiff makes multiple claims or pursues under only one of a number of possible options. Others have looked more closely at these finer distinctions. See for example, Graeme Dinwoodie, 'Concurrence and Convergence of Rights: The Concerns of the US Supreme Court' and Antoon Quaedvlieg, 'Concurrence and Convergence in Industrial Designs: 3-Dimensional Shapes Excluded by Trademark Law'; both articles can be found in F. Willem Grosheide & Jan J. Brinkhof, eds, *Intellectual Property Law: Crossing Borders between Traditional and Actual* (Antwerp: Intersentia, 2004) at 5 and 23 respectively.

[4] See generally, John McKeown, *Fox Canadian law of Copyright and Industrial Designs*, 4th ed. (Toronto: Carswell, 2003); Kelly Gill & R. Scott Jolliffe, *Fox on Canadian Law of Trade-Marks and Unfair Competition*, 4th ed. (Toronto: Thomson-Carswell, 2000); Harold G. Fox, *Canadian Patent Law and Practice*, 4th ed. (Toronto: The Carswell Company, 1969).

[5] Brad Sherman & Lionel Bently, *The Making of Modern Intellectual Property Law* (Cambridge, UK: Cambridge University Press, 1999).

of intellectual property right became defined by its structure and form. The prevailing assumption was that the different legal treatment was rationally connected to the different subject matter and that each of these laws served fundamentally different policy purposes. As such, possible inter-relationships between these various bodies of law would not have appeared obvious to the nineteenth and early twentieth century jurist.

Modern intellectual property jurists share this same legacy. Like their Victorian predecessors, they will identify the nature and purpose of the various forms of intellectual property in relation to their formal differences. Copyright protects aesthetic expressions, patents useful inventions, designs aesthetic features of useful articles while trademarks shield consumers from misrepresentations as to the source of goods. All but copyright involve registration systems[6] although trademarks enjoy both unregistered and registered rights. Copyright and trademark benefit from generous terms of protection whereas patent and designs rights are much more limited in duration. Only patent is an absolute monopoly – the others are restricted to prohibitions against copying or misrepresenting to the public. In this way, contemporary lawmakers have avoided having to address the more profound metaphysical questions surrounding the immutable 'essence' of each body of law and whether there is or ought to be a coherent and comprehensive policy to bind them one to the other.

However, as intellectual property right holders become more aggressive and, indeed, more creative in seeking to prolong their periods of exclusivity, Canadian courts, like their counterparts around the world, are increasingly having to come to terms with new permutations and possibilities – whether it be the assertion of copyright in design drawings of functional articles, trademark rights in the shapes of patented products or copyright in trademarks affixed to consumer goods. In the words of the Supreme Court of Canada:

> The economic value of intellectual property rights arouses the imagination and litigiousness of rights holders in their search for continuing protection of what they view as their rightful property. Such a search carries with it the risk of discarding basic and necessary distinctions between different forms of intellectual property and their legal and economic functions.[7]

In the absence of any comprehensive theoretical foundation upon which to draw, any 'basic and necessary distinctions' underlying each form of intellectual

---

6 Of course, copyright originally required registration. This formality was abolished in Canada with the enactment of *The Copyright Act,* S.C. 1921, c. 24 (in force in 1924).

7 *Kirkbi AG v. Ritvik Holdings*, [2005] 3 S.C.R. 302 at para. 37 [*Kirkbi*].

property right must be elicited 'case by case' and 'law by law'. It is therefore the aim of this chapter to examine the phenomenon of coexisting intellectual property rights in an effort to tease out, from the existing record, greater understanding of their individual contours through the prism of their convergences.

OVERLAPPING INTELLECTUAL PROPERTY RIGHTS

Copyright – Industrial Design

Industrial designs, ornamental designs applied to articles of commerce, closely mirror the subject matter protected under copyright law. However, consistent with the position in other jurisdictions within the British Commonwealth[8] that industrial designs warrant a different remedial scheme than copyright, Canadian law protects industrial designs under the *Industrial Design Act*[9] and expressly prohibits copyright protection under the *Copyright Act*.[10] In essence, the triggering factor to exclude a design from the purview of copyright is whether the article of manufacture embodying it is to be multiplied for mass consumption. It is believed that more limited protection through dedicated industrial design legislation is better calibrated to meet the competing interests of designers, competitors and consumers. As a result, industrial design legislation in Canada protects a design for a period of ten years upon registration.

> Full copyright protection is…life of the creator, plus 50 years. That is a very strong form of protection. It would be quite inappropriate and certainly not good for the economy to extend this type of protection for examples of work that would only receive the lesser protection of industrial design.[11]

---

[8] Canadian industrial design laws have followed closely early British law. However, modern reform of industrial design law such as that undertaken in England with the *Copyright, Designs and Patents Act 1988* (UK), 1988, c. 48 has yet to occur in Canada. For developments in other jurisdictions see for example, Tana Pistorius, 'Aesthetics and Economics? An Overview of the Copyright Protection of Utilitarian Works in South Africa' in Ysolde Gendreau, ed., *Intellectual Property: Bridging Aesthetics and Economics* (Montreal: Thémis, 2006) 67; Eric Setliff, 'Copyright And Industrial Design: An "Alternative Design" Alternative' (2006) 30 Colum. J. & Arts 49; David Rolph, 'News from Australia Legislation and Cases' (2005) 19 I.P.J. 245; Estelle Derclaye, 'The British Unregistered Design Right: Will it Survive its New Community Counterpart to Influence Future European Case Law' (2004) 10 Colum. J. Eur. L. 265.

[9] *Industrial Design Act*, R.S.C. 1985, c. I-9.

[10] *Copyright Act,* R.S.C. 1985, c. C-42.

[11] *House of Commons Debates* (26 June 1987) at 7692 (Lynn McDonald).

The assumption being made of course is that industrial design law as it stands is wholly appropriate to meet the various interests at stake. And yet, it is generally agreed that the existing legislative scheme in Canada is inadequate and in need of significant reform.[12] Indeed, industrial design legislation in Canada has had a chequered history. First passed in 1861 prior to Canadian Confederation by the Province of Canada, industrial design law was later subsumed within trademark law under the *Trade Mark and Design Act* of 1906. It regained its status as an independent piece of legislation in 1953. However, in substance, design law in Canada has remained largely faithful to its initial pre-Confederation iteration.[13] It is small wonder that designers have aggressively pushed at the boundaries of copyright law in order to protect their interests. Copyright is a more desirable alternative as it arises without the need for registration, enjoys a lower threshold for eligibility and a much more generous term of protection.

In the early 1980s, a series of court decisions afforded greater scope for copyright protection in industrial designs by restrictively construing the prohibitions against overlap in the existing *Copyright Act*.[14] This line of reasoning led Parliament to more clearly delineate the exclusion of industrial designs from the ambit of copyright. In 1988, the *Copyright Act* was amended to disallow claims of copyright infringement in respect of designs applied to useful articles that were multiplied in 50 copies or more.[15] The provisions, contained in ss. 64 *et seq.*, are crafted in such a way that the design drawings themselves remain the subject of copyright but it is not an infringement of that copyright for competitors to reproduce the manufactured article embodying the design.

It would appear that, for the most part, these amendments have had their desired effect as cases decided after the legislative change have usually interpreted the interface between copyright and industrial design as being mutually exclusive[16] except where the design in question falls within one of the enumerated exceptions. These exceptions, found in s. 64(3), were concessions to special interests and include, among other things, designs used as trade-

---

12 See Amy Muhlstein & Margaret Ann Wilkinson, 'Whither Industrial Design' (1999–2000) 14 I.P.J. 1.

13 See McKeown, *supra* note 4.

14 *Royal Doulton Tableware Ltd v. Cassidy's Ltd* (1984), [1986] 1 F.C. 357 (F.C.T.D.); *Bayliner Marine Corporation v. Doral Boats Ltd.*, (1985) 5 C.P.R. (3d) 289 (F.C.T.D.), later overturned on appeal [1986] 3 F.C. 421 (F.C.A.). For further discussion see Myra J. Tawfik, 'The Law of Copyright and Industrial Designs in Canada' (1991) 7 C.I.P.R. 133.

15 *An Act to Amend the Copyright Act*, S.C. 1988, c. 15.

16 Example, *Milliken & Co. v. Interface Flooring (T.D.)*, [1998] 3 F.C. 103 (F.C.T.D.); *Canadian Private Copying Collective v. Amico Imaging Services Inc.* (2004), 249 F.T.R. 312 (F.C.T.D.).

marks, drawings or photographs applied to the face of useful articles or images of real or fictional characters used as features of shape. These designs enjoy full copyright protection even though mass-produced.

It is worth noting that in making the recommendations that ultimately led to the 1988 copyright amendments, the Sub-Committee on the Revision of Copyright had cautioned that:

> Undue delay in revising design legislation could result in transforming the Copyright Act into umbrella legislation for the protection of works never envisaged nor warranting copyright protection. …it is reasonable to fear that this result would have enormous repercussions on all intellectual property laws, possibly even rendering everything except copyright law obsolete.[17]

This call for action has not yet been acted upon. Thus, in the absence of significant industrial design reform in Canada, designers who remain dissatisfied with the terms of the antiquated *Industrial Design Act* continue to have an incentive to seek more advantageous alternatives. And so, in 2004, the Federal Court of Appeal was seized of a motion for summary judgment involving a claim of copyright infringement in the design of jewellery multiplied in 50 copies or more. The court refused to grant the motion finding a genuine issue to be tried as to whether jewellery was a 'useful article' to which the exclusion in s. 64 would apply.[18] Without commenting on the merits of this argument, one cannot help but find the Appeal Court's discussion of the 1988 copyright amendments puzzling:

> In the earlier legislation, section 46 of the *Copyright Act* had stated that 'This act does not apply to designs capable of being registered under the *Industrial Design Act*'. This restriction no longer appears in the current legislation (see section 64). It is obvious, therefore, that it is now possible for the *Copyright Act* to apply to the designs capable of being registered under the *Industrial Design Act*, that is, dual protection may now be possible in some situations.[19]

Nothing in the language of the 1988 amendments to the *Copyright Act* was intended to modify the pre-existing position that designs capable of being registered under the *Industrial Design Act* were *not* to benefit from copyright. Rather, the amendments were intended to broaden the scope of the exclusion

---

[17] House of Commons Standing Committee on Communications and Culture, *Report of the Sub-Committee on the Revision of Copyright – A Charter of Rights for Creators* (Ottawa: Supply and Services Canada, 1985) at 26 [*Sub-Committee on the Revision of Copyright*].

[18] *Pyrrha Design Inc. v. 623735 Saskatchewan Ltd.* (2004), 36 C.P.R. (4th) 432 (F.C.A.).

[19] *Ibid.* at para. 15.

by making it clear that copyright infringement could not be claimed in respect of all mass-produced designs whether or not they were strictly capable of industrial design registration.

It would seem then that in spite of Parliament's best efforts, the segregation of industrial design and copyright has not been entirely successful – and indeed, will not likely be fully achieved unless and until a systematic review of Canadian industrial design law is undertaken that includes a full analysis of its interface with copyright law.

Copyright – Patent

The 1988 copyright amendments were not limited to setting a more clearly defined boundary between copyright and ornamental designs applied to useful articles. They were intended to forestall the type of claim that had been made in the UK in the case of *British Leyland Motor Corp. v. Armstrong Patents Co.*[20] In *British Leyland*, the plaintiffs took an action for copyright infringement against the defendants who had reproduced their car exhaust pipes without permission. They claimed that the reproduction by the defendants of the three-dimensional object infringed the copyright in the underlying design drawings. As has been seen, under the existing Anglo-Canadian rules, copyright legislation expressly prohibited protection of ornamental designs applied to articles of manufacture. No similar legislative proscription existed for copyright in design drawings of purely *functional* articles – in many cases, design drawings of patentable inventions but not exclusively so. The inevitable logic was that functional designs would benefit from copyright protection for life of the author plus 50 years *post mortem* whereas ornamental designs would be granted a much more limited term of protection. Given the undesirable implications of upholding the plaintiff's claim, the House of Lords in *British Leyland* fashioned a 'spare parts' exception to the existing copyright principles to permit competitors to manufacture the functional products.

Similar disquieting events were occurring in Canada as one court found that the reproduction of an unpatented pump coupler by reference to the object itself was an infringement of copyright in the underlying design drawings. The court in *Spiro-Flex Industries Ltd v. Progressive Sealing Inc.*[21] did not consider the policy implications of allowing copyright in such a functional item and it remains an open question whether the court would have decided differently had the plaintiffs held patent rights in the coupler. In fact, prior to

---

20 [1986] 1 All. E.R. 850. See as well, Tawfik, *supra* note 14 and Jean-Phillippe Mikus, 'Of Industrious Authors and Artful Inventions: Industrial Works and Software at the Frontier of Copyright and Patent Law' (2004) 18 I.P.J. 187.

21 (1986), 32 D.L.R. (4th) 201 at 211–2 (B.C.S.C.).

the 1988 amendments, few Canadian courts had examined the precise question of patent-copyright overlap.

The most authoritative decision on point was the 1986 Federal Court decision in *Rucker Co. v. Gavel's Vulcanizing Ltd.* wherein the court pronounced itself forcefully on the subject:

> …to give the wide interpretation sought by Defendant to copyright protection for the drawings would defeat the time limitation provided for in the *Patent Act*. Most mechanical patents have drawings in connection therewith and the drawings can readily be copyrighted, but when patent infringement protection is no longer available to the owner of the patent it is not desirable that he should be able to extend this protection by application of the *Copyright Act* to the drawings from which the physical object covered by the patent was constructed, and thereby prevent anyone else from manufacturing the same device, even without the use of the drawings. I strongly believe that it was not the intention of Parliament nor from a practical view is it desirable that the *Patent Act*, the *Copyright Act*, and the *Industrial Design Act* should be interpreted so as to give overlapping protection. Something suitable for industrial design cannot be registered for copyright, as that statute states, and something for which a patent is granted should not also be given double protection for an extended period of time by registering for copyright drawings from which the patented object was made. Moreover in the present case the patent has not yet expired.[22]

A similar opinion was expressed in an earlier judgment of the Exchequer Court of Canada (now the Federal Court) in *Cuisenaire v. Southwest Imports* in a claim for copyright infringement in coloured rods used for teaching math:

> There must…I believe be some limitation to what is protected by copyright as it cannot conceivably have been the intention of Parliament to protect by way of copyright, material of any kind or any type of object. Nor must it have been intended that all original productions in the scientific field be given protection for the life of the author plus fifty years thereafter when they can also be patented as inventions and given protection for seventeen years only even if the rights of a patentee are not entirely similar to those of a holder of copyright.[23]

However, in *Interlego AG v. Irwin Toy Ltd.*, the court, seized of a motion for interlocutory injunction to prevent the defendant from infringing the plaintiff's copyright in the design drawings of an expired patented product, observed that:

> It is at best a question yet undecided in Canadian courts as to whether the fact that the product in question was originally the subject of a patent which has since expired is in any way a bar to the plaintiffs in preventing the reproduction of that

---

22 (1985), 7 C.P.R. (3d) 294 at 312 (F.C.T.D.) [*Rucker*].
23 [1968] 1 Ex. C.R. 493 at 507 [*Cuisenaire*].

product on grounds of breach of copyright of the drawings from which it was originally produced.[24]

And so matters stood until the 1988 copyright amendments included the following provision:

> s. 64.1 (1) The following acts do not constitute an infringement of the copyright or moral rights in a work:
> (a) applying to a useful article features that are dictated solely by a utilitarian function of the article;
> (b) by reference solely to a useful article, making a drawing or other reproduction in any material form of any features of the article that are dictated solely by a utilitarian function of the article;
> (c) doing with a useful article having only features described in paragraph (a), or with a drawing or reproduction made as described in paragraph (b), anything that the owner of the copyright has the sole right to do with the work; and
> (d) using any method or principle of manufacture or construction.

Although this section does not speak directly to the question of the coexistence of patent and copyright, the intent of Parliament in enacting s. 64.1 was to make it clear that '...copyright does not and never did apply to functional articles...[s. 64.1] states what the law was always intended to say.'[25] Presumably the prohibition against copyright protection for functional articles would not be limited to unpatentable products and a purposive construction of these sections would certainly capture most if not all cases involving patented or patentable inventions. Unfortunately however, uncertainty lingers. Although some recent judgments have endorsed the principle in *Rucker* and held that '...scientific inventions which are the subject of patents are not also capable of copyright protection',[26] plaintiffs continue to press the point and courts continue to raise doubts.

In *Energy Absorption Systems Ltd v. Y. Boissonneault et Fils Inc.*, the plaintiff sued for copyright infringement in the underlying drawings of a patented invention, in this case, impact absorbing safety cushions. The defendant had

---

24 (1985), 3 C.P.R. (3d) 476 at 485–6 (F.C.T.D.). This case parallels similar attempts by Interlego in other jurisdictions. See for example, *Interlego A.G. v. Tyco Industries Inc.* (1989), 1 A.C. 217.

25 *House of Commons Debates* (3 February 1988) at 12588 (Roger Clinch).

26 *North West Marine Technology Inc v. Crosby (c.o.b Micro Mark)* (1998), 75 C.P.R. (3d) 491 at 518 (B.C.S.C.). See as well *Matrox Electronic Systems v. Gaudreau*, [1993] QJ No. 1228 (Que. S.C.) at para. 48: 'It is not the intention of Parliament (nor is it desirable) to interpret the *Patent Act* and the *Copyright Act* to give overlapping protection'. See as well, Mikus, *supra* note 20; Robert J. Tomkowicz & Elizabeth F. Judge, 'The Rights of Exclusive Access: Misusing Copyright to Expand the Patent Monopoly' (2006) 19 I.P.J. 351.

reproduced and sold similar cushions. Not only did the court uphold the patent infringement claim, it also upheld the claim in copyright on a strict reading of s. 64.1:

> Section 64.1, however, may apply in a case such as the present case provided the defendants can establish that their drawings were made 'by reference solely to a useful article', i.e. an article that has a utilitarian function.
>
> Now, the drawings at issue in the Safety Impact Road's manual were not all made 'by reference solely' to the plaintiff's crash cushion, but were rather copied from the plaintiff's G-R-E-A-T System design and installation manuals, which is clearly prohibited copyright infringement. Under such circumstances, taking into account the above amendments to the *Copyright Act*, the plaintiff ought not to lose copyright protection because of the existence of patents that it owns.[27]

Presumably, the impact of this decision is to encourage competitors to 'refer solely to the useful article' in future in order to reproduce the product with impunity. Unfortunately, the case is notable for its absence of meaningful reflection on the implications of allowing copyright and patent to coexist in spite of the issue having been raised at trial with defence counsel proffering the *Rucker* decision to the court. In response, the judge appeared to assume that *Rucker* no longer had any relevance because it was decided before the passage of the 1988 amendments. The court interpreted s. 64.1 as it did without relying on any authority whatsoever to justify its position.

A more recent decision is even more troubling. In *R. v. Boutin*, involving an accused charged under the criminal provisions of the *Copyright Act*, the court took issue with the principle espoused in *Rucker* commenting that:

> Avec beaucoup de déférence pour l'opinion contraire, je ne peux comprendre pourquoi la protection de la Loi sur le droit d'auteur serait annulée par l'obtention d'un brevet. La Loi ne le stipule pas. Je ne crois pas non plus que la Loi empêche celui qui détient un droit d'auteur d'obtenir un brevet s'il y voit un avantage. A tout événement, je suis persuadé que si Jacques Bilodeau détient des droits d'auteur, il peut bénéficier de la protection de cette loi si les autres conditions sont rencontrées.[28]

Although this opinion is *obiter dictum*, if the effect of allowing cumulative patent and copyright protection would be to prevent a competitor from repro-

---

27 (1990), 30 C.P.R. (3d) 420 at 467–8 (F.C.T.D.).

28 [1997] AQ no. 3111 (Que. C.A.) at para. 37. Author's translation: 'With deference to the contrary opinion, I do not understand why copyright protection would be unavailable with the granting of a patent. The Act doesn't stipulate this. I also do not think that the Act prevents someone who holds copyright from also obtaining a patent if he finds an advantage to doing so. In any event, I am persuaded that if Jacques Bilodeau holds copyright, he is entitled to protection if the other conditions are met.'

ducing the invention for the lengthy copyright term, thereby extending the patent monopoly beyond its 20-year lifespan, such a policy must be called into question. More dubious still, what this case illustrates is that the coexistence of copyright would permit the invocation of the criminal remedies provisions under the *Copyright Act*[29] – an unduly harsh method of deterring competition in an invention, that finds no parallel within the *Patent Act*.[30]

Happily for Mr Boutin, he was acquitted on all counts. Although he had reproduced the *idea* of the unexpired patented invention – in this case, scratch cards – the court found that he had not copied their expression in that he had produced a different work. Although felicitous for the accused, this result offers only small comfort in addressing the larger question of the legitimacy of patent and copyright convergence. A situation may well present itself in which, in order to reproduce a product upon the expiry of the patent, a substantial reproduction of the work may have to be made. In such a case, raising a claim under copyright law would be as contra-indicated as it is in cases involving industrial designs.

If the policy concern governing this area of law is to avoid unduly hindering industry, the ability to assert copyright over engineering drawings to prevent competitors from manufacturing the three-dimensional object itself would be a most glaring example of what must be scrupulously avoided. As such, the overarching principle espoused in *Rucker* makes good sense. If, however, the courts are more inclined to root this principle within the statutory language of the *Copyright Act*, s. 64.1 ought to be sufficient in its drafting to permit competitors to produce the same product without fear of retaliation under copyright law especially in cases involving expired patents. It is to be hoped that the courts will clarify the scope and application of s. 64.1 in cases involving technical drawings of patented objects in the not too distant future.

Patent – Industrial Design

In principle, these two forms of protection should be mutually exclusive given that patent protection relates to the functional features of a useful object while industrial design protection attaches to its ornamental features expressly precluding protection over functional designs. Section 5.1 of the *Industrial Design Act* mirrors the language of s. 64 of the Copyright Act by providing that:

---

29 Ss. 42ff.

30 *Patent Act,* R.S.C. 1985, c. P-4, ss. 75–76. The Act provides only for very few criminal sanctions relating to making false representations and a specific offence in relation to patented medicines. These provisions are not as sweeping in their breadth and in the severity of their sanctions as those found in the *Copyright Act*, *supra* note 10.

5.1. No protection afforded by this Act shall extend to
(*a*) features applied to a useful article that are dictated solely by a utilitarian function of the article; or
(*b*) any method or principle of manufacture or construction.

Of course, one could obtain design protection for 10 years over the design features of a patented invention as a separate aspect of the same object.[31] However, according to the Federal Court in *Mainetti SpA v. E.R.A Display Co.*[32] where the ornamental design is merely an incidental feature of an invention, industrial design protection should give way to patent protection.

> If the primary purpose served by the article in question is one of function the decorative ornamentation being merely incidental, the article should be patentable under the *Patent Act*, if it is patentable, rather than seeking an industrial design registration for it.[33]

The court identified the principal objectives underlying industrial design law, patent law and trademark law in strong public interest terms asserting that these laws exist 'for the protection of the public against being misled into the belief that an infringing article is in fact that of the party whose design, patent or trade mark had been registered. It is only secondarily intended to protect the commercial interests of the parties…'. [34] The court is here suggesting that a claimant should be channelled exclusively towards the most appropriate form of protection on the basis that the primary aim of intellectual property law is consumer, rather than right holder, oriented. Although fairly unique within the Canadian legal context, this line of reasoning offers an alternate approach to the question of convergence that merits further consideration.

Finally, the ability to assert industrial design rights *after* the expiry of a patent registration would also appear to be a non-starter given that the *Industrial Design Act* requires that an application for registration be made within one year of the publication of the design.[35] Presumably, any window for registering an industrial design in a formerly patented product would be foreclosed since the design would have been published during the 20 year life of the patent (and vice versa).

---

31 See for example *Comstock Canada v. Electec Ltd* (1989), 28 C.P.R. (3d) 495 (F.C.T.D.).
32 (1984), 80 C.P.R. (2d) 206 (F.C.T.D.).
33 *Ibid.* at 224–5.
34 *Ibid.* at 226.
35 Section 6(3).

Patent – Trademark

It is in relation to the overlap between patents and trademarks that the question of convergence has had its most fulsome discussion and has been, for all intents and purposes, resolved by the Supreme Court of Canada in the 2005 decision of *Kirkbi AG v. Ritvik Holdings*[36] involving a claim in passing-off in relation to the shape of children's interlocking toy bricks.

From the moment that Canadian law recognized that trademark rights could be acquired in and registration obtained for the distinctive shapes of products or their packaging, [37] potential overlap with other forms of intellectual property became inevitable including claims of trademark rights in the shapes of expired patented products. The difficulties inherent in permitting convergence with patents were clearly understood by both Parliament and the courts. In order to function as a trademark, the shape of a product must be distinctive, that is, it must serve to distinguish one manufacturer's wares or services from another's. If the features of shape are exclusively dictated by function, then the shape could never become distinctive and so, should never acquire trademark rights. Even if such a shape could acquire distinctiveness, the effect of trademark protection would be to effectively prevent competitors from manufacturing the object itself. Finally, even if the shape were not exclusively dictated by function, where the effect of conferring trademark rights in the shape would nevertheless prevent competitors from entering the market in the same or similar goods, legal protection under the circumstances would be unwarranted as an undue restraint on competition.

As a result, Parliament explicitly set out the parameters for the registration of shapes as trademarks, referred to in the statute as 'distinguishing guises':

> 13(1) A distinguishing guise is registrable only if
> (a) it has been so used in Canada by the applicant or his predecessor in title as to have become distinctive at the date of filing an application for its registration; and
> (b) the exclusive use by the applicant of the distinguishing guise in association with the wares or services with which it has been used is not likely unreasonably to limit the development of any art or industry.

---

[36] *Supra* note 7. For background on the case leading up to the Supreme Court decision see Myra J. Tawfik 'Follow the LEGO Brick Road: The Doctrine of Functionality under Canadian Trademark Law' in Grosheide & Brinkhof, *supra* note 3 at 71.

[37] Early on in its history, Canadian common law recognized trademark rights in the packaging of products. In addition, the 1868 *Trade Mark and Design Act*, 31 Vic., c. 55 provided for registration of distinctive packaging of a product as a trademark. This was later expanded by the *Unfair Competition Act,* S.C. 1932, c. 38 to any distinguishing guise and the registrability of distinguishing guises as trademarks takes its modern form by virtue of the 1953 *Trade Marks Act*, S.C. 1952–53, c. 49. See Gill and Jolliffe, *supra* note 4.

Effect of registration
(2) No registration of a distinguishing guise interferes with the use of any utilitarian feature embodied in the distinguishing guise.

Not to limit art or industry
(3) The registration of a distinguishing guise may be expunged by the Federal Court on the application of any interested person if the Court decides that the registration has become likely unreasonably to limit the development of any art or industry.[38]

Registration is made contingent upon the distinguishing guise being both 'distinctive' and not 'likely to unreasonably limit the development of any art or industry'. Even when registered, the protection afforded is limited – others are free to use any utilitarian features of the registered distinguishing guise with impunity. In 1953, the Trade Mark Law Revision Committee, deliberating on whether to extend the benefits of trademark registration to distinguishing guises, observed that:

> The reaction of trade and commerce generally has not wholly favoured this policy [of registration] of the law and it has been felt that while certain modes of shaping…might be properly monopolized as indicia of origin, great care should be exercised that registration will not hamper industry in its employment of newly developed processes, materials or methods of merchandizing.[39]

Given the concerns about the potential anti-competitive consequences of registered distinguishing guises, it is not surprising that a good number of shapes have not enjoyed much success at securing or maintaining registration.[40]

Equally wary of the effects of conferring trademark rights on utilitarian objects, the courts independently developed a pre-emptive doctrine through which to assess all cases involving guises, regardless of whether they have

---

[38] *Trade-marks Act,* R.S.C. 1985, c. T-13. The term 'distinguishing guise' is defined in s. 2 as either the shape of wares or containers or the mode of packaging or wrapping wares 'the appearance of which is used by a person for the purpose of distinguishing or so as to distinguish wares or services manufactured, sold, leased, hired or performed by him from those manufactured, sold, leased, hired or performed by others.'

[39] *Report of the Trade Mark Law Revision Committee to the Secretary of State of Canada*, 1953, reprinted in Harold G. Fox, *The Canadian Law of Trade Marks and Unfair Competition*, 2nd ed. (Toronto: Carswell, 1956) 1142 at 1151.

[40] For example, *Remington Rand Corp v. Phillips Electronics NV* (1995), 64 C.P.R. (3d) 467 (F.C.A.) [*Remington Rand*]. The stakes are just too high. Under s. 19 of the Act, a registered trademark holder can prevent anyone from using the same or a confusingly similar trademark anywhere in Canada.

been registered or not. The doctrine of functionality acts as a complete bar to the acquisition of trademark rights in shapes that are primarily functional. [41] It has had a long and solid history culminating in its robust endorsement by the Supreme Court of Canada in the *Kirkbi* decision.

The origins of the doctrine lie in the 1939 decision in *Imperial Tobacco Co. v. Registrar of Trademarks*.[42] At issue was whether the plastic outer wrapper on a package of cigarettes could be registered as a distinguishing guise. In denying the registration, the court concluded that: '…any combination of elements which are primarily designed to perform a function…is not fit subject-matter for a trade mark, and if permitted would lead to grave abuses.'[43] The grave abuses that the doctrine was developed to counter have been alternately described as 'restraint on manufacturing and trade',[44] '[unfairness] to the public if a patentee could, after the expiry of the patent…give itself a monopoly over the shape'[45] and 'abuses of monopoly positions in respect of products and processes'.[46]

In *Kirkbi*, the thrust of the case before the Supreme Court was whether the doctrine of functionality applied equally to claims for passing-off as it did to claims involving registered distinguishing guises. The plaintiffs argued that Parliament had only chosen to restrict primarily functional distinguishing guises from registration. It had therefore left the exercise of rights in unregistered shapes unaffected by functional considerations. The court rejected this line of reasoning arguing that 'granting such a claim in these circumstances would amount to recreating a monopoly contrary to basic policies of the laws and legal principles which inform the various forms of intellectual property in our legal system'.[47] It further held that the law of passing off 'did not develop to protect monopolies in respect of products but of guises, get-ups, names and symbols which identify the distinctiveness of the source'.[48]

In reaffirming the doctrine of functionality as the critical safeguard to preventing abuses of monopoly, the court reminded competitors that

---

41 The doctrine excludes only those guises that are primarily functional namely 'a mark which goes beyond distinguishing the wares of its owner to the functional structure of the wares themselves.' *Remington Rand*, supra at 478. See as well *Pizza Pizza Ltd. v. Canada* (1998), 26 C.P.R. (3d) 355 (F.C.A.) and *Samann v. Canada's Royal Pinetree Mfg Co. Ltd.* (1986), 9 C.P.R. (3d) 223 (F.C.A.).

42 [1939] 2 D.L.R. 65 (Ex. Ct.).

43 *Ibid.* at 67.

44 *Remington Rand, supra* note 40 at 477.

45 *Thomas Betts v. Panduit Corp.*(2000), 4 C.P.R. (4th) 498 at paras. 23–4 (F.C.A).

46 *Kirkbi, supra* note 7 at para. 44.

47 *Ibid.* at para. 69.

48 *Ibid.* at para. 67.

'competition between products using the same technical processes or solutions, once patent rights are out of the way, is not unfair competition. It is simply the way the economy and the market are supposed to work in modern liberal societies.'[49]

In other words, there is some rational coherence to our intellectual property laws that limits their reach and the role of the courts is to monitor their borders against unwanted incursions – in this case, where such incursions result in overextensions of monopolies to the detriment of open competition in the marketplace. The Supreme Court's decision in *Kirkbi* is not only consistent with the lengthy body of jurisprudence on the question of patent-trademark interface, it serves as an affirmation of the underlying policy necessitating their mutual exclusion that is manifested in both legislative and jurisprudential intervention.

Industrial Design – Trademark

In contrast with the case of patent-trademark convergence and in spite of opinion to the contrary, current legal thinking would generally allow trademark and industrial design rights to subsist in the design features of a product so long as the respective requirements for protection are met.[50] In *WCC Containers Sales Ltd v. Haul-All Equipment Ltd* [51] the court expressly rejected the defendant's assertion that industrial designs and trademarks were intended to be mutually exclusive including the argument that extending industrial design protection through trademark law was a breach of an implied bargain with society that, upon expiry of the registered design right, the design would belong in the public domain.

This position is in contrast with earlier policy recommendations. In its 1958 *Report on Industrial Designs*, the Royal Commission on Patents, Copyright, Trade Marks and Industrial Designs recommended most emphatically that dual protection be denied – at least for a defined period of time. According to the Commission, a designer '…should not be permitted under the cover of his design monopoly to build up distinctiveness of his design, or these features of it, so that it or they can be registered as a distinguishing guise and thereby prolong his monopoly beyond the period of the design protection.'[52] The final recommendation was that, once expired, a registered industrial design should

49 *Ibid.* at para. 54.

50 See for example, McKeown, *supra* note 4 but see contra, Gordon J. Zimmerman, 'Extending the Monopoly? The Risks and Benefits of Multiple Forms of Intellectual Property Protection' (2001) 17 C.I.P.R. 345.

51 [2003] F.C. 962 (F.C.T.D.) [*WCC Containers*].

52 (Ottawa: Queen's Printer, 1958) at 33.

not be registered as a distinguishing guise for a period of three years. Trademark registration would be subsequently permitted but only where the design remained distinctive as to source. In its 1971 *Report on Intellectual and Industrial Property*, the Economic Council of Canada endorsed the position taken by the Royal Commission on the premise that '…it is considered inconsistent with the logic of a short term of protection for a registered industrial design to permit such a potential'.[53] Of course, this presumes that there is a 'logic of a short term of protection' that governs industrial design law.

To the extent that asserting trademark rights in designs has the potential to hinder others from making the product itself, allowing these distinct intellectual property rights to coexist raises similar concerns to those relating to patents. In *Remington Rand*,[54] the court described the mischief that the doctrine of functionality was designed to remedy in terms of unwarranted extensions of *both* patent and industrial design monopolies.

However, given that both schemes preclude the acquisition of rights in functional designs, one could argue that the risk to competition of allowing overlapping rights would likely be minimal. Indeed, although the court in *WCC Containers* refused to expunge the registered trademark in the design of a rubbish bin on policy grounds, it did expunge the registration under s. 13(3) of the *Trade-marks Act* on the basis that the registration was 'likely unreasonably to limit the development of any art or industry'.

In sum, while as a matter of principle it would appear that industrial design rights and trademark rights can coexist, this coexistence is premised on each of these bodies of law containing sufficient safeguards to prevent deleterious outcomes and on the courts interpreting the legislative texts accordingly.

Copyright – Trademark

By virtue of s. 64(3), the *Copyright Act* implicitly recognizes copyright in trademarks when it specifically exempts them from the application of the industrial design exclusions. Further, under trademark law, a mark can consist of a literary, artistic work and, potentially, a musical work so long as the mark is distinctive and used in association with wares or services. Thus, under Canadian law one can claim copyright in a trademark if it meets the criteria for copyright protection and trademark protection for a copyright work that serves the function of a trademark. The *Trade-marks Act* also makes it clear that the wares upon which the trademark can be affixed can include 'printed publications'. The reason for this inclusion in the definition

53 (Ottawa: Information Canada, 1971) at 125.
54 *Supra* note 40.

of wares in s. 2 has bearing on the question of copyright and trademark overlap and is of some historical interest.

In the late nineteenth and early twentieth centuries, a series of cases were taken before Canadian courts in which claims of 'passing-off' were being made in respect of titles of literary works.[55] These decisions are somewhat reminiscent of the more famous US case of *Clemens v. Belford and Clark*,[56] a trademark infringement claim initiated by American humorist Samuel Clemens to prevent the unauthorized publication of one of his works. Clemens argued that he held trademark rights in his nom de plume 'Mark Twain' which the defendants infringed when they used it, without his permission, on their reprints of his literary works. In denying the claim, the court discussed the conceptual inappropriateness of invoking trademark principles under the circumstances:

> ...This is the first attempt which has ever come under my notice, to protect a writer's exclusive right to literary property under the law applicable to trade marks.
>
> ...an author can not...be allowed to defeat the well settled rules of the common law in force in this country, that the 'publication of a literary work without copyright is a dedication to the public, after which any one may republish it.'[57]

The facts were somewhat different in the Canadian cases in that the defendants did not reproduce a substantial portion of the literary works themselves but merely their title. Although the courts did not, as a matter of principle, deny trademark rights to the titles of the literary works, the issue of copyright was, inescapably, a subtext of these decisions. In *Canada Publishing Co. v. Gage*, the majority of the Supreme Court of Canada upheld the plaintiff's claim to passing-off for the title of its copy-book where the defendant used a confusingly similar one for its own copy-book. However, the dissenting judge would have offered no remedy in the absence of a claim in copyright over the plaintiff's book. [58]

The later decision of the same court in *New York Herald* v. *Ottawa Citizen Co.* is particularly instructive. Here, the court explicitly deliberated on the question of overlapping copyright and trademark rights in a case involving the

---

[55] *Canada Publishing Co. v. Gage* (1885), 11 S.C.R. 306; *Rose v. McLean Publishing Co.* (1897), 24 O.A.R. 240 (Ont. C.A.); *New York Herald Co. v. Ottawa Citizen Co.* (1909), 41 S.C.R. 229 [*NY Herald*]; *McIndoo v. Musson Book Co.* (1916), 35 O.L.R. 342 (Ont. C.A.).

[56] *Clemens v. Belford, Clarke & Co.* (1883), 14 F. 728 (N.D. Ill.).

[57] *Ibid.* at 731–2.

[58] *Canada Publishing Co. v. Gage*, *supra* note 55 at 311 (Henry J., dissenting): 'There was no copyright in Gage's book...Here the copy book of the appellants did not infringe any right in the book published and sold by Gage.'

trademark registration of the title of a comic strip. In holding that the title did not meet the definition of a trademark under the relevant statute, Justice Iddington, speaking for the majority, opined:

> ...when we look at the general scope and purpose of the [Trade Mark and Designs] Act, it seems quite impossible to suppose it was ever intended to protect property in a distinguishing mark such as this when applied to the kind of goods appellant vends...The production which the appellant sells is not a kind of paper, or of paper coloured in any particular way or covered with a peculiar kind of ink or set forms or figures. It is the nonsense that is produced by the brain of the man writing for the diversion of the idle that in truth is sold.
>
> It may be that kind of brain product that copyright might amongst other things be extended to or that copyright might cover.
>
> I am not, however, going to wander into the field of whether or not a trade mark can exist in such a name or names, or in the name of or title given any literary production of any kind, for I am quite sure it never was intended that this section should apply to such a thing.
>
> If it did, all that would be needed for a publisher of copyrighted works, when the copyright was about to expire, in order practically to add twenty-five years to the term of copyright, would be to register the title and defy any one to use it, though then at liberty to sell the thing itself without a title.
>
> I think the distinction between copyright and trade mark registration was intended by the legislature to be, and that it must be, observed in applying this Act.[59]

The majority decision is notable for looking beyond the terms of the legislative text to the consequences of allowing the plaintiff's claim for trademark infringement. Compromising the 'essence' of the different forms of intellectual property rights and allowing copyright holders to extend their monopoly through the use of trademark law were clearly considered undesirable. In contrast, Justice Duff, in dissent, found no legitimate justification for the exclusion of titles from the purview of trademark protection.

> There is nothing in the statute or in the subject matter with which the statute deals seeming to require us to give to these words any signification less narrow than they import in their ordinary use; and we should not, of course, be justified in restricting their operation on any vague surmise respecting the policy of the Act.[60]

The disquiet that the majority expressed over the intersection of copyright and trademark, that Duff J., dismissively characterised as 'vague surmise', has not been echoed either by Parliament or the courts since. Indeed, Canadian law has accommodated the coexistence of these rights almost as a matter of

---

59 *New York Herald Co. v. Ottawa Citizen Co.*, *supra* note 55 at 233–4.
60 *Ibid.* at 236.

course.[61] Thus, when a striking labour union reproduced a modified image of the famous 'Michelin Man' on its picket signs and other materials, the employer, Michelin & Co. sued for copyright infringement in the image as an artistic work and trademark infringement in the image as its trademark.[62] Although the court dismissed the allegation of trademark infringement on the basis that the defendant was not a competitor and was not using the trademark in a commercial context, it upheld the copyright claim. The court rejected the union's defence that their parody of the plaintiff's artistic work constituted fair dealing for the purpose of criticism. Similarly, in *Société des Loteries du Québec v. Club Lotto International CLI Inc.*,[63] the court determined that the activities of the defendant in reproducing the plaintiff's lottery tickets and official marks in their advertising did not amount to passing-off or unfair competition but did constitute copyright infringement. In this way then, the plaintiff was able to achieve its desired aim, which had less to do with seeking to prevent the reproduction of the copyright work *per se* and more to do with bringing an end to the defendant's advertising strategy.

In each of these cases, the courts accepted that copyright and trademark rights could be invoked concurrently and rendered their decisions based strictly on the statutory language. They appear never to have questioned why it should be that trademark law permits many more 'fair uses' than copyright law and whether this parsimony in copyright is at all sound policy.[64] They also failed to inquire as to whether the mischief complained of related to the copyright work *qua* work or whether the claim was primarily directed towards restricting competition within the marketplace – a context that might require a more nuanced analysis. And although it is true that some of these fundamental questions were raised very recently before the Supreme Court of Canada in a copyright infringement claim against a parallel importer, this latest judgment of the highest court leaves much to be desired on the question of intersecting rights.

---

[61] Jean-Phillippe Mikus, 'Chevauchements des droits en propriété intellectuelle – Deuxième partie: la cavalcade du droit d'auteur et du droit des marques de commerce' 15 I.P.J. 167.

[62] *Compagnie Générale des Établissements Michelin-Michelin & Cie v. National Automobile, Aerospace, Transportation and General Workers Union of Canada* (1996), 71 C.P.R. (3d) 348, [1997] 2 F.C. 306 (F.C.T.D.).

[63] (2001), 13 C.P.R. (4th) 315 (F.C.T.D.).

[64] See Teresa Scassa, 'Intellectual Property on the Cyber-Picket Line: A Comment on *British Columbia Automobile Assn. v. Office and Professional Employees' International Union, Local 378*' (2002) 39 Alta. L. Rev. 934. See also Jane Bailey, 'Deflating the Michelin Man: Protecting Users' Rights in the Canadian Copyright Reform Process' in Michael Geist, ed., *In the Public Interest: The Future of Canadian Copyright Law* (Toronto: Irwin Law, 2005).

The plaintiff in *Kraft Canada Inc v. Euro-Excellence Inc.*[65] was the exclusive Canadian distributor of certain brands of chocolate bars and the defendant was a competitor who purchased the same products directly from the European manufacturer and imported them for sale in Canada. The goods in question bore the manufacturer's trademarks on their packaging. Under existing trademark law principles, exclusive distributors have been unsuccessful at preventing parallel imports from circulating in the Canadian market.[66] However, under s. 27(2) of the *Copyright Act*, it is an infringement of copyright to import a copyright work for the purpose of sale if the imported works are infringing copies or copies that would be infringing if 'made in Canada by the person who made it'. Therefore, Kraft pursued Euro-Excellence exclusively under the terms of the *Copyright Act*, claiming copyright in the design mark as an artistic work and, indeed, the plaintiff enjoyed success at both trial and appellate levels of the Federal Court of Canada.

In both of these lower level decisions, the courts summarily rejected the defendant's policy argument that copyright should not be used to inhibit the free flow of goods, presumably satisfied that they had dispensed justice by allowing Euro-Excellence to continue to sell the chocolate bars in Canada upon the removal of the infringing labels. Assuming that it was economically feasible for Euro-Excellence to comply with such a ruling, is it necessarily good policy to have the defendants assume the risk in this type of case?

It is not unreasonable to surmise that Kraft's primary concern was to prevent the defendant from competing with it in the sale of chocolate bars rather than to prohibit the importation of the artistic works *per se*. The implications of upholding the plaintiff's claim come perilously close to preventing competition in the marketplace for an activity that would not be prohibited under trademark law. Was it clearly the intention of Parliament when it enacted the importation restrictions in the *Copyright Act* to prevent this particular type of parallel importation from occurring? The drafting language is somewhat tortured but it is not at all obvious that s. 27(2) should be interpreted to permit an exclusive licensee, that is, not a copyright holder to claim against a parallel importer where the copy of the work that was imported was made by the person authorized to make it namely the European copyright holder.

Further, a trademark is, by definition, a mark that is affixed to an article of commerce. The copyright work is therefore primarily intended to serve an industrial or commercial function. Copyright in a trademark raises analogous

---

65 *Euro-Excellence Inc. v. Kraft Canada Inc.*, 2007 SCC 37 [*Kraft SCC*] (judgment rendered 26 July 2007), rev'g *Kraft Canada Inc. v. Euro Excellence Inc.* (2005), 47 C.P.R. (4th) 113 (F.C.A.), rev'g *Kraft Canada Inc. v. Euro Excellence Inc.* (2003), 25 C.P.R. (4th) 22 (F.C.T.D.).

66 *Smith & Nephew v. Glen Oak Inc* (1996), 68 C.P.R. 3d 153 (F.C.A.).

difficulties to copyright in industrial designs and yet, for political rather than policy reasons, trademarks continue to enjoy its full benefits. If the courts are genuinely preoccupied with ensuring that intellectual property rights do not unduly hinder competition, then the effect of granting Kraft's claim should have elicited stronger reaction or at least more considered discussion from the lower courts.

The facts presented in the *Kraft* case required greater reflection on the 'essence' of copyright and challenged the simplistic assumption that its overlap with trademarks is benign. It asked the courts to read into the language of the *Copyright Act* limitations justified on the basis of overriding public policy considerations. In this way then, the case was an ideal litmus test for determining how far the Supreme Court was prepared to go in order to delineate the boundary between these two bodies of intellectual property law.

Regrettably, the decision of the Supreme Court is most disappointing in this respect. Although the ultimate outcome was to allow the appeal thereby permitting Euro-Excellence to legitimately import the goods bearing the copyright work, the Bench split in a number of ways on a number of key issues – evidencing the discomfort of the Supreme Court when tested with a particularly difficult case.

The only issue that the entire Bench agreed on was that Parliament intended that copyright and trademark should overlap. The judges differed markedly however on the appropriate legal principles to govern the outcome. Three members of the Bench allowed the appeal based purely upon an interpretation of the *Copyright Act* – denying to an exclusive distributor who was not the copyright holder the ability to pursue a parallel importer.[67] Two judges dissented, finding no legal basis to deny Kraft's claim.[68] However, three other members of the Bench rendered their decision in terms of overarching policy, censuring the unwarranted extension of copyright into the realm of trademark.[69] In the words of Justice Bastarache '[t]he protection offered by copyright cannot be leveraged to include protection of economic interests that are only tangentially related to the copyrighted work.'[70] Finally, although Justice Fish concurred with those who dismissed the claim on the basis that a licensee could not pursue a parallel importer under the terms of the *Copyright Act*, he wrote in *obiter* commentary: '…I express grave doubt whether the law governing the protection of intellectual property rights in Canada can be trans-

67 Justices Rothstein, Binnie, Deschamps with Justice Fish writing concurring reasons.

68 Justices Abella and McLachlin.

69 Justices Bastarache, LeBel and Charron with Justice Fish adding obiter remarks advancing similar policy arguments.

70 *Kraft SCC*, *supra* note 65 at para. 83.

formed in this way into an instrument of trade control not contemplated by the *Copyright Act*'.[71]

In the final analysis, as a result of the wide divergence of opinions and in spite of some strong language from some of the judges on the question of copyright-trademark policy, it is very difficult to claim with any confidence that the Supreme Court has adequately resolved some of the more nagging questions surrounding this combination of overlapping rights.

EXTRAPOLATING NORMATIVE PRINCIPLES?

In light of the above, one must ask just how far a piecemeal approach of 'case by case' and 'law by law' can go towards providing meaningful solutions to the sorts of difficulties raised in cases like *Kraft*. Can one glean from the existing body of law any normative principles that can offer a full and complete answer to the vexing question of the intersection of intellectual property rights? I would suggest not.

What the current Canadian legal context does teach us, however, is that the courts will presume coexistence of rights unless the legislature has expressly intervened to prohibit a specific combination or where the outcome of allowing convergence is so obviously unacceptable, as in the case of trademark protection for functional shapes. Whether justified so as not to 'limit art or industry' or not to 'impede competition' or in order to 'encourage learning' or 'the progress of useful arts', the courts and Parliament will sever the connection between two forms of intellectual property where the end result of allowing them to coexist would be anti-competitive. This rationale is borne out by the treatment of the copyright-industrial design interface and should presumably govern in cases involving combinations of copyright-patent and patent – industrial design as well. It is also very evident in the trademark–patent convergence and underlies the trademark-industrial design connection. It can also be discerned in the reasoning of four of the nine judges in the *Kraft* decision, especially in Justice Fish's remarks about the misuse of copyright as an instrument of trade control.

It is not at all surprising that Canadian jurists are guided by competition concerns as a matter of overarching policy. After all, intellectual property rights are monopoly rights and concern over abuses of monopoly is as deeply ingrained as is the desire to reward and encourage innovation. In the Canadian legal tradition there remain the echoes of the *Statute of Monopolies* permitting only those patent uses not 'contrary to the law, nor mischievous to the State,

71 *Ibid*. at para. 56.

by raising prices of commodities at home, or hurt of trade, or generally inconvenient'[72] and of the *Statute of Anne* curbing usurious book pricing under the watchful eye of the Archbishop of Canterbury.[73]

In other instances, however, decision-making on questions involving overlapping rights is less explicit about identifying a governing public policy rationale. Rather, the focus appears more squarely rooted in identifying the nature and purpose of the particular body of intellectual property law at issue. Here the discussion revolves around the assumption that intellectual property laws were designed to meet a core set of constants such that although they may have expanded or been reshaped through the course of time, their fundamental purpose has not shifted. Rather than studying the outcome of allowing coexistence in a given case, the question of overlap is measured in light of the foundational principles governing each form of intellectual property right. In other words, while intellectual property laws can adapt and grow, they nevertheless have a basic intrinsic integrity that must not be distorted although their boundaries are not clearly mapped out and their contours vague at best.

This approach is characteristic of earlier court decisions and Government policy documents but not exclusively so. It is manifested in statements such as 'works never envisaged nor warranting copyright protection',[74] 'not the intention of Parliament nor from a practical view is it desirable…';[75] 'there must…be some limitation to what is protected by copyright';[76] 'it was never intended that this section should apply to such a thing'[77] – presented without any further elaboration as if the broad assertion itself could constitute a complete answer to resolving the particular claim. The 'essence' of the law is here being defined in fairly abstract and formal terms – in much the same way as was the case in the late nineteenth century when jurists distinguished between the various intellectual property laws by citing their formal and structural differences rather than their underlying policy objectives.

Interestingly, the more recent decisions of the Supreme Court of Canada have been offering a less embryonic, more nuanced and ultimately more helpful exploration of the 'essence' of the laws. The highest appellate court in Canada has, increasingly, been taking greater care to more clearly delineate each form of intellectual property right in terms of its structure and its intrinsic purpose as well as in relation to overarching intellectual property policy. As but one example, the Supreme Court in *Kirkbi* suggested that '[i]n order to

72 1624, 21 Jac. I, c. 3, s. 6.
73 1710, 8 Anne, c. 19, s. 4.
74 *Sub-Committee on the Revision of Copyright*, *supra* note 17 at 26.
75 *Rucker*, *supra* note 22 at 312.
76 *Cuisenaire*, *supra* note 23 at 507.
77 *NY Herald*, *supra* note 55 at 234.

understand the role and relevance of the doctrine of functionality in the law of trade-marks, some comments of the nature and function of patents and trade-marks will be useful'.[78] Throughout its judgment the Court went to great lengths to compare and contrast the rationales underlying patents on the one hand and trademarks on the other in order to arrive at the conclusion that functional shapes should be barred from trademark protection as a matter of competition policy.

Indeed, in both convergence and non-convergence cases, the Supreme Court has been clarifying not only the scope of a particular intellectual property right but its boundaries as well – whether these boundaries are characterized as necessary to encourage the free flow of ideas and knowledge or to ensure a healthy competitive marketplace for goods and services.[79] The 'essence' of a given form of intellectual property law is increasingly being considered and expressly defined in both formal and policy terms.

Ultimately, however, even the most enlightened judicial approach can advance the law only so far because the normative principles at play can only be invoked *a posteriori*. In the absence of a broad view of the intellectual property system from the outset and in its entirety, the silo effect of settling each combination as it presents itself inevitably generates paradoxes that can never be properly resolved.

For instance, why are the courts so emphatic about preventing patent and trademarks overlapping on the grounds of anti-competitive outcomes but not similarly exercised over patent and copyright overlap? Why are they eager to find copyright infringement in activities that would otherwise be acceptable uses under trademark law without questioning the underlying policies that have led to such a result? Why is competition policy not front and centre in cases involving copyright in trademarks when this same concern is at the forefront of the relationship between copyright and industrial designs? Further, what public policy consideration is being served by allowing patent holders to invoke the criminal provisions of the *Copyright Act*? A 'case by case' and 'law by law' approach can never hope to fully address these issues. It is instructive to reflect on the fact that in the *Kraft* case the Supreme Court was stymied in its ability to fix, with any degree of certainty, the trajectory of Canadian intellectual property policy in cases of overlapping trademark and copyright rights.

---

78 *Kirkbi*, *supra* note 7 at para. 37.

79 Similar expressions of the essential nature of intellectual property rights can be found in non-convergence cases. See for example, on copyright and user's rights *CCH Canadian Ltd. v. Law Society of Upper Canada*, [2004] 1 S.C.R. 339; on patenting higher life forms, *Harvard College v. Canada (Commissioner of Patents),* [2002] 4 S.C.R. 45 and on the limits of trademark law in famous marks *Veuve Clicquot Ponsardin v. Boutiques Cliquot Ltée*, [2006] 1 S.C.R. 824.

I would suggest that the unsatisfactory nature of the *Kraft* decision best exemplifies the fundamental problem surrounding the current approach.

Of course, it is ultimately for Parliament to settle questions of policy. Unfortunately, in spite of the growth in importance of intellectual property over the past 20 years or so, Canadian policy-makers appear unwilling to undertake a comprehensive examination of the intellectual property law system as a whole and have paid scant attention to issues of critical concern. Sadly, the Royal Commission on Patents, Copyright, Trademarks and Industrial Designs established in the 1950s to study Canadian intellectual and industrial property finds no parallel in the twenty-first century. The mandate of this earlier Commission is impressive in its breadth, scope and balance:

> …to inquire as to whether Federal legislation relating in any way to patents of invention, industrial designs, copyright and trade marks affords reasonable incentive to invention and research, to the development of literary and artistic talents, to creativeness, and to making available to the Canadian public scientific, technical, literary and artistic creations….in a manner and on terms adequately safeguarding the paramount public interest, the whole in the light of present day economic conditions, scientific, technical and industrial developments, trade practices and any other relevant factors or circumstances…[80]

It must be stressed though that, however laudable the mandate of the Commission, the Federal Government never acted upon the Commission's findings. This failure to act quickly and decisively in matters relating to intellectual property is one that continues to afflict current policy-makers. As but one glaring example, the much-needed full-scale review of industrial design law, both in its own right and in light of its intersection with copyright, continues to languish. Further, I would suggest that in light of the *Kraft* case, Parliament must now look more closely at the intersection of trademark and copyright and reconsider its advisability. In addition, cases of intersecting rights bring to the fore the uneven legislative drafting of the various intellectual property statutes and the attendant uncertainty this generates. For example, if functionality is a primary consideration in setting limits for some forms of intellectual property rights, then it is not at all helpful that the various statutes that address functional concerns do so in very different terms. While one statute speaks of excluding 'utilitarian features' from protection another

80 *Report on Industrial Designs*, *supra* note 52 at 5. The Commission was established in 1954 by Order in Council. It issued 3 Reports, commonly referred to as the 'Ilsley Reports' after its Chair. J.L. Ilsley. The Report on Copyright was issued in 1957, followed by the Report on Industrial Designs in 1958 and the Report on Patents of Invention in 1959. It is to be noted that the Commission requested that it be relieved of its mandate to study trademarks.

refers to preventing rights from 'unreasonably limiting the development of art or industry'. Are these terms intended to be expressions of the same prohibitions or are they to catch different but related concerns?[81] To add to the confusion, the courts themselves do not often look closely at these linguistic distinctions, ascribing to each phrase the broad gloss of 'functionality'. If there are sound policy reasons to recognize variations on 'functionality' depending on the particular form of intellectual property right in question, these must be identified and articulated more clearly by Canadian policy-makers. Unnecessary complexity and doubt are generated when the statutory texts are not rationalized in some fashion.

Perhaps more egregious still, the fragmented 'case by case' and 'law by law' approach leaves unanswered the more fundamental question of whether coexistence of intellectual property rights is, in and of itself, desirable policy. After all, what underlying intellectual property policy objectives are being served by allowing rights to overlap in the first place? Because converging intellectual property rights are manifestations of the overall intellectual property expansionism that has become so endemic in recent years, careful attention must be paid to fully assessing the legitimacy of this phenomenon. As David Vaver has suggested, 'multiple protection is usually overprotection'[82] and he asks:

> Given that innovation levels are hardly enhanced by the prospect of adventitious multiple protection, the question may be asked whether this rule of 'take as many as you can carry' should be replaced by a rule of 'only one per customer'.[83]

Viewed in this light, adopting a policy of prohibiting overlapping rights except where there are clear public policy reasons to permit coexistence in a given case – in other words turning the current thinking on its head – would appear to be a much more salutary approach. Unfortunately, this essential question has not yet been seriously considered either by those who set intellectual property policy in Canada or by those who interpret it.

---

81 A case in point is *WCC Containers*, *supra* note 51 in which the design at issue was registrable and therefore *not* 'functional' under the *Industrial Design Act*, *supra* note 9 but was unregistrable for being 'functional' under the *Trade-marks Act*, *supra* note 38.

82 David Vaver, *Intellectual Property Law* (Toronto: Irwin Law, 1997) at 15.

83 David Vaver, 'Canada's Intellectual Property Framework: A Comparative Overview' 17 I.P.J. 125 at 132. See too, Viva R. Moffat, 'Mutant Copyrights and Backdoor Patents: The Problem of Overlapping Intellectual Property Protection' (2004) 19 Berkeley Technology Law Journal 1474.

CONCLUSION

The current state of Canadian law on convergence of intellectual property rights can be characterized as disjointed – limited to judicial and legislative treatment of case specific combinations. Although one can glean from the record some understanding as to when and why jurists will intervene in a given case – most notably where allowing coexistence would be anti-competitive – the piecemeal approach remains mired in confusion and uncertainty. Progress in this area of law remains dependent on the vagaries of the litigation process, a poor mechanism for the development of meaningful normative principles. If, as is likely, courts will continue to be challenged by cases of multiple rights, a more concerted effort will have to be made at the policy level to delineate the contours of each form of intellectual property in a systematic way. A good first step would be to eschew the belief that a 'case by case' and 'law by law' approach is sufficiently capable of resolving all the complexities, paradoxes and inconsistencies that will undoubtedly continue to present themselves.

12. Surfacing: the Canadian intellectual property identity

Ysolde Gendreau

To assert one's own voice in the concert of nations: here is an endeavour that may seem almost foolhardy in the contemporary world of intellectual property. In an age of increasing globalisation – to use a worn out phrase – few countries are able to express loudly their identity and run counter to the waves of international harmonisation. Who, indeed, can afford to be isolated? Increasingly, the positions that may be exemplified by one country's stance are perceived as representative of positions that are shared by a recognised community of nations. To wit, the debate in South Africa on the price exacted on patented anti-HIV drugs in the 1990s has been emblematic of the views held by developing countries on drug patents and even patents in general. After all, which country does not elaborate intellectual property policies in light of its overall political and commercial alliances?

Of course, such political and commercial contexts do not by themselves account for all the policy decisions that a country may make. The degree of integration with others that countries experience is one factor that can influence the situation: it is easy to appreciate that the intellectual property laws of a European Community country are much more dictated on an on-going basis by community principles than those of a member country of the *North American Free Trade Agreement* can be by the terms of that text.[1] Moreover, the strength of that country's intellectual property heritage will also bear upon its integration of those common norms. Being a member of a group need not entail a loss of individuality and the looser the connections, the easier it will be to maintain and forge one's own identity within that group.

A case on point is Canada. The geopolitical position of that country can lead an uninformed observer to presume that Canadian intellectual property laws are even subsumed into those of its immediate neighbour. Dwarfed by an

[1] For an account of the differences in copyright harmonisation between these two trading blocks, see Ysolde Gendreau, 'Copyright Harmonisation in the European Union and in North America' (1995) 20 Columbia-VLA Journal of Law & Arts 37; [1995] European Intellectual Property Review 488.

economic superpower with a population that is almost ten times its own south of the longest undefended border, Canada shares with the United States a British colonial heritage and the current lingua franca of trade. Even when it has been the first to introduce certain schemes, whether it be moral rights in copyright countries,[2] an administrative tribunal to oversee the setting of copyright royalties,[3] or compulsory licences for the exportation of patented drugs to developing countries,[4] these measures have not been recognised as trail-blazing breakthroughs that were meant to be followed by other countries.

Yet, the existence of some innovative contributions do not *per se* constitute a system's identity: Canadian intellectual property law as a whole has been shaped by general considerations that are characteristic of this nation. If, on the one hand, the internalisation of foreign influences has been an inevitable component of the process (A), this exercise has not prevented it from finding room for home-grown approaches (B). The result is an almost surprising affirmation of individuality.

A THE INTERNALISATION OF FOREIGN INFLUENCES

A country that is the by-product of two colonisation periods from two colonial superpowers can hardly be immune to foreign influences. Since the early periods of Canadian history involved important settlements of colonists from both mother countries, the path toward the achievement of a modern government led to a preference for a federal structure that would be able to accommodate the interests of the local population. The *British North America Act of 1867*, which laid the foundation for today's Canada, thus left the jurisdiction over private law matters to the provincial governments so that, in particular, the population of Quebec, the high majority of which is of French stock, could continue to live according to civil law rules. Among the exceptions to this scheme were patents and copyrights, relatively well identified categories of intellectual property law at the time,[5] which became the responsibility of the federal government.[6] Given the dominance of the British influence at the

---

2 Canada was the first copyright country to introduce Berne-style moral rights provisions in 1931: *An Act to amend the Copyright Act*, 21–22 Geo. V., c. 8, s. 5.

3 The Copyright Appeal Tribunal was created in 1936, some 21 years before the British Performing Rights Tribunal: *An Act to amend the Copyright Amendment Act, 1931*, 1 Edw. VIII, c. 28, s. 2.

4 *An Act to amend the Patent Act and the Food and Drugs Act (The Jean Chrétien Pledge to Africa)*, S.C. 2004, c. 23.

5 See Brad Sherman & Lionel Bently, *The Making of Modern Intellectual Property Law* (Cambridge: Cambridge University Press, 1999) at 101–28.

6 *Constitutional Act, 1867* (UK), 30 & 31 Vict., c. 3, ss. 91(22) and (23).

federal level, as well as in the other Canadian provinces, it is to be expected that the basic model for federal legislation should be British legislation.

History has shown, however, that this premise has nevertheless allowed for the incorporation of non-British influences in the make-up of Canadian intellectual property law. Different techniques have brought about this incorporation: statutory drafting, whether at the initial stage or through later amendments, and judicial interpretation, of course; but the bijural character of the country, which can be identified more precisely as one of the explanations for some of these achievements, also includes the interplay with provincial law as a source of suppletive legal rules (1). In such a context, it is no surprise that the resort to comparative law has almost become a second nature for all actors in this process (2).

1 The Bijural Nature of the Country

The bijural character of Canadian intellectual property law has evolved since its early days. At the beginning, in the absence of indigenous legislations, models for intellectual property regimes were to be found in England, naturally, but also in the United States. Both were thus rooted in the common law tradition. Today's understanding of bijuralism in Canada, however, rather refers to a mixture of common law sources, from whatever such country, with civil law ones. Moreover, its effect is felt not only in statutory drafting, but also in the search for suppletive rules as well as in the interpretation of this overall scheme.

In this broad picture, trademark legislation stands out as a regime that was adopted before England legislated on this matter and before a federal trademark statute was enacted in the US.[7] Indeed, up until 1954 when the Canadian legislation was entirely revised to become what is still today's *Trade-Marks Act*, hardly any foreign influences could be noted. The drafters of the 1954 statute, however, were not shy about borrowing from US and UK sources when they felt that these could provide useful solutions. For instance, registration for service marks, which then existed in the US but not in England, could henceforth be effected. If the Canadian trademark regime can be clearly identified as one that belongs to the common law tradition, through its allowance for common law trademarks in addition to registered ones, the fact that the statute also addresses unfair competition sets the field for some civil law inroads.[8]

---

[7] The 1860 and 1861 statutes predate the 1861 UK Act and the 1870 US Act. See A. Kelly Gill & R. Scott Jolliffe, *Fox on Canadian Law of Trade-Marks and Unfair Competition,* 4th ed. (Toronto: Carswell, 2006) at 1–3ff.

[8] See, below, the text accompanying notes 36ff.

A propensity for US law has also been the hallmark of the Canadian patent regime ever since the first statute in Lower Canada (now Quebec) in 1824.[9] Without necessarily being exact copies of the US statutes, the various patent statutes have, in particular, featured the first-to-invent system up until 1989.[10] Some typically Canadian features have, however, been introduced over the years.[11] To a certain extent, one of them is the long-standing openness towards British case law for their interpretation despite the US legislative influence and the Europeanisation of UK patent law.[12]

There is another pronounced mixture of US and British features in the early years of Canadian copyright law until the 1921 revision of the law. The first statute in the colony, in 1832, was very similar to the 1831 US legislation.[13] However, it had to be applied in conjunction with some UK copyright statutes whose application was extended to the Canadian dominions. This pattern of copyright legislations of mixed origins continued as both London and Ottawa voted new statutes until the Imperial *Copyright Act, 1911*.[14] With that *Act*, the British colonies, if they so wished, were invited to enact legislations that would fully govern copyright matters in their countries. Canada chose to do so and adopted in 1921 the *Copyright Act*[15] that came into force in 1924 and which still forms the basis of today's legislation.

This 1921 *Act* was heavily inspired by the British 1911 *Act* and was thus very much a product of the copyright tradition. Two important amendments would however alter this nature. In 1931, the Canadian Parliament voted the first implementation of moral rights in a copyright country.[16] Towards the end of the twentieth century, another author's right institution found its way into the *Act*: 'Rome-style' neighbouring rights were introduced.[17] The bijural nature of the Canadian copyright legislation has thus evolved from a US/UK origin to a UK/author's rights mix.

---

9 *An Act to promote the progress of useful Arts in this Province*, 4 Geo. IV, c. 25. See William L. Hayhurst, 'Intellectual Property Laws in Canada: The British Tradition, the American Influence and the French Factor' (1996) 10 I.P.J. 265 at 269–76.

10 *An Act to amend the Patent Act and to provide for certain matters in relation thereto*, S.C. 1987, c. 41.

11 See, below, the text accompanying note 46.

12 On this issue, see, among others, Jacques A. Léger, 'Why do We Still Refer to English Decisions in the Interpretation of the Canadian Patent Act?' in Gordon F. Henderson, ed., *Patent Law of Canada* (Toronto: Carswell, 1994) at 263.

13 *An Act for the protection of Copy Rights*, 2 Will. IV., c. 53.

14 *Copyright Act, 1911*, 1 & 2 Geo. V, c. 46.

15 *The Copyright Act, 1921*, 11 & 12 Geo. V, c. 24.

16 *Supra*, note 2.

17 *Act to Amend the Copyright Act*, S.C. 1997, c. 24.

Canadian bijuralism is not a disembodied concept which exists only as a consequence of historical events that are recognised in a legal environment. It is an approach to law that lives through the persons who contribute to its shaping. Every Canadian reader of the *Théberge*[18] decision by the Supreme Court of Canada has immediately noticed that the Court split along linguistic/legal traditions lines: the majority were judges from the common law provinces, while all three Quebec (civilist) judges dissented. This is certainly an extreme manifestation – and, to a certain extent, not the most constructive one – of the impact of bijuralism on the interpretation of copyright law; but there have nevertheless been other signs of openness towards 'the other' system over the years. The Quebec/civilist presence is not limited to the physical presence of jurists from that province in the judiciary, in Parliament, or in the civil service, for instance, but is also reflected in the fact that its ready presence may bring common law/anglophone jurists to consider author's rights/civilist theories in their reasonings. As early as 1911, the then anglophone Chief Justice of the Supreme Court of Canada did not hesitate to rely heavily on French doctrine to resolve a case pertaining to the rights over a manuscript.[19] An early anglophone commentator was quick to recognise that French/civil law played an important role in the understanding of Canadian copyright law.[20] Similarly, francophone judges can demonstrate much openness towards the use of copyright/anglophone sources.[21]

A common law/civil law pairing is very much the typical representation of bijuralism that one can expect from Canada. Yet, while it exists in copyright law and, to a much lesser extent, in trademark law, it is absent from patent law. If one looks at the overall picture of Canadian intellectual property law, however, one must recognise that US law plays an important role in its make up: one half of the contemporary bijural components is itself of a dual nature and it is thus possible to play upon two definitions of bijuralism in this context. Whatever content is given to this duality – which may even be considered a threesome – this phenomenon increasingly supposes that the intellectual property legal community has been resorting to comparative law in order to determine its rules.

---

18 *Théberge v. Galerie d'art du Petit Champlain inc.*, [2002] 2 R.C.S. 336 (concerning the 'reproduction' of posters and greeting cards onto canvases).

19 *Morang and Co. v. LeSueur* (1911), 45 S.C.R. 95.

20 See S. E. Dawson, 'Copyright in Books, An Inquiry into its Origin, And an Account of The Present State of The Law In Canada' (A Lecture Delivered Before The Law School of Bishop's College, at Sherbrooke, P.Q., Thursday, 26 January 1882) (Montreal: Dawson Brothers Publishers, 1882) at 10.

21 *Tele-Direct (Publications) Inc. v. American Business Information, Inc.* (1997), 76 C.P.R. (3rd) 296 (F.C.A). Décary J., of the Federal Court of Appeal, relied on the US decision *Feist Publications, Inc. v. Rural Telephone Service Co.*, 499 U.S. 340 (1991) to buttress his interpretation of originality.

2 The Resort to Comparative Law

The evolution of Canadian intellectual property has revealed that very few statutes have been extemporised without regard for what is done elsewhere. In many instances, of course, this consideration of foreign law is mandated by the international agreements to which Canada has adhered. For example, the particular implementation of new rules may result from their imposition by a commercial partner,[22] just as the decision *not* to enact measures that are made possible by an agreement may come from an examination of the workings of these rules in other countries.[23] These are situations that can be identified fairly easily. Of a more diffuse ambivalence are the trends that take shape through caselaw.

Some of the most obvious starting points for comparative law analysis may perhaps be found in copyright law. As mentioned before, moral rights and neighbouring rights are two institutions that are historically foreign to copyright countries, but which have found their way into the Canadian *Copyright Act*. The mechanism through which this happens, however, may vary considerably. When moral rights were introduced in the *Act* in 1931, their formulation paraphrased Article 6 *bis* of the Berne Convention and can almost be reckoned as a general statement of liability such as can be found in a Civil Code. As the need for its revision became an issue because of its vagueness,[24] the new text that emerged displays a much greater sensibility to the concerns of the copyright tradition and to the style of common law legislative drafting.[25]

An inverse process can be said to characterise the evolution of neighbouring rights. As a by-product of the Imperial *Copyright Act, 1911*, the 1921

---

[22] The implementation of the cable retransmission right in Canada, which flowed from the *Free Trade Agreement between the Government of Canada and the Government of the United States of America*, 2 January 1988, Can. T. S. 1989 No.3, reflects a 'new audience' basis for the creation of a statutory licence, as in US law, while the language of Article 11 *bis* (1)(ii) of the Berne Convention on this matter refers to communications made 'by an organisation other than the original one'. See *Copyright Act*, R.S.C. 1985, c. C-42, s. 31.

[23] With respect to terms of protection, Canada has not extended basic copyright term from life plus 50 years to life plus 70 years, as in the United States or in the European Union, nor has it introduced a 'supplementary protection certificate' scheme for pharmaceutical patents to compensate for time lost as a result of regulatory controls for these products.

[24] It has been described by an eminent specialist as 'conceived in vagueness, poorly drafted, sententious in utterance, and useless in practical application': Harold G. Fox, 'Some Points of Interest in the Law of Copyright' (1945–1946) 6 U.T.L.J. 100 at 126.

[25] See *Copyright Act*, *supra*, note 22, ss. 14.1, 14.2, 28.1, 28.2 and 34(2).

Canadian *Act* contained a provision that protected sound recordings, 'records, perforated rolls, and other contrivances by means of which sounds may be mechanically reproduced', as if they were works.[26] Later on, when performers' rights were introduced because of the 1994 implementation of the *TRIPs Agreement*, the national text closely followed the international one.[27] It is with the modifications that were brought about with Phase II of the revision of the *Act* in 1997 that Rome-style neighbouring rights replaced the earlier provisions.[28] One can thus observe that the degree of approximation to the author's rights approach can increase or decrease differently with time depending on the issue at stake.

Variations in attitudes towards foreign law can also be perceived in the jurisprudence. It is perhaps more difficult to account for them because there is a much greater number of players who are involved in the process and pronouncements by judges of courts of all levels can moreover be influenced by the willingness and ability of a multitude of legal professionals. Another factor which tempers the tendency to refer to foreign law is outright nationalism. The Supreme Court of Canada has made no bones about saying that foreign conceptions must be considered with great care:

> As this Court recognized in *Compo, supra,* at p. 367, U.S. copyright cases may not be easily transferable to Canada given the key differences in the copyright concepts in Canadian and American copyright legislation.[29]

There is, of course, a difference between the indiscriminate adoption of ideas from other jurisdictions and their rational consideration. Examples of the latter kind abound in Canadian case law, whether it be in patent law,[30] trademark law,[31] or copyright law.[32] They can result in a rejection[33] as much as in

[26] *Copyright Act, 1921*, *supra*, note 15, s. 4(3).

[27] *World Trade Organization Agreement Implementation Act*, S.C. 1994, c. 47, s. 68.

[28] *Act to Amend the Copyright Act*, *supra*, note 17, ss. 14ff. See also, *infra* at 307.

[29] *CCH Canadian Ltd. v. Law Society of Upper Canada*, [2004] S.C.R. 339 at 355.

[30] See Mark Perry, 'From Pasteur to Monsanto: Approaches to Patenting Life in Canada' in Ysolde Gendreau, ed., *An Emerging Intellectual Property Paradigm* (Cheltenham, UK and Northampton, MA, USA: Edward Elgar, 2008) at 67.

[31] Robert G. Howell, 'A Watershed Year for Well Known or Famous Marks' in Gendreau, *ibid.* at 22.

[32] See A. Drassinower, 'Canadian Originality: Remarks on a Judgment in Search of an Author' in Gendreau, *ibid.* at 139.

[33] The Supreme Court of Canada declared itself against the patenting of the onco-mouse, which is patented in the United States: *Harvard College v. Canada (Commissioner of Patents)*, [2002] 4 S.C.R. 45.

an acceptance[34] of the foreign experience. Whatever the outcome may be, the overall effect is an indication of an awareness of global developments and, given the drafting style of judgments in common law countries, of an increasing participation in the worldwide conversation on intellectual property law. When the specific issue which is discussed is one where the Canadian experience is particularly rich, its case law could even in turn be exported.[35]

The consequences of this citizenship of the intellectual property world may not always be positive. Naturally, the ideal goal in any country is the formulation of a well articulated position that provides a reliable guideline. However, as a starting point, one may say that in a federal state where the suppletive private law is split between provinces, which are themselves divided between common law and civil law traditions, there is no guarantee that the overall solution for a particular case that involves such a mixture of legal rules will be the same across the country. When the notion to be developed is one that is itself the object of such divisions, the result is a very fragmented picture indeed. It seems to be the fate of the concept of unfair competition.[36] Partly codified in a federal statute, the *Trade-Marks Act*, its primary foundations remain in provincial law.[37] It thus becomes a real challenge to develop a consolidated identity when, despite some intranational, albeit lopsided, exchanges, the foreign materials that are used come from very separate sources and would contribute to the reinforcement of the inherent tendencies of each system.[38] One may regret that this fragmentation – or, at least, this lack

---

[34] The same Supreme Court of Canada referred approvingly to US case law on the blurring and tarnishment of trademarks for the interpretation of the Canadian provision on the depreciation of the goodwill attached to a trademark: *Veuve Clicquot Ponsardin v. Boutiques Cliquot Ltée*, [2006] 1 S.C.R. 824.

[35] It is suggested that this turn of events may happen with respect to the Canadian caselaw on moral rights in other copyright jurisdictions, particularly in the Commonwealth: E. Adeney, 'Moral Rights in Canada: An Historical and Comparative View' in Gendreau, *supra* note 30 at 163.

[36] See Teresa Scassa, 'The Challenge of Trademark Law in Canada's Federal and Bijural System' in Gendreau, *supra* note 30 at 3.

[37] See, *infra*, note 41.

[38] Despite a continuous debate about this issue, it is commonly acknowledged that there is no 'federal' common law. On this question in general, see Roderick A. Macdonald, 'Harmonizing the Concepts and Vocabulary of Federal and Provincial Law: The Unique Situation of Quebec Civil Law' in Department of Justice, ed., *The Harmonization of Federal Legislation with Quebec Civil Law and Canadian Bijuralism* (Ottawa: Department of Justice, 1999) 27 at 42ff. The federal *Interpretation Act*, R.S.C. 1985, c. I-21, ss. 8.1 and 8.2, corroborates this vision:

> **8.1** Both the common law and the civil law are equally authoritative and recognized sources of the law of property and civil rights in Canada and, unless otherwise provided by law, if in interpreting an enactment it is necessary to refer to a

of cohesion – manifests itself in an area of the law whose function can so often be to complement an intellectual property right or even to help articulate one that has not yet formally taken shape.

Despite some drawbacks, the resort to foreign law is likely to remain a characteristic feature of Canadian intellectual property law:[39] the bijural nature of the country invites it; its historical and geopolitical makeup makes it inevitable. One can surmise that it is more likely to occur when the law is considered unsettled, but even a mature consensus may be in want of some periodic 'reality check' with the rest of the world in order to comfort its position or to justify a change of heart. After all, one's own interests will always be the primary motivation for the choice of any course of action and there are notable instances when Canada has paid less attention to foreign trends in order to forge its own solutions.

B THE CREATION OF NATIVE APPROACHES

The resort to foreign law, whether statutory or jurisprudential, as a source of inspiration, whether accepted or rejected, can only be useful if it is meant to enlighten the decision-making process. There are instances, however, where the policy decision cannot be directly traced to such a particular exercise, but rather results from taking stock of specific national preoccupations. It is when these concerns are paramount that homegrown approaches spring forth more consistently.[40] Such national traits, which can be identified more easily in

---

province's rules, principles or concepts forming part of the law of property and civil rights, reference must be made to the rules, principles and concepts in force in the province at the time the enactment is being applied.

8.2 Unless otherwise provided by law, when an enactment contains both civil law and common law terminology, or terminology that has a different meaning in the civil law and the common law, the civil law terminology or meaning is to be adopted in the Province of Quebec and the common law terminology or meaning is to be adopted in the other provinces.

[39] For a discussion with respect to copyright law, see Pierre-Emmanuel Moyse, 'Importing Foreign Standards into Canadian Law: Caught Between Closed and Open Doors' in AFPIDA, ed., *Regards sur les sources du droit d'auteur/Exploring the Sources of Copyright Law* (Paris: ALAI, 2007) 260.

[40] For example, the *Trade-Marks Act* contains several provisions on 'official marks', i.e. marks 'in respect of which the Registrar has, at the request of Her Majesty or of the university or public authority, as the case may be, given public notice of its adoption and use.' (*Trade-Marks Act*, R.S.C. 1985, c. T-13, s. 9(1).) The status that the *Act* recognises to these marks creates a parallel regime within the trademarks system whose full implications have not yet been totally explored. The conceptual framework at the root of this system has probably facilitated the decision to enact a specific trademark legislation for Olympic and Paralympic marks with a view to the winter Olympic Games of 2010 (*Olympic and Paralympic Marks Act*, S.C. 2007, c. 25).

statutory schemes, have manifested themselves through administrative institutions (1) and the Canadian stance on international policy (2).

1 The Administrative Institutions

It would be impossible today to imagine a modern intellectual property system without the essential institutions that are patent and trademarks offices. Indeed in Canada, the existence of a regulatory agency that continually oversees the application of the *Trade-Marks Act* contributes to the constitutional validity of the *Act*.[41] But apart from these traditional bodies, Canada has created other agencies that have been entrusted with specific mandates in the field of copyright law as well as in patent law.

The oldest one is the Copyright Board. Created in 1936 as the Copyright Appeal Tribunal, the Copyright Board is an increasingly essential component of Canadian copyright law. It was originally designed to supervise the setting of royalties for the public performances of musical works by collecting societies. Its duties were considerably extended in 1989 because of the expansion of collective management. Nowadays, it oversees three other regimes of collective management in addition to those related to performing rights in musical works and to some neighbouring rights: regimes for some exceptions (retransmission and some educational uses); a private copying regime for music; and a general 'residual' regime. Its role has been redefined 'from simply protecting users against the potential misuse of monopoly power by CMOs (a view which still seems to inform the work of several national copyright tribunals) to regulating the balance of market power between copyright holders and users'.[42]

Apart from these duties related to collective management, the Copyright Board is also responsible for issuing licences to users who have been unable to locate the copyright owners from whom they would have obtained a permission to use a work or object of a neighbouring right.[43] This mechanism, the Canadian answer to the 'orphan work' problem, is poised to continue to gain momentum as more works are transmitted over the internet.

---

41 *Kirkbi AG v. Ritvik Holdings Inc.*, [2005] 3 S.C.R. 302 at 313–17. The Constitution is silent on the designation of a legislative authority to be responsible for trademarks legislation. Because of this void, there has been constant debate on the legitimacy of the federal *Trade-Marks Act* in general and of the provisions on unfair competition that are included in it.

42 Daniel J. Gervais, 'A Uniquely Canadian Institution: The Copyright Board of Canada' in Gendreau, *supra* note 30 at 211.

43 *Copyright Act*, *supra* note 22, s. 77.

Indeed, decisions by the Copyright Board have been attracting greater attention over the years. As it is called to approve tariffs in an increasing number of situations, the Copyright Board is confronted with new issues which require legal interpretations that the judicial courts may not have already tackled. The scope of its decisions can thus extend beyond the mere determination of royalties to encompass fundamental legal reasoning. The Copyright Board was among the first to confirm that the transmission of a work over the internet qualifies as a 'communication to the public by telecommunication',[44] and to accept that the non-removable memory that is permanently embedded in an MP3 player is a 'blank audio recording medium' and is therefore subject to a levy within the private copying scheme for music.[45]

Patent law also has its own administrative tribunal: the Patented Medicine Prices Review Board (PMPRB).[46] For many years, Canada had a compulsory licence regime for patented drugs that gave birth to a thriving generics industry. Licences were available as soon as the drugs were available in exchange for a very low royalty rate. The situation had become so untenable for the pharmaceutical research companies that the modification of the Canadian *Patent Act* became a condition for the negotiation of the Canada–United States Free Trade Agreement in 1987. As its name implies, the PMPRB controls the prices of patented medicines in Canada. It functioned together with an 'improved' statutory licence regime until 1993 when that regime was itself abolished. Since then, however, it has been the sole entity to determine whether the price of a patented medicine in Canada is 'excessive' and, thus, to be empowered to direct a drug patentee to lower its price if necessary.[47] The administrative system that is set up under the aegis of these provisions appears to be very efficient as there are very few cases that have required the quasi-judicial intervention of the Board.

The very existence of the PMPRB hinges on the patent status of the medicines which it controls. It is precisely because the power to legislate over patents belongs to the federal Parliament that the latter is entitled to create this Board. One of the consequences of this premise is that the price of drugs that are produced after the patents have expired is not subject to the evaluation of

---

44 *SOCAN v. Canadian Association of Internet Providers* (1999), 1 C.P.R. (4th) 417 at 445 (Cop. Bd.), aff'd *SOCAN v. Canadian Association of Internet Providers*, [2004] 2 S.C.R. 427 at para. 30.

45 *Re Private Copying 2003–2004, Tariff of Levies to be Collected by CPCC* (2003), 28 C.P.R. (4th) 417, rev'd *Canada (Canadian Private Copying Collective) v. Canadian Storage Media Alliance*, [2005] 2 F.C. 654 (F.C.A.).

46 See Mélanie Bourassa Forcier & Jean-Frédéric Morin, 'Canadian Pharmaceutical Patent Policy: International Constraints and Domestic Priority' in Gendreau, *supra* note 30 at 81.

47 *Patent Act*, R.S.C. 1985, c. P-4, s. 83.

the Board. It also means that a pharmaceutical company may avoid the jurisdiction of the PMPRB by deciding not to patent a drug that it wants to market. This kind of strategic decision-making is not available to copyright owners who would like to avoid the compulsory licence regimes that the Copyright Board oversees.

While it has been more manifest in the case of the Copyright Board, time has witnessed the expansion of the powers that are exercised by both Boards. Both institutions appear firmly entrenched in the Canadian intellectual property landscape. Because of their official status, their role in the working of the law is clearly identifiable. Shedding light on Canada's international policy in intellectual property unfortunately depends on more conjecture.

2 The International Policy

The *TRIPs Agreement* of 1994 has fundamentally altered our understanding of international intellectual property law. Up till then, an international intellectual property instrument was negotiated 'for its own sake'. Relationships with other such instruments were of course considered,[48] but there was no emphasis on the overall picture of international intellectual property law. With the assemblage of intellectual property rights regulation in the *TRIPs Agreement*, it has now become more common to make a global assessment of a country's policy in this respect, but not to the detriment of the specificities of each right. Similarly, the inclusion of the *TRIPs Agreement* in a multilateral trade agreement stresses the commercial diplomacy component of intellectual property foreign relations. A perspective on Canada's international policy in intellectual property matters in general is thus a more recent kind of exercise which simply recasts older observations in a slightly different light.

Canada's current stance on the 1996 WIPO treaties, the WIPO Copyright Treaty and the WIPO Performances and Phonograms Treaty, is a typical illustration of the usual process. Even though it was one of their signatories more than ten years ago, the country has yet to adopt implementing legislation that would allow it to ratify them.[49] This deferment of action is just one manifes-

---

48 A prime example would be the *International Convention for the Protection of Performers, Producers of Phonograms and Broadcasting Organisations* (the Rome Convention of 1961), whose very first article states that the protection it grants 'shall leave intact and shall in no way affect the protection of copyright in literary and artistic works'.

49 Bill C-60, which was introduced in Parliament in June 2005, died on the order paper when elections were called for the autumn. See Bill C-60, *An Act to amend the Copyright Act*, 1st Sess., 38th Parl., 2005. The same fate seems to await Bill C-61 which was tabled in June 2008. See Bill C-61, *An Act to amend the Copyright Act*, 2nd Sess., 39th Parl., 2008.

tation of the minimalist approach to international intellectual property relations. It is in keeping with the long delays in the ratification of the latest Acts of the Paris and Berne conventions: although it became a party to the *Paris Convention* in 1925, Canada signed on to the 1967 Act in 1996; similarly, it was only in 1998 that Canada adhered to the 1971 Paris Act of the *Berne Convention*, even though its status had not changed since it became a member of that Union with the Rome Act of 1928. These updates obviously resulted from the requirements of the *TRIPs Agreement*.

Indeed, apart from the *International Convention for the Protection of New Varieties of Plants*, Canada is not a member of many 'non-trade' intellectual property agreements. The *International Convention for the Protection of Performers, Producers of Phonograms and Broadcasting Organisations*, the Rome Convention of 1961, is a notable exception. Canada became a party to that convention in 1998 when it proceeded with Phase II of the revision process of its *Copyright Act*. What is striking about that decision is that it marked an adoption of an author's rights approach to neighbouring rights in a traditionally copyright country. Moreover, it seems to have resulted from a purely national policy decision rather than from some external pressure. This international positioning did not turn Canada into a full member of the author's rights tradition, but it does point to its ability to bridge two variations on the same intellectual property right. The same can be said about the change in its patent law, effective on 1 October 1989, from a first inventor system to a first-to-file one.

A minimalist approach to international protection offers the advantage of allowing Canada to raise more easily its level of protection whenever it feels that it is in its interest. This can happen through adhesion to instruments like the *Rome Convention* or through a more generous implementation of its treaty obligations, like its protection of the right to anonymity within the general concept of moral rights in the *Berne Convention*[50] or the eight-year data protection term that can be traced to the *NAFTA Agreement*.[51] Indeed, regional and especially bilateral trade agreements provide increasing opportunities to negotiate intellectual property rights in the broader framework of commercial interests: a recent instance has been the 2003 Canada–EU Agreement on geographical indications which raises the level of Canada's obligations in this area above the requirements of the *TRIPs Agreement*.[52]

---

50 See Adeney, *supra*, note 35.

51 See Bourassa Forcier & Morin, *supra*, note 46.

52 See Norbert Olszak, 'L'évolution du droit des appellations d'origine et indications de provenance au Canada' (2003) 56 Rev.trim.dr.com.&dr.éc. 617; Dianne Daley, 'Canada's Treatment of Geographical Indications: Compliant or Defiant? An International Perspective' in Gendreau, *supra* note 30 at 35.

In any event, the pursuit of one's own interests has always been any country's policy and its ability to do so successfully depends on the real freedom of action it enjoys at any given time. If its geopolitical position in the nineteenth century put it between England's imperialist policies and the United States' nationalistic assertions,[53] Canada today remains at the crossroads of European and North American interests that have evolved since then. The marching of time also means that it has gained a maturity that enables it to be open to the influences of its traditional partners with discernment, while the breadth of its outlook can extend beyond them.[54]

This maturing of Canadian intellectual property law brings with it the same consequences as elsewhere. As this branch of the law takes on a greater role in the commercial policies of a country, its expansion nurtures issues that have always plagued it, albeit perhaps in a less publicised manner than today. One of them is the relationship of the various intellectual property rights among themselves. The recent Supreme Court decision in *Kraft Canada*,[55] which highlights a conflict between trademark law and copyright law, is but one example[56] of a continuing evolution in the shaping of intellectual property law.[57] Another one is the encounter with rights or values, other than intellectual property rights, that may come in conflict with any one of them. Because of the inherent abilities of these rights to create monopolies, competition law is a natural antagonist in this respect. Although there is not much case law on this interaction,[58] the matter has caught the attention of some scholars[59] and of

---

53 For an example of this situation with respect to copyright law, see Pierre-Emmanuel Moyse, 'Canadian Colonial Copyright: The Colony Strikes Back' in Gendreau, *supra* note 30 at 107.

54 Canada was the first country to implement the 2003 WTO decision on access to patented medicines by developing countries. See Bourassa Forcier & Morin, *supra* note 46. Indeed, the very first notification to the World Trade Organisation that such a regime would be used has been made by Canada too. See WTO, *Council for Trade-Related Aspects of Intellectual Property Rights – Notification under Paragraph 2(c) of the Decision of 30 August 2003 on the Implementation of Paragraph 6 of the Doha Declaration on the TRIPS Agreement and Public Health – Canada*, WTO Doc. IP/N/10/CAN/1 (8 October 2007), online: <http://docsonline.wto.org>.

55 *Euro-Excellence Inc. v. Kraft Canada Inc.*, 2007 SCC 37.

56 For a more complete picture of the Canadian situation, see Myra J. Tawfik, 'When Intellectual Property Rights Converge – Tracing the Contours and Mapping the Fault Lines Case by Case and Law by Law' in Gendreau, *supra* note 30 at 267.

57 See Sherman & Bently, *supra* note 5.

58 See, for example, *Director of Investigation and Research v. NutraSweet & Co.* (1990), 32 C.P.R. (3d) 1 (Comp. Trib.); *Director of Investigation and Research v. Warner Music Canada Ltd.* (1997), 78 C.P.R. (3d) 321 (Comp. Trib.).

59 Among several works, see in particular the papers published in Robert D. Anderson & Nancy T. Gallini, ed., *Competition Policy and Intellectual Property Rights in the Knowledge-Based Economy* (Calgary: University of Calgary Press, 1998).

the Competition Bureau.[60] More recently, human rights, in all their manifestations, have emerged as an important antagonist. They can be individual ones, such as privacy rights that clash with gene patenting or with copyright control mechanisms,[61] as well as collective rights, like those that form the basis of the claims by developing nations about access to medicines or by native groups in the quest for the recognition of traditional knowledge.

Far from a sign of diffidence, Canada's minimalist attitude springs from an awareness of the multiple influences that are at play when it is deciding on the orientation of its intellectual property laws. A federal state that must respect the constitutional division of powers that affect intellectual property laws, it is bound from the start by certain constraints. As a bijural and bilingual country, it is a living laboratory for the mixing of different approaches. As a former colony and the neighbour of a contemporary superpower, the assertion of its identity will continue to be an ongoing process.

---

60 Competition Bureau, *Intellectual Property Enforcement Guidelines* (2000), online: <http://strategis.ic.gc.ca/pics/ct/ipege.pdf>.

61 On the latter issue, see an example of an application in Margaret Ann Wilkinson, 'Battleground Between New and Old Orders: Control Conflicts Between Copyright and Personal Data Protection' in Gendreau, *supra* note 30 at 227.

Index